TO IMPROVE THE ACADEMY

TO IMPROVE THE ACADEMY

Resources for Faculty, Instructional, and Organizational Development

Volume 31

James E. Groccia, Editor

Laura Cruz, Associate Editor

Published by Jossey-Bass/Higher and Adult Education Series

A Wiley Imprint
One Montgomery Street, Suite 1200, San Francisco, CA 94104-4594—
www.josseybass.com

ISBN: 978-1-118-25781-4
ISBN: 978-1-11828285-4 (epub)
ISBN: 978-1-118-28462-9 (emobi)
ISBN: 978-1-118-28610-4 (epdf)

Printed in the United States of America
FIRST EDITION
PB Printing 10 9 8 7 6 5 4 3 2 1

To Improve the Academy is published annually by the Professional and Organizational Network in Higher Education (POD) through Jossey-Bass Publishers and is abstracted in ERIC documents and in Higher Education Abstracts.

Ordering Information

The annual volume of *To Improve the Academy* is distributed to members at the POD conference in the autumn of each year. To order or obtain ordering information, please contact:

John Wiley & Sons, Inc.
Customer Care Center
10475 Crosspoint Blvd.
Indianapolis, IN 46256
Phone: 877-762-2974
Fax: 800-597-3299
E-mail: custserv@wiley.com
Web: www.josseybass.com

Permission to Copy

The contents of *To Improve the Academy* are copyrighted to protect the authors. Nevertheless, consistent with the networking and resource-sharing functions of POD, readers are encouraged to reproduce articles and cases from *To Improve the Academy* for educational use, as long as the source is identified.

Instructions to Contributors for the Next Volume

Anyone interested in the issues related to instructional, faculty, and organizational development in higher education may submit manuscripts. Manuscripts are submitted to the current editor early in December of each year and selected through a double-blind peer review process.

Correspondence, including requests for information about guidelines and submission of manuscripts for Volume 32, should be directed to:

James E. Groccia, Ed.D.
Director, Biggio Center for the Enhancement of Teaching and Learning

Auburn University
Auburn, AL 36830
Phone: 334-844-8530
Fax: 334-844-0130
E-mail: tia@auburn.edu

Mission Statement

As revised and accepted by the POD Core Committee, April 2, 2004

Statement of Purpose

The Professional and Organizational Development Network in Higher Education is an association of higher education professionals dedicated to enhancing teaching and learning by supporting educational developers and leaders in higher education.

Mission Statement

The Professional and Organizational Development Network in Higher Education encourages the advocacy of the ongoing enhancement of teaching and learning through faculty and organizational development. To this end, it supports the work of educational developers and champions their importance to the academic enterprise.

Vision Statement

During the twenty-first century, the Professional and Organizational Development Network in Higher Education will expand guidelines for educational development, build strong alliances with sister organizations, and encourage developer exchanges and research projects to improve teaching and learning.

Values

The Professional and Organizational Development Network in Higher Education is committed to:

- Personal, faculty, instructional, and organizational development
- Humane and collaborative organizations and administrations

- Diverse perspectives and a diverse membership
- Supportive educational development networks on the local, regional, national, and international levels
- Advocacy for improved teaching and learning in the academy through programs for faculty, administrators, and graduate students
- The identification and collection of a strong and accessible body of research on development theories and practices
- The establishment of guidelines for ethical practice
- The increasingly useful and thorough assessment and evaluation of practice and research

Programs, Publications, and Activities

The Professional and Organizational Development Network in Higher Education offers members and interested individuals the following benefits:

- An annual membership conference designed to promote professional and personal growth, nurture innovation and change, stimulate important research projects, and enable participants to exchange ideas and broaden their professional network
- An annual membership directory and networking guide
- Publications in print and in electronic form
- Access to the POD Web site and listserv

Membership, Conference, and Programs Information

For information, please contact:

Hoag Holmgren, Executive Director

The POD Network

P.O. Box 3318

Nederland, CO 80466

Phone: 303-258-9521

Fax: 303-258-7377

E-mail: podoffice@podnetwork.org

Web: podnetwork.org

CONTENTS

PART THREE

Building Effective Relationships

PART FOUR

Practicing Innovative Teaching and Learning

PART FIVE

Assessing Student Learning

PART SIX

Setting a Context for Promoting Diversity

PART SEVEN

Integrating Technology into Teaching, Learning, and Faculty Development

ABOUT THE AUTHORS

The Editors

James E. Groccia is director of the Biggio Center for the Enhancement of Teaching and Learning and associate professor of higher education in the Department of Educational Foundations, Leadership, and Technology at Auburn University. In addition to faculty development work, he teaches graduate courses on teaching and higher education and coordinates the university's Graduate Certificate in College and University Teaching. He is a former POD Network president and received his Ed.D. in educational psychology and guidance from the University of Tennessee. He is coauthor with Mary Stuart Hunter of *The First-Year Seminar: Designing, Implementing, and Assessing Courses to Support Student Learning and Success: Volume II—Instructor Training and Development* (2012), and author of *The College Success Book: A Whole-Student Approach to Academic Excellence* (1992). He is coeditor with Mohammed Alsudairi and Bill Buskist of *The Handbook of College and University Teaching: A Global Perspective* (2012); with Bill Buskist of *Evidence-Based Teaching* (2011); and with Judy Miller of *On Becoming a Productive University: Strategies for Reducing Costs and Increasing Quality in Higher Education* (2005), *Student Assisted Teaching: A Guide to Faculty-Student Teamwork* (2001), and *Enhancing Productivity: Administrative, Instructional, and Technological Strategies* (1998). He can be reached at groccje@auburn.edu.

Laura Cruz is associate professor of history and director of the Coulter Faculty Commons at Western Carolina University, a large and productive teaching and learning center that won a national award in 2010 from *Campus Technologies* magazine. In addition to publications in her discipline, European history, she is the author of articles on faculty development, educational technology, history pedagogy, graduate student development, peer review, and (especially) the Boyer model of scholarship. She currently serves as editor-in-chief of *MountainRise*, the international journal of the scholarship of teaching and learning (SoTL). Cruz has won multiple teaching and engagement awards and is the principal organizer of an annual nationwide retreat on the Boyer model of scholarship. She regularly participates in professional organizations including POD, Southern Regional Faculty and Instructional Development, International Scholarship of Teaching and Learning, and those related to her discipline of history. She is frequently invited to present, provide workshops and invited sessions, or consult on topics of SoTL, the Boyer model of scholarship, and faculty center organizational models. She can be reached at lcruz@email.wcu.edu.

The Contributors

Dorothe J. Bach is associate professor and assistant director at the University of Virginia's Teaching Resource Center where she directs the Excellence in Diversity Fellows Program for new and underrepresented faculty and supports initiatives designed to advance excellence in teaching and learning. She also teaches literature courses in the university's German Department and Comparative Literature Program. Her publications include articles on teaching and learning, as well as faculty development. She can be reached at bach@virginia.edu.

o

Daniel Barbezat is professor of economics at Amherst College. He has been a visiting professor at Northwestern University and Yale University and has taught in the summer program at Harvard University. In 2004, he won the J. T. Hughes Prize for Excellence in Teaching Economic History from the Economic History Association. His approach to teaching economics classes has been featured in the *Boston Globe* and *U.S. News & World Report*, as well as on NPR's program *Here and Now*. He is executive director of the Center for Contemplative Mind in Society and is currently writing a handbook of contemplative practices in higher education with Mirabai Bush, editing a collection of papers with Arthur Zajonc, and working on a book provisionally entitled *Wanting*. He can be reached at dpbarbezat@amherst.edu.

o

Nancy H. Barry is professor of music education in the Auburn University College of Education. She also served as professor, graduate coordinator, and chair of music education at the University of Oklahoma, where she received the Henry Daniel Rinsland Memorial Award for Excellence in

Educational Research and was awarded a Presidential Professorship. Her research interests include faculty professional development, curriculum, and arts education. She can be reached at barrynh@auburn.edu.

o

Allison Boye is the director of the Teaching Effectiveness and Career enHancement (TEACH) Program at Texas Tech University's Teaching, Learning, and Professional Development Center. She is the chair of the POD Innovation Award Committee and on the 2012 POD Conference Team and also currently serves on the executive council of the Texas Faculty Development Network. Her recent publications focus on consulting practices, graduate student development, peer observation, and instructor response to feedback. She can be reached at allison.p.boye@ttu.edu.

o

Edward J. Brantmeier is assistant director of the Center for Faculty Innovation and assistant professor in the Learning, Technology, and Leadership Education Department at James Madison University. A former Fulbright Scholar, he teaches multicultural education courses, faculty development work, and researching issues related to curriculum development, diversity, critical theoretical approaches, technology, sustainability, and contemplative practices in K–20 contexts. He can be reached at brantmej@jmu.edu.

o

Allison BrckaLorenz is an assistant research scientist at the Indiana University Center for Postsecondary Research working primarily with the National Survey of Student Engagement and the Faculty Survey of Student Engagement. Her research interests include the teaching and learning of college students and accompanying issues that faculty face, as well as the socialization and professional development of graduate students and faculty members. She can be reached at abrckalo@indiana.edu.

o

Derek Bruff is director of the Vanderbilt University Center for Teaching and a senior lecturer in the Department of Mathematics. Bruff consults regularly with faculty in a variety of disciplines about educational technology and other teaching and learning topics. His research interests include classroom response systems (clickers), visual thinking, student motivation, and social pedagogies. He blogs on these topics at derekbruff.com, and his book, *Teaching with Classroom Response Systems: Creating Active*

Learning Environments, was published by Jossey-Bass in 2009. Bruff has taught at Harvard University and has a Ph.D. in mathematics from Vanderbilt University. He can be reached at derek.bruff@Vanderbilt.edu.

o

William E. Buhro is professor and chair of chemistry and George E. Pake Professor in Arts and Sciences at Washington University in St. Louis. He teaches general chemistry, inorganic chemistry, and solid-state and materials chemistry. His research investigates quantum confinement effects and exciton/charge transport in colloidal semiconductor nanocrystals, including quantum dots, rods, wires, and belts. He can be reached at buhro@wustl.edu.

o

Eddie Cole is a project associate for the Faculty Survey of Student Engagement and a doctoral candidate in higher education at Indiana University, where he also holds a master's degree in higher education. His primary research focus is on the rhetoric of college presidents and student unrest in the 1960s and the historical roots of and current issues faced by distinct mission institutions. He can be reached at coleer@indiana.edu.

o

Michelle Corvette holds a doctorate in educational psychology, an M.F.A. in studio art, and is currently pursuing a second doctoral degree in visual art research at Goldsmiths, University of London. She previously served as the assistant director of the Tennessee Teaching and Learning Center. She can be reached at michellecorvette@nyu.edu.

o

Amber Dailey-Hebert is an associate professor of adult education at Park University and serves as an international consultant for educational projects in Europe and Africa. Her work and research is focused on adult learners, distance education and training, and grant-funded projects that serve working professionals. She chairs the Research Committee for the Association of Continuing and Higher Education, has published numerous articles and book chapters, and was the founding director of the Center for Excellence in Teaching and Learning, which serves over sixteen hundred full- and part-time faculty worldwide. She can be reached at adailey@park.edu.

o

Dannielle Joy Davis, a graduate of the University of Illinois at Urbana-Champaign and associate professor of educational leadership, policy, and law at Alabama State University, has studied and conducted research in Ghana, South Africa, Egypt, Germany, the Netherlands, and Belgium. Her interdisciplinary, K–20 research examines the experiences of marginalized groups in educational settings and the role of organizational policy and practice in the promotion or inhibition of egalitarian academic and occupational outcomes. She serves as an associate editor for *Learning for Democracy: An International Journal of Thought and Practice,* which is sponsored by the American Educational Research Association Special Interest Group, Democratic Citizenship in Education. She can be reached at djdavis@illinoisalumni.org.

o

Michele DiPietro is executive director of the Center for Excellence in Teaching and Learning and associate professor of statistics at Kennesaw State University. His research interests focus on learning sciences, diversity and inclusion, the consultation process, statistics education, student evaluations of teaching, and teaching in times of tragedies. He is the 2012–2013 president of the POD Network. He can be reached at mdipietr@kennesaw.edu.

o

Emily Donnelli-Sallee is an associate professor of English at Park University, where she also serves as faculty director of the Center for Excellence in Teaching and Learning. In this role, she devises resources and programs to support teaching excellence across disciplines and instructional modalities, and she provides leadership for a cross-disciplinary faculty advisory council. She teaches courses in writing and rhetoric and serves as editor of Missouri Campus Compact's *Journal of Public Scholarship in Higher Education.* Her research examines the ways that public sphere theory can inform civic engagement pedagogies, particularly in first-year composition. She can be reached at emilyd@park.edu.

o

Peter E. Doolittle is director of the Center for Instructional Development and Educational Research and associate professor of educational psychology in the Department of Learning Sciences at Virginia Tech. He is also the executive editor of the *International Journal of Teaching and Learning in Higher Education*, co-executive editor of the *International Journal of ePortfolio*, and associate editor of the *International Journal of Cyber Behavior, Psychology and Learning*. His current research focuses include multimedia learning, working memory capacity, and the learning efficacy of Web 2.0 technologies. He can be reached at pdoo@vt.edu.

o

Elizabeth L. Evans is the director of the Center for Excellence in Learning and Teaching and an assistant professor of business at Concordia University Wisconsin. Her chapter is based on her doctoral research at the University of Wisconsin-Milwaukee and her presentation on this work, which was recognized with the POD Network's 2011 Robert J. Menges Award. She serves as a Teagle Assessment Scholar with the Center of Inquiry in the Liberal Arts at Wabash College. She can be reached at elizabeth.evans@cuw.edu.

o

Hyacinth E. Findlay is professor of instructional leadership at Alabama State University. Her main areas of research include teacher concerns, educational leadership, and succession planning. She has served as a public school and higher education administrator. She has traveled widely on international educational trips, including a Fulbright award to Senegal and the Gambia. She can be reached at hfindlay@alasu.edu.

o

Beth A. Fisher is associate director of the Teaching Center and Lecturer in Women, Gender, and Sexuality Studies at Washington University in St. Louis. Her work focuses on helping graduate students develop pedagogical knowledge and expertise and on developing teaching methods that can help undergraduates and graduate students improve their writing skills. She teaches courses in American literature and gender studies. She can be reached at bfisher@wustl.edu.

o

Deborah J. Frank is a science writer in the Department of Obstetrics and Gynecology at Washington University in St. Louis. Her work focuses on improving the quality of research manuscripts and grant proposals in terms of both the science and the writing. She can be reached at DFrank22@wustl.edu.

o

Regina F. Frey is professor of the practice in chemistry, director of the Teaching Center, and associate director of the Center for Integrative Research in Cognition, Learning, and Education at Washington

University in St. Louis. She teaches general chemistry, Women in Science, and a peer leader training course. She works with colleagues in chemistry, cognitive science, and education to conduct research focused on group-oriented, student-centered pedagogies for the teaching of science, technology, engineering, and mathematics. She can be reached at gfrey@wustl.edu.

o

Chutney Guyton holds a Ph.D. in educational leadership and policy and an M.B.A. degree. She is an academic adviser at North Carolina Central University, Durham. Previously she was a graduate researcher with the Tennessee Teaching and Learning Center. She can be reached at chutney.guyton@nccu.edu.

o

Cameron J. Harris is an associate instructor in the School of Education and graduate assistant in the Office of the President, Indiana University, Bloomington, where he is completing his Ph.D. in higher education and student affairs. His research interests include the faculty profession, the educational pipeline to the professoriate, African Americans in higher education, and curriculum in higher education. He can be reached at harriscj@indiana.edu.

o

Natasha Haugnes is a faculty developer at the Academy of Art University in San Francisco. She holds an M.A. from San Francisco State University in Teaching English to Speakers of Other Languages and has authored two English as a Second Language textbooks. Her recent professional presentations and research focus on fostering creativity in the classroom, as well as using and creating rubrics to effectively assess art and design work. She can be reached at nhaugnes@gmail.com.

o

Jennifer H. Herman is director of instructional support at Niagara University. She holds a master's degree in international training and education from American University and a Ph.D. in higher education from the State University of New York at Buffalo. Her research focuses on online education, faculty development, organizational development in higher education, and curriculum design. She has developed extensive curricula and training programs for the U.S. Department of State and the

New York State Small Business Development Center. She can be reached at jherman@niagara.edu.

o

Matthew Holley is a visiting lecturer at the Indiana University School of Medicine, where he serves as the curriculum and instructional design director for the Department of Family Medicine. He is completing his Ph.D. in higher education and student Affairs at Indiana University, Bloomington. His research focuses on curriculum development, college teaching and learning, and the faculty profession, with a particular emphasis on the experiences of lesbian, gay, bisexual, and transgender faculty members. He can be reached at maholley@iupui.edu.

o

Hoag Holmgren is executive director of the POD Network in Higher Education. His professional interests include collaborative leadership, higher education and the arts, and assessment and the arts. He taught creative writing for several years at the University of Colorado-Boulder and has published and presented on assessing student work in the arts. His nonfiction, fiction, and poetry have appeared in numerous literary journals. He can be reached at hoag.holmgren@gmail.com.

o

Jillian Kinzie is associate director of the Indiana University Center for Postsecondary Research and NSSE Institute. She leads project activities on the effective use of student engagement data to improve educational quality, and serves as a research associate on the National Institute for Learning Outcomes Assessment, an initiative to study assessment in higher education and assist institutions in adopting promising practices in the assessment of college student learning outcomes. She can be reached at jikinzie@indiana.edu.

o

Melissa Langridge is the user education coordinator at Niagara University Library. She has a master's degree in library science and is obtaining a master's degree in teacher education at Niagara University. A strong foundation in educational theory and practice, along with her interest in technology, supports the ongoing development of the library's instruction curriculum. Other interests include information literacy, online learning, and instructional game design. She can be reached at mlangridge@niagara.edu.

Carol Lauer is chair and professor of anthropology at Rollins College. She received her Ph.D. in anthropology from the University of Michigan and teaches courses on human evolution and medical anthropology. As a result of her work evaluating the quality of her colleagues' teaching as a department chair and member of her college's tenure and promotion committee, she has developed an academic interest in assessment of teaching by students. She can be reached at clauer@rollins.edu.

Virginia S. Lee is principal and senior consultant of Virginia S. Lee & Associates, a consulting firm specializing in educational development in higher education. Previously she held administrative positions with teaching centers at the University of North Carolina at Chapel Hill and North Carolina State University. She is a former president of the Professional and Organizational Development Network in Higher Education. She edited *Inquiry-Guided Learning* (2012) and *Teaching and Learning Through Inquiry: A Guidebook for Institutions and Instructors* (2004). She can be reached at vslee@virginiaslee.com.

Cuiting Li, born in China, received elementary to college education in China. After teaching in a university for three years, she was admitted to Auburn University to obtain her master's and Ph.D. in human development and family studies. After graduation, she worked as an assistant professor in the State University of New York, Oneonta. Currently she is an assistant professor at the University of Wisconsin, Stevens Point. She can be reached at cli@uwsp.edu.

Marty Loy is dean of the College of Professional Studies at the University of Wisconsin-Stevens Point, where he also served as associate dean in the School of Health Promotion and Human Development and as the Focus on Teaching program coordinator. His research areas are stress management, childhood grief, and faculty development. He is the author of *Childhood Stress: A Handbook for Parents, Teachers and Therapists* (2009). He won the University Excellence in Teaching Award in 2001. He can be reached at mloy@uwsp.edu.

B. Jean Mandernach is a research professor and director of the Center for Innovation in Research and Teaching at Grand Canyon University. Her research focuses on enhancing student learning through assessment and innovative online instructional strategies. In addition, she has interests in examining the perception of online degrees, the quality of online course offerings, and the development of effective faculty evaluation models. She received her B.S. in comprehensive psychology from the University of Nebraska at Kearney, an M.S. in experimental psychology from Western Illinois University, and a Ph.D. in social psychology from the University of Nebraska at Lincoln. She can be reached at jean.mandernach@gcu.edu.

o

Kathryn G. Miller is professor and chair of biology at Washington University in St. Louis. She is conducting a study of the pedagogical methods she developed in an upper-division, writing-intensive course in developmental biology. Since 2004, she has been the principal investigator on a Howard Hughes Medical Institute grant supporting improvements in undergraduate science education. Her research investigates structural components of cells that mediate movement, shape, and organization. She can be reached at miller@wustl.edu.

o

Richard N. Muthiah is dean of learning support services at George Fox University, where he is responsible for disability services and the student learning center. He received a Ph.D. in higher education from Indiana University, Bloomington, while working as a project associate for the NSSE Institute. His areas of interest include student learning, cocurricular contributions to student learning, service-learning, campus cultures, and Christ-centered thought and practice in higher education. He can be reached at rmuthiah@georgefox.edu.

o

Rachel K. Niemer oversees digital publicity efforts and leads the graduate student instructor teaching orientation and the University of Michigan's involvement in the Center for the Integration of Research, Teaching and Learning Network. Previously she taught chemistry at Gustavus Adolphus College and courses on pedagogy to undergraduate peer leaders at University of Rochester. She has a Ph.D. in chemistry from Caltech and did postdoctoral work at the University of Rochester. She can be reached at rkniemer@umich.edu.

Linda B. Nilson is founding director of the Office of Teaching Effectiveness and Innovation at Clemson University and a previous editor of *To Improve the Academy* (Vols. 25–28). She is also author of *The Graphic Syllabus and the Outcomes Map: Communicating Your Course* (2007) and *Teaching at Its Best: A Research-Based Resource for College Instructors*, now in its third edition (2010). She gives keynotes and workshops at conferences, colleges, and universities both nationally and internationally. She can be reached at nilson@clemson.edu.

Megan M. Palmer is assistant dean for faculty affairs and professional development at the Indiana University (IU) School of Medicine. She is also an assistant professor of general internal medicine and educational leadership and policy studies at the IU School of Education in Indianapolis. Along with her colleagues Genevieve Shaker and Nancy Chism, she was selected for POD's Robert Menges Award. Her research focuses on college teaching, faculty development, and faculty vitality. She can be reached at mmpalmer@indiana.edu.

Allison Pingree is director of professional pedagogy at the Harvard Kennedy School, after serving as director of the Vanderbilt University Center for Teaching for thirteen years. She holds a Ph.D. in English and American literature from Harvard; taught there in English, history, literature, and expository writing; and served as an acting associate director at the Derek Bok Center for Teaching and Learning. Her research interests include interdisciplinary teaching, learning, and collaboration; leadership and organizational change; and contemplative pedagogy. Her passion as an educator lies in cultivating ways to integrate cognitive, affective, and embodied forms of learning to promote individual and social change. She can be reached at allison_pingree@harvard.edu.

Kristen A. Renn is associate professor of higher, adult, and lifelong education at Michigan State University. Her teaching and research focus on areas of identity in higher education. She has published books, articles, and chapters on the topics of mixed-race college students; lesbian, gay, bisexual, and transgender issues; and promoting success for diverse learners in the United States and other countries. She is associate editor for international research and scholarship of the *Journal of College Student*

Development and a member of the governing board of the American College Personnel Association. She can be reached at renn@msu.edu.

Tony Ribera is a project associate for the NSSE Institute for Effective Educational Practice and a doctoral candidate in higher education at Indiana University. His dissertation explores the formal student affairs master's curriculum and how future professionals are prepared to gather, analyze, interpret, and disseminate evidence of teaching and learning. He can be reached at aribera@indiana.edu.

Kelly Schoonaert is assistant professor of health promotion and human development at the University of Wisconsin Stevens Point. She earned her Ed.D. at Ball State University in 2003 with a cognate in wellness. She is a certified intrinsic coach and enjoys helping people find their strengths and inspirations. She can be reached at Kelly.Schoonaert@uwsp.edu.

David W. Schumann is the inaugural director of the Tennessee Teaching and Learning Center and holds the William J. Taylor Distinguished Professorship of Business at the University of Tennessee. His research interests are focused on consumer attitudes and persuasion and his teaching on leadership and teaching preparation of Ph.D. students. He has a master's degree and Ph.D. in social psychology, a master's degree in counseling education, and a bachelor's degree in education. He can be reached at dschuman@utk.edu.

Genevieve G. Shaker is assistant professor of philanthropic studies at the Center on Philanthropy at Indiana University and director of communications and creative services for the IU School of Liberal Arts at IUPUI. With her colleagues Nancy Chism and Megan Palmer, she was selected for POD's Robert J. Menges Award. Her work was also recognized as the Association for the Study of Higher Education's Bobby Wright Dissertation of the Year. Her current research interests center on philanthropy and faculty work. She can be reached at gshaker@iupui.edu.

Martin Springborg is a faculty member in the Minnesota State Colleges and Universities System (MnSCU), where he teaches photography and art history. He has also worked in the field of educational development for eight years, at Inver Hills Community College, and later as a program director at MnSCU's system office. His current photographic work is focused on teaching and learning in higher education. Other research interests include assessment methods used in arts disciplines. He can be reached at martin.springborg@gmail.com.

○

Dorian Stiefel is a doctoral student in political science at the University of Tennessee and a community volunteer with the Tennessee Teaching and Learning Center. She can be reached at dstiefel@utk.edu.

○

Suzanne Tapp is director of the Teaching, Learning, and Professional Development Center at Texas Tech University. She is a member of the POD Core Committee (2011–2014) and the past chair of the Texas Faculty Development Network. She can be reached at suzanne.tapp@ttu.edu.

○

Krista Terry is assistant professor of instructional technology in the Department of Leadership and Educational Studies at Appalachian State University. She is an associate editor of the *International Journal of Teaching and Learning in Higher Education* and the publications officer for the Applied Research in Virtual Environments for Learning SIG of the American Educational Research Association. Her current research focus includes aspects of community and collaboration in virtual learning environments, as well as issues related to cognition in technology-mediated learning environments. She can be reached at terrykp@appstate.edu.

○

Roben Torosyan is associate director for the Center for Academic Excellence and assistant professor of educational studies and teacher preparation at Fairfield University. He has facilitated seventy-eight workshops at conferences and institutions, including Columbia, New York University, and Harvard, on topics such as facilitating controversial conversations, giving critical feedback on teaching, and managing resistance. He holds a Ph.D. in cultural studies, philosophy, and education from Teachers College, Columbia University. He can be reached at rtorosyan@fairfield.edu.

○

Katherine Valle is a graduate student earning a master's of public policy and master's of arts in higher education at the Gerald R. Ford School of Public Policy and the Center for the Study of Higher and Postsecondary Education at the University of Michigan. She has worked in policy development in both the United States and abroad. Her interests center on polices that increase student success such as access, college affordability, and the promotion of civic engagement and leadership development opportunities. She can be reached at kvalle@umich.edu.

o

Nancy Van Note Chism is professor emerita of higher education and student affairs in the Indiana University School of Education, Indianapolis. She has worked in professional and organizational development at both Ohio State University and Indiana University-Purdue University Indianapolis for over twenty-five years. Her interests include professional and organizational development, the faculty profession, international higher education, and college teaching and learning. She can be reached at nchism@iupui.edu.

o

Sterling K. Wall, associate professor of family and consumer sciences, has taught ten years in family science in the University of Wisconsin System and has led his college students on several service-learning trips to Mexico and Nicaragua. He seeks to simultaneously increase students' awareness of the world outside the United States, while helping them to see themselves, their families, and their own culture more clearly. He can be reached at Sterling.Wall@uwsp.edu.

o

C. Edward Watson is associate director of the Center for Instructional Development and Educational Research at Virginia Tech. He holds a Ph.D. in instructional design and technology. His current research interests include digital native mythologies, e-portfolio pedagogies and practices, distance learning, and the pedagogy of things. He is the founding co-executive editor of the *International Journal of ePortfolio* and the managing editor of the *International Journal of Teaching and Learning in Higher Education*. He can be reached at edwatson@vt.edu.

o

Mary Wright is director of assessment and an associate research scientist at the Center for Research on Learning and Teaching. In this capacity, she works with the University of Michigan's faculty and academic units on assessment of student learning, evaluation of educational initiatives, and the scholarship of teaching and learning. She is the author of *Always at Odds? Creating Alignment Between Faculty and Administrative Values* (2008). She is a member of POD's Core Committee and cochairs the Graduate and Professional Student Development Committee. She has a Ph.D. in sociology from the University of Michigan. She can be reached at mcwright@umich.edu.

PREFACE

Volume 31 of *To Improve the Academy: Resources for Faculty, Instructional, and Organizational Development (TIA)* contains twenty-one chapters from authors across an array of institutions on a variety of topics. We have organized the chapters into seven parts based on our subjective reading of the issues they describe. This organization reflects our attempt to provide some structure to assist understanding and application of the content presented and was done after the chapters have been accepted. We have tried to fit part titles to chapter content so as not to constrain author creativity by forcing them to fit our predetermined structure. In this way, *TIA* best reflects the various levels at which our work as developers has impact—broadening our scope; reaching out to new populations; building effective relationships; practicing innovative teaching, learning, and faculty development techniques; assessing student learning; setting a context for promoting diversity; and integrating technology into teaching and learning practice.

Part One: Broadening Our Scope

Chapter One, by Emily Donnelli-Sallee, Amber Dailey-Hebert, and B. Jean Mandernach, reports on a study that identified emergent trends in faculty development programming, including an emphasis on collaborative course and program development, virtual learning communities and mentoring, and professionalism of contingent faculty roles. The authors' findings highlight the importance of decentralized, networked development models for geographically dispersed faculty.

David Schumann, Dorian Stiefel, Michelle Corvette, and Chutney Guyton in Chapter Two provide a case study of a strategy for initiating and maintaining a university learning consortium. The consortium brings together center directors, faculty scholars, and administrators to operate as an independent think tank on campus in ways that enhance dialogue, generate creative ideas, and design and propose policies and practices that reflect desired change.

In Chapter Three, Elizabeth Evans investigates the experiences of faculty who self-identified as engaged, a term used to describe attitudes of excitement as well as participatory behaviors. To encourage faculty engagement and recognize the learning process that engagement embodies, she suggests that institutions provide faculty development, an environment that values assessment work, support for learning, and opportunities for faculty members to make contributions using what they have learned.

Part Two: Reaching Out to New Audiences

In Chapter Four, Natasha Haugnes, Hoag Holmgren, and Martin Springborg examine several assumptions about artists and how these assumptions can be overcome for the benefit of educational developers, faculty-artists, and students. To this end, they provide suggestions for generating dialogue about teaching and learning with faculty-artists and for making these dialogues fruitful.

Virginia Lee, Dorothe J. Bach, and Richard Muthiah examine in Chapter Five higher education's current malaise through an exploration of midcareer faculty. After summarizing selected studies on midcareer faculty, they draw on alternative literature and developmental frameworks to shed light on the spiritual dimension of the midcareer faculty experience. They offer recommendations on appropriate interventions and discuss their wider implications for a postindustrial paradigm of academic renewal.

In Chapter Six, Genevieve Shaker and Megan Palmer provide information on faculty and staff giving, review the related literature, share findings from a new study on faculty major donors, and provide a series of recommendations, based on the literature and a study of major donors, to inform fundraising efforts by faculty development centers.

Part Three: Building Effective Relationships

Nancy Barry in Chapter Seven discusses faculty mentoring as a way of preparing new faculty to function effectively within the culture of the department to deal with increased professional expectations brought about through digital technology, budget issues, and other factors that contribute to a stressful and complex working environment. She concludes that investing time and effort in a formal, structured mentoring program can ultimately increase productivity for all faculty, new and veteran.

Allison Boye and Suzanne Tapp in Chapter Eight discuss the "provocative" consultation approach, where the faculty developer adopts a more direct role and seeks to address perceived challenges in a frank discussion. This chapter uses three case studies focusing on a graduate student, a pretenured faculty member, and a multidisciplinary course to discuss how faculty developers can effect change in difficult consultations through the use of a more confrontational style.

In Chapter Nine, Nancy Van Note Chism, Matthew Holley, and Cameron Harris review 138 studies on the impact of educational development practices and present an overview of findings on the impact of workshops, formal courses, communities of practice, consultation, mentoring, and awards and grants programs. The authors conclude that although the studies vary in quality, the sheer volume of results offers guidance for development practice.

Part Four: Practicing Innovative Teaching and Learning

In Chapter Ten, Allison BrckaLorenz, Tony Ribera, Jillian Kinzie, and Eddie Cole explore the frequency of student exposure to teaching clarity behaviors and the extent to which these behaviors relate to student engagement, deep approaches to learning, and students' self-reports of gains in college. They report that students exposed to clear teaching behaviors, such as explaining course goals and requirements, had positive relationships with all of these outcomes.

Michele DiPietro in Chapter Eleven examines societal trends that have shaped today's millennial students and connects these findings to insights from the learning sciences. This analysis uncovers how students' experiences affect readiness for college and attitudes about learning. DiPietro suggests that the current sociocultural context leaves students ill equipped for certain cognitive functions, particularly metacognitive awareness and progress toward mature stages of intellectual development, and he suggests strategies to support development of those functions.

In Chapter Twelve, Daniel Barbezat and Allison Pingree provide an overview of the definition of, intention, and benefits from contemplative exercises, showing how these practices can build and sustain attention, deepen understanding of the material presented, support and increase connection and interrelatedness, and inspire inquiry and insight. Following that, they provide approaches to fostering these sorts of practices through university teaching and learning centers, as well as offer a cautionary note on possible problems with this approach.

Part Five: Assessing Student Learning

In Chapter Thirteen, Carol Lauer presents a comparison of students and faculty perceptions of the meanings of several terms commonly used in narrative course evaluation. Both groups produced complex and multifaceted definitions for these terms, and instructors were frequently incorrect in inferring common student definitions. Based on these misunderstandings, they question the usefulness of forms for evaluative or developmental purposes. Faculty peer review of class meetings and course materials are suggested as ways to help provide the necessary filter for interpreting evaluation comments.

Linda Nilson in Chapter Fourteen continues the discussion of student ratings of teaching, questioning their validity in light of changes in college students and societal realities. Drawing on recent research conducted on students, she examines the relationship between student ratings and student learning, the biases found in these ratings, and their factual accuracy and apparent truthfulness. She also addresses why findings of early and recent studies differ, the sorts of information that student ratings now provide, and how institutions and faculty have consolidated the effects on ratings that students initiated.

In Chapter Fifteen, Jennifer H. Herman and Melissa Langridge discuss the need for professional development for faculty teaching online courses explaining how small group individual diagnosis was adapted to the online environment. They report surprising challenges that emerged when the technique was adapted to the online environment.

Part Six: Setting a Context for Promoting Diversity

Cuiting Li, Sterling Wall, Marty Loy, and Kelly Schoonaert in Chapter Sixteen present an account of a Chinese faculty member's experiences integrating into American higher education. Told from three points of view, her story emphasizes the importance of openness and willingness to talk about cultural issues. The authors highlight that it is not enough to recruit diverse faculty; ongoing communication and support must take place, especially after the contract is offered.

In Chapter Seventeen, Kristen A. Renn describes an ecological model and uses it to analyze how diversity and identities interact with the processes of teaching and learning. Examples from research with students of color and lesbian, gay, bisexual, and transgender students illustrate barriers to learning and opportunities to use diverse identities to engage students more effectively. She concludes by offering recommendations for faculty developers for improving the classroom climate for diverse learners.

Dannielle Joy Davis, Edward Brantmeier, Roben Torosyan, and Hyacinth Findlay in Chapter Eighteen draw on autoethnographic narrative reflections to explore the experiences of members of the Professional and Organizational Development Network in Higher Education and the HBCU Faculty Development Network during the organizations' first joint conference. Using the theory of professional interaction as a framework, they describe how effectively the organizations manifested their interest in increased racial inclusion and collaboration.

Part Seven: Integrating Technology into Teaching, Learning, and Faculty Development

In Chapter Nineteen, C. Edward Watson, Krista Terry, and Peter Doolittle discuss the perceived changes in the learning profile of today's students that includes multitasking. The belief in these skills has mistakenly led some to encourage pedagogies that require multitasking. They consider the lineage of the multitasking narrative, examine empirical research associated with multitasking, and chart a path forward for faculty, students, and developers to improve learning.

Mary Wright, Rachel Niemer, Derek Bruff, and Katherine Valle in Chapter Twenty analyze the ways in which participants in the 2011 joint conference of the Professional and Organizational Development Network and the Historically Black Colleges and Universities Faculty Development Network used Twitter to communicate about the annual meeting. Many messages mapped onto key faculty development priorities that were established in a prior large survey of faculty developers. However, important distinctions also arose, namely emphasis among tweeters on how faculty and students learn, faculty roles and rewards, and approaches to effectively engage in educational development work. They suggest that Twitter served an important communicative function through development of social networks and resource sharing.

In Chapter Twenty-One, Beth Fisher, Kathryn Miller, William Buhro, Deborah Frank, and Regina Frey conclude with a description of a collaboration among faculty and teaching center staff that produced in-class, active learning methods to help students learn visualization, problem-solving, critical thinking, and communication skills as they develop disciplinary knowledge. Preliminary evaluations suggest evidence of improved learning and high levels of student engagement. They conclude that this collaboration has produced insights into teaching and learning that are widely applicable, helping to make teaching innovation visible and to transform teaching into an act of scholarship.

o

TIA continues to be a primary source for faculty development professionals to disseminate their expertise, best practice, and research in the continuing effort to enhance teaching, learning, and the effectiveness of higher education. The true spirit of POD is reflected in the peer review process used to select the chapters in this book, as well as the willingness of our colleagues to share their wisdom with others. We hope this book serves as a handy and helpful resource in efforts so that our practice has more impact and more effective teaching and learning.

ACKNOWLEDGMENTS

A book of this type represents the cumulative and collaborative work of numerous members of the POD community whose work it reflects and documents. We received thirty-six manuscripts, all worthy of dissemination. Due to space limitations however, we had to make difficult choices in selecting twenty-one for publication in this book. We did this by distributing each manuscript for review by peers across the faculty development community. One hundred reviewers participated in the review process, thereby providing each manuscript with between five and six reviews. Most of these volunteer reviewers had prior experience, but we were also able to include a number of new reviewers in the process. The reviews were, for the most part, timely, thorough, and thoughtful, and they yielded constructive feedback for revision or resubmission. Without doubt, the peer review process for *To Improve the Academy, Vol. 31* reflected the diversity of perspectives that is a characteristic and strength of the POD Network.

We acknowledge and thank all reviewers who provided one of the essential characteristics of academic scholarship, peer review, to the manuscripts submitted to this volume of *To Improve the Academy*: Karen Adsit, Roberta Ambrosino, Pamela Arrington, Kola Babarinde, David Babb, Dorothe Bach, Donna W. Bailey, Pamela Barnett, Gabriele Bauer, Danilo Baylen, A. Page Beetem, Victoria Bhavsar, Phyllis Blumberg, Karen Bovenmeyer, Beverly Brehl, Mary Breslin, Kate Brinko, Neal Bryan, Karen Bull, Susanna Calkins, Rosemary Capps, S. Raj Chaudhury, G. Christopher Clark, Jeanette Clausen, Eli Collins-Brown, Kathryn Cunningham, Bonnie Daniel, Michele DiPietro, Angeles L. Eames, Sally Ebest, Phillip Edwards, Joshua Eyler, Bonnie Farley-Lucas, Beth Fisher, Richard Freishtat, Brenda Frieden, Christopher Garrett, Judy Grace, Brian Greenwood, Nira Hativa, Aeron Haynie, Jason Hendryx, Jennifer Herman, Susan Hines, Katherine Hoffman, Matthew Holley, Mikaela Huntzinger, Carol Hurney, Kathy Jackson, Wayne Jacobson, Kathleen Kane, Bruce Larson, Jean Layne, Virginia Lee, Donna Gardner Liljegren, Kathryn Linder, Deandra Little, Debra Rudder Lohe, Jean Mandernach, Jean Martin-Williams, Christopher Mayer, Leslie McBride, Jeanette

McDonald, Lillian McEnery, Sal Meyers, Cheryl Miller, Linda B. Nilson, Linda Noble, Edward Nuhfer, Patrick O'Sullivan, Michael Palmer, Donna Petherbridge, Stacie Pittell, Susan M. Polich, Patricia Pulver, Emily C. Richardson, Michael Rogers, Cathy Ryan, Brian Rybarczyk, Derina Samuel, David W. Schumann, Peter Shaw, Ike Shibley, Julie Sievers, D. Lynn Sorenson, Susan Sullivan, Suzanne Tapp, Krishna Thomas, Brigitte Valesey, William Vanderburgh, Kam Vat, Karen Ward, Patricia White, Stacie Williams, Laurel Willingham-McLain, Mary-Ann Winkelmes, Eva Wong, Mary Wright, Olena Zhadko.

We acknowledge the continued support of the POD Publication Committee and Hoag Holmgren, the executive director of the POD Network. Working with Jossey-Bass's publication staff has been a delight. Everyone we have listed here was responsive to our queries and supportive of our requests for clarification and assistance. Special thanks go to Amy Vaughan, Emad Ismail, and Chenzi Wang for their technological, logistical, and editorial support with this publication.

My associate editor, Laura Cruz, has made a seamless transition to the editorial team. This volume is truly a team effort as Laura and I have shared decision making, review, and editing tasks throughout the process.

Auburn, Alabama
June 15, 2012

James E. Groccia
Auburn University

ETHICAL GUIDELINES FOR EDUCATIONAL DEVELOPERS

Preamble

As professionals, educational developers (faculty, teaching assistant, organizational, instructional, and staff developers) have a unique opportunity and a special responsibility to contribute to the improvement of the quality of teaching and learning in higher education. As members of the academic community, they are subject to all the codes of conduct and ethical guidelines that already exist for those who work or study on campuses and those who belong to disciplinary associations. Educational developers have special ethical responsibilities because of the unique and privileged access they have to people and often to sensitive information. This document provides general guidelines to inform the practice of professionals working in educational development roles in higher education.

Educational developers in higher education come from various disciplinary areas and follow different career tracks. Some work as educational developers on a part-time basis or for simply a short time, but for others, educational development is a full-time career. The nature of their responsibilities and prerogatives as developers varies with their position in the organization, their experience, interests, and talents, and the special characteristics of their institutions. This document attempts to provide general ethical guidelines that should apply to most developers across a variety of settings.

Ethical guidelines indicate a consensus among practitioners about the ideals that should inform their practice as professionals, as well as those behaviors that would constitute misconduct. Between the ideal of exemplary practice and misconduct lies a gray area where dilemmas arise: choices may seem equally right or wrong; different roles and responsibilities may place competing, if not incompatible, demands on developers; or certain behaviors may seem questionable but no consensus can determine that those behaviors are examples of misconduct.

It is our hope that these guidelines complement typical programmatic statements of philosophy and mission and that educational developers can use the guidelines effectively to promote ethical practice. This document describes the ideals of practice, identifies specific behaviors that typify professional misconduct, and provides a model to think through situations that present conflicting choices or questionable behavior.

Guidelines for Practice

Ideals of Practice

Ideals that should inform the practice of educational developers include the following areas of professional behavior: providing responsible service to clients, demonstrating competence and integrity, ensuring that the rights of others are respected, maintaining the confidentiality of any information regarding contact with clients, and fulfilling responsibilities to the profession of educational development as a whole. It is expected that educational developers will understand and integrate these ideals into their daily practice. Even though the following categories are viewed as ideals of practice, many of the individual statements are quite concrete and practical, while others encourage educational developers to attain a high standard of excellence.

Educational developers evince a high level of responsibility to their clients and are expected to:

1. Provide services to everyone within their mandate, provided that they are able to serve all clients responsibly
2. Treat clients fairly, respecting their uniqueness, their fundamental rights, dignity and worth, and their right to set objectives and make decisions
3. Maintain appropriate boundaries in the relationship, avoid exploiting the relationship in any way, and be clear with themselves and their clients about their specific role
4. Protect all privileged information, obtaining informed consent from clients before using or referring publicly to client cases in such a way that the client could be identified
5. Continue service only as long as the client is benefiting, discontinue service by mutual consent, and suggest other resources to meet needs they cannot or should not address

Competence and Integrity

Aspects of competence and integrity discussed in these guidelines include the behavior of educational developers, the skills and the boundaries they should respect and enforce, and the need for them to ensure the rights of their clients. Educational developers should also interact competently and with integrity in relationships with their coworkers, supervisees, and the community.

BEHAVIOR. In order to ensure evidence of competence and integrity, educational developers should:

a. Clarify professional roles and obligations
b. Accept appropriate responsibility for their behavior
c. Make no false or intentionally misleading statements
d. Avoid the distortion and misuse of their work
e. Clarify their roles and responsibilities with each party from the outset when providing services at the behest of a third party
f. Accept appropriate responsibility for the behavior of those they supervise
g. Model ethical behavior with coworkers and those they supervise and in the larger academic community

SKILLS AND BOUNDARIES. To practice effectively, educational developers need an awareness of their belief systems, personal skills, and personal knowledge base and cognizance of their own and their clients' boundaries. Ethical practice requires that educational developers:

a. Be reflective and self-critical in their practice
b. Seek out knowledge, skills, and resources continually to undergird and expand their practice
c. Consult with other professionals when they lack the experience or training for a particular case or endeavor or if they seek to prevent or avoid unethical conduct
d. Know and work within the boundaries of their competence and time limitations
e. Know and act in consonance with their purpose, mandate, and philosophy, integrating the latter insofar as possible
f. Strive to be aware of their own belief systems, values, biases, needs, and the effect of these on their work
g. Incorporate diverse points of view
h. Allow no personal or private interests to conflict or appear to conflict with professional duties or clients' needs

i. Take care of their personal welfare so they can facilitate clients' development
j. Ensure that they have the institutional freedom to do their job ethically

CLIENTS' RIGHTS. Because educational developers work in a variety of settings with a variety of clients and interact within different teaching and learning contexts, they must be sensitive to and respectful of intellectual, individual, and power differences. Educational developers should thus:

a. Be receptive to different styles and approaches to teaching and learning and to others' professional roles and functions
b. Respect the rights of others to hold values, attitudes, and opinions different from their own
c. Respect the right of clients to refuse services or to request the services of another professional
d. Work against harassment and discrimination of any kind, including race, ethnicity, gender, class, religion, sexual orientation, disability, age, nationality, etc.
e. Be aware of various power relationships with clients (e.g., power based on position or on information) and not abuse their power.

Confidentiality

Educational developers maintain confidentiality regarding client identity, information, and records within appropriate limits and according to legal regulations. Educational developers should:

a. Keep confidential the identity of clients, as well as their professional observations, interactions, or conclusions related to specific clients or cases
b. Know the legal requirements regarding appropriate and inappropriate professional confidentiality (e.g., for cases of murder, suicide, or gross misconduct)
c. Store and dispose of records in a safe way; and comply with institutional, state, and federal regulations about storing and ownership of records
d. Conduct discreet conversations among professional colleagues in supervisory relationships and never discuss clients in public places

Responsibilities to the Profession

Educational developers work with colleagues in the local, national, and international arena. In order to ensure the integrity of the profession, they:

a. Attribute materials and ideas to their creators or authors
b. Contribute ideas, experience, and knowledge to colleagues
c. Respond promptly to requests from colleagues
d. Respect colleagues and acknowledge collegial differences
e. Work positively for the development of individuals and the profession
f. Cooperate with other units and professionals involved in development efforts
g. Are advocates for their institutional and professional missions

Professional Misconduct

The professional misconduct of educational developers would reflect gross negligence and disdain for the Guidelines for Practice stated above. Unethical, unprofessional, and incompetent behaviors carried out by educational developers should be brought to the attention of the association. Individual educational developers should take responsibility if or when they become aware of gross unethical conduct by any colleague in the profession.

Ethical Conflicts in Educational Development

CONFLICTS ARISING FROM MULTIPLE RESPONSIBILITIES, CONSTITUENTS, RELATIONSHIPS, AND LOYALTIES. Educational developers may encounter conflicts that arise from multiple responsibilities, constituents, relationships, and loyalties. Because educational developers are responsible to their institutions, faculty, graduate students, undergraduate students, and themselves, it is inevitable that conflict will arise. For example, multiple responsibilities and relationships to various constituencies, together with competing loyalties, may lead to conflicting ethical responsibilities. The following examples point out situations in which conflicts may arise and identify the specific conflict:

> *Example 1:* An instructor is teaching extremely poorly, and students in the class are suffering seriously as a result. *Conflict:* In this

situation, the educational developer is faced with a conflict between the responsibility of confidentiality to the client-teacher and responsibility to the students and the institution.

Example 2: A faculty member wants to know how a teaching assistant with whom the educational developer is working is progressing in his or her consultation or in the classroom. *Conflict:* In this situation, the educational developer is faced with a conflict between responding to the faculty member's legitimate concern and with maintaining confidentiality vis-à-vis the teaching assistant.

Example 3: The educational developer knows firsthand that a professor-client is making racist or sexist remarks or is sexually harassing a student. *Conflict:* In this situation, the educational developer is faced with a conflict between confidentiality vis-à-vis the professor-client and not only institutional and personal ethical responsibilities but responsibility to the students as well.

Example 4: A fine teacher who has worked with the educational developer for two years is coming up for tenure and asks that a letter be written to the tenure committee. *Conflict:* In this situation, the educational developer is faced with a conflict between rules regarding client confidentiality and the educational developer's commitment to advocate for good teaching on campus and in tenure decisions.

In such instances of conflict, educational developers need to practice sensitive and sensible confidentiality. It is best that they:

1. Consult in confidence with other professionals when they are faced with conflicting or confusing ethical choices.
2. Inform the other person or persons when they have to break confidentiality, unless doing so would jeopardize their personal safety or the safety of someone else.
3. Break confidentiality according to legal precedent in cases of potential suicide, murder, or gross misconduct. In such cases, to do nothing is to do something.
4. Decide cases of questionable practice individually, after first informing themselves to the best of their ability of all the ramifications of their actions.
5. Work to determine when they will act or not act, while being mindful of the rules and regulations of the institution and the relevant legal requirements.

CONFLICTS ARISING FROM MULTIPLE ROLES. Educational developers often assume or are assigned roles that might be characterized as teaching police, doctor, coach, teacher, or advocate, among others. They are expected to be institutional models or even the conscience for good teaching on their campuses. Yet in their work with professors and graduate students, they endeavor to provide a safe place for their clients to work on their teaching. Another potential area for conflict arises from the fact that educational developers may serve as both faculty developers and as faculty members. As developers, they support clients in their efforts to improve their teaching; in their role as faculty, they often serve on review committees that evaluate other faculty. Either role may give them access to information that cannot appropriately be shared or communicated beyond the committee or the consultation relationship (even if it would be useful for the other role).

An important area of potential conflict exists in the case of the summative evaluation of teaching. Departmental faculty and campus administrators (chairs, deans, etc.) are responsible for the assessment of teaching for personnel decisions. Educational developers should not generally be placed in this situation because of the confidentiality requirements noted in the section on Guidelines for Practice. In general, educational developers do not make summative judgments about an individual's teaching. In particular, they should never perform the role of developer and summative evaluator concurrently for the same individual unless they have that person's explicit consent and with proper declaration to any panel or committee involved. However, educational developers may:

1. Provide assessment tools
2. Collect student evaluations
3. Help individuals prepare dossiers
4. Educate those who make summative decisions
5. Critique evaluation systems

Conclusion

This document is an attempt to define ethical behaviors for the current practice of educational development in higher education. In creating this document the POD Network has referred to and borrowed from the Ethical Guidelines of the American Psychological Association, the American Association for Marriage and Family Therapy, Guidance

Counselors, the Society for Teaching and Learning in Higher Education in Canada, and the Staff and Educational Development Association in the United Kingdom. The association will continue to refine these guidelines in light of the changes and issues that confront the profession. The guidelines will be updated on a periodic basis by the Core Committee of the Professional and Organizational Development Network in Higher Education.

TO IMPROVE THE ACADEMY

PART ONE

BROADENING OUR SCOPE

1

PROFESSIONAL DEVELOPMENT FOR GEOGRAPHICALLY DISPERSED FACULTY

EMERGING TRENDS, ORGANIZATIONAL CHALLENGES, AND CONSIDERATIONS FOR THE FUTURE

Emily Donnelli-Sallee, Amber Dailey-Hebert
Park University

B. Jean Mandernach
Grand Canyon University

The growth of distance education programs has significantly influenced learner demographics and dispositions; however, often overlooked is its concomitant *effect on the characteristics and needs of faculty. As institutions continue to diversify their educational offerings and faculty appointments, innovative, inclusive professional development models are vital for faculty success. A qualitative study of thirty institutions identified trends in faculty development programming, including an emphasis on collaborative course and program development, virtual learning communities and mentoring, and professionalism of contingent faculty roles. Findings*

This research was generously supported by a grant from the Professional and Organizational Development Network in Higher Education.

highlight the importance of decentralized, networked development models for geographically dispersed faculty.

o

It is seldom disputed that the growth of online and distance education has significantly influenced learner demographics and dispositions; however, often overlooked is its concomitant effect on the characteristics and needs of faculty. Consequently, faculty developers are challenged to support audiences beyond the full-time and adjunct faculty who teach courses on their institutions' primary physical campuses. Institutions now include a diverse faculty body comprising many full-time and adjunct faculty who work remotely, are not required to serve physically at their institution's flagship campus, have instructional release time for varied projects, and occupy diverse contractual agreements. As a result, faculty developers now work with faculty from geographically dispersed locations, including faculty teaching online or otherwise remotely at branch campus locations. These faculty possess varying levels of physical and psychological connection to their institutions, hold diverse appointments, and often face limited opportunities for professional development (Bower, 2001; Eaton, 2001; Gappa, Austin, & Trice, 2007; National Center for Education Statistics, 2007). As institutions continue to diversify their educational offerings and faculty positions, innovative, inclusive professional enhancement models become even more vital.

To pursue a deeper understanding of effective professional development programming for this expanded faculty audience, researchers from two universities with large distance learning programs undertook a qualitative study of thirty institutions across the spectrum of Carnegie Basic Classifications (including private, public, and nonprofit institutions). The study yielded information about emergent trends in faculty development, primarily in the areas of collaborative course and program development, virtual learning communities, and professionalization of contingent faculty roles, as well as examples of innovative programming across institutional type. However, most significant, and surprising given our focus on identifying strategies and best practices, were interviews that overwhelmingly focused on the impact of organizational factors on faculty development and the pragmatic and epistemological considerations surrounding various models for supporting geographically dispersed faculty.

Thus, in this chapter, we address ways that institutional dynamics constrain and propel the growth of faculty development initiatives and the benefits and costs associated with centralized, decentralized, and hybrid organizational models. This knowledge can aid faculty development stakeholders in determining how to best integrate diverse faculty development goals and programs across academic departments, teaching centers, and distance learning administrative offices. Our contention is that an analysis of institutional organizational dynamics is a requisite first step to developing and sustaining effective, inclusive development programs for geographically dispersed faculty.

Geographically Dispersed Faculty: Context and Growth Factors

The context and characteristics of higher education are changing dramatically as we experience a significant paradigm shift in the academy. Gappa et al. (2007) identified four major forces currently affecting higher education institutions and their faculty members: "1) fiscal constraints and increased competition, 2) calls for accountability, 3) growing enrollment and increasing diversity of students, and 4) the rise of the Information Age, with its continuous expansion of new technologies" (p. 15). Certainly online learning is a primary influence on Gappa et al.'s (2007) observations about the role of new technologies. Based on a survey of twenty-five hundred colleges and universities nationwide, the Sloan Consortium found that approximately 5.6 million students were enrolled in at least one online course in fall 2009, representing a growth of over 1 million online students from the previous year (Allen & Seaman, 2010). The ever-increasing student interest in online education has mandated more involvement from adjunct and full-time faculty. According to the National Center for Education Statistics (2010), 49 percent of instructional staff in degree-granting postsecondary institutions hold part-time or contingent positions. A study by the Association of Public and Land-Grant Universities (Seaman, 2009), which included both full-time and adjunct faculty at sixty-nine public institutions across the country, indicated that more than one-third of public university faculty have taught an online course.

Further diversifying faculty roles and the locations for faculty work is the growth of other forms of distance education, specifically the trend toward branch or satellite campuses. In addition to domestic branch campuses, typified by institutions such as Penn State and the University of California system, international branch campuses are on the rise, up 43 percent in just three years according to a 2009 study by the Observatory on Borderless Higher Education (Jaschik, 2009). Unlike state or even nationwide branch campuses, international campuses particularly accentuate the phenomenon of geographically dispersed faculty: some of these faculty may never, or very rarely, set foot on their institution's flagship campus. As a result of these factors and the varied instructional modalities now available, the traditional faculty role and related professional development needs are being redefined for both full-time and adjunct faculty.

Beyond Training to Development: The Challenges of Working with Geographically Dispersed Faculty

Conversations about the needs of geographically dispersed faculty typically focus on training faculty, primarily adjunct faculty, to teach and develop courses online (Cranton, 2005). The Association of Public and Land-Grant Universities' report (Seaman, 2009), The Paradox of Faculty Voices: Views and Experiences with Online Learning, which assessed campus support structures for full-time and adjunct faculty teaching online, affirms this well-established emphasis on technology training. Faculty respondents ranked only one of eight faculty support dimensions as acceptable: technology infrastructure. Tellingly, support dimensions related to curriculum development, student support, incentives for course development, and promotion, retention, and recognition were ranked below average. In addition, in her survey of faculty development programs in distance education, McQuiggan (2007) found that most programs center on "step-by-step" training processes, "dissemination of information," or the "development of specific skills" (para. 39). She offered that "while there is evidence of faculty changes, there is little reporting of reflective thought, questioning of prior beliefs and assumptions about their classroom teaching, or rethinking their teaching philosophy" (para. 2). These activities (reflecting on and improving pedagogical practice, reenvisioning one's instructional role and philosophy) move beyond training to align with the aims and transformative potential of faculty and instructional development.

Findings from Bartley's (2001) study of twenty-seven higher education institutions within Ohio also confirm the tendency of faculty development programs in distance education to stress training over development. After surveying distance learning faculty and administrators and analyzing exemplary programs, Bartley concluded that "distance teaching is not just about using technology; it is about perfecting a pedagogical art for effective learning" and requires a systematic approach to "institutional collaboration and innovation" (para. 1). Indeed, calls for collaboration across academic and administrative units are prevalent in conversations about online faculty development, as well as support for face-to-face teaching at branch campuses. The American Association of University Professors and the Canadian Association of University Teachers' 2009 joint statement asserted, "Continued pursuit of this path [establishing branch campuses, particularly internationally] will accelerate the casualization of the academic workforce, taking its toll on the quality of instruction as well as adversely affecting faculty rights." The statement concluded that faculty involvement and collaboration to create standards for curriculum development and faculty evaluation are paramount to the ongoing vitality of higher education (Jaschik, 2009, para. 2). The Association of Public and Land-Grant Universities echoed: "Campus leaders should maintain consistent communication with all faculty and administrators regarding the role and purpose of online learning programs as they relate to academic mission and academic quality . . . and use communication strategies *that target and engage all faculty members*" (Seaman, 2009, p. 50, emphasis added).

As numbers of courses and academic programs offered by distance education modalities continue to increase, faculty developers face new opportunities and challenges to traditional models of faculty development and distance faculty training. Academic and administrative units are compelled to augment traditional technology training–oriented programs with new approaches that draw on the potential of faculty and instructional development and that work toward the goal of integrating geographically dispersed faculty.

Purpose of the Study

Our work in faculty development at institutions with multicampus structures and large online learning programs compelled the design of a research study that would connect us with campus leaders facing similar opportunities to design pedagogically focused, inclusive faculty development programs. Moreover, with two researchers personally experiencing working from a distance, we have observed firsthand the need for faculty at a distance to connect and interact with their on-campus peers in shared faculty development endeavors. Thus, we sought to:

- Identify faculty developers from diverse institutions across the country who have developed strategies for inclusive faculty development programming
- Identify the features of effective, inclusive faculty development programming
- Obtain a more comprehensive understanding of the challenges and opportunities presented by the diversification of faculty roles and geographical locations

Participants and Method

Recognizing the complex contextual factors that affect the priorities and outcomes of faculty development at any institution, qualitative research was emphasized, consisting primarily of individual interviews with faculty developers who agreed to participate in the study by invitation. A list of potential participant institutions was compiled based on the Carnegie Basic Classifications and the Professional and Organizational Development Network in Higher Education (Professional and Organizational Development Network in Higher Education, 2007) faculty development program types: faculty committee–run programs, programs run by a single individual, centralized programs, and decentralized programs. Given our focus on learning from institutions with established distance learning programs, we cross-referenced institutional member lists from the Sloan Consortium and the Western Cooperative of Educational Technologies. Volunteer participants were recruited through e-mail invitation and asked to complete an informed-consent form prior to the interview.

A range of institutional classifications and faculty development program types was involved in the study. The majority of the institutions (approximately 70 percent) were POD members. In total, thirty institutions were involved in the study, with interviewees providing information on institutional dynamics and faculty development initiatives for geographically dispersed faculty. Represented in the sample are the following institution types: 73.3 percent public, 20 percent private nonprofit, and 6.7 percent private for profit. Using the ATLAS.ti qualitative analysis software, we coded interview transcripts and researcher notes and identified content themes based on the frequency of terms and topics, as well as themes suggested by the interview questions (see the appendix at the end of the chapter).

Results

The topics emerging from the interview transcript analysis resulted in five overarching categories (with percentage of total responses for each category indicated):

- Guiding perceptions of faculty development needs (11 percent)
- Emergent trends in inclusive faculty development programming (27 percent)
- Scope of faculty development (18 percent)
- Institutional position of faculty development (32 percent)
- Integration of faculty development with academic departments (12 percent)

For the purposes of presenting these data, we collapsed these five topics into two overarching content themes correlated to the study objectives: guiding perceptions and emerging trends, and organizational challenges.

Guiding Perceptions and Emerging Trends

Interview participants provided contextual information about their institutions, including number of full-time and adjunct faculty teaching in various modalities and the support structures in place for distance faculty. Emerging structures revealed through the interviews were consistent with trends noted in the literature: although the majority of full-time faculty at the institutions participated in some way in distance education, most notably online teaching and course development, most of the geographically dispersed faculty were adjuncts teaching online or at branch campuses. In addition to faculty demographics, two data themes surfaced that directly related to our objective of uncovering inclusive faculty development strategies:

- Theme 1: Guiding perceptions of faculty development needs
- Theme 2: Emergent trends in inclusive faculty development programming

A significant amount of interview dialogue addressed the underlying assumptions commonly held about the needs of geographically dispersed faculty. Consistent with the literature reviewed, the guiding perceptions of geographically dispersed faculty development centered on technology training and orientation to institutional policies and procedures. These perceptions were most evident when the directors of centralized teaching centers referred us to campus distance and continuing education offices or instructional technology offices when asked to talk about their support of geographically dispersed faculty. Even when discussed in the context of centralized faculty development, geographically dispersed faculty needs were almost exclusively described in terms of technology training. For example, one participant shared: "The idea is to prepare them to teach online and they are all over the range in terms of their current skills and abilities, but ultimately we have a series of outcomes we want to get all [of] our faculty to—toward teaching online and that's what we work towards."

Another interviewee highlighted the importance of training based on the university's learning management system (LMS):

> The university is encouraging people to go hybrid and to use the [LMS] system as a supplement for readings, course scheduling, and so

> forth. But what we're recognizing is that the model that we've used to do LMS training and course design, which have kind of come together in a lot of ways for the online faculty, is just not scalable when you are dealing with the whole campus.

Another interviewee echoed:

> I think most faculty need to know how to use the learning management system (the basics, such as Gradebook, etc.). They also need a lot of pedagogical support when they first start, and our instructional designers work with those who are going to be teaching students through [the LMS system] and we've been asked to help all of our faculty who will be using the system.

To be sure, interview participants shared practical strategies for measuring such needs, including use of Web-based surveys and focus groups. Importantly, participants cautioned against the assumption that geographically dispersed faculty necessarily desire online training. However, it is clear that much outreach to geographically dispersed faculty comes in the form of encouragement to use the technologies their institutions have adopted. The pressure to implement mandated trainings for faculty at a distance often results in little time for conversations about how technology can directly affect and improve student learning or dialogue among diverse faculty constituents about how they have used such technologies to improve teaching and learning.

The interview data also uncovered emergent trends in faculty development and examples of innovative programming across institution types. Although a vast majority of these trends pertained to technology training, of particular note were efforts involving the use of various technologies (for example, LMS and virtual conferencing software) to deploy inclusive, dialogue, and constructivist-oriented approaches to training, specifically those that integrated technology training with pedagogical application. For example, some institutions have replaced individual online course development with a program development approach in which an instructional designer works with groups of faculty to envision and create an entire program. An interviewee described such a program:

> The way we've worked with faculty in the past is through one-on-one relationships where we identify a course or program that we are going to help. What we started doing is having *program development* rather than *individual course development* . . . where we would have groups of faculty coming together with one instructional designer to talk about the best approach for that program. And what we anticipate,

> what we think we found this first semester trying that, is the faculty actually serve as much as a resource as the designer and they are able to bounce ideas off one another and it saves us. . . . Instead of seven or eight individual conversations, presentations, and discussions we now have one that serves many folks.

This collaborative approach productively disrupts the dyad of traditional course development and allows room for faculty to collaboratively generate not only content but also programwide pedagogical strategies. Several institutions reported involving adjunct faculty who routinely teach a course online or at a branch campus to participate in course redesign and redevelopment with a full-time faculty content developer.

In addition to such task-specific collaborations, other institutions reported virtual, asynchronous teaching and learning conferences, which serve to link affiliate faculty from across the country (and even the world) with their academic departments to discuss student outcomes and curriculum consistency across instructional modalities and locations. Online special interest groups housed within an LMS are encouraged at some institutions; forming organically around instructor-identified topics of interest, these groups blur the line between on- and off-campus faculty. Some institutions are creating ways to reach their faculty through their own networked learning communities, as one study participant described:

> We have a series of podcasts that will be posted to our Web site . . . and the vision is for our center to be a place where faculty can come anytime they want to be able to hear about what we do so they can download presentations/podcasts to their smart phones and listen to them . . . and some of their resources will be unique to the Web site where faculty can also be pointed to other resources online and to access resources directly.

Another participant added, "We've created something called 'the village' for a virtual faculty open forum and discussion area; some are general discussion areas, and some are by discipline."

Open access academic commons or community-constructed repositories of pedagogical tips also acknowledge the expertise and contributions of distributed and contingent faculty. And certificate programs, both intra- and cross-institutional, most often facilitated through LMSs, were cited as a means of professionalizing contingent faculty roles and restoring the pedagogical and professional development dimensions to adjunct faculty hiring and preparation. Thus, despite a persistent emphasis on technology, there is evidence that some institutions are increasingly prioritizing pedagogy over training.

Organizational Challenges

Over half of the data themes related to the organization of and resource allocation for faculty development at participants' institutions. Approaching the interviews, we assumed that discussion of organizational dynamics would be little more than a naturally occurring outcome of our research. Our principal goal was to uncover strategies and best practices for inclusive faculty development—that is, faculty development designed for and accessible to both full-time and adjunct faculty, regardless of instructional modality or geographical location. We perceived that discussions about the infrastructure of faculty development would be limited to information gathering about institutional models and demographics. However, several of the final data themes related to organizational dynamics:

- Theme 3: Scope of faculty development
- Theme 4: Institutional position of faculty development
- Theme 5: Integration of faculty development with academic departments

The scope of faculty development for distance faculty directly correlated to the institutional position of faculty development entities. We found, overwhelmingly, that geographically dispersed faculty were rarely considered a primary audience for centralized faculty development centers, even those including adjunct faculty in their mission statements. Instead and certainly tied to the guiding perceptions of distance faculty development, most faculty development professionals referred us to administrative leadership within distance and continuing education offices for more information about support for geographically dispersed faculty. This pattern proved significant: it suggested that traditional teaching and learning centers are not equipped for, or do not see as part of their responsibilities, supporting full-time and adjunct faculty who are geographically removed from the institution's flagship campus. One participant said:

> The center handles the faculty development initiatives for our face-to-face trainings. Academic Affairs oversees the training, hiring, and supervision of the distance faculty. Most distance faculty are adjuncts that are working from a distance. All distance faculty are required to complete a moderated three-week training course and are subject

> to ongoing peer review. Course development happens as a separate process that is done out of Curriculum Services.

Another interviewee explained:

> We mostly work with faculty who are on campus. We've been sensitized, as we have an outreach school responsible for the distance learning, and they have moved more and more to the model that the faculty who teach in the outreach courses are supposed to be faculty who are hired by departments.

Varying functions and roles also exist within each faculty development center as described by this study participant: "Academic parts all belong to the academic departments; we just provide support services. We do market analysis, marketing, recruiting, course design and development, student services, advising, and financial aid." This organizational dynamic could help explain the persistent emphasis on technology training and policy orientation we uncovered.

To address this fragmentation of technologically and pedagogically oriented development initiatives, several institutions have begun to forge intentional partnerships and networks among leaders from perennially disparate campus entities (for example, department heads, faculty developers, instructional technologists, assessment experts, and administrative personnel in extended, continuing, and distance studies). These partnerships are often realized by creating new roles or collaborations—for instance, faculty who are granted instructional release time to serve as liaisons or translators of distance learning procedures and policies to their department colleagues; administrative positions, funded by the distance learning administrative office, that "live" in the academic departments; faculty development positions for branch campuses; and university committees that routinely bring together administrative leaders from distance learning, academic technologies, and faculty development centers to assess duplication of services, resources, and initiatives. These models work against a top-down or unilateral approach to emphasize an inclusive, collaborative dynamic for identifying and addressing the needs of all faculty, regardless of location.

Discussion

Our conversations with faculty developers and distance education administrative leaders about the scope, organization, institutional position, and audiences for faculty development belied larger epistemological issues related to the purposes and outcomes of such efforts. As a way of framing such issues, the literature on knowledge management offers language for identifying and articulating a distinction between training and development, between explicit and tacit knowledge prioritization. This research has been used to theorize a number of issues in higher education (Carlson, 2002; Kidwell, Vander Linde, & Johnson, 2000; Serban & Luan, 2002) and can capture the epistemological and related structural issues that emerged from our study.

Through the lens of knowledge management, we generalized that most faculty development programs operating out of traditional, centralized university teaching centers privilege tacit knowledge, understood as the combination of "information with experience" (Carlson, 2002, p. 8). Cultivation of tacit knowledge requires programs and venues that engage faculty in mentoring relationships and provide opportunities for ongoing, informal dialogue about teaching scenarios and challenges, placing the explicit knowledge of policy and procedure into a meaningful context. Such initiatives foster a sense of loyalty to the institution by conveying a regard for the professional growth of full-time and adjunct faculty and the ongoing improvement of curriculum and student learning. Inherent in this orientation toward tacit knowledge is an emphasis on creating a community of scholars and valuing each faculty member as a contributor to larger, more inclusive faculty development efforts. Conversely, faculty development programs emanating from administrative units within distance learning offices possessed more strengths in the domain of explicit knowledge. As such, focus is often placed on disseminating how-to technical knowledge and performance expectations, as opposed to fostering an integrated faculty community. In this orientation, faculty are passive recipients of explicit knowledge, with few opportunities to contribute their expertise or build their professional skills. To be sure, both tacit and explicit knowledge are essential for well-rounded professional development, which suggests a need for models that take advantage of both knowledge paradigms. As expressed in Table 1.1, hybridizing or networking centralized and decentralized resources involves grounding faculty in the explicit knowledge they need to succeed in particular institutional and disciplinary contexts, while also fostering the tacit knowledge that derives from experience and is generated in communities.

Implications

Devising inclusive faculty development initiatives starts with interrogating persistent and limiting assumptions about the needs of geographically dispersed faculty. Such assumptions include privileging the transmission of explicit knowledge, especially in the form of technological and procedural

Table 1.1 Knowledge Management Analysis of Professional Development Paradigms for Geographically Dispersed Faculty.

	Explicit Knowledge	Tacit Knowledge
Features	Easily codified Storable Transferable Easy to capture and share Orients Transmits knowledge Reflects institutional identity Overemphasized	Personal Context specific and situational Difficult to formalize Difficult to capture and share Equips Facilitates community Creates institutional loyalty Deemphasized or neglected
Sources, scope	Scripted, formal Institutional perspectives Current understandings Administratively driven University centered	Informal, organic Personal faculty experiences Historical understandings Faculty and department driven Discipline centered
Venues	Instructions Policy statements Training modules, Webinars Static Web site content Newsletters Tips and strategies Technology help pages	E-mentoring Interactive, application-oriented modules Dynamic Web site content Discussion boards Instructor blogs Community wikis
Institutional models	Centralized	Decentralized

Source: *Adapted from Serban and Luan (2002, p.10).*

support (for example, how to use an LMS; how to respond to student incivility, a grade challenge, or an instance of plagiarism), over engaging distance faculty in conversations about disciplinary content and pedagogical strategy.

Explicit knowledge in the form of technology training and instructional policies and procedures, for example, equips faculty with the resources to perform effectively and uphold institutional practice. This type of explicit knowledge is especially important to the process of orienting new faculty, but it should not comprise the whole of faculty development programming. Explicit knowledge in the form of best practices for pedagogy should be captured from across the faculty communities (full time, adjunct, distance, and local) and disseminated in ways that support the general and discipline-specific pedagogical effectiveness of all faculty. In addition, tacit knowledge—that which is constructed through interaction and builds community at the same time that it advances practice—must be far from a secondary concern. Faculty development initiatives must be equally concerned with capturing and disseminating explicit knowledge and fostering tacit knowledge, recognizing that, "ironically, in most of today's human systems, enormous quantities of explicit knowledge may actually hinder the emergence of tacit knowledge in individuals, as members of the organization struggle just to keep from drowning in the flood of information" (Carlson, 2002, p. 8).

A final, overarching implication of this study points to the value of leveraging collaboration to create hybrid models for faculty development. Faculty development initiatives should strive to move beyond information transfer to help faculty build communities of practice around academic disciplines and instructional modalities. While communities of practice can be administrated in a centralized manner, they are decentralized by nature. Velez (2009) summarized the foundational research on communities of practice:

> Members of a Community of Practice are brought together through *joint enterprise*, which is a set of common activities and common goals that are understood and continually renegotiated by the members. . . . *MUTUAL ENGAGEMENT* sustains the Community of Practice because they are bound by their common goals and become a social entity. . . . [Finally,] the Community of Practice has a *shared repertoire* of *communal resources* like routines, language, styles, habits, that the group members develop over a period of time [para. 3].

Faculty development professionals can take their cues from the community of practice approach by seeking to collaborate across institutional divisions (academic and administrative) and organizing opportunities around common problems and authentic contexts.

Conclusion

Our study suggests there is much value in creating structures and programs that incorporate flexibility for both integration and differentiation of faculty communities, academic disciplines, and administrative units—dependent on the audience, topic, and learning objective of the training or development. The study points to a need for initiatives that more substantially support the pedagogical effectiveness of geographically dispersed faculty, full-time and adjunct, as well as that help faculty build communities of practice around academic disciplines and instructional modalities. While technology training and practical orientation are necessary, the cultivation and dissemination of tacit knowledge, that is, lived wisdom, draw on the potential of professional and instructional development integrating faculty with diverse appointments and locations.

Appendix: Interview Questions

- What are the mission and goals of your faculty development center? How do these relate to your institution's mission, goals, and culture?
- Whom does your center serve? Is the center a centralized academic resource, serving all disciplines and instructional modalities?
- Does the scope of your faculty development programming extend to faculty working at a distance? Both those teaching online and face-to-face?
- How is distance education coordinated at your institution? To what extent is it centralized through the academic departments? How does the organization of distance education affect faculty development services?
- What specific professional development needs do you perceive (or perhaps that you have learned from assessment) relevant to faculty working from a distance? How do these compare to the needs of other faculty?
- What are some of the challenges that you've encountered in supporting the work of faculty working from a distance?
- Are these challenges similar or different across full-time and adjunct faculty populations?
- What faculty development resources do you offer to faculty working from a distance? Do you attempt to make all flagship/central/main campus resources available to those off-campus, or is the programming distinct?
- Which of your faculty development resources/programs/initiatives has been most used by faculty working from a distance?

- Based on your experiences, which faculty development programming features work best for faculty working from a distance, and which do not?

REFERENCES

Allen, I. E., & Seaman, J. (2010). *Class differences: Online education in the United States.* Sloan Consortium. Retrieved from http://sloanconsortium.org/sites/default/files/class_differences.pdf

Bartley, J. M. (2001). *Faculty training and development initiatives for effective instruction in distance education.* Cincinnati, OH: University of Cincinnati Press.

Bower, B. (2001). Distance education: Facing the faculty challenge. *Online Journal of Distance Learning Administration*, 2(1). Retrieved from http://www.westga.edu/~distance/ojdla/summer42/bower42.html

Carlson, P. (2002). A community of practice: Web portals and faculty development. *Journal of Computing in Higher Education, 13*(2), 4–24.

Cranton, P. (2005). Not making or shaping: Finding authenticity in faculty development. In S. Chadwick-Blossey & D. R. Robertson (Eds.), *To improve the academy: Resources for faculty, instructional, and organizational development, Vol. 24* (pp. 70–85). San Francisco, CA: Jossey-Bass/Anker.

Eaton, J. (2001). *Distance learning: Academic and political challenges for higher education accreditation.* Retrieved from http://www.chea.org/pdf/mono_1_dist_learning_2001.pdf

Gappa, J. M., Austin, A. E., & Trice, A. C. (2007). *Rethinking faculty work: Higher education's strategic imperative.* San Francisco, CA: Jossey-Bass.

Jaschik, S. (2009). Scrutiny and standards for branch campuses. *Inside HigherEd.* Retrieved from http://www.insidehighered.com/news/2009/04/09/branch

Kidwell, J., Vander Linde, K., & Johnson, S. (2000). Applying corporate knowledge management practices in higher education. *EDUCAUSE Quarterly, 23*(4), 28–33.

McQuiggan, C. A. (2007). The role of faculty development in online teaching's potential to question teaching beliefs and assumptions. *Online Journal of Distance Learning Administration, 10*(3). Retrieved from http://www.westga.edu/~distance/ojdla/summer122/velez122.html

National Center for Education Statistics. (2010). *Digest of education statistics, 2010: Table 255.* Retrieved from http://nces.ed.gov/programs/digest/d10/tables/dt10_255.asp?referrervreport

Professional and Organizational Development Network in Higher Education. (2007). *What is faculty development?* Retrieved from http://www.podnetwork.org/faculty_development/definitions.htm

Seaman, J. (2009). *The paradox of faculty voices: Views and experiences with online learning.* Washington, DC: Association of Public and Land-Grant Universities. Retrieved from http://sloanconsortium.org/sites/default/files/APLU_online_strategic_asset_vol2–1.pdf

Serban, A. M., & Luan, J. (2002). Overview of knowledge management. In A. M. Serban & J. Luan (Eds.), *New directions for institutional research, No. 113. Knowledge management: Building a competitive advantage in higher education* (pp. 5–16). San Francisco, CA: Jossey-Bass.

Velez, A. (2009). The ties that bind: How faculty learning communities connect online adjuncts to their virtual institutions. *Online Journal of Distance Learning Administration, 12*(2). Retrieved from http://www.westga.edu/~distance/ojdla/summer122/velez122.html

2

IMPLEMENTING A UNIVERSITY LEARNING CONSORTIUM FOR SHARED COMMUNICATION AND PROACTIVE CAMPUS CHANGE

David W. Schumann, Dorian Stiefel
University of Tennessee

Michelle Corvette
Goldsmiths, University of London

Chutney W. Guyton
North Carolina Central University

One problem that large, comprehensive universities often share is the lack of communication and synergistic creativity between units and services related to teaching and student learning. Moreover, large universities have difficulty creating and reinforcing needed change. This chapter provides a case study of a strategy for initiating and maintaining a university learning consortium. The consortium brings together center directors, faculty scholars, and administrators to operate as an independent think tank on campus. The members engage in dialogue, generate creative ideas, and design and propose policies and practices that reflect desired change.

A number of consequences ensue when university units charged with faculty development work independently and do not communicate with one another. Obvious negative repercussions include duplication of services, lack of knowledge about other units, and missed opportunities to work together to better serve individual faculty needs. At a higher level, three problems emerge. First, the lack of community around teaching and learning leaves people unsupported and working alone. Second, important projects are not addressed, either because people do not have time or because the projects fall into the gaps between individuals' responsibilities; there is work that everyone means to handle but nobody does. Third, many of the teaching and learning problems require maturity and strategic thinking. For each of these problems, working together as a group produces far more creative alternatives than working individually. The remedy to these failures of communication is the learning consortium, described in this chapter, that provides faculty development leaders with expanded opportunities, collaborations, and leverage.

Many large public universities provide multiple support services focused on teaching and student learning: student success centers, teaching and learning centers, libraries, instructional technology (if independent of teaching and learning centers), centers for international education, public policy centers, organized outreach centers and programs, and housing (such as learning communities), for example. In addition, these large institutions have multiple structures with responsibility for curriculum to include central administration (often the provost), college administrators, and faculty senate representatives. In most cases, these services and structures often appear to work independently. By their very nature, such separate services and structures reinforce less-than-optimal between-group communication and decrease the potential for synergistic creativity.

One way to encourage increased communication across these learning-focused units and university structures is to create an entity that is inclusive of all relevant units and is focused on interactive dialogue. In 2008, the University of Tennessee initiated the Tennessee Teaching and Learning Center (TENN TLC). With a new center came the opportunity to create a vehicle to bring multiple units together, all involved in the support of teaching and student learning. The vehicle employed was a learning consortium (LC).

The overall purpose in establishing the consortium was twofold. First, it was thought that encouraging direct communication would increase understanding of roles and practices and contribute to intercenter communication, engagement, and potential for synergistic approaches to new initiatives. Second, such a representative group could consider some critical issues and concerns related to teaching and student learning and the related need for improvement and change. This chapter focuses on the supportive literature, purpose, design, membership, implementation and maintenance, and results to date of the University of Tennessee's learning consortium.

Literature Review

Consortia represent a sharing of governance among directors of centers, key faculty members, administrators, and graduate students collaborating as change agents to influence the culture and policies of an institution (Baron, 2006; Chism, 1998; Cox, 2001; Dawson, Mighty, & Britnell, 2010; Howe & Strauss, 2007; Lieberman & Guskin, 2003; Marshall, 1999; Schroeder & Spannagel, 2006). The concept of collaboration, the grouping and pairing of individuals for the purpose of achieving a goal by relying on each other, has been widely researched and advocated throughout the academic literature (Bruffee, 1993; Dawson, Britnell, & Hitchcock, 2009; Garrison & Vaughan, 2008; Gerlach, 1994; Kerka, 1997; Peters & Armstrong, 1998; Saltiel, 1998; Wildavsky, 1986). Proponents of collaboration point out that the active exchange of ideas within small groups not only increases interest but may also promote critical thinking, greater effectiveness, efficiency, and a better campus environment (Gokhale, 1995; Kezar & Lester, 2009; Mattessich & Monsey, 1992). Likewise, collabora tion among individuals and groups who share a common vision is essential for developing, sustaining, and reshaping educational systems. Fullan (1993, 1995) observed that collaboration is necessary for ongoing learning; without collaborative skills and relationships, change can be a slow process.

Collaboration between faculty developers and support system staff can provide great value. Faculty members often travel from one center to another (for example, those for teaching and learning, library, and instructional technology), searching for the right tools to facilitate student learning in their classrooms. Many faculty scholars and administrators believe that integration and collaboration improve the quality of teaching, research, and service (Bakker, 1995; Clark, 1997; Garrison & Akyol, 2009; Jenkins, 2000; Taylor, 2005). Integrated services bring together faculty members' teaching, research, and services more effectively (Colbeck, 1998; Ferren & Stanton, 2004; Maehr & Braskamp, 1986; Martin, Schermerhorn, & Larson, 1989). Furthermore, integrated services reinforce the wise use of faculty resources, which ultimately benefits students and other beneficiaries of college and university work (Kezar & Lester, 2009; Krahenbuhl, 1998).

Developing Commitment for a Learning Consortium

As the inaugural director of the TENN TLC was interviewing for his position, it became apparent to him that the units responsible for various aspects of teaching and student learning were not provided the opportunities to communicate with one another. This led him to the idea of a learning consortium (LC) where center directors, creative faculty, and progressive administrators could have meaningful conversations and form joint ventures. To initiate the consortium at the university, the inaugural director identified key potential participants: other center directors (director-level individuals from the Student Success Center, University Libraries, Center for International Education, Office of Information Technology's Educational Support Group, and Howard H. Baker Jr. Center for Public Policy). He met with each one individually to discuss the idea of a learning consortium. Receptivity for the idea was universally strong.

The next step was to advise the provost's office of the desire to create the LC. Because three of the center directors were on the provost's staff, the idea was strongly supported by the central administration.

Once initial buy-in was established, a list was generated of other key administrators and faculty scholars who were deemed to be thought leaders and appropriate candidates for membership in the consortium. Drawing from the literature and research on collaboration (Bergman, 1992; Mattessich & Monsey, 1992), careful attention was given to the selection and organization of the LC membership. An initial decision was also made to limit the group to fifteen members in order to keep it to a manageable size. In addition to the center directors, the remaining members of the LC were the associate dean of the College of Arts and Science (representing the largest college), the chair of the Faculty Senate Teaching Council, the assistant provost for student success (which included responsibility for student advising), and a set of innovative faculty involved in a high level of student engagement through experiential, collaborative, and distance learning pedagogies. Over the past three years, the group has added director representation from the Undergraduate General Education Committee, Undergraduate Policies Committee, graduate school, Chancellor's Honors Program, academic deans, Department of Student Housing, and university president's staff (systems level).

The rationale for identifying and adding key participants reflects several distinct needs that include campuswide representation, diverse information sources, knowledge of campus personnel, and the ability to facilitate action. More than a traditional university committee or council, the learning consortium mixes people at different job levels and from different types of units. Whereas administrative units are often brought together by a central administrator reflecting the responsibilities of that central administrator, the learning consortium was developed to reinforce the communication and collaboration between a combination of entities. Moreover, because the consortium does not have to operate as would a unit resembling a functional silo, its independent and broad-based nature represents more diverse thinking and the ability to consider a greater number of alternatives for forwarding the teaching and learning effort at the university.

Learning Consortium Structure

The structure of the learning consortium was developed over time with the input and involvement of a wide range of participants and perspectives.

Stage I Meetings: Getting Started and a Strategic Plan

To facilitate the collaborative approach, the learning consortium began meeting in October 2008 with the specific purpose of addressing concerns, issues, and activities related to the question of how students at the university learn best. In the initial meeting, the decision was made that all members would commit to being full participants in the consortium discussions and full collaborators in the design and implementation of actions, and they would have an equal voice regarding all group decisions. The role of the facilitator would be a shared responsibility among the group members.

The first meeting began with each person sharing his or her thoughts with regard to his or her own interest in the group and how each perceived its purpose. This facilitated a co-constructed understanding of shared mission and purpose. The initial facilitator, the TENN TLC inaugural director, reflected on the importance of maintaining mutual respect, trust, flexibility, openness, and shared communications. All agreed, and meetings were set at a three-week interval.

In order to open up the discussion and begin to understand the areas of concern that could be the focus of the learning consortium, the group participated in an affinity exercise where each member was asked to share the issues, thoughts, or activities that were important to improving an understanding of student learning. The results of the affinity exercise revealed a set of learning-related clusters: vision, support, incentives, learning advances, pedagogical research, communication, assessment, students, and faculty. It became apparent that a systematic planning approach (Kaufman & Herman, 1991) was needed to address these interests. Between the first and second meeting, the results of the affinity exercise informed a working group that authored a strategic planning document. It was agreed that the strategic plan, which emphasizes collaborative decision making, should include the following components: developing a cocreated mission (purposes and beliefs), identifying appropriate objectives and respective strategies for addressing those objectives, and addressing the needs and issues derived from the affinity exercise.

During the second meeting, a significant amount of time was spent on refining the mission statement. It was clear that all members wanted to make sure the preferred language was correct because this statement would potentially represent the group with other university stakeholders. The following mission statement was adopted:

> The purpose of the University of Tennessee Learning Consortium (UTLC) is to support and facilitate the enhancement of learning at the University of Tennessee through the purposeful interaction of individual learning facilitators across the UT faculty and administration. The UTLC is comprised of learning related center directors, faculty, and college administrators directly involved in the design and delivery of creative learning pedagogy.
>
> The UTLC will provide an independent voice offering guidance and support to the University community in order to create a better learning environment. By working as a group and through partnerships with other learning facilitators in the University community and outside of the University, the UTLC will generate ideas, approaches, processes, research and propose policy that addresses the state of current and future learning. This accumulated knowledge will be disseminated to the University community through a number of means (e.g., workshops, presentations, papers, articles, workbooks). The UTLC will also foster continuous improvement of teaching and learning through ongoing review and discussion of each other's activities, practices, and policies, as well as other related teaching and learning initiatives. It is envisioned that this will lead to creation of a culture of teaching and learning excellence that is facilitated, integrated, and reinforced throughout the University community.

During the second meeting, members suggested changes to the strategic plan such as editing the objectives, the language of the strategies, and the order and specifics of the tactics. In the third and final meeting of stage I, each objective and the resultant strategies and tactics were examined closely and revised in final form as necessary. The following objectives were finalized:

1. Create a professional learning community environment within the UTLC where all perspectives can be voiced and considered.
2. Research new integrated learning strategies and the changing characteristics and needs of our students.
3. Develop new pedagogical models and inform critical stakeholders.
4. Improve assessment of teaching and learning.
5. Create cultural change within units to reinforce engagement in the understanding and facilitation of student learning.

Given that each objective had multiple strategies and each strategy had one or more tactics, implementing the plan required leadership from the learning consortium members. Thus, during the third meeting, each person voiced one or more objectives in which he or she was willing to lead a working group that would address the needed strategies. It was believed that these working groups should be inclusive and reach out to others in the university community.

During this first stage of meetings it was also important to discuss the specific products from the work. The group decided on four major outputs:

- Sharing creative ideas within the LC that could be adopted relatively quickly by one or more of the centers as well as by individual faculty participants
- The creation by each working group of a product (for example, a white paper, guide, checklist) that would provide policy or practice recommendations
- The use of specific information from these products and, where appropriate, the development of faculty development modules for professional training (for example, workshops, presentations, papers, articles, and workbooks)
- The need to pool both personnel and financial resources, as appropriate, to be used to bring in external speakers and provide faculty and students with meaningful cosponsored learning activities

Stage II Meetings: Implementation and Continued Generation of Ideas

After completion of the initial strategic planning work came the need to develop a structure for all subsequent meetings. It was decided that all meetings would last ninety minutes. Two main types of presentation content were envisioned. The first included working group updates, sharing new ideas, reports on recent and forthcoming events, and presentations of existing learning and faculty development strategies. The second included meetings that would focus primarily on revising a targeted product.

Although the objectives in the strategic plan were broad, several initial work groups reflecting one or more objectives were initiated, and more have been generated over the past three years of the learning consortium's existence.

Finally, and perhaps of greatest importance, meetings are an excellent venue for ongoing conversations about teaching and learning topics. Every meeting begins with an update from two or three of the center directors or other members, and each update sparks further conversation and new ideas. Many of these ideas reflect ways in which two or more of the represented units or members can work together more effectively. This represents the initial reason for forming the consortium, and it now appears to be a highly valued aspect.

Discourse in the learning consortium is advanced through problem-solving activities, playful discussions, and challenging questions. Fundamentally, respect for each other and the mission of improving teaching and learning influences everyone's approach to the meetings and each other. The collaborative philosophy of the group was developed early and is reinforced consistently by members and the facilitator.

This approach to discourse and collaboration leads to new insights by allowing people to work together, play off each other, share multiple perspectives, and incorporate different views. One early insight was the value of listening to what people had to say, which in turn provided individuals with new ways of thinking; another is the importance of attempting to carry the conversations that learning consortium members are having beyond the group. Finally, members admit that multiple ways to effect change and multiple outcomes can be acceptable. In one case, discussions in the group provoked a proposal for a teaching academy consisting of creative faculty across campus who meet together and then return to their departments with new ideas and potential guest speakers. Membership in the teaching academy will rotate over time to include different departments and faculty.

Examples of the Learning Consortium Work and Results to Date

One issue that was raised early in the learning consortium's existence was the development of consistent standards for two emerging types of pedagogical delivery: online learning and service-learning. Two working groups were formed to review the existing literature, benchmark other schools, and author appropriate documents for faculty guidance. The former (types of online delivery) resulted in a comprehensive checklist for faculty of steps to consider and needs to address. This checklist for service-learning was presented to several faculty leaders with significant online teaching experience, then vetted by the consortium, and revised; it is now available on multiple university Web sites. This checklist served as a guiding structure for a summer institute in course design, a collaborative effort of two units represented in the consortium, employing three tracks for faculty (face-to-face, blended or hybrid, and pure online).

The focus on service-learning has sparked two initiatives. First, the learning consortium facilitator was asked by the provost's office to lead a task force to develop a business plan around service-learning for the campus. This task force, composed in part of learning consortium members, authored a proposal for a new center for community engagement that would incorporate service-learning but go much further to serve as a portal between the university and the community. This plan was vetted by the learning consortium members, was submitted to the provost, and is now under consideration for funding. Second, the emerging checklist for service-learning has spurred multiple faculty training workshops on the topic.

In addition, the learning consortium has made significant progress in addressing one of its initial objectives, assessment of teaching effectiveness and of student learning. To do so, it established two committees, both of which created documents useful to the university. First, a peer teaching evaluation guide was researched and authored. This document was approved by the provost and faculty senate as a guide and was disseminated to all department heads. Numerous anecdotal comments from department heads reflect that this document was essential, welcomed, and now widely employed across the various units on campus. Second, and perhaps the most meaningful learning consortium initiative to date, is addressing the challenging topic of improving institutional assessment of learning. A working group of the consortium collected research on the topic and developed an initial set of recommendations to the vice provost for academic programs. The learning consortium working group leader was then asked to convene a larger group as an official provost's task force on the topic. This group, working with the vice chancellor overseeing university accreditation, developed a comprehensive set of recommendations that connects directly to accreditation requirements of the university. This proposal has been accepted by the vice chancellor in charge of our upcoming accreditation process. As a result, the teaching and learning center has a search under way for an assistant director for research, assessment, and program evaluation. A primary function of this position is to lead department-level faculty training that directly addresses assessment of learning concerns.

The learning consortium has continued to use the first meeting of each academic year to generate new ideas. For example, at the beginning of the second year, the consortium voiced a desire to engage with students. A student forum on learning (SFL) was initiated under the sponsorship of the Tennessee Teaching and Learning Center (TLC). The SFL became active, meeting every three weeks, and it settled on two purposes. First, it serves to inform both the TLC and the learning consortium about students' needs regarding teaching and learning. Students from the group are invited to present their thoughts to the TLC staff and the learning consortium on a regular basis and react to the learning consortium members' ideas. Second, the SFL, with the learning consortium's encouragement, has generated its first white paper focused on student perceptions and student needs. This white paper was vetted by the learning consortium members, who proposed a widespread dissemination of the paper across campus. The paper was then submitted to the provost. Not only has the paper received significant attention by central administration and been widely disseminated to the administration, but the SFL has been asked by numerous groups to make a presentation. Furthermore, the provost has asked that members of the SFL serve as student representatives on key strategic planning committees and task forces. The SFL, with support and shared dialogue from the learning consortium, provides another vehicle for student voices to be heard.

The learning consortium is currently pursuing a number of projects:

- A teaching certification program for Ph.D. students (joint effort between the TENN TLC and the graduate school)
- A university cultural statement of shared values (for example, about civility, respect, desire to learn, and desire to improve) of those who study or work at the university
- A plan to increase the numbers of students studying abroad
- A common "university syllabus" available for faculty to include within course syllabi

- An assessment of the learning consortium's impact, including a discussion of the strengths and weaknesses of the University of Tennessee learning environment (broadly defined)

Conclusion: Potential Constraints and Review of Benefits

The development of a learning consortium, which in theory sounds like a logical idea to improve communication and take a more active role as a change agent within the university, contains certain inherent constraints and threats. Given the multiple roles the learning consortium members have on campus, each is extremely pressed for time. This has manifested itself in occasional absence from meetings and delay in completing projects. The consortium has addressed this constraint in three ways. It has increased its membership to create more working capacity. Next, it employs a few hours of time from a TENN TLC staff member who is responsible for taking and distributing minutes, arranging the schedule of meetings, and facilitating communication. Finally, it charged the consortium facilitator with keeping a careful eye on the progress of each working group and encouraging movement as appropriate.

A potential threat that exists is the ongoing question of how willing other campus entities are to allow a relatively independent think tank to exist on campus and have significant input into change. Several factors can mitigate this threat. Keeping both the provost's office and the faculty senate apprised of the learning consortium's activities is critical to sustaining this group's effectiveness and importance on campus. Over time, as a result of the quality of the products provided, trust can develop. Furthermore, by having key people from both faculty and administration as members of the consortium, the threat of a movement to centralize this effort under a central administrator is diminished although never erased. As the consortium becomes more visible with regard to suggesting practices and policy that guide change, it is possible that a reporting structure may be required. However, to date, the learning consortium has operated independent of a direct reporting line.

To best respond to this threat, the consortium is considering an assessment of its impact. While individual centers assess their activities as do cofacilitated projects between centers, no overall assessment of impact has been undertaken yet. As this chapter goes to press, the consortium has determined measures of assessment of impact that reflect adoption of recommendations and the extent of the adoption.

While certain constraints and threats are likely to exist for a learning consortium, four significant benefits can be identified and outweigh any concerns. First, by meeting on a regular basis, center directors are able to have a time set aside to communicate with one another and share new ideas that can potentially lead to integrated activities (such as shared workshops and shared funding of events) as well as improvement of the base services each center provides. Second, by recruiting innovative and creative participants, the group can serve as a think tank with regard to improvement of teaching and learning. New ideas can be discussed and considered for action. Third, the university benefits through the efforts of the group to consider needed changes in practices and policies. Fourth, through careful composition and inclusion, numerous units and individuals are represented, generating a wealth of perspectives and creative ideas.

A question to be posed is whether the learning consortium model transfers to multiple types of higher education institutions. We believe that the concept is generalizable across all types of colleges and universities. Although the learning consortium described in this chapter was initiated at a research-intensive institution, the underlying value proposition reflects a desire for joint communication and collaboration among entities to continuously improve the state of student learning. It seems logical that this value should be held in common across all types of higher education institutions. Such efforts can only enhance the student educational experience.

In sum, this chapter has offered faculty development leaders insights and a pathway for designing, promoting, and implementing the learning consortium concept. During its three-year existence, the University of Tennessee's learning consortium has engaged in numerous important activities and has created meaningful changes important to teaching effectiveness and student learning. It has intentionally and carefully built its membership to reinforce inclusivity. Each year it generates new ideas and builds on previous ones. The group remains energetic and highly focused. The philosophy of strategic inclusion, openness to ideas, the proactive nature of the group, and the creativity that comes from collaboration make it a desirable organizational entity on which to serve.

REFERENCES

Bakker, G. (1995, March 17). Using "pedagogical-impact statements" to make teaching and research symbiotic activities. *Chronicle of Higher Education*, B3.

Baron, L. (2006). The advantage of a reciprocal relationship between faculty development and organizational development in higher education. In S. Chadwick-Blossey & D. R. Robertson (Eds.), *To improve the academy: Resources for faculty, instructional, and organizational development, Vol. 24* (pp. 29–43). San Francisco, CA: Jossey-Bass/Anker.

Bergman, A. (1992). Lessons for principals from site-based management. *Educational Leadership, 50*(1), 48–51.

Bruffee, K. A. (1993). *Collaborative learning, higher education, interdependence and the authority of knowledge.* Baltimore, MD: Johns Hopkins University Press.

Chism, N.V.N. (1998). The role of educational developers in institutional change: From basement office to the front office. In M. Kaplan & D. Lieberman (Eds.), *To improve the academy: Resources for faculty, instructional, and organizational development, Vol. 17* (pp. 141–153). San Francisco, CA: Jossey-Bass/Anker.

Clark, B. R. (1997). The modern integration of research activities with teaching and learning. *Journal of Higher Education, 68,* 241–255.

Colbeck, C. L. (1998). Merging in a seamless blend: How faculty integrate teaching and research. *Journal of Higher Education, 69*(6), 647–671.

Cox, M. (2001). Faculty learning communities: Change agents for transforming institutions into learning organizations. In D. Lieberman & C. Wehlburg (Eds.), *To improve the academy: Resources for faculty, instructional, and organizational development, Vol. 19* (pp. 69–93). San Francisco, CA: Jossey-Bass/Anker.

Dawson, D., Britnell, J., & Hitchcock, A. (2009). Developing competency models of faculty developers: Using world café to foster dialogue. In L. Nilson & J. E. Miller (Eds.), *To improve the academy: Resources for faculty, instructional, and organizational development, Vol. 28* (pp. 3–24). San Francisco, CA: Jossey-Bass/Anker.

Dawson, D., Mighty, J., & Britnell, J. (2010). Moving from the periphery to the center of the academy: Faculty developers as leaders of change. In J. McDonald & D. Stockley (Eds.), *New directions for teaching and learning: No. 122. Pathways to the profession of educational development* (pp. 69–78). San Francisco: Jossey-Bass.

Ferren, A. S., & Stanton, W. W. (2004). *Leadership through collaboration: The role of the chief academic officer.* San Francisco, CA: Jossey-Bass.

Fullan, M. G. (1993). *Change forces: Probing the depth of educational reform.* New York: Falmer.

Fullan, M. G. (1995). The limits and the potential of professional development. In T. R. Guskey & M. Huberman (Eds.), *Professional development in education: New paradigms and practices* (pp. 253–267). New York: Teachers College Press.

Garrison, D. R., & Akyol, Z. (2009). Role of instructional technology in the transformation of higher education. *Journal of Computing in Higher Education, 21*(1), 19–30.

Garrison, D. R., & Vaughan, N.D. (2008). *Blended learning in higher education: Framework, principles, and guidelines.* San Francisco, CA: Jossey-Bass.

Gerlach, J. M. (1994). Is this collaboration? In K. Bosworth & S. J. Hamilton (Eds.), *New directions for teaching and learning: No. 59. Collaborative learning: Underlying processes and effective techniques* (pp. 5–14). San Francisco, CA: Jossey-Bass.

Gokhale, A. A. (1995). Collaborative learning enhances critical thinking. *Journal of Technology Education, 7*(1), 22–30.

Howe, N., & Strauss, W. (2007). *Millennials go to college* (2nd ed.). Great Falls, VA: Lifecourse Associates.

Jenkins, A. (2000). The relationship between teaching and research: Where does geography stand and deliver? *Journal of Geography in Higher Education, 24*(3), 325–351.

Kaufman R., & Herman, J. (1991). *Strategic planning in education: Rethinking, restructuring, revitalizing.* Lancaster, PA: Technomic Publishing Company.

Kerka, S. (1997). *Developing collaborative partnerships.* Columbus, OH: ERIC Clearinghouse on Adult, Career, and Vocational Education, Center on Education and Training for Employment, Ohio State University.

Kezar, A. J., & Lester, J. (2009). *Organizing higher education for collaboration: A guide for campus leaders.* San Francisco, CA: Jossey-Bass.

Krahenbuhl, G. S. (1998). Faculty work: Integrating responsibilities and institutional needs. *Change, 30*(6), 18–25.

Lieberman, D. A., & Guskin, A. F. (2003). The essential role of faculty development in new higher education models. In C. M. Wehlburg & S. Chadwick-Blossey (Eds.), *To improve the academy: Resources for faculty, instructional, and organizational development, Vol. 21* (pp. 257–272). San Francisco, CA: Jossey-Bass/Anker.

Maehr, M. L., & Braskamp, L. A. (1986). *The motivation factor: A theory of personal investment.* Lexington, MA: Heath.

Marshall, W.J. (1999). University service. In V. Bianco-Mathis & N. Chalofsky (Eds.), *The full-time faculty handbook* (pp. 113–128). Thousand Oaks, CA: Sage.

Martin, T. N., Schermerhorn, J. R., & Larson, L. L. (1989). Motivational consequences of a supportive work environment. In M. L. Maehr & C. Ames (Eds.), *Advances in motivation and achievement* (pp. 179–214). Greenwich, CT: JAI Press.

Mattessich, P. W., & Monsey, B. R. (1992). *Collaboration: What makes it work.* St Paul, MN: Amherst H. Wilder Foundation.

Peters, J. M., & Armstrong, J. L. (1998). Collaborative learning: People laboring together to construct knowledge. In I. R. Saltiel, A. Sgroi, & R. G. Brockett

(Eds.), *New directions for adult and continuing education: No. 79. Using consultants to improve teaching* (pp. 75–85). San Francisco: Jossey-Bass.

Saltiel, I. M. (1998). Defining collaborative partnerships. In I. R. Saltiel, A. Sgroi, & R. G. Brockett (Eds.), *New directions for adult and continuing education: No. 79. Using consultants to improve teaching* (pp. 5–11). San Francisco, CA: Jossey-Bass.

Schroeder, U., & Spannagel, C. (2006). Supporting the active learning process. *International Journal on E-Learning, 5*(2), 245–264.

Taylor, K. L. (2005). Academic development as institutional leadership: An interplay of person, role, strategy, and institution. *International Journal for Academic Development, 10*(1), 31–46.

Wildavsky, A. B. (1986). *Budgeting: A comparative history of budgetary processes.* New Brunswick, NJ: Transaction Books.

3

FACULTY ENGAGEMENT IN PROGRAM-LEVEL OUTCOMES ASSESSMENT

A LEARNING PROCESS

Elizabeth L. Evans
Concordia University Wisconsin

Faculty are often not seen as engaged in the work of program-level student learning outcomes assessment. This study investigates the experiences of faculty who self-identified as engaged, a term used to describe attitudes of excitement as well as participatory behaviors. To encourage faculty engagement and recognize the learning process that engagement embodies, institutions can provide faculty development or role catalysts, an environment that values assessment work, support for learning, and opportunities for faculty members to make contributions using what they have learned.

Public pressure to measure quality in higher education has emerged in the past two decades as higher education has come to be perceived as an economic necessity for students and the nation rather than as an "optional indulgence" for some students (Suskie, 2006, p. 15). The slipping competitive position of the United States compared to other countries has led to broader bipartisan agreement on the need for increased educational attainment, and higher education institutions are now being asked to respond with transparency in sharing results of student performance on student learning outcomes (Ewell, 2009). One example, *Measuring Up 2000* (National Center for Public Policy and Higher Education, 2009), created a report card for each state on higher education benchmarks of student success.

In 2006, the Spellings Commission (U.S. Department of Education, 2006) called on higher education institutions to demonstrate accountability through improvement in access, affordability, and assessment of learning outcomes. Outcomes assessment at the program level is undertaken for two perceived purposes: accountability and improvement (Ewell, 1987). In a survey of provosts and chief academic officers, Kuh and Ikenberry (2009) found that on a scale of 1 = not at all used and 4 = used very much, assessment data were most frequently used for institutional (3.27) and program (3.24) accreditation. By contrast, improving instructional performance and improving the general education curriculum were each rated at approximately 2.5 out of 4.0 in this survey. Faculty development offerings related to outcomes assessment showed a high level of discrepancy between importance and availability in a survey of faculty developers on top teaching and learning issues by Sorcinelli, Austin, Eddy, and Beach (2006). Respondents agreed that delivery of outcomes assessment programs was and would continue to be important, but one respondent noted that "assessment is increasingly being used to measure institutional accountability . . . rather than to assist faculty in clarifying teaching goals and understanding student needs" (p. 82). Accordingly, faculty developers who integrate knowledge about effective outcomes assessment practice with teaching and learning work already recognized as crucial to student learning (for example, course redesign or general education development) may be more successful in assisting in the development of faculty engagement in outcomes assessment.

Most institutions lag in fully implementing assessment processes and using outcomes data to improve student learning. Blaich and Wise (2011) found that even with guidance and support, only about 25 percent of the 2006 cohort of institutions participating in the Wabash National Study of Liberal Arts Education developed active responses to outcomes assessment data after four years. Blacklaw (2008) found only moderate success in demonstrating that outcomes assessment data were being used to improve classroom instruction in eight universities in one system. If these indicators are the norm, institutions and faculty need to improve their assessment processes to use assessment data for improving student learning in order to meet the continuing escalation of accountability pressure.

Higher education institutions are looking for opportunities to engage faculty in the work of outcomes assessment at the program and general education levels. Knowledge of assessment practices and pitfalls is necessary, but active interest and involvement by faculty who are responsible for the process of improving teaching and learning in their departments or programs are key to both institutional effectiveness and continued accreditation. Kuh and Ikenberry (2009) found that 66 percent of institutional leaders who responded felt that increased faculty engagement would be helpful in more effectively assessing and using student learning outcomes on their campuses.

Unfortunately, the institutional effectiveness literature suggests that faculty are resistant to this type of work, which they often see as a requirement of external accountability and an additional burden to their roles of teaching, research, and service. Faculty satisfaction with institutional approaches to measuring institutional effectiveness (Grunwald & Peterson, 2003), involvement (Jacobson, 2001), or participation has been examined, but no definition of faculty engagement appears in the practitioner or research literature on outcomes assessment. Little is therefore known about faculty who are engaged in outcomes assessment or what is meant by the term *engagement*, though it is used repeatedly in the practitioner literature on outcomes assessment (see Banta, 2004). Two studies have included interviews with faculty about positive experiences with assessment (Johnson, 2007; Verberkmoes, 2006) and found the work benefited their teaching or administrative duties within their departments and colleges. Promisingly, Ewell (2009) found that "a sizeable minority of faculty have wholeheartedly embraced assessment as useful in improving undergraduate instruction—a constituency of adherents that did not exist a quarter century ago" (p. 6).

A Qualitative Study of Engaged Faculty

I examined the experiences of higher education full-time faculty members at teaching-intensive institutions who described themselves as already engaged in program-level outcomes assessment to learn how they described their engagement and what factors they associated with it. By focusing research on this emerging group of adherents, I hope to launch further research to refine the preliminary definition of *engagement* developed in this study; give voice to their experiences; and identify patterns of attitudes, behaviors, or contextual factors that assist in the development of engagement in outcomes assessment work. Research on these faculty experiences will provide faculty leaders, administrators, and assessment leaders with more information and tools to address the exigencies of today's higher education environment regarding the engagement of faculty in outcomes assessment at their campuses.

Study Participants and Methods

To determine whether there was a common experience of engagement among participants and to capture the phenomenological essence of their experience, this study used purposeful sampling to identify individuals who could describe experiences of engagement (Evans, 2010). Eligible participants were full-time faculty members at nonprofit private or public baccalaureate or master's institutions regionally accredited by the Higher Learning Commission, either teaching or working in an academic administrative role such as assessment director, who described themselves as taking initiative in and feeling a commitment to the work of program-level student learning outcomes. These parameters were chosen to create some level of similar background among participants in assessment expectations and the experience of a teaching-intensive institution. Potential participants were identified through my networks, institutional Web sites, the POD listserv, conference attendee lists, or referral. A recruitment letter was sent to individuals identified through these methods to determine if they fit study parameters; referrals were also sought through the letter.

Ultimately I identified ten individuals available for interviews in fall 2009. I conducted in-person interviews with six of them and telephone interviews with the others. Five of the participants were men and five were women; eight had Ph.D.s, one had an Ed.D., and one had an M.A. as the highest earned degree. Phenomenological interviews were conducted inquiring about the history and context of experiences with engagement and the meaning they ascribed to those experiences. All participants were or had been involved in some institutional responsibility for program-level assessment.

Findings

After analysis of the data through a phenomenological process, described by Giorgi (1997), involving bracketing, description, and the search for the essence of experiences, I discerned themes related to a common experience of engagement among participants that included both affective and behavioral elements. Participants were either role oriented (those whose catalyst related to assessment-related roles) or teaching and learning oriented (those whose catalyst arose out of faculty development experiences or conversations with colleagues about teaching and learning).

Participants collectively defined engagement as a set of both positive attitudes and dedicated behaviors involved in using assessment as a process to improve student learning. All embraced improvement of student learning as the primary purpose of assessment (Ewell, 1987, 2009), seeing learning and student performance as having greater value than institutional accountability. Participants overcame the notion that assessment was being done primarily for external purposes and desired to participate in assessment activities as a benefit to student learning. At the same time, they recognized the need to conduct outcomes assessment as a requirement from accrediting bodies. Participants described their engagement in terms connoting energy and enthusiasm for the work, including *eager*, *enthusiastic*, and *excited*. Engagement was found to include such affective elements, distinguishing it from mere participation. Engaged faculty described both positive attitudes and dedicated behaviors, were excited about outcomes assessment as a means to improve student learning, and sought and found the opportunities to have conversations with colleagues about student learning meaningful. Engaged faculty members were also interested in proactively improving the processes they used and believed assessment was an opportunity to think systematically about institutional improvement. Attitudes and behaviors of engagement as described by participants and identified as themes by the researcher are displayed in Table 3.1.

Table 3.1. Faculty Engagement Attitudes and Behaviors.

Attitudes	Behaviors
Believing that outcomes assessment is a process for improving student learning	Spending time and energy on assessment work
Being excited about assessment as an opportunity for improvement	Integrating classroom assessment with program-level assessment
Caring about the process and improving it	Contributing to the successful work of assessment on campus, including seeking ways to improve it
Viewing assessment as a way to work collaboratively with colleagues	Participating in meaningful conversations about using assessment data to improve teaching, learning, and the institution at both departmental and institutional levels
Seeing assessment as a way to think systematically about institutional improvement	

One participant, for example, suggested that although she had always been interested in student learning as a faculty member, her own learning about and engagement with assessment allowed her to become more intentional about student learning in individual class sessions. Another's view of engagement focused on her habit of thinking about student outcomes and student performance at the department level that developed in her engagement process. She thinks about student assessment and student outcomes first, and since becoming engaged with assessment she makes decisions about teaching methods based on the outcomes she wants students to achieve at the end of the course. Previously she had felt driven more by the need to cover a certain amount of content than by the ability to affect student performance.

Two Paths of Engagement

Two groups emerged among study participants. One group was teaching and learning oriented, finding interest in outcomes assessment initially within a context of faculty development experiences or through dialogue and conversation with colleagues about student learning. The other, a role-oriented group, began learning about assessment because of their responsibility for outcomes assessment within their department or institution. Identification of these divergent paths is valuable in informing leaders, administrators, and faculty developers on how to locate faculty who might be moving toward engagement and encourage development of positive attitudes toward engagement through the three phases of engagement: catalyst, learning, and contribution (Figure 3.1).

Phase 1: Encountering a Catalyst

Role-oriented faculty experienced the catalyst that began their engagement when they accepted a departmental or institutional leadership role

Figure 3.1 The Three Phases of Engagement: Catalyst, Learning, and Contribution.

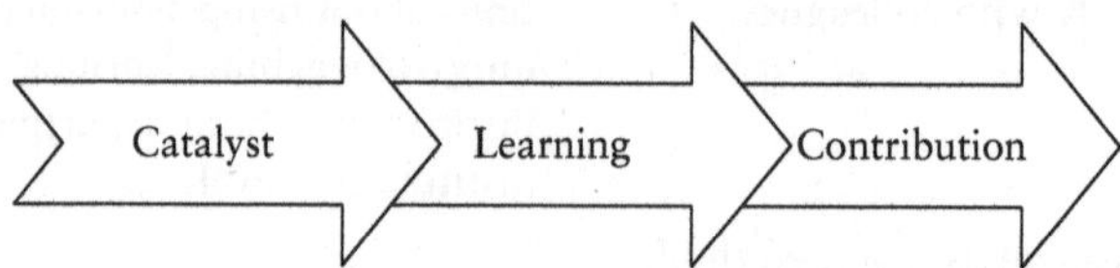

in assessment activities. When study participants began this work, they felt compelled to learn about assessment at the program level and effective assessment practice. In contrast, the catalysts for teaching-and-learning-oriented faculty were moments of sudden awareness or new learning paradigms they discovered while working to improve their teaching. They began the process of engagement in outcomes assessment during faculty development opportunities related to teaching and learning or during conversations with departmental colleagues about what their students were learning.

Phase 2: Learning and Discovery

Most teaching-and-learning-oriented faculty began their path to engagement through faculty development programs providing experiences in which they developed a greater understanding of their own teaching, particularly learner-centered teaching. As they began thinking about pedagogy and student learning, they realized that program-level assessment beyond the classroom was an important part of their responsibility for improving student learning. This group was thus already engaged in outcomes assessment when they accepted institutional assessment roles.

Learning was more focused and time delimited in the role-oriented group, whose members embraced a time of learning and discovery about outcomes assessment after they accepted an institutional role of responsibility for assessment. Faculty in this group took on roles such as faculty coach for a grant on outcomes assessment and interactive learning, department chair, departmental or divisional assessment representative charged with carrying out program-level assessment and serving on a faculty assessment committee, assessment committee member or chair of such a committee, or assessment director charged with oversight of all academic assessment within a school or across the institution. This group focused on self-directed learning such as reading books, attending conferences, seeking out peers and mentors, and working with consultants. The period of learning was more distinct for the role-oriented faculty: they often sought out learning within the first six months of accepting an assessment role. Phase 2 for teaching-and-learning-oriented faculty overlapped with phase 3. Both groups continued to learn and develop as they moved into the next phase.

Recognizing a need for learning, one participant immersed herself in books and conferences and learned through colleagues in other schools and by completing her own department's assessment. She explained that learning was the antidote to the initial confusion she felt on accepting the position of assessment coordinator. Another highlighted the support he received from senior administrators in providing resources for learning, including time and financial resources. A third stepped up to serve as the director of assessment because no one else seemed to be willing. He explained that his prior service on the committee had begun his education in assessment, but once he began attending conferences, reading books, and undertaking the work of assessment director, he "really started to learn."

All participants described their engagement as the interplay between self-directed learning and experiential learning throughout the phases. Both of these learning processes were well represented in the initial catalytic phase; self-directed learning was more prominent in the second phase, and experiential learning was more prominent in the third phase.

Phase 3: Sustained Contribution

Whereas the paths of teaching-and-learning-oriented faculty and role-oriented faculty diverged in phases 1 and 2, both groups worked toward the improvement of student learning through sustained contributions to their institutions using their knowledge and engagement. Activities included leadership on committees, serving as a first-year-experience director, moving into administrative roles, and working to improve general education. Participants continued learning as in earlier phases, but experiential learning was particularly evident in this phase as participants used what they had learned about effective assessment process as they participated in and led academic work in which knowledge of outcomes assessment was beneficial.

Participants valued assessment work with colleagues as an opportunity to create meaningful conversations about teaching and learning. For example, one participant saw that working on assessment "in a smart efficient way would facilitate conversations about teaching and learning that would form the collegial bonds I like, the collegium, and the collaboration." Another felt that having meaningful conversations at both the faculty and the administrative levels was an important part of being engaged in assessment. Another participant indicated that while she could think by herself about her own courses, she needed to be in communication and conversation with her departmental colleagues on how her courses fit within the program.

Encouraging and Hindering Factors

While much of the experience of engagement was an internal one, factors within the institutional context were perceived as either encouraging or hindering participants' engagement. In the first phase, opportunities for catalytic experiences required institutional investment in faculty development and an infrastructure supporting assessment processes within departments and general education. One participant's experience at a faculty development seminar was possible because she had received a grant to participate. Progress through the second phase depended on the presence of opportunities for reflection to occur, included being given sufficient time and financial support for learning (purchase of books, attendance at conferences, the opportunities to interact with peers outside the institution). While faculty members at her own campus were not yet finding value in assessment work, another participant found support and encouragement from peers outside her institution during work on a multicampus grant project. Another's phases of engagement were supported by the positive energy from colleagues; "one of the smarter things" he ever did was to look up and network with peers at sister institutions. Encouraging factors in the phases of engagement included support in the form of mentoring relationships, a cadre of interested faculty peers, positive attitudes toward assessment as an improvement process in the organization, and senior institutional leaders who invested resources and financing for learning opportunities and publicly acknowledged the value of the work done by those engaged in outcomes assessment work.

Several participants recognized lack of financial support or other demonstrations of support for assessment by senior institutional leaders as a challenge, and resistance from faculty peers as a barrier, to effective collaborative work. Prior to her engagement, one participant felt that no one in the academic office was paying attention to her assessment reports, but once meaningful feedback was offered by administrators and expectations made of her department to be accountable for their assessment work, she became more interested. Another participant sighed during the interview when talking about lack of respect for assessment demonstrated by faculty and administrators at his prior employer. He felt that his efforts to get faculty engaged at that institution failed because of a culture that placed a lower value on assessment than other faculty work. Resistance by faculty peers to assessment was a formidable challenge for other participants, who stated that interest seemed to wax and wane with the accreditation cycle instead of being recognized as an important recurring process. Thus, institutional culture affected engagement through the context surrounding participants and the level of support they received from peers and administrators.

Implications

This study presents attitudes and behaviors that engaged a small group of faculty members in outcomes assessment. While qualitative research is not necessarily generalizable beyond localized contexts and cases (Patton, 2002), these faculty stories illustrate key factors in engagement and indicate that viewing assessment work as a systematic opportunity to improve student learning was the strongest motivator for becoming engaged. This finding should inform faculty and assessment leaders, senior administrators, and faculty developers in seeking to create an environment in which faculty members might become engaged. With faculty who are moving toward engagement in outcomes assessment appearing as role oriented or teaching and learning oriented, a successful approach to engagement involves deploying resources for both faculty development (to draw out potential teaching-and-learning-oriented faculty) and the creation of structures of faculty roles of responsibility within departments supported by resources for learning (as a means to develop role-oriented faculty on the path toward engagement). The study further recommends the use of responsibility, resources, and rewards (Palomba & Banta, 1999) within an intentional framework of learning opportunities for faculty.

Perhaps the easier approach to fostering engagement is to assign roles of responsibility for coordinating assessment activities to one person in each department. Since the doorway to periods of intense learning for many of the participants came when they were given such responsibilities, identifying an assessment coordinator to take on responsibility in each department would seem to be one way to begin the process of increasing engagement on campus. Faculty development and learning resources should follow.

Internal Motivation and Culture

Faculty who saw improvement as the most important purpose of outcomes assessment found personal meaning in their contributions to improving their students' learning through outcomes assessment work. A sense of personal ownership, or engagement, included the affective elements of attitude, energy, and enthusiasm, which are triggered by interior individual experiences. Engaged faculty members individually embraced the improvement purpose of assessment and desire to use assessment to improve student learning despite elements opposing this within the culture of their organizations. Engagement cannot be mandated, but it can be fostered by a culture that shows concern for student learning and attitudes that value outcomes assessment work, supported by investing in those outcomes.

Participants in this study described organizational cultures that contributed to their learning or hindered their engagement. Faculty colleagues and administrative leaders played important roles in creating an environment fostering collaboration and dialogue about student learning. Individuals in leadership positions can emphasize the view of assessment on campus as an improvement process rather than focusing on accountability as the primary driver of the work. A faculty and organizational culture that values learning about assessment and leadership in improvement of student learning could give faculty the opportunity to discover outcomes assessment as an improvement process and provide support to transform an interest into engagement.

A Teaching and Learning Process

The development of positive attitudes toward assessment in faculty can be seen as a teaching and learning process to be planned and implemented by campus leaders and faculty developers. Leaders need to demonstrate their own interest and engagement in the activities of assessment on campus. Outcomes assessment is asking a series of important questions about teaching and learning (Hutchings & Marchese, 1990). Accordingly, institutional leaders can ask: what do we want our faculty to know, do, and value so they can embrace outcomes assessment as a meaningful way to improve their teaching and their students' learning? When leaders see engagement as a faculty learning process, they can identify the tools available to support adult learning in the form and practices of adult education and development. Faculty developers are knowledgeable in these areas and in helping to create effective learning environments. When leaders see engagement as a faculty learning process, they will want to deploy resources to support that learning—an experiential, cyclical learning process that requires practice, reflection, and process improvement.

Responsibility, Resources, and Rewards

Palomba and Banta (1999) suggested that the three Rs of responsibility, resources, and rewards are necessary to overcome faculty resistance to work on outcomes assessment. The rewards that faculty receive from the institution affect their perception of the value of assessment work. Hutchings (2010) suggested that an obstacle to faculty involvement in outcomes assessment work is that the work does not fit typical institutional reward systems and is undervalued.

Outcomes assessment work has often been seen as service within the faculty work of teaching, research, and service (Johnson, 2007; Schilling & Schilling, 1998). Brocker (2007) found that this categorization did not promote participation. Instead, if faculty could perceive assessment as related to their teaching or their scholarship, their resistance might drop. Angelo (2002) suggested reframing assessment as scholarship akin to the scholarship of teaching and learning (SoTL), so that faculty might publish and present their findings to peers. Ewell (2002) described the emergence of a scholarship of assessment as one of the precursors to the further development of assessment as faculty work which is valued.

Organizational reward systems that do not embrace outcomes assessment as an important part of teaching or scholarship are unlikely to foster faculty engagement in that area. Scholarship on outcomes assessment has the potential to improve student learning and should be considered in promotion and tenure decisions, particularly in teaching-intensive institutions. Among the resources that can be brought to support assessment are assigning responsibility for implementation, providing reading materials, and bringing consultants to campus for presentations. Opportunities for reflection on learning and networking with other faculty interested in assessment encourage engagement. Resources can be allocated to reward faculty to develop assessment projects using stipends, release time from teaching, or travel fund grants (Palomba & Banta, 1999). Attending conferences is valuable, as nine of the ten participants in this study reported.

What Faculty Developers Can Do

The faculty development literature has not embraced a thoughtful and integrative approach to improving faculty engagement in outcomes assessment as a faculty development intervention at the group level of organization development. Hutchings (2010) opined that outcomes assessment inquiry should grow out of faculty questions about student learning and the regular ongoing work of teaching. To this end, faculty developers might also seek to develop collaborative learning opportunities such as communities of inquiry within programs, those who teach general education courses, or across campus. The purpose of collaborative inquiry is to explore individual and group responses to a dilemma they face (Kasl & Yorks, 2002). In such learning experiences, questions are asked, answers are sought, and reflection and dialogue on the questions and answers foster learning. Faculty engaged in collaborative inquiry strategies about teaching and learning are more likely to find assessment conversations to be worth their time and investment.

Scholarship of Teaching and Learning

Hutchings, Huber, and Ciccione (2011) argued that there has been a wide chasm between the grassroots, classroom-focused, data-driven practice of the SoTL and the institution-focused need for effective program-level outcomes assessment practice. Yet they saw possibilities and bridges across this rift being formed. Centers can integrate teaching and learning with outcomes assessment in a number of effective ways. Learning through reflective practice can be brought to a scholarly level by encouraging faculty to share experiences through SoTL, other action research projects, the practice of learning communities, or collaborative inquiry (Bray, 2002). SoTL and action research projects can be disseminated in publications or presentations. Faculty developers working with individual faculty members on their course-level assessment could expand this work to the department level. They can include reference to program-level learning outcomes when they teach course redesign workshops, highlighting for faculty the connection between individual course and programmatic outcomes.

Systematic and Sustained

When faculty developers frame course, program, general education, and institutional-level learning outcomes as interconnected, faculty will be more prepared to work toward outcomes assessment processes at the program and general education levels. Faculty developers can also work directly with assessment leaders to provide learning support for faculty about the processes of outcomes assessment at the program level. Huba and Freed (2000) argued that faculty development that supports assessment must be systematic and sustained. They suggested that faculty need to understand multiple assessment elements such as developing measurable outcomes, designing rubrics to evaluate student work, conducting data analysis, and documenting the work.

While developing programs that develop faculty who become and remain engaged in outcomes assessment is complex and unfolds over time, the potential rewards in student improvement, faculty satisfaction, and institutional accountability seem well worth the efforts.

REFERENCES

Angelo, T. A. (2002). Engaging and supporting faculty in the scholarship of assessment: Guidelines from research and best practice. In T. W. Banta (Ed.), *Building a scholarship of assessment* (pp. 185–200). San Francisco, CA: Jossey-Bass.

Banta, T. W. (2004). That second look at student work: A strategy for engaging faculty in outcomes assessment. In T. W. Banta (Ed.), *Hallmarks of effective outcomes assessment* (pp. 37–42). San Francisco, CA: Jossey-Bass.

Blacklaw, S. T. (2008). Affecting change in the State University of New York: Linking the locus of commitment to effective assessment. *Dissertation Abstracts International, 69*(08). (UMI No. 3060501)

Blaich, C., and Wise, K. (2011, January). *From gathering to using assessment results: Lessons from the Wabash National Study* (NILOA Occasional Paper No. 8). Champaign, IL: National Institute for Learning Outcomes Assessment. Retrieved from http://www.learningoutcomeassessment.org/documents/Wabash_001.pdf

Bray, J. N. (2002). Uniting teacher learning: Collaborative inquiry for professional development. In L. Yorks & E. Kasl (Eds.), *New directions for adult and continuing education: No. 94. Collaborative inquiry as a strategy for adult learning* (pp. 83–91). San Francisco, CA: Jossey-Bass.

Brocker, J. (2007). Involving faculty in assessment activities associated with AACSB assurance of learning standards. *Dissertation Abstracts International, 68*(3). (UMI No. 3253731)

Evans, E. L. (2010). Experiences of higher education faculty engaged in undergraduate student learning outcomes assessment. *Dissertation Abstracts International, 72*(03). (UMI No. 3441983)

Ewell, P. T. (1987). *Assessment, accountability, and improvement: Managing the contradiction.* American Association for Higher Education Assessment Forum. ED 287330.

Ewell, P. T. (2002). An emerging scholarship: A brief history of assessment. In T. W. Banta (Ed.), *Building a scholarship of assessment* (pp. 3–25). San Francisco, CA: Jossey-Bass.

Ewell, P. T. (2009, November). *Assessment, accountability, and improvement: Revisiting the tension* (Occasional Paper No. 1). Champaign, IL: National Institute for Learning Outcomes Assessment Retrieved from http://www.learningoutcomeassessment.org/occasionalpaperone.htm

Giorgi, A. (1997). The theory, practice, and evaluation of the phenomenological method as a qualitative research procedure. *Journal of Phenomenological Psychology, 28*(2), 235–260.

Grunwald, H., & Peterson, N. W. (2003). Factors that promote faculty involvement in and satisfaction with institutional and classroom assessment. *Research in Higher Education, 44,* 173–204.

Huba, M. E., & Freed, J. E. (2000). *Learner-centered assessment on college campuses: Shifting the focus from teaching to learning.* Needham Heights, MA: Allyn & Bacon.

Hutchings, P. (2010, April). *Opening doors to faculty involvement in assessment* (NILOA Occasional Paper No. 4). Champaign, IL: National Institute for Learning Outcomes Assessment. Retrieved from http://www.learningoutcomeassessment.org/occasionalpaperfour.htm

Hutchings, P., Huber, M. T., & Ciccione, A. (2011). *The scholarship of teaching and learning reconsidered: Institutional integration and impact.* San Francisco, CA: Jossey-Bass.

Hutchings, P., & Marchese, T. (1990). Watching assessment: Questions, stories, prospects. *Change, 22*(5), 12–38.

Jacobson, A. B. (2001). Involvement of faculty in higher education assessment practices. *Dissertation Abstracts International, A62*(05). (UMI No. 3015411)

Johnson, L. G. (2007). Faculty involvement in scholarly assessment: A phenomenological study. *Dissertation Abstracts International, 69*(03). (UMI No. 3305926)

Kasl, E., & Yorks, L. (2002). Collaborative inquiry for adult learning. In L. Yorks & E. Kasl (Eds.), *New directions for adult and continuing education: No. 94. Collaborative inquiry as a strategy for adult learning* (pp. 3–12). San Francisco: Jossey-Bass.

Kuh, G. E., & Ikenberry, S. (2009). *More than you think, less than we need: Learning outcomes assessment in American higher education.* National Institute for Learning Outcomes Assessment. Retrieved from http://www.learningoutcomeassessment.org/NILOAsurveyresults09.htm

National Center for Public Policy and Higher Education. (2009). *Measuring up 2006.* Retrieved from http://measuringup.highereducation.org/about/

Palomba, C. A., & Banta, T. W. (1999). *Assessment essentials: Planning, implementing, and improving assessment in higher education.* San Francisco, CA: Jossey-Bass.

Patton, M. Q. (2002). *Qualitative research and evaluation methods* (3rd ed.). Thousand Oaks, CA: Sage.

Schilling, K. M., & Schilling, K. L. (1998). *Proclaiming and sustaining excellence: Assessment as a faculty role.* ASHE-ERIC Higher Education Report 26(3). Washington, DC: George Washington University, Graduate School of Education and Human Development.

Sorcinelli, M. D., Austin, A. E., Eddy, P. L., & Beach, A. L. (2006). *Creating the future of faculty development: Learning from the past, understanding the present.* San Francisco, CA: Jossey-Bass/Anker.

Suskie, L. (2006). Accountability and quality improvement. In P. Hernon, R. E. Dugan, & C. Schwartz, (Eds.), *Revisiting outcomes assessment in higher education* (pp. 13–38). Westport, CT: Libraries Unlimited.

U.S. Department of Education. Secretary of Education's Commission on the Future of Higher Education. (2006). *A test of leadership: Charting the future of U.S. higher education.* Retrieved from http://www.ed.gov/about/bdscomm/list/hiedfuture/reports/final-report.pdf

Verberkmoes, J. F. (2006). Student outcomes assessment: A study of the organizational factors that foster or inhibit progress in establishing a culture of assessment within graduate theological schools. *Dissertation Abstracts International, 67*(05). (UMI No. 3216183)

PART TWO

REACHING OUT TO NEW AUDIENCES

4

WHAT EDUCATIONAL DEVELOPERS NEED TO KNOW ABOUT FACULTY-ARTISTS IN THE ACADEMY

Natasha Haugnes
Academy of Art University

Hoag Holmgren
Professional and Organizational Development Network in Higher Education

Martin Springborg
Minnesota State Colleges and Universities

Both educational developers and faculty-artists share the same goal: significant learning. Yet effective dialogue and collaboration between the two can be undermined without the educational developer's knowledge of signature pedagogies and discipline-specific terminology in the various disciplines of art. We examine several assumptions about artists and how these assumptions can be overcome for the benefit of educational developers, faculty-artists, and students. To this end, we provide suggestions for generating dialogue about teaching and learning with faculty-artists and for making these dialogues fruitful.

The work of faculty who teach art in the academy (for example, theater and dance, fine arts, creative writing, music) is often misunderstood by nonartist educational developers. As a result, educational developers are less likely to learn about the signature pedagogies of various artistic disciplines, as defined by Shulman (2005), and are less likely to be able to deeply or broadly support faculty-artists in their teaching and scholarship. This misunderstanding is reflected in, if not influenced by, the promulgation of artist stereotypes in popular culture. In most films, for example, artists are portrayed as self-absorbed, mentally unstable, morally suspect, and highly skeptical of institutions, the academy most of all. Such stereotypes extend to the work faculty-artists do in the classroom. We might be tempted to believe such work is unplanned and undisciplined, privileging intuition over reason (and is thus immune to assessment or evaluation and so not to be taken seriously).

In the film *Barfly* (1987), Mickey Rourke plays a poet named Henry Chinasky, based on real-life poet Charles Bukowski, who lives in squalor and spends most of his time drinking, fighting, and writing. The film *Pollock* (2000) depicts the painter Jackson Pollock as essentially tortured, alcoholic, and self-destructive. *Amadeus* (1984) portrays Mozart as a rebellious savant with wild mood swings whose dedication to his work led to exhaustion and an early death. Many other popular films about art and artists highlight or exaggerate the darker realms of the artist's psyche—to name just a few, *Black Swan* (2010), *Basquiat* (1996), *Frida* (2002), *Vincent and Theo* (1990), *The Rose* (1979), *The Shining* (1980), *Art School Confidential* (2006), *American Splendor* (2003), *The Piano Teacher* (2001), *Wonder Boys* (2000), *Crumb* (1994), and *Camille Claudel* (1988). While many of these films feature accurate biographical events, it is also true that stories about stable, sober, and successful artists do not necessarily make popular movies, with *Rivers and Tides* (2001) being a notable exception.

Within the "unruly artist" family of films, a subcategory further highlights the artist's rebellious spirit by placing him or her in an academic setting, populated by stiff, rule-bound "academics," determined to force the artist to conform to the academic mold, and seemingly determined to destroy the artist's spirit. *School of Rock* (2003) and *Mona Lisa Smile* (2003) fit this pattern. In *Mona Lisa Smile*, the exceedingly uptight academic administrators admonish a new faculty-artist to "submit all lesson plans for approval and revision at the beginning of each semester," after learning that the newly hired artist teacher was exposing Wellesley University women of the 1950s to Jackson Pollock's nonconformist artwork.

None of these films offers particularly admirable examples of faculty-artists, administrators, or students. But the simplified characters and situations highlight a very real conflict: the struggle of artists to hold on to their passion in an academic setting and the struggle of the academy to understand and integrate artists into the scholarly context. While the focus of this chapter is what educational developers can learn about real faculty-artists and their world in order to support them in their teaching and scholarship, educational developers may note that "academics" in the film examples do not come out looking so great either. We hope that the following information may help to open conversations and mitigate unhelpful expectations that both parties may bring to the educational development table.

Artist Traits

We have found a family of traits that tend to set faculty-artists apart from their peers in other departments, although they are not as extreme as the cinematic depictions of artists. The point of sharing this list of traits is not to show how "special" artists are (indeed, any discipline could publish such a list), but rather to reveal opportunities for educational developers to begin dialogue and collaboration.

Artists Are Risk Takers

To create is to take risks. As a result, artists must be able to accept risk and mitigate fear. "If you don't create an atmosphere in which risk can be easily taken, in which weird ideas can be floated, then it's likely you're going to be producing work that will look derivative," says Pixar University dean Randy Nelson (Hempel, 2003).

> **Tip:** Ask how faculty-artists get students to take creative risks in the classroom. Ask for input in planning a workshop or panel discussion on creativity.

Artists Are Intrinsically and Tirelessly Curious

Martha Breen, a faculty-artist member at the Academy of Art University, defines an artist as a person who has a vision and will do anything he or she has to—or learn anything necessary—in order to realize that vision. Judy Chicago studied pyrotechnics in order to realize her vision for her Multi-Colored Atmosphere series, essentially sculptural performance art with fireworks. Christo, for every temporary installation he creates, files a mountain of bureaucratic permits and environmental impact reports that would certainly discourage a person with less vision. Many ceramicists become experts in chemistry in their pursuit of specific textures and colors in glazes. An artist will never say, "That's not part of my job," when pursuing an artistic goal. Artists will not be deterred by permit processes, or lack of skills in a field.

> **Tip:** Be curious. Attend departmental readings, openings, and performances. Introduce yourself; ask about the pockets of knowledge outside art that faculty-artists have acquired along the way. Ask about their work and their students' work.

Artists Tend to See Holistically Rather Than in Parts

Artists tend to see relationships, rather than differences, among seemingly unrelated elements. They look for underlying patterns that may not have been obvious to all of the casual observers who have gone before them. This trait is highlighted by a study that found that when looking at paintings, nonartists tend to focus on the objects and the people in the paintings, while visual artists' eyes move all around the canvas (Vogt and Magnussen, 2007). The artists are presumably seeing patterns in light and color or composition in the whole canvas. They are seeing the background as much as they are the objects and figures.

> **Tip:** Ask faculty-artists if they have suggestions for how art-related resources, content, or teaching methods might be useful to faculty in the sciences, social sciences, or other disciplines. Solicit their ideas for a workshop, article, blog, or tweet on this topic.

Artists Embrace Ambiguity

Artists tend to thrive in the qualitative arena more than in the linear, logical arena. They embrace ambiguity and nuance instead of attempting to explain it away. The nineteenth-century poet John Keats, in talking about Shakespeare, called this quality negative capability: "That is when a man is capable of being in uncertainties, Mysteries, doubts, without any irritable reaching after fact & reason" (Heath, 1973, p. 1105). Creative writing teacher Allyson Ritger brings this trait to the foreground by classifying her students in terms of how clear their writing is and how attached they are to whether the audience gets their message: "If a student is very attached to whether an audience is getting their message and they are very clear or obvious with their message, then sometimes it is not so interesting to read" (Flanagan & Shaffner, 2007). This analysis helps her to work with student writers within their own goals, although even she admits that in the academic context, coaching can be difficult if a student is unattached and unclear.

> **Tip:** Ask to observe an instructor in the classroom in order to learn more about how art is taught. Art instructors are likely as interested in this topic as you.

A Composite of Traits

The list is not meant to imply that artists don't struggle with these traits personally or that the faculty-artists know how to nurture these qualities in their students. Faculty-artists, like postsecondary teachers everywhere, usually have little more than an "apprenticeship of observation" (Shulman, p. 57) by way of teacher training. That is, the only training they have, powerful as it may be, is from watching their own teachers teach in their many years of schooling; they tend to teach the way they were taught.

These traits begin to suggest what makes the "artist-ness" of an artist. We believe that it is this family of traits that academic institutions are often unprepared to support, nurture, and learn from.

You Say Tomato; I Say Tomahto

The language that educational developers use when engaging faculty-artists is crucial in establishing a trusting relationship where learning can occur on both sides. An anecdote helps illustrate this point.

Before meeting with external accreditors, the administrator-liaison of an arts and design university handed out translation cards to the faculty-artists who would be involved. The cards said:

Accreditors Say	We Say
Assessment strategies	Critiques, rubrics, portfolios, reels, thesis projects
Program learning outcomes	What students learn in your department
Course learning outcomes	What students learn in your class

The meeting went more smoothly than anticipated. The faculty-artists were able to adapt readily to accreditor jargon, and the university earned its accreditation with positive reviews. The translation cards made it clear, in a good-humored way, that both administrators and artists are involved in similar practices while employing different terms.

But while the simple replacement of *assessment* with *critique* in an educational developer's vocabulary is a good start to opening conversations with faculty-artists, the translation is inadequate. There is a place for the educational developer to instruct a faculty-artist in well-researched and established best practice, but it is equally important for the educational developer to let go of structures that he or she uses to make sense of classroom teaching and be open to the apparent ambiguity of an arts classroom. We must remember that a lot of these established best practices originated in the fields of geology, education, math, literature, and physics—not art. This is not to suggest that educational developers must use only discipline-specific tactics, but that there is a lot to learn from arts faculty that has the potential to inform the work we do with faculty in other disciplines. Because faculty-artists' scholarly work is less likely to take the form of citable, published academic articles, there is scant research in the teaching and assessment of art in higher education. Therefore, we need to be willing to suspend preconceptions about what is best practice in the arts classroom since so few of the best practices for teaching and assessing art have been codified.

The following sections explore what signature pedagogies and signature scholarship in the arts look like, as well as how educational developers can work with faculty-artists once a connection is established.

Assessment = Critique?

The critique is sacred to an arts education and assumes many forms as a signature pedagogy in the arts, from professional pitches for a commission, to creative writing workshops. It is not simply an oral assessment of a product. Ask an art teacher what the goal of her or his critique is, and precious few will say, "To deliver grades and clear feedback." While many faculty do use critiques to assess work, the critique is also an end in itself. An analysis of critique as a signature pedagogy indicates that "it is more accurate to think of each critique as a step on the path toward the more ambitious project of the students' development of mature artistic practice" (Klebsadel & Kornetsky, 2009, p. 102).

That path to mature artistic practice involves nurturing many of the traits outlined in the previous section, and all in a very public learning environment. While much of twentieth-century academia saw students with blue books seated at every other seat so that they could not copy others' work during exams, the logistical requirements in an arts classroom would never allow that type of individual, secretive activity. Imagine a drawing classroom where students could not see others' newsprint sketch pads.

Students' work and feedback in the critique are displayed for the entire class to experience.

Given this environment, the critique has to be about more than assessment. It should push students to work as hard as they can to achieve their vision but without paralyzing them with fear. It should engage students in conversations and teach them to think for themselves. It should encourage students to discover how others see their art. It should be about learning to graciously accept feedback and ultimately make their own choices.

An educational developer observing a traditional art critique through the assessment lens may be baffled at the seemingly open-ended, inconclusive discussion about a piece of art. The developer may be listening for the criteria and discussion about the piece, while the art teacher may be paying attention to the student-artist's process: his or her engagement, tenaciousness, willingness to take risks, or ability to incorporate feedback while maintaining ownership over the final piece.

An educational developer might also find herself observing what she perceives to be a very focused critique in an art class, perhaps with an extensive rubric or objective checklist to guide clear feedback. In the developer's excitement over clear objectives and feedback tools, she might miss the fact that this art teacher might not be nurturing the all-important artist traits listed above. A student in the video series *Fostering Creativity in the Classroom* voiced this sentiment well in her description of what had happened to her own artistic creative process prior to arriving in a particularly gifted faculty-artist's class: "I had been overly critiqued on my designs. It was just work now. It wasn't even fun anymore. It was like—gotta get stuff done" (Flanagan & Shaffner, 2007).

Educational developers should be able to support teaching artists in both situations. To establish trust and gain some knowledge of the artist-faculty's intent, the developers need to ask the instructor questions and perhaps exhibit a few of the artist trait themselves: they need to be curious and comfortable with ambiguity. They need to ask the types of questions that serve them in any discipline in which they might be observing teachers—for example: "Tell me about your critiques." "What do you want students to walk away from your class with that they did not have before?"

Tips: Once this communication is established, there are a few ways educational developers may support faculty-artists in critiques. They may:

- Work with faculty-artists to develop assessment criteria or learning outcomes based on process if that is indeed the focus.

Rubrics can include criteria such as "responsiveness to feedback" or "design process."

- Work with overly focused skill-based instructors to embed the skill teaching in bigger questions about art, or more authentic art projects that nurture the artistic problem-solving traits and intrinsic motivation so central to being an artist.
- Assist faculty-artists to be clear and supportive in feedback.
- Assist teachers in developing grading systems that foster risk taking while holding students accountable for skills mastery. We know that too much emphasis on grading will extinguish students' intrinsic motivation.
- Help set up peer critiques using principles of group work or cooperative learning (though we do not need to call it that). Guidelines for task-based group work or even a jigsaw can be used in a critique setting. One art and design school encourages faculty to experiment with role playing in critiques with a model called "your creative director is stopping in."
- Support faculty-artists in building accountability into their critiques. Faculty-artists often say that students who are not being critiqued should be "listening and learning from the other critiques." Educational developers can help the faculty check in on this learning by setting up a classroom assessment technique or other follow-up activity: summarizing the most common points made in a critique journal, taking critique notes for each other, or synthesizing the whole critique in at the end.

Active Learning = Making Art

New faculty often enter the academy thinking they need to "act like professors." Whether stemming from encounters with instructors in real life or in film, this tendency to try to overintellectualize one's field can drain the excitement out of any classroom. Faculty-artists are no exception to this tendency. Richard Swan's film *Professor Dancealot* (2009), a dramatization of the dance professor who teaches his craft solely in a traditional lecture format, provides a humorous case in point. Faculty-artists can forget that it is better to pique and nurture students' curiosity through hands-on learning experiences than to rely on the more conventionally accepted lecture format associated with academe.

Educational developers can remind instructors that their natural inclinations to have students make art in the classroom is a traditionally effective way to teach. While it is rarely referred to as active learning, this practice is nonetheless a signature pedagogy in the arts.

> **Tip:** Educational developers can help faculty-artists with scaffolding projects, breaking the "doing art" down into smaller chunks, so that students can be successful.

> **Tip:** Developers can help instructors incorporate low-stakes projects into lessons. For example, allow time to play with a new tool or experiment with a new medium in order to discover its possibilities.

Scholarship: Do Not Call It Scholarship

Generally *scholarship* refers to faculty members' contributions to their fields—whether that is in the form of new published research in the physical and biological sciences, books or publication credits positing new viewpoints in the social sciences and humanities, or the exhibition of new work in the arts. Many similarities exist across disciplines in terms of scholarly activity, but while faculty in the social sciences and humanities are more prone to speak in terms of research and scholarship, often faculty in the arts are not.

A perception among artists is that good art cannot be produced within the confines of the academy and therefore falls outside the realm of scholarship as it is traditionally defined. While an astrophysicist may wish that she could dedicate all her time to research and not teach in the classroom at all, the artist wishes she could spend more time in the studio or in the theater. She may fear losing her creative outlets and thereby lessening her chances of making significant contributions to her field; in fact, a common belief among artists is that "lifelong adherence to institutions of higher learning . . . puts the poet, daily, class-wise, office-wise, library-wise, before the dragons of respectability and caution" (Eshleman, 1989, p. 39). Similarly, Bayles and Orland (1993, pp. 79–80) describe the associations that artists have with academia: "Indeed, the thought of working in the art education system either as student or faculty may sound about as attractive as standing beneath a steady drizzle of dead cats." This is one reason that so many artists who work in the academy cast the net of inspiration far beyond the ivory towers. Indeed, the evidence of the faculty-artist's scholarship may be absent altogether from the university setting.

Traditional Forms of Scholarship in the Arts

As educational developers, we need to familiarize ourselves with examples of scholarship in the arts if we are to encourage faculty colleagues to incorporate their scholarly work into their teaching, disseminate their work within the institution, and, in the case of early-career faculty, document their scholarship for the purposes of promotion and tenure down the road.

Table 4.1 and the lists that follow can serve as an introductory taxonomy of scholarship within arts disciplines:

Table 4.1. A Taxonomy of Scholarship in the Arts.

	Performances	Publications	Exhibits	Commissioned Work
Creative writing	X	X		
Music and theater	X			X
Visual arts		X	X	X

Creative Writing

- The publication of new poetry, fiction, nonfiction, and drama
- Readings or performances
- Editing, publishing, and distributing a literary journal (departmental or national)
- Editing an anthology

Music, Theater, and Dance

- Performances in which the faculty member has played a role
- Productions in which the faculty member has served in the role of director or writer
- Composition of music—either by the faculty member along or commissioned for a larger production or purpose

Visual and Fine Arts

- The creation and exhibition or dissemination of new work. Solo exhibitions are typically held in higher regard than participation in group exhibitions, although there may be exceptions to this depending the extent to which the show was collaborative.

- Exhibitions in which the faculty member served as curator.
- Commissioned work for public exhibition, such as work that is incorporated into new building projects, or private collection.

Although these categories are by no means a comprehensive view of scholarly activity within all arts disciplines, they provide a foundation of understanding that can lead to productive conversations and consultations with faculty in the arts.

A good entry into discussions of scholarship with all faculty colleagues, regardless of discipline, is to get to know their work. In the arts, this means researching arts faculty members for evidence of the types of work listed. We can use the knowledge to assist faculty in framing their work as scholarship so as to gain the recognition they deserve from their institutions. We can also support faculty in seeing and enhancing connections between scholarship and teaching.

> **Tip:** Begin conversations with faculty-artists about what precedes their scholarly activity in terms of research and work production. These don't show up in footnotes as they often do in other disciplines' scholarly publications.
>
> **Tip:** Ask faculty-artists how they incorporate their own work or their colleagues' work in the classroom.

Undergraduate Research

One direction we might take conversations with faculty-artists is toward undergraduate research. This is an unfamiliar term to many arts faculty, which is perhaps the reason that many have not embraced undergraduate research as a way to bring together their creative and teaching lives. The barrier for many faculty members to bringing their research into the classroom as a teaching method is not being able to envision the positive impacts on student learning or on their own research.

The following is an example of how one of us (M.S.) describes doing this in a course. An educational developer could support this type of project in any number of disciplines:

> *Community Education* was a photographic essay that I conducted as a faculty member at Inver Hills Community College in Inver Grove Heights, Minnesota. What preceded this project was an acknowledgment that in teaching four or five courses per semester, I had almost entirely lost sight of my own work. The lack of engagement in my

work outside of the classroom was having a negative effect on my teaching. In short, I was losing my "spark" as an instructor.

I gave my students and myself an assignment: to document in photographs our lives and the lives of their peers outside the classroom doors. In doing this work, my students and I saw first-hand the many challenges facing our respective groups, and the result was the development of a mutual respect for our workloads as well as the many challenges we face in becoming model students and instructors.

By semester's end, I had gathered hundreds of student photographs on the multitude of issues facing them both in and out of the classroom. I had also established a considerable body of my own work on the topic of teaching at a community college. Students who participated in this project developed an interest in photography unlike I had experienced in other beginning photography students.

Tip: Help faculty conceptualize and design undergraduate research projects. Opportunities include mentorships or apprenticeships in the form of departmental publications, exhibits, and readings. Assist in incorporating these projects into course design, curriculum, and assessment methods.

Going Meta: The Scholarship of (Arts) Teaching and Learning

Embedded within the enterprise of the scholarship of teaching and learning (SoTL) is the dissemination of findings to colleagues for the betterment of those involved in the teaching and learning process—faculty and students alike. SoTL is central to the learning paradigm, as opposed to the instruction paradigm, as defined by Barr and Tagg (1995). This vision is of "the institution itself as learner—over time, it continuously learns how to produce more learning with each graduating class, each entering student" (p. 14)."

Talk to any faculty-artist for long, and you're bound to arrive at some deep thinking about the practice of teaching in the arts. A number of common questions arise between colleagues at departmental meetings and during art conferences—for example:

"Can art be taught?"

"What is good art?"

"Should I grade for effort?"

"What is the role of talent?"

"Can skills be taught in the absence of creativity?"

"How can instructors quantifiably measure students' growth as artists?"

"Do I have the right to judge my students' art?"

"How do I assess creativity?"

"Can I assess and nurture creativity simultaneously?"

Tip: Engage faculty-artists in conversations about teaching and learning within the arts. Tap into what they are already thinking about, and nudge them to formalize their interests into true SoTL research projects.

Tip: Host faculty learning community meetings to fertilize the seeds of SoTL projects within arts disciplines.

Conclusion

By opening conversations and strengthening ties with faculty-artists, educational developers not only support their artist colleagues in the areas of teaching and learning but also enrich their own understanding of effective teaching, learning, and scholarship. With creativity and initiative, this new understanding may ultimately be extended to support the enterprises of teaching and learning in disciplines beyond the arts: "We can learn a great deal by examining the signature pedagogies of a variety of professions and asking how they might improve teaching and learning in professions for which they are not now signatures" (Shulman, 2005, p. 58).

REFERENCES

Barr, R. B., & Tagg, J. (1995, November/December). From teaching to learning: A new paradigm for undergraduate education. *Change*, 12–25.

Bayles, D., & Orland, T. (1993). *Art and fear: Observations on the perils (and rewards) of artmaking*. Santa Cruz, CA: Image Continuum.

Eshleman, C. (1989). *Novices: A study of poetic apprenticeship. Los Angeles*, CA: Mercer & Aitchison.

Flanagan, M., & Shaffner, M. (Directors). (2007). *Fostering creativity in the classroom*. Retrieved from http://elixr.merlot.org/case-stories/understanding—meeting-students-needs/creativity/fostering-creativity2

Heath, W. (Ed.). (1973). *Major British poets of the romantic period*. New York, NY: Macmillan.

Hempel, J. (2003, June 4). Pixar university: Thinking outside the mouse. *San Francisco Chronicle*. Retrieved from http://articles.sfgate.com/

2003–06–04/bay-area/17493262_1_pixar-s-emeryville-technical-director-bill-polson-pixar-president-edwin-catmull/2

Klebsadel, H., & Kornetsky, L. (2009). Critique as signature pedagogy in the arts. In R.A.R. Gurung, N. L. Chick, & A. Haynie (Eds.). *Exploring signature pedagogies: Approaches to teaching disciplinary habits of mind* (pp. 99–117). Sterling, VA: Stylus.

Shulman, L. (2005). Signature pedagogies in the professions. *Daedalus, 134*(3), 52–59. Retrieved from http://search.proquest.com/docview/210573746?accountidv27957

Swan, R. (2009, September). *Professor Dancealot.* Retrieved from http://www.youtube.com/watch?vv1k8aeDUC9XQ

Vogt, S., & Magnussen, S. (2007). Expertise in pictorial perception: Eye-movement patterns and visual memory in artists and laymen. *Perception, 36*(1), 91–100.

5

AN EXPLORATION OF THE SPIRITUAL ROOTS OF THE MIDCAREER FACULTY EXPERIENCE

Virginia S. Lee
Virginia S. Lee & Associates

Dorothe J. Bach
University of Virginia

Richard N. Muthiah
George Fox University

In this time of intense pressure on institutions of higher education, the realities and needs of faculty working in them are often not very high on the list of concerns. This chapter examines the current malaise of the academy through an exploration of midcareer faculty. After summarizing selected studies on midcareer faculty, we draw on alternative literature and developmental frameworks to shed light on the spiritual dimension of the midcareer faculty experience. We offer recommendations on appropriate interventions in light of the alternative analysis and discuss their wider implications for a postindustrial paradigm of academic renewal.

The current critique of higher education, intense and far ranging, spans a host of issues ranging from the rising cost of higher education to the vulnerability of the humanities. In this time of intense pressure on institutions of higher education, the realities and needs of faculty working in them are often not very high on the list of concerns. However, a close look at the experiences of people whose careers, dreams, and aspirations are intricately linked to the well-being of our institutions may deepen our understanding of the roots of the crisis in higher education and lead to insights into how to respond with renewed wisdom.

A gathering conversation on college campuses, a series of conferences, and a growing strand of research acknowledge hollowness beneath the frenetic surface of contemporary academic life. At its center is a divided and conflicted faculty. According to Astin and Astin's research (1999), faculty members report that their own personal quest for meaning and purpose within the academy is important, but that it is neither appropriate nor is there sufficient time to pursue such questions with students in their classes. Furthermore, although they derive a sense of meaning and purpose from their research, they frequently sacrifice personal health and time with family, friends, and community to meet the perceived demands of their research agenda. Faculty members also report difficulties in being "authentic," lack of clarity regarding what is "enough" and what constitutes "quality," multiple sources of stress, lack of collegiality, and lack of time. There is reason to assume that a community driven by external metrics such as grant dollars, number of publications, and institutional rankings is in danger of losing its bearings, moral compass, and ultimately its ability to assume a leadership role in discussions about what matters most in the academy, in society, and for students. Given that the intellectual capital of universities is still their biggest asset, a faculty divided and driven in these ways may have severe consequences.

In this chapter, we examine the current malaise of the academy, including the phenomenon of a divided and conflicted faculty, through an exploration of midcareer faculty. (There are various definitions of *midcareer,* and we refer here to the period after the pretenure probationary stage and before imminent retirement; see Baldwin, Lunceford, & Vanderlinden, 2005.) While we value the experience of all faculty members, the projects of securing tenure and planning for imminent retirement tend to skew the experiences of junior and senior faculty, respectively. By contrast, midcareer constitutes the longest and often most productive phase of academic life, normally a period of fifteen to twenty-five years. Due to its length, the midcareer phase encompasses a significant period of the life span, a time when most faculty members also experience a range of crises and rites of passage of adult experience. It is not surprising that various developmental frameworks suggest that the middle years are dynamic and complex (Baldwin et al., 2005).

A Selective Literature Review of Midcareer Faculty

Midcareer faculty remained largely unexamined in the research literature until Baldwin et al.'s review (2005). Using data from the National Study of Postsecondary Faculty (National Center for Education Statistics, 2002), one of the largest and most representative databases on U.S. faculty, the researchers found that midcareer faculty distinguished themselves from early- and late-career faculty with respect to the percentage of time spent on different categories of scholarly activity and general productivity, but not dramatically so. Furthermore, there was great within-group variability, not surprising in a group as large and diverse as midcareer faculty. However, general dissatisfaction is highest during the middle years.

In a later study conducted at Michigan State University, Baldwin, DeZure, Shaw, and Moretto (2008) interviewed two groups: twenty midcareer professors (ten who were one to five years posttenure and ten who were six to twenty years posttenure years) and twenty department chairs and school directors (nine focused on faculty members one to five years posttenure and eleven on six to twenty years posttenure). The qualitative study yielded a more nuanced picture of the dissatisfaction of midcareer faculty and insights into the variability of their experience. Among the challenges noted were high expectations, including a sometimes daunting workload; neglect; lack of clarity on immediate next steps and longer-term goals once tenure had been achieved; adapting to change and remaining competitive; and special challenges related to race, ethnicity, sexual orientation, and age.

Baldwin and his collaborators draw on both career and general adult development theories to support their research findings. Super's (1986) classic theory of career development describes a movement from an "establishment stage" (twenty-five to forty-four years old) to a "maintenance stage" (forty-five to sixty-four years old), when work becomes stable and routine. He later added the idea of career recycling to the theory, acknowledging the phenomenon of reassessment even during the middle years. Hall's (1986) model of organizational career stages portrays midcareer as a complex stage that can lead to maintenance, growth, or stagnation. Career routines can inhibit experimentation and career revision, but various triggers can disrupt career routine and stimulate new exploration. Similarly, Levinson (1986) characterizes the middle years as alternating between stable periods of achievement and advancement and transitional periods characterized by questioning, reassessment, redirection, and renewal. These theories also suggest that broad developmental forces are at play in the lives of midcareer faculty.

Midcareer Faculty and Spiritual Development

Although the literature hints at deeper developmental shifts underlying the experience of midcareer faculty, it falls short of addressing them head-on. Career and general development theories describe reliable patterns in the experience of midcareer faculty, but these are often symptoms rather than causes. In contrast, literature related to spiritual development sheds light on the deeper experience of midcareer faculty and the ultimate source of their malaise.

In the 1990s, Hansen (1993) identified the search for purpose and meaning as a deeper current that influences career development across the life span: "Career decision-making is not only logical and rational but intuitive" (pp. 20–21). In addition, spirituality has received growing attention in the academy in the past decade (Astin, Astin, & Lindholm, 2011; Chickering, Dalton, & Stamm, 2006; Palmer & Zajonc, 2010):

> In recent years, at colleges and universities around the country, an expanding and increasingly vigorous dialogue has begun, centered on examining personal values, meaning, and purpose—including religious and spiritual values—as part of the educational experience. . . . Faculty are increasingly communicating their own need to find a place in the institutional environment to express their deeper values and hopes for societal change as they engage in the enterprise of producing and conveying knowledge [Chickering et al., 2006, pp. 1–2].

The term *spiritual* may be off-putting to some, particularly in an academic context (Chickering et al., 2006). Part of the problem is that discussions of spiritual development often confuse religion and spirituality, but recent research defines them as distinctly different constructs. Religion concerns the beliefs or practices of a particular faith community. In contrast, spirituality refers to an orientation of the whole person that gives meaning and purpose to life. Drawing on a range of sources, Astin et al. (2011) developed a consensus definition of *spirituality* as "an animating, creative, energizing, and meaning-making force—a 'dynamic expression' of who we are" (p. 28). Fundamental existential questions—Who am I? What is my purpose? Who will I become?—are spiritual questions. Their answers are rooted in "a lifelong, internal process of seeking personal authenticity; developing a greater sense of connectedness to self and others through relationship and community; [and] deriving meaning, purpose, and direction in life" (p. 27). Throughout this chapter, when we use the terms *spirituality* and *spiritual*, this consensus definition of *spirituality* is what we mean. Understood in this way, openness to and expressions of spirituality have practical implications for faculty members and the colleges and universities in which they work.

Over time, people's deepest concerns tend to shift in predictable ways. The shift is often particularly acute during the midlife period, which also falls within the span of midcareer faculty. The rewards of individual striving and self-authorship provide motivation and some satisfaction for a period of time. But for any number of reasons, the foundation of commitment on which that motivation and satisfaction rest may change. For example, some faculty members experience a loss of motivation after attaining a professional goal that had long been the target, such as promotion; in time, they will need to determine a new purpose for their work while simultaneously adding new responsibilities. A second common response involves achieving a goal but not experiencing the satisfaction expected to come with it. Faculty who have invested significant energy into climbing the academic ladder may find that disillusionment or even depression sets in once they have reached the top rung of becoming full professor. Other life changes are also occurring related to marriage, children, and parents. Negotiating these and other challenges often leads to introspection concerning the larger questions of life purpose (Loder, 1998).

In order to negotiate challenges of middle age successfully, adults must come to terms with new ways of seeing themselves and the world (Vogel, 2003). Being able to envision and try alternative approaches to making meaning portends a satisfactory resolution of the later-life conflicts of generativity versus stagnation and integrity versus despair that Erikson identified (1963). And according to Fowler (1981), the fifth of his six stages of faith development may emerge sometime during the midlife period. In this stage, individuals enter a "second naïveté," an opening to the voices of their "deeper self." At the same time, they become critically aware of their social unconscious—the myths and ideals inherited from social class, ethnic background, and religious group. Others have noted a similar transition in the middle years. Kegan (1994) sees a transition from the "self-authoring" to "self-transforming" mind with its embracing of paradox and contradiction; Hollis (1993), a Jungian analyst, explores the dynamics of midlife development, individuation, and the transition from the provisional to the authentic or true self; and Lightfoot (2009) examines the dynamics and characteristics of development in a small number of highly accomplished men and women in the years between fifty and seventy, including significant shifts in their sources of meaning and purpose.

Toward a Postindustrial Paradigm of Academic Renewal

Taking seriously the underlying spiritual development of faculty including periods of uncertainty, confusion, and reassessment of personal values calls for a radical reassessment of the traditional paradigm in the academy that focuses on productivity and the implicit ethical equivalency of "more" and "better." In its place, a postindustrial paradigm substitutes a metric of sustainability, "enough," and the underlying ethical foundation that healthier and more connected with one's self and the world around, not bigger and more, is "better." This alternate paradigm trusts that people who live out their authentic life purpose will revitalize institutions for the common good.

A Comprehensive Midcareer Faculty Development Process: Baldwin and Chang's Model

The emphasis on a vital sense of meaning as the driver of faculty members' scholarly work, learning, and professional engagement has practical implications for faculty and career development processes and interventions. In response to the challenges that midcareer faculty face, a variety of best practices in midcareer faculty development have been recommended. Baldwin and Chang (2006) provide a model for a comprehensive process (see Figure 5.1) comprising career reflection and assessment, career planning (both short and long term), and career action and implementation. Supporting each stage is an essential building block: collegial support including mentoring, networking, collaborating; resources, including information, time, and funding; and reinforcement, including recognition and rewards.

Baldwin et al. (2008) offer an extensive list of promising practices related to training and development, resources, and assessment and planning for institutions, department chairs, personnel and promotion and tenure committees, and midcareer faculty members themselves. Together these practices describe a coordinated process of career reflection and assessment at multiple levels of the institution. While many institutions have pieces of such a process in place, we believe few institutions have systems as comprehensive as the one described by Baldwin and his colleagues. Undoubtedly institutions would benefit from such coordination, as would midcareer faculty.

As promising as such comprehensive systems are, however, the literature on spiritual development suggests that they may fall short of

Figure 5.1. Midcareer Faculty Development Process.

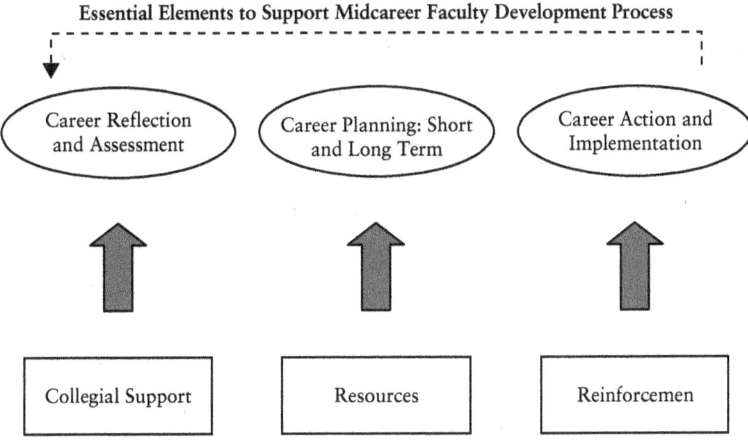

Source: *Reprinted with permission from "Reinforcing Our 'Keystone' Faculty: Strategies to Support Faculty in the Middle Years of Academic Life" (Liberal Education, 92 (4)). Copyright 2006 by the Association of American Colleges and Universities.*

realizing the full potential of professional revitalization for midcareer faculty and, more broadly, institutional transformation. Referring back to the Baldwin and Chang model, if career reflection and assessment are shallow and perfunctory, resources limited, and reinforcement absent or available for only a limited range of professional activities such as research, even a seemingly comprehensive system will fail to reap its intended benefits. The literature on spiritual development and the growing literature on spirituality in higher education provides a source of guidance on promising practices for each stage of the Baldwin and Chang model. These practices are grounded in authentic self-reflection that recognizes the deeper sources of faculty members' evolving sense of meaning and purpose, supportive community, creative uses of time, and the power of intrinsic motivation coupled with a flexible incentive structure.

Career Reflection and Assessment

The first element of Baldwin and Chang's model of a comprehensive career assessment process is career reflection and assessment. The potential of this element is particularly rich if the career reflection involves contemplation of one's most deeply held values and priorities as a vehicle for sustained faculty satisfaction, productivity, and vitality. Addressing ideas contrary to institutional norms, connecting passion and values to one's work, and fostering support among colleagues are among the ways that such deep reflection and assessment are enacted.

SPEAKING THE UNSPEAKABLE. As a foundation for authentic self-reflection, members of the academy need permission to speak the unspeakable: that is, acknowledge that they are whole persons with a sense of meaning and purpose that their lives as faculty members should support and sustain. For example, in a recent national survey of faculty, 81 percent consider themselves to be spiritual to "some" or "great" extent, 60 percent engage in prayer or meditation to "some" or "great" extent, and 70 percent seek opportunities to grow spiritually. Only 47 percent feel that integrating spirituality into their lives is "very important" or "essential," and only 30 percent believe that colleges and universities should be concerned with students' spiritual development (Astin et al., 2011).

As we noted, there is an expanding dialogue across the country on examining personal values, meaning, and purpose as a central part of the educational experience for both faculty and students (Chickering et al., 2006). Others have advanced simple but powerful ways of encouraging collegial conversations on college campuses concerning personal values, meaning, and purpose (see Palmer & Zajonc, 2010).

IDENTIFYING PASSIONS AND VALUES AS A FOUNDATION FOR SCHOLARLY WORK AND LEARNING. With growing permission to speak the unspeakable, faculty members and the institutions in which they reside can begin to acknowledge the importance of personal passions and values as a foundation for scholarly work. Following forty recently tenured faculty at four U.S. institutions over a three-year period, Anna Neumann (2009) argues that understanding and nurturing the passions that underlie scholarly work and learning is central to the promise of higher education in contemporary society because professors are "the central carriers and cultivators of that promise" (p. 231). In contrast to the expectation of radical objectivism in traditional scholarship, Neumann defines learning as "the construction of knowledge, scholarly and otherwise, that a person experiences through mental processes," and it assumes "the thinker's inner engagement" with a subject (p. 6). Thus, scholarly learning draws on life experience, including inner experience, personal values, and passions.

Neumann encourages professors to find a subject of study that is meaningful to them and to explain it publicly, including its larger significance. She reminds professors that the subject of their study "is a statement to yourself of who you are, what you care about, and what you want to know" (p. 227). In fact, fueled by current research in positive psychology, more and more faculty development centers (for example, the one at the University of Virginia) offer opportunities for faculty to consider their ultimate concerns, write personal purpose and mission statements, and develop ways to stay focused on their vision. Colleges and universities also may wish to look to faith-based institutions for inspiration. For example, George Fox University asks faculty members to describe the intersection of individual values and beliefs with their discipline and their teaching as part of pre- and posttenure review. Faculty developers at secular institutions could invite faculty members to engage in similar reflection about the integration of values, beliefs, discipline, teaching, and career.

FOSTERING COLLEGIAL SUPPORT. Baldwin and Chang identify collegial support as the essential building block for career reflection and assessment. Faculty members reside in social systems—classrooms, departments, schools, colleges and universities, and their wider scholarly communities; it is important to engage these networks of relationships in the process of authentic self-assessment. In fact, encouraging relationships around personal disclosure and authentic self-assessment can have powerful transformational effects for institutions as a whole (Palmer & Zajonc, 2010). Austin (2010) notes the important role of chairpersons in "nurturing, encouraging, and challenging mid-career faculty members to stay vibrant" (p. 373). In addition, some institutions are formalizing supportive relationships in the form of new approaches to mentoring: the midcareer faculty member can function as either the mentor to an early-career faculty member or the mentee of a more senior member. Either way, the relationship can foster deeper self-reflection for both parties and, with it, career revitalization. Furthermore, some institutions (for example, Towson University, University of Massachusetts Amherst, University of Minnesota, and University of Virginia) have formed faculty learning communities for midcareer faculty to explore issues commonly shared by members of this cohort. Finally, adopting pedagogies that foster deeper student engagement in the classroom can also be revitalizing and foster authentic self-reflection, not only for students but for faculty as well. This is particularly the case when classroom discussions entertain the big questions concerning life meaning and purpose that preoccupy students and faculty alike, but which are frequently unacknowledged in the academy (see Astin et al., 2011). The contemplative pedagogy movement (see Association for Contemplative Mind in Higher Education, an initiative of the Center for Contemplative Mind in Society that promotes the emergence of a broad culture of contemplation in the academy) inspires a growing number of faculty members to bring questions of meaning and purpose into disciplines that are traditionally uninterested in such explorations.

Career Planning

Authentic self-reflection grounded in midcareer faculty members' evolving sense of meaning and purpose is the basis for the second element in the Baldwin and Chang model: short- and long-term career planning. Ideally the aim of career planning should be sustaining faculty members' vital and evolving sense of purpose through their scholarly work during a long and productive career that also contributes to the fulfillment of the mission of their college or university.

Baldwin and Chang identify resources in the form of information, time, and funding as the essential building blocks for this element of their model. Below we expand on two of these types of resources, information and time, recognizing that institutions must provide adequate funding to support the programs and initiatives we describe.

INFORMATION. As midcareer faculty members engage in career planning, they would benefit from knowing about theories of development such as those developed by James Fowler, Robert Kegan, James Hollis, and Erik Erikson, as well as the underlying conditions that support healthy human development over the life span. Changing perspectives on core concepts such as authority, identity, self, and commitment over the life span are normal and natural and can have extensive consequences in terms of career performance and satisfaction, as well as other spheres of life. Knowing about these overarching patterns of human development puts one's own struggles and periods of disillusionment in perspective and alleviates one's sense of isolation. Furthermore, career planning, which often occurs in the academic department, should recognize and allow shifts in motivation and interest as midcareer faculty negotiate common crises of human development.

For a variety of reasons, the academy tends to ignore the importance of physical and emotional well-being in a satisfying and sustainable career. Not the least of these reasons is the mind-body schism, a relic from earlier philosophical traditions that still permeates academic life (Kronman, 2007). Holistic well-being requires a healthy diet, physical exercise, rest, and supportive relationships. Recent research reveals that many faculty members sacrifice their health and supportive relationships with family, friends, and colleagues in the relentless pursuit of productivity required by today's academy (Astin et al., 2011). In response, some institutions (for example, Northwest Arkansas Community College) offer wellness sessions for faculty on topics such as exercise, diet, mindfulness, and recognizing core values. And some faculty development centers have incorporated a broad array of wellness programs as a central part of their mission; one of them is Appalachian State University, although its center's mission has narrowed in recent years. These efforts are valuable, but they ultimately are not a substitute for systematic culture change.

TIME. Time is arguably the most basic, elusive, and misunderstood resource in the academy. Certainly there is never enough of it in an environment that emphasizes productivity and doing above all else. But in the context of midcareer faculty members sustaining a vital sense of meaning and purpose as the primary driver of scholarly work and learning, we need to think about time differently and more creatively. Neumann (2009) reminds us that following one's passions and engaging in continued meaningful scholarly learning takes time and effort. To "see and ponder" (p. 224) does not equal productivity, but not attending to this important dimension risks cutting off the root of vibrant and sustainable scholarship.

In the new paradigm, time is a resource that is preserved and protected as a source of refreshment, vitality, and renewal like an oasis in a desert. Various practices protect and extend time for rest, greater awareness, and meaningful reflection as the ultimate source of insight and creative and sustainable scholarly work, learning, and full participation in the academy and in all of society. In contrast to objective and analytical ways of knowing that dominate the academy, a growing number of researchers, practitioners, and commentators on higher education are advocating for the many benefits of practices such as contemplation and mindfulness training (Kuh & Gonyea, 2004; Palmer & Zajonc, 2010) for both faculty members and students. They remind us that contemplative insight has a role in scientific inquiry and that introducing contemplative practices into academic life creates an opening and spaciousness for insight, learning, and renewal. Inspired by the mindfulness movement, leading medical schools have established centers that teach mindfulness-based meditation to health care professionals. Some universities (for example, University of Virginia and Vanderbilt University) have followed the lead of their medical centers and have brought opportunities for faculty to explore the benefits of contemplative practice for student learning and faculty work.

The modern academy has institutionalized rest in the sabbatical—a paid leave, typically for a semester or a full year, granted to tenured faculty members every six to seven years, in order to work on a major research or other professional project that requires sustained time and unbroken attention. The roots of the word *sabbatical,* however, have been all but forgotten. The concept of a sabbatical has biblical roots: Genesis 2:2–3 recounts that God rested on the seventh day after creating the universe. The Hebrew *Shavat VaYinafash* means "ceased" or "rested physically" and "spiritually renewed." The biblical sabbath, derived from the Hebrew word *Shavat*, is the origin of the practice of the "weekend" in which there is no scheduled work. While the academy also recognizes the weekend, vacations, and, for many faculty members, a nine- or ten-month appointment, the sheer weight of responsibilities and expectations for productivity often means that faculty members work during these times meant for rest. In other words, the idea of sabbatical and rest as times of retreat and replenishment has been lost in the existing paradigm. The new paradigm calls for their reinstatement as a source of faculty members' vitality, renewal, and sustainable scholarly work and contribution.

Career Action and Implementation

The final stage of the Baldwin and Chang development process is career action and implementation in which midcareer faculty members conduct the courses, projects, research, and other aspects of professional engagement they have identified in planning. According to the model, reinforcements such as various forms of rewards and recognition support this stage of the process.

Certainly it is important that colleges and universities develop effective incentive structures. On the other hand, our discussion suggests that intrinsic sources of motivation such as passions, values, and a sense of meaning and purpose are the ultimate source of sustainable scholarly work, learning, and professional engagement. For example, Neumann (2009) argues that "professors' desire to learn subjects that matter to them personally, and their strivings to do so, are important, but largely undiscussed (and underused) resources that higher education leaders could more fully deploy—for the good of students, the university, society and indeed, humanity" (p. 224). In fact, policymakers might not need to champion productivity and engagement as strenuously if they attended more openly to what professors already want to do in service to the university's benefit. Neumann also reminds leaders that faculty are rarely motivated by pay and that rewards are unlikely to "spur professors to action that is as thoughtful and imaginative as the promised opportunity to advance one's scholarly learning" (p. 229).

These insights point to the need to create more flexible reward structures, which recognize a range of viable career paths that may evolve as faculty members' passions, values, and sense of purpose shift over the years. Recognizing the unique contributions of individual faculty members will go a long way in enhancing midcareer faculty members' experience that is currently marked too often by a sense of being undervalued and disrespected.

Conclusion

Recent research studies point to widespread alienation of faculty members from their most deeply held values and an authentic sense of meaning and purpose as the foundation for scholarly work, engagement with students, and societal realities. In addition, the demands of the modern academy often compromise faculty members' health, well-being, and personal relationships. This malaise is symptomatic of the traditional paradigm of the academy, whose underlying metaphor is industrial with a metric of productivity and the belief that more is better.

The experience of midcareer faculty members provides a window into the dynamic of widespread alienation in the academy. Research conducted over three decades confirms that this experience is distinct from that of junior and senior faculty members. Furthermore, the persistence of an underlying affect of ambivalence, uncertainty, discontent, and periodic unsettledness in midcareer faculty members points to deeper developmental sources. We believe the roots are ultimately spiritual. Alternative frameworks offered by the spiritual development literature can deepen faculty developers' understanding of the midcareer faculty experience and help them design more meaningful interventions.

Career development processes such as those advanced by Baldwin and Chang incorporate stages of reflection and assessment, planning, and implementation. Each of these stages offers opportunities to incorporate practices that recognize midcareer faculty members as whole persons whose spiritual development is essential to the evolution of their careers.

Incorporated bit by bit over time, these practices have the power to transform the academy. In place of the current industrial paradigm, they introduce a metric of sustainability and "enough" and an underlying ethical foundation that "better" is the result of being healthier, happier, and more connected with one's self and the rest of the world. A renewal paradigm, we believe, will enable midcareer faculty to live a holistic life calling, leading to revitalization of their work and increased benefit to their institutions and the greater good of society.

REFERENCES

Astin, A. W., & Astin, H. S. (1999). *Meaning and spirituality in the lives of college faculty: A study of values, authenticity, and stress.* Los Angeles: University of California, Los Angeles, Higher Education Research Institute.

Astin, A. W., Astin, H. S., & Lindholm J. A. (2011). *Cultivating the spirit: How college can enhance students' inner lives.* San Francisco, CA: Jossey-Bass.

Austin, A. (2010). Supporting faculty members across their careers. In K. J. Gillespie, D. L. Robertson, & Associates. *A guide to faculty development* (2nd ed., pp. 363–378). San Francisco, CA: Jossey-Bass.

Baldwin, R. G., & Chang, D. A. (2006, Fall). Reinforcing our strategies to support faculty in the middle years of academic life. *Liberal Education,* 38–35.

Baldwin, R., DeZure, D., Shaw, A., & Moretto, D. (2008, September/October). Mapping the terrain of mid-career faculty at a research university: Implications for faculty and academic leaders. *Change,* 46–55.

Baldwin, R. G., Lunceford, C. J., & Vanderlinden, K. E. (2005). Faculty in the middle years: Illuminating an overlooked phase of academic life. *Review of Higher Education, 29*(1), 97–118.

Chickering, A., Dalton, J., & Stamm, L. (Eds.). (2006). *Encouraging authenticity and spirituality in higher education.* San Francisco, CA: Jossey-Bass.

Erikson, E. (1963). *Childhood and society* (2nd ed.). New York, NY: Norton.

Fowler, J. (1981). *Stages of faith: The psychology of human development and the quest for meaning.* San Francisco: HarperSanFrancisco.

Hall, D. T. (1986). *Breaking career routines: Mid-career choice and identity development.* In D. T. Hall & Associates (Eds.), *Career development in organizations* (pp. 120–159). San Francisco, CA: Jossey-Bass.

Hansen, L. S. (1993). Career development trends and issues in the United States. *Journal of Career Development, 20*(1), 7–24.

Hollis, J. (1993). *The middle passage: From misery to meaning in mid-life.* Toronto, Canada: Inner City Books.

Kegan, R. (1994). *In over our heads: The mental demands of modern life.* Cambridge, MA: Harvard University Press.

Kronman, A. T. (2007). *Education's end: Why our colleges and universities have given up on the meaning of life.* New Haven, CT: Yale University Press.

Kuh, G. D., & Gonyea, R. M. (2004, Winter). Spirituality, liberal learning, and college student engagement. *Liberal Education,* 40–47.

Levinson, D. J. (1986). A conception of adult development. *American Psychologist, 41,* 3–13.

Lightfoot, S. L. (2009). *The third chapter: Passion, risk and adventure in the twenty-five years after fifty.* New York, NY: Farrar, Straus and Giroux.

Loder, J. (1998). *The logic of the spirit: Human development in theological perspective.* San Francisco: Jossey-Bass.

National Center for Education Statistics. (2002). *National Study of Post-Secondary Faculty (NSOPF: 99) methodology report.* Washington, DC: Author.

Neumann, A. (2009). *Professing to learn: Creating tenured lives and careers in the American research University.* Baltimore, MD: John Hopkins University Press.

Palmer, P., & Zajonc, A. (2010). *The heart of higher education: A call to renewal: Transforming the academy through collegial conversations.* San Francisco, CA: Jossey-Bass.

Super, D. E. (1986). Life career roles: Self-realization in work and leisure. In D. T. Hall & Associates (Eds.), *Career development in organizations* (pp. 95–119). San Francisco, CA: Jossey-Bass.

Vogel, L. J. (2003). Spiritual development in later life. In M. A. Kimble, S. H. McFadden, J. W. Ellor, & J. J. Seeber (Eds.), *Aging, spirituality, and religion* (pp. 74–86). Minneapolis, MN: Fortress Press.

6

THE DONORS NEXT DOOR

RAISING FUNDS FROM FACULTY FOR FACULTY DEVELOPMENT CENTERS

Genevieve G. Shaker
Megan M. Palmer
Indiana University Purdue University-Indianapolis

As a result of waning institutional support and charitable foundation interest, teaching and learning centers and other faculty development units may have little choice but to turn to private donors. Although faculty and staff giving is an important part of higher education fundraising, considering faculty as potential donors for faculty development centers is uncommon. In this chapter, we provide information on faculty and staff giving, review the related literature, share findings from a new study on faculty major donors, and provide a series of recommendations, stemming from the literature and the major donor study, to inform fundraising efforts by faculty development centers.

o

A quick review of the headlines in the *Chronicle of Higher Education* and *Inside Higher Education* yields results such as: "Financing for Higher Education Shifts to Private Sector Worldwide," "State Budgets Weaken, and May Get Worse," "NSF Budget Would Remain Flat Under House Bill, Despite Earlier Promises," "Where Universities Can Be Cut," and

"Welcome, Now Start Slashing." Although financial struggles are not new to institutions of higher education (Thelin, 2004), the recent recession has created additional financial pressures, resulting in cuts to university budgets as well as to funding organizations such as the National Institutes of Health and National Science Foundation (Basken, 2011).

In recent years, institutions like the University of California at Berkeley and the University of North Carolina at Chapel Hill have hired management consultants to analyze their university budgets and identify potential savings. The consultants' findings revealed that major savings could occur if cuts were made in administration (Kiley, 2011). Similarly, other institutions are working to protect the academic core and trim the fat by focusing on cuts to administrative units. Despite the importance of teaching centers and other faculty development units, it is not unusual for them to be subject to major fiscal cuts or to function with small budgets (Gray & Hohnstreiter, 2010).

In the past, faculty development units were able to secure funding from external sources such as the Bush, Ford, and Lilly foundations (Ouellet, 2010). In some cases, however, financial support from foundations has also been on the decline (Preston, 2010), and in other cases, the focus of these foundations has shifted from funding teaching innovations ("Bush Foundation Announces New Priorities," 2008). In Dotson and Bernstein's (2010) comparison of teaching centers at large state universities, 82 percent of the centers in their study reported that 90 percent or more of their total budgets were from institutional sources.

It is evident that teaching and learning centers and other faculty development units may have little choice but to turn to alternate sources of support, most prominently private donors. Faculty and staff donors make significant contributions to higher education (Council for the Advancement and Support of Education, 2011). Faculty and staff fundraising therefore should be a foundational component of faculty development center strategies for building support.

In this chapter we provide information on faculty and staff giving, review the related literature, share findings from a new study on faculty major donors, and provide a series of recommendations, based on the literature and study of major donors to inform fundraising efforts by faculty development centers.

Data on Faculty and Staff Giving

Employee giving campaigns are a regular occurrence at many colleges and universities (March, 2005), as is calculating faculty and staff participation within larger campuswide campaigns. Faculty, staff, and retirees are known to give millions of dollars back to their departments, schools, and campuses. A series of examples from multiyear and single-year campaigns, as well as from public and private institutions, is revealing in its scope and significance. At the University of Minnesota, eleven thousand faculty, staff, and retirees gave $67 million during the Campaign for Minnesota (Palmer, 2004), and at Penn State they gave $41 million during an equivalent campaign (Penn State University, 2010). In the mid-1990s, the University of Georgia reported that faculty and staff gave $4.4 million during their annual campaign, accounting for just over 10 percent of all giving that year. Furthermore, over 73 percent of their faculty and staff contributed to this campaign (Bailey, 1994). Around that same time, 91 percent of Wittenberg University employees contributed to its annual campaign (Bailey, 1994). At our institution, Indiana University Purdue University-Indianapolis, hundreds of retired and current faculty and staff gave $2.4 million during fiscal year 2011.

Data drawn from the Voluntary Support for Education survey show that at research and doctoral institutions, 18.5 percent of faculty and staff gave, with an average total per institution of $685,997; at master's institutions, 24.5 percent gave, with an institutional average of $103,418; at baccalaureate institutions, 26.3 percent gave, with an institutional total average of $64,716; and at associate institutions, 43.7 percent gave, averaging $27,793 per institution (Council for the Advancement and Support of Education, 2011).

From these examples and figures, it is evident that faculty and staff giving varies by institutional type and that it has been an important source of support for all colleges and universities for at least two decades. What we know about which faculty and staff give, and where, how, and why, comes from only a handful of studies focused at the individual, unit, and institutional levels. Although the majority of the studies we review here are not focused specifically on giving to faculty development units, it is important to understand the motivations for giving and conditions under which faculty and staff give. This information can then underpin any fundraising efforts made by those in faculty development.

Literature on Faculty and Staff Giving

A mid-1990s study explored who gives and why through a survey of 183 full-time faculty at a research university, a comprehensive university, and a liberal arts college (Holland, 1997; Holland & Miller, 1999). Senior, tenured faculty who were not alumni of the institution were the most likely to give. The top giving motives, as selected from a list of thirty options, were altruism, social responsibility to the institution, self-fulfillment, professional attitude, conviction, and institutional loyalty; of these, institutional loyalty was most prevalent. Although there were institutional differences in the motivating factors, especially between the research university and the other institutions, differences in motives by faculty rank, tenure status, or length of service were muted. In response to questions about preferred means of solicitation before e-mail was common, mailed correspondence was deemed important, and telephone calls and visits from fundraising professionals were not.

When staff were added into the equation in a mixed-method study conducted at Bowling Green State University, giving was most likely among those in full-time administrative professional positions than among full-time faculty, part-time faculty, or hourly staff (Knight, 2004). Those who had worked at the institution longer, received higher salaries, gave previously, lived in the town of Bowling Green, or were alumni of the university were also more likely to be current donors. The qualitative portion of the study consisted of twelve faculty interviews in which the participants posited that the top reasons others gave were allegiance, especially at the department and school levels, and connectivity. Barriers were thought to include poor morale, lack of community spirit, low salaries, limited resources, and philosophical concerns related to fundraising priorities and employee campaigns.

March (2005) surveyed chief advancement officers at 164 public universities, seeking institutional differences in faculty and staff philanthropy. Institutions with fewer than one thousand students and Carnegie-classified baccalaureate institutions had higher levels of giving. Furthermore, faculty members at midwestern institutions were more likely to give than elsewhere. Department chairs and faculty and staff campaign cochairs were deemed the most effective solicitors of funds. March concluded that faculty and staff were more likely to restrict their giving rather than rely on the institution to determine how to use their contributions, a finding that mirrors overall trends in philanthropic giving to higher education (McClintock, 2000).

A recent study focused on giving by faculty and staff in two annual on-campus campaigns, but rather than examining giving to the institution, both campaigns encouraged employees to support external nonprofit organizations (Agypt, Christensen, & Nesbit, 2011). One campaign aimed at raising funds for local arts organizations and the other for human and social services. The longitudinal study at a large public university explored various individual characteristics in relation to donations between 2001 and 2008. Higher salaries were found to be a constant in predicting giving, while longer lengths of service were an accurate predictor only in one of the two campaigns. Neither sex nor age was found to have significant effects on giving. When the two campaigns were looked at together, hourly staff gave more money than did full professors, assistant professors, and salaried staff; however, their giving was somewhat consistent with that of associate professors. Although the giving was external, these findings may have some value for those raising money for internal purposes.

Two case studies, one of a fundraising model developed by a faculty development center (Gray & Hohnstreiter, 2010) and the other of a redesign of a faculty and staff campaign at Southern Utah University (Cardon, 2009), show how practitioners are working to create and refine fundraising programs and provide information on the results of their efforts. In 2008, Southern Utah sought to increase the number of employees donating to the campaign. Through a well-designed program that involved training faculty and staff to cochair the campaign, engaging faculty and staff to serve on the steering committee, and designing specific fundraising materials for employees, Southern Utah saw its participation rate increase from 27 percent to 85 percent. The effectiveness of friendly competition, importance of promoting departmental fundraising successes, ability to build on the momentum of campus events, centrality of methods for gift designation, and importance of employee giving for external fundraising efforts are among the lessons learned in the study (Cardon, 2009).

In a 2010 POD session, Gray and Hohnstreiter presented a fundraising strategy fine-tuned by one teaching center over five years that included development of a case for support and a fundraising plan built around mail appeals, one-on-one solicitations, pitches at workshops, and special events. In their subsequent chapter in 2011 in *To Improve the Academy*, the researchers revealed that teaching center "alumni"—university faculty—with ten or more hours of participation a year in center programs were not only the first to be asked for support but 30 percent of them became donors (Hohnstreiter & Gray, 2011). In 2010, the center had one hundred faculty and community donors who gave $30,000, an amount that constituted nearly one-third of the center's budget. The largest commitments came from two community members who together pledged more than $300,000 in future support. Nevertheless, they conclude, "Your center's most natural donors are its participants, but they don't know how to give, and they haven't been asked" (Hohnstreiter & Gray, 2011, p. 274). The case that Hohnstreiter and Gray presented shows that as at the institutional level, faculty are an important population of potential donors for faculty development centers.

These studies give faculty developers important baseline information about faculty and staff donors and a window on strategies for increasing giving from this population. In response to the lack of literature on faculty and staff giving, particularly qualitative literature and literature focusing on those who make larger gifts, one of us interviewed faculty who are major donors. This study, which took place in one school within a single institution, can help faculty developers delineate the best prospects for large gifts and, building on the prior research, determine how a culture of giving can be fostered among our faculty and staff that will support both annual giving and major gift fundraising.

A Study of Faculty Major Donors

To learn more about faculty donors, one of us interviewed six women and four men who were senior and retired faculty and administrators who had made significant gifts and pledges directed toward a large school with more than three hundred faculty and staff on an urban university established in the latter half of the twentieth century. The individuals considered for this study had made at least one gift or bequest at or above twenty-five thousand dollars (and therefore they were deemed by the institution to be major gift donors). In the institutional review board–approved study, interviews were conducted until the point of saturation, when additional conversations produced little new knowledge (Kvale, 1996). Participants took part in sixty- to ninety-minute, digitally recorded interviews and answered questions about their professional histories, institutional experiences, and philanthropic activities. A semistructured protocol created a conversational exchange, which encouraged openness by the participants and allowed interviewer flexibility (Burgess, 1984; Seidman, 2006). A cross-case analysis served as the method for examining the interviews collectively and in a strategic manner (Eisenhardt, 2002). A series of analytical techniques including clustering, categorizing, reduction, and drawing comparisons generated the set of common characteristics among the faculty donors that follows. An illustrative quote highlighting one or more aspect follows each characteristic. Reviewing these results, from the lens of a faculty developer provides insight on the motivations for giving and circumstances under which faculty made major donations:

1. All of the participants had worked between fifteen and forty years at their institution and had successful and fulfilling careers. This created a meaningful institutional bond and sense of gratitude and responsibility.

> "Except for my family of origin, I've [probably] been in a relationship with [the university] longer than just about anyone else."

2. The participants were deeply involved in the life of the university throughout their careers, serving on committees, participating in institutional governance, creating new programs, and helping to shape the institution's development.

   > "I've always been a strong believer that wherever you are, you participate in what makes it go."

3. All participants served in administrative positions at one time or another, at one level or another. Although not all of them enjoyed these appointments, the positions gave them a perspective beyond individual disciplines and some experience with fundraising and philanthropy.

   > "I think that the faculty who have made larger gifts are primarily citizens of the campus more than of the discipline, who see the potential of [the university] to make a difference, who see the potential of gifts to make a difference. And, I think it's because most of them have had assignments that have taken them outside of their department."

4. The professional and personal lives of the participants were integrated through friendships, interests that spanned work and home, and spousal connections to higher education. Distinctions were rarely drawn between work activities and private life.

   > "We always feel like we're ambassadors for the university even when we're out in other social venues. So, frequently, a lot of events or things we might attend, you meet people where you can find there are things you could do with them or some person you could get in contact with at the university that would help. So, I tend to carry my business cards with me for most of those occasions."

5. The donors believed in the importance of higher education as a public good. Most shared an interest in scholarship with a community connection and were civically engaged, incorporating this commitment into their teaching, research, and service activities.

   > "It was my idea when the [state] bicentennial came along that our department do something for the bicentennial. So, I thought we should do a book [on the state]. I got all my department people, Latin American people as well as European people, to do

some [state] topics. . . . That book came out and was made into a [traveling] exhibit."

6. Most of the participants were generous annual donors who realized that philanthropy could perpetuate their professional values. Though they gave outside of the university, higher education emerged as their philanthropic priority.

   "[Philanthropy] gives you the feeling that you're doing something longer lasting for the campus and the program. It's satisfying."

7. The philanthropy of colleagues and mentors inspired the participants to make significant gifts of their own. The behaviors of colleagues and friends led the faculty to consider whether they could and should do something similar. They wished also to inspire philanthropy in others.

   "I don't want to suggest that some of the faculty who gave similar size gifts were persuaded by what we did but I think that we all had similar kinds of thoughts about what will this represent and what will this say to other people who are potential donors."

Reviewing these results from the lens of a faculty developer provides insight into the motivations for giving and circumstances under which faculty made major donations. Although this study did not focus specifically on faculty who gave to teaching centers or faculty development units, the findings reveal patterns about those who give, which are similar to what studies presented in the review of literature found. As a result, this information can be used to navigate the fairly uncharted waters of fundraising for faculty development units.

The recommendations in the next section are directed to faculty developers interested in raising funds from faculty and staff. These recommendations are based on our review of the common themes in the literature, as well as the seven characteristics of faculty who are major donors. Because a goal of fundraising is to inspire annual givers to become major donors, it makes sense to apply lessons learned from major donors to overall approaches to cultivating giving prospects and stewarding annual supporters.

Recommendations: Building a Culture of Giving

Why should a teaching center director, dean of faculties, or associate dean for academic and faculty affairs engage in fundraising? Eckert and

Pollack (2000) point out several reasons that faculty and administrators should be central players in this effort. Faculty development leaders are in the best position to articulate the vision for the faculty development unit. A development officer would be hard-pressed to convey the enthusiasm of faculty developers for the work or to as effectively delineate the value of philanthropic resources in advancing student learning. Faculty donors want to know that their gifts will support, improve, and shape educational efforts, and faculty developers are best positioned to tell them how this will happen. Moreover, while fundraising personnel would likely be thought of as administrators with only loose ties to academic work, faculty developers would be more likely to be considered faculty peers and thus could inspire colleagues to give in a different manner. This is not to say that faculty developers should not partner with development professionals in these efforts. Indeed the subsequent set of recommendations begins with building connections to existing fundraising efforts. The main lesson here, however, is that fundraising efforts for faculty development programming and needs will be more successful when faculty developers are involved.

The following framework focuses on developing strategies within faculty development units for creating cultures of giving and inspiring major gifts. Many of these strategies apply to both faculty outside the center and to those with even closer affiliations—your own staff, leadership, advisory board, and faculty fellows, all of them among your faculty and staff prospects.

Explore Existing Institutional Fundraising Resources and Programs

Start by finding out what support for fundraising is available to you through your college or university. A development professional may already be charged with faculty and staff fundraising; if not, someone who specializes in annual gift fundraising may be able to work with you to build a strategy for your center. Whether or not you can obtain this kind of support, faculty development leaders must understand institutional policy and practice when it comes to fundraising. Therefore, getting to know your local development officer or institutional foundation is critical.

It is likely that your institution already holds an annual campaign to raise money from its own faculty and staff, and your center staff may be participants. Piggybacking on an existing initiative with an established time line, materials, and approach will make getting started much less daunting and may inspire additional giving by your colleagues in the center, as well as developing new donors from elsewhere on campus. Gifts from these campaigns are likely to be made close to home, so reminding faculty about your center as their home for professional development may go a long way.

Seek and Provide Education About Philanthropy

Faculty developers who decide to become fundraisers (if even modestly so) should consider getting training about fundraising or perusing some of the many books, articles, and electronic resources on the subject. Opportunities may be available through home institutions or local fundraising organizations for those who want to understand the basic tenets of the field. For example, the Center for Philanthropy at Indiana University offers the Fund Raising School that teaches "the historical and philanthropic context, the current issues, and the art and science of fundraising and philanthropy" (Indiana University Center on Philanthropy, 2011). The Council for the Advancement and Support of Education (CASE) provides trainings and materials specifically directed at fundraising for higher education (http://www.case.org/), and your institution may well already be a CASE member. A range of articles about faculty and staff giving, as well as many about partnering with faculty and staff on fundraising efforts, has also appeared in the organization's magazine, *Currents.*

Training and self-driven education will not only prepare faculty developers to raise money; it will develop their own philanthropic awareness. Furthermore, once they are trained, this new knowledge can be passed on to faculty, and as we learned from the major donors, some experience with philanthropy is a plus when it comes to learning to make gifts of your own. The average faculty member likely lacks a strong understanding—and even may have big misconceptions—about fundraising practices, administrative processes, and avenues for giving. Education can take place through planned internal communications as well as informal individual conversations.

Develop Giving Opportunities

Regularly asking faculty to give will establish philanthropy within the life of the center. Although mini-campaigns for a teaching center require significant effort, it is for these most personal purposes that faculty may make their first gifts or will be persuaded to make more than an obligatory contribution. For many teaching centers, non-tenure-track and part-time faculty who do a majority of the teaching are the most likely to benefit from the services provided. As a result, they may see the teaching center as a unit that closely matches their interests and may be inclined to give—even if they do not give elsewhere.

By providing opportunities for faculty and staff to give, centers can get over what is typically the largest hurdle in raising funds: failing to ask for support. Creating a community of giving will allow interested faculty to come together in support of shared priorities and self-determined initiatives.

Promote Involvement in Fundraising Among Center Staff and Faculty Users

From helping set campaign priorities to involvement with external fundraising efforts, involving center staff, faculty users, or advisory board members in the fundraising process will educate everyone involved about fundraising. Moreover, developing fundraising friends and allies among the faculty will expand your circle of influence and have a ripple effect. Inviting faculty to serve as volunteers during annual fundraising efforts may lead to more gifts and inspire the faculty to begin making gifts of their own. Once a faculty member has made a significant gift, involve that person in your fundraising activities because that gift will likely inspire others to contribute. As Collins (2000) writes, "If faculty and staff members want to help out, don't limit their involvement to signing appeal letters or soliciting each other. Let them get to know your prospects by including them in campaign events and activities. . . . They can be your most valuable partners in making the case for support" (p. 6).

Make Philanthropy Visible

The ways in which philanthropy enhances the work of your center is a story worth telling again and again. Hosting special events or providing print or electronic venues for recognition of faculty and staff support, for example, can provide others with models of giving. Writing about the activities of one teaching center, Hohnstreiter and Gray (2011) explain how an online and classroom wall of honor, fundraising pitches at workshops, luncheons for campus and community prospects, and a yearly gala all provide venues for sharing stories of philanthropy and its outcomes.

As a faculty developer, you have credibility in the eyes of faculty donors. Eckert and Pollack (2000) discuss faculty members' (and faculty developers') firsthand knowledge of what is happening in the classroom and awareness of the challenges faculty and students face as significant assets in fundraising: "As a result, faculty will listen to you, even when you're just chatting with them at a cocktail party. A few well-considered remarks could lead you into the process of cultivating the next gift to your department" (p. 12).

Treat All Faculty—and Center Staff—as Potential Donors

Faculty development professionals tend to form strong and lasting relationships with faculty and administrators on campus. Individuals with a relationship with the potential donor should be the ones to ask for support (Eckert & Pollack, 2000). Think about the faculty member who was asked to create an online program and turned to your center for ongoing support; the senior faculty member who continues to win teaching awards year after year; the department chair who sought counsel and support to become an inspiring leader. Center staff should also be considered among those with the greatest proclivity to give; indeed, gifts by center leadership and staff may be among the first you seek.

A casual interaction in passing with someone may have an effect that you do not expect, particularly if that person has been quietly considering making a gift. Formal and informal conversations and behavior can influence these important decisions. Pay attention to important events in the professional lives of your faculty because these may set the time frame for their gifts. Remember that everyone may be a future donor.

When Fundraising for Major Gifts, Begin with the Right People

Let the literature be your guide when it comes to identifying possible major donors. As Hohnstreiter and Gray (2011) suggest, begin your annual fundraising efforts by soliciting faculty who are regular participants in your faculty development offerings and seeking funds from your colleagues in the center. The same principle holds for major donors: those with an established relationship to your center are more likely to give because the opportunity is closely related to their work and values. Identify faculty who are currently, or have in the past, served as administrators. As discussed in the major donor study and as in Knight's (2004) research, faculty who hold administrative appointments are more likely to understand the big picture, realize the importance of fundraising, and be willing to contribute at higher levels. Furthermore, ongoing annual gifts most often precede larger gifts; therefore, it is wise to consider those who become consistent donors to your program as your best prospects for large gifts. Remember that faculty with many years on campus as well as those with strong local connections to the community may be more philanthropically inclined. Consider what you know about where your faculty and staff prospects are in life, including their current financial obligations (for example, their children may be in college, or their partner may be out of work) and capacity; your development professional can help out with this information, But as the annual giving data (Agypt et al., 2011; Holland & Miller, 1999) demonstrate, do not be too hasty in eliminating prospects based solely on what you know about their salaries or professorial rank. Call on fundraising staff when you are ready to review your list of potential donors, discuss next steps, and plan individual strategies.

Conclusion

Applying the seven principles strategically and intentionally can lead to a cohort of faculty and staff donors who give year after year, become significant supporters, and emerge as strong partners in fundraising. Moreover, as you gain financial support, you will also be strengthening your professional ties to those you serve and building their investment, philanthropic and intellectual, in the work of your center. Fundraising is not easy, and it requires a commitment of time and resources. It is, however, an undertaking with a significant return, and looking for the faculty and staff donors next door is the best place to begin.

REFERENCES

Agypt, B., Christensen, R. K., & Nesbit, R. (2011). A tale of two charitable campaigns: Longitudinal analysis of employee giving at a public university. *Nonprofit and Voluntary Sector Quarterly.* Retrieved from http://nvs.sagepub.com/content/early/2011/09/02/0899764011418836.abstract

Bailey, A. L. (1994). Giving begins at home: The hows and whys of faculty-staff fund-raising campaigns. *CASECurrents, 10*(6), 26–30. Retrieved from http://www.case.org/Documents/protected/GoodQuestion/FacultyStaffFRGiving/Giving-Begins-at-Home_June-1984.pdf?downloadIdvf4f60631–3c69–4993–9276-f412c81aa4ee

Basken, P. (2011, February 3). House Republicans set deep targets for budget cuts, alarming universities. *Chronicle of Higher Education.* Retrieved from http://chronicle.com/article/House-Republicans-Set-Deep/126249/

Burgess, R. (1984). *In the field: An introduction to field research.* London: George Allen and Unwin.

Bush Foundation announces new priorities. (2008, July 30). *Chronicle of Philanthropy.* Retrieved from http://philanthropy.com/blogs/philanthropy today/bush-foundation-announces-new-priorities/15384

Cardon, R. (2009). *Developing and implementing a successful employee giving campaign: A case study from Southern Utah University* (Master's thesis). Retrieved from http://www.suu.edu/hss/comm/masters/Capstone/Project/R_Cardon.pdf

Collins, M. E. (2000). Campaign strategies: drawing together. *CASECurrents, 26*(7), 13–14. Retrieved from http://www.case.org/Publications_and_Products/CURRENTS/CURRENTS_Archive/2000/September_2000/Campaign_Strategies_Drawing_Together.html

Council for the Advancement and Support of Education. (2011). *Faculty and staff giving data for 2010.* Retrieved from http://www.case.org/Samples_Research_and_Tools/Good_Question_Archive/Faculty_Staff_FR_Giving/Faculty_Staff_VSE_Data.html

Dotson, W. H., & Bernstein, D. J. (2010). A model for putting a teaching center in context: An informal comparison of teaching centers at larger state universities. In L. B. Nilson & J. E. Miller (Eds.), *To improve the academy: Resources for faculty, instructional, and organizational development, Vol. 28* (pp. 82–97). San Francisco, CA: Jossey-Bass/Anker.

Eckert, G., & Pollack, R. H. (2000). Sowing the seeds of philanthropy. *CASECurrents, 26*(7), 46–49. Retrieved from http://www.case.org/Publications_and_Products/CURRENTS/CURRENTS_Archive/2000/September_2000/Sowing_the_Seeds_of_Philanthropy.html

Eisenhardt, K. M. (2002). Building theories from case study research. In A. M. Huberman & M. B. Miles (Eds.), *The qualitative researcher's companion* (pp. 5–36), Thousand Oaks, CA: Sage.

Gray, T., & Hohnstreiter, M. (2010, October). *Go for the gold: Fund-raising for teaching centers.* Paper presented at the Professional and Organizational Development Network Annual Conference, St. Louis, MO.

Hohnstreiter, M., & Gray, T. (2011). Go for the gold: Fundraising for teaching centers. In J. E. Miller & J. E. Groccia (Eds.), *To improve the academy: Resources for faculty, instructional, and organizational development, Vol. 30* (pp. 262–276). San Francisco, CA: Jossey-Bass/Anker.

Holland, A. P. (1997). Faculty motivations for giving to their employing to their employing institutions. *Dissertation Abstracts International.* (UMI No. 9735711)

Holland, A. P., & Miller, M. T. (1999). *Faculty as donors: Why they give to their employing institutions.* (ERIC Document Reproduction Service No. ED439648)

Indiana University Center on Philanthropy. (2011). *The fund raising school.* Retrieved from http://www.philanthropy.iupui.edu/thefundraisingschool/

Kiley, K. (2011, September 16). Where universities can be cut. *Inside Higher Education.* Retrieved from http://www.insidehighered.com/news/2011/09/16/unc_berkeley_cornell_experience_show_where_administrative_cuts_can_be_made

Knight, W. E. (2004). Influences on participation in a university faculty and staff annual giving campaign. *CASE International Journal of Educational Advancement, 4*(3), 221–232.

Kvale, S. (1996). *InterViews: An introduction to qualitative research interviewing.* Thousand Oaks, CA: Sage.

March, K. S. (2005). *A descriptive study of faculty and staff giving practices at public institutions of higher education within the United States* (Doctoral dissertation). (UMI No. 3173632)

McClintock, B. R. (2000). Trends in educational fundraising. In P. M. Buchanan (Ed.), *Handbook of institutional advancement* (3rd ed., pp. 367–373), New York, NY: Council for Advancement and Support of Education.

Ouellet, M. (2010). Overview of faculty development: History and choices. In K. J. Gillespie, D. L. Robertson, & Associates (Eds.), *A guide to faculty development* (pp. 3–20). San Francisco, CA: Jossey-Bass.

Palmer, T. (2004, January). AdvanceWork: Giving begins at home. *CASECurrents.* Retrieved from http://www.case.org/Publications_and_Products/CURRENTS/CURRENTS_Archive/2004/January_2004/AdvanceWork_Giving_Begins_at_Home.htm

Penn State University. (2010). *Faculty and staff giving boosts programs in college of agsciences.* Retrieved from http://live.psu.edu/story/45593

Preston, C. (2010, March 18). Grants budgets take hit at many small foundations. *Chronicle of Philanthropy.* Retrieved from http://philanthropy.com/article/Grants-Budgets-Take-a-Hit-at/64753/

Seidman, I. (2006). *Interviewing as qualitative research: A guide for researchers in education and the social sciences* (3rd ed.). New York, NY: Teachers College Press.

Thelin, J. R. (2004). *A history of American higher education.* Baltimore, MD: Johns Hopkins University Press.

PART THREE

BUILDING EFFECTIVE RELATIONSHIPS

7

THE GENTLE ART OF MENTORING IN HIGHER EDUCATION

FACILITATING SUCCESS IN THE ACADEMIC WORLD

Nancy H. Barry
Auburn University

Senior faculty working together to support the professional development of new faculty colleagues is a much more efficient use of time and effort in comparison to dealing with a new faculty member who flounders because he or she has not been prepared to function effectively within the culture of the department. Increased professional expectations brought about through digital technology, budget issues, and other factors are contributing to a stressful and complex working environment for all faculty, and new faculty are particularly vulnerable. Investing time and effort in a formal, structured mentoring program can ultimately increase productivity for all.

o

College programs across the United States produce graduates who are generally well trained in the techniques of their content disciplines, scholarship, and research. However, most of these students complete their degree programs and embark on academic careers with no formal training in how to be a productive and successful faculty member. Although there is no sure way to guarantee a successful academic career, mentoring programs can provide needed support in negotiating the challenges of successfully balancing the responsibilities of teaching, research, creative work, outreach, service, and collegiality, not to mention the daunting realities of navigating the pitfalls of university politics and protocol (Mullen & Forbes, 2000; Mullen & Hutinger, 2008). This chapter provides a brief review of the literature and a review of selected successful mentoring programs as frameworks for discussing practical implications of mentoring as professional practice in college teaching.

In a formal academic mentoring relationship, the novice faculty member receives support and guidance from a more experienced colleague (Luna & Cullen, 1995; Mullen & Hutinger, 2008). The term *mentor* is generally attributed to the story of Odysseus (Harnish & Wild, 1994). According to Greek mythology, when Odysseus departed for the Trojan War, he charged his old friend Mentor with looking after his son, Telemachus, as well as watching over his wife, household, and possessions. Mentor's influence over Odysseus's son was so profound that when the goddess Athena visited Telemachus, she disguised herself as Mentor to gain the young man's trust. In this guise, she advised Telemachus to stand against his mother's suitors and go abroad to discover his father's fate ("Mentor," 2010). Roberts (2000), however, disputes the popular notion that the modern use of *mentor* originated with *The Odyssey*, citing Fénélon's *Les aventures de Télémaque*, written in 1699, as the more contemporary origin of the term.

Review of the Literature

Savage, Karp, and Logue (2004) define *mentoring* as "a process in which one person, usually of superior rank and outstanding achievement, guides the development of an entry-level individual" (p. 21). The ways in which mentoring occurs in higher education vary, ranging from natural and spontaneous professional relationships that develop between individuals, to very formal and systematic programs with clearly defined roles, expectations, and evaluation processes (Leslie, Lingard, & Whyte, 2005; Mullen & Hutinger, 2008). These different types of mentoring are not mutually exclusive. It is not unusual to see situations in which the same individual participates in a formal university mentoring program while also seeking counsel from an informal mentor, either on- or off-campus (Leslie et al., 2005; Mullen & Hutinger, 2008; Savage et al., 2004).

Opportunities for developing mentoring relationships with on-campus colleagues may be becoming more limited. The decline of the tradition of faculty clubs and faculty common rooms, coupled with increasing dependence on electronic communication and the Internet, have contributed to a culture in which "professors often feel greater allegiance to fellow specialists across the country than to their colleagues down the hall" (Schneider, 1997, p. A12). The literature depicts situations in which junior faculty frequently report feelings of isolation and disenfranchisement at their own institutions (Driscoll, Parkes, Tilley-Lubbs, Brill, & Bannister, 2009; Mandernach, 2006; Trower & Gallagher, 2008; Tysome, 2007), forcing them to look elsewhere for "support from a community of scholars that they have not found" on their own campuses (Savage et al., 2004, p. 22).

While opportunities for on-campus interaction with colleagues may be declining, those for virtual interaction are expanding. Innovations in digital technology, coupled with economic concerns for both students and degree-granting institutions, are triggering changes in the way that a college campus and the academic culture within a college, department, or program are being defined (Finkelstein, Frances, Jewett, & Scholz, 2000). These changes may have a profound impact on faculty role development and socialization. As a result of the virtual classroom, new understandings of collegiality and what it means to be a faculty member are emerging and expanding beyond the brick-and-mortar classroom. Just a few years ago, many academic professionals viewed virtual degrees from online institutions with skepticism and concern that academic rigor may have been compromised. In contrast, today we see the top academic institutions in the United States offering (and expanding) their distance programs. Distance education provides both advantages and challenges for students and faculty (Conciecao-Runlee, 2001). However, on many campuses, the reward structure for faculty has not yet caught up with the increasing demands on faculty to develop and maintain distance programs (Orr, Williams, & Pennington, 2009; Simpson, 2010). New faculty may need mentoring to help them balance the contemporary challenges of the virtual classroom with traditional expectations within their unit.

This trend toward distance instruction represents a significant paradigm shift in terms of the traditional on-campus faculty academic culture and the ways in which teaching, collegiality, and service have been defined. This situation is compounded by the fact that these changes have happened relatively quickly. It is likely that the field of college teaching will eventually reconcile new faculty expectations regarding technology and distance instruction within the traditional on-campus culture of the institution and the tenure and promotion process. However, it appears that at present, the opportunity, or expectation, to teach courses using distance technology may be contributing to social isolation and a level of remoteness from colleagues and may compromise a faculty member's ability to participate fully in the on-campus culture and traditional expectations of the department and institution (Conciecao-Runlee, 2001; Mandernach, 2006).

Despite some of these challenges, successful mentoring in higher education is possible. Certainly many individuals seek out informal mentoring relationships, which may be quite beneficial. An important advantage of informal mentoring is that usually both the mentor and mentee self-selected to engage in the process and therefore are less likely to experience interpersonal conflict or communication problems (Leslie et al., 2005; Mullen & Forbes, 2000).

Leslie et al. (2005) identified several advantages associated with informal peer-based mentoring within the medical profession. Mentoring among peers provides professional guidance and support within the relative safety of nonhierarchical relationships, as opposed to a situation in which the mentor may hold political power over the mentee. Informal mentoring among peers may also promote a supportive environment within the workplace and contribute to a generalized attitude among physicians that help is available from colleagues when needed.

However, while research acknowledges that informal mentoring relationships can be highly beneficial and productive, the consensus among most scholars is that a more formalized mentoring process is necessary to ensure that all junior faculty have equitable access to mentoring (Harnish & Wild, 1994; Leslie et al., 2005; Mullen & Hutinger, 2008; Savage et al., 2004). Formal mentoring has been identified as an important tool for achieving professional socialization for new academic colleagues (Mullen & Forbes, 2000) and has been encouraged by leading professional associations. The American Association for Higher Education, for example, had endorsed mentoring by senior faculty as good practice at colleges and universities (Sorcinelli, 2000).

Numerous studies have addressed the importance of providing formal mentoring processes for entry-level college faculty, but the research also points out that the mentoring of our new faculty colleagues should begin before they take that first college-level position (Gibson, 2006; Mullen & Hutinger, 2008; Savage et al., 2004). The process of mentoring colleagues should begin with doctoral students: "Professional socialization (including ethical issues) needs to be built into the academic mentoring of doctoral students who typically do not realize what is required of faculty in order to be successful in the academy" (Mullen & Forbes, 2000, p. 45). However, not all scholars support the notion that formal mentoring should be provided for university faculty. In their essay in *Teaching of Psychology*, Selby and Calhoun (1998) express an alternative view, stating that formal mentoring programs drain time and resources that should be invested in other professional endeavors and arguing that this type of professional preparation should be the responsibility of the graduate program: "If colleges and universities are now systematically producing psychologists who are not ready to take their places as fully functioning colleagues, then perhaps what is needed is not the formalized paternalism of mentoring programs, but an improvement in the quality of doctoral training in psychology" (p. 211).

Despite possible pitfalls (such as Selby and Calhoun's concern about mentoring as a type of "formalized paternalism"), the research literature strongly supports the need for providing structured mentoring for our future colleagues while they are still graduate students as well as a formalized mentoring process for new faculty. But what is the best way to achieve this?

In their article describing a successful mentoring program at Clarion University of Pennsylvania, Savage et al. (2004) provide a useful summary of the literature. According to this literature review, a mentoring program should:

- Empower new and continuing faculty by supporting their professional growth and renewal.
- Promote faculty satisfaction through what has been described in recent literature as a dialectical relationship with peers and senior faculty that can foster a sense of community.
- Attract, retrain, and facilitate promotion of new faculty by thoroughly explaining the university's tenure and promotion systems and by introducing new faculty to unique organizational cultures and definitions of work responsibilities.
- Provide opportunities for interactions between junior and senior faculty to facilitate mutual respect and avoid counterproductive divisions between old and young professors.
- Meet "entry level survival needs" of new faculty by providing information about departmental and university sociopolitical culture.
- Assist new faculty members in developing and balancing their professional commitments to research, creative activity, teaching, outreach, and service.

This list provides useful guidelines for developing successful mentoring programs, but formal pairings between mentees and mentors do not always work out well. Differences in goals, experience, dispositions, and perceived power relationships (Donnelly & McSweeney, 2011; Hansman, 2009) raise ethical dilemmas and may contribute to conflict between the mentee and the mentor. Certainly most experienced university faculty and administrators are aware of dismal stories in which a mismatch between mentor and mentee yielded unproductive or even tragic results. However, despite some possible pitfalls, as the roles and expectations of college faculty become increasingly complex in a world where new communications technologies may be contributing to physical isolation in the workplace, it is clear that a structured approach to mentoring is necessary to ensure the professional socialization and ultimate academic success of our graduate students and our colleagues.

Examples of Successful Mentoring Programs

In preparing this chapter, I searched both the Internet and academic databases to identify models of mentoring programs in colleges and universities across the United States. This search revealed that mentoring programs currently in place at higher learning institutions around the country vary widely. Some are very informal and unofficial, such as the program at the University of Iowa's College of Engineering, which explicitly states, "The main purpose of the mentor program is to provide unofficial, informal, and confidential assistance and suggestions to tenure-track faculty members.... Suggestions made by a mentor are informal and unofficial. All participants are free to terminate their participation in the program at any time" (University of Iowa College of Engineering, n.d.).

Other programs are much more formal and structured, with regularly scheduled events and ongoing evaluation, such as the faculty mentoring program in the College of Education at Kansas State University, which includes "formal mentor-mentee matches, monthly lunches, and other activities" (Kansas State University College of Education, n.d.). After being interviewed and participating in a discussion with the director and the mentoring committee, new tenure-track faculty are matched with one or two mentors. This program includes scheduled events and formal evaluation, but the exact nature of the mentoring relationship is determined by each mentor and mentee team.

The College of Education New Faculty Mentoring Program at the University of South Florida is another example of a "formalized, systematic approach to mentoring" (Mullen, 2006, p. 3). Each new faculty member is assigned two mentors, one from her or his own department (assigned by the department chair) and one from outside the department (assigned by the college's faculty mentoring coordinator). The faculty mentoring coordinator organizes collegewide events such as a meet-and-greet luncheon each fall, faculty research panels, grant-writing workshops, and other specialized activities. Faculty mentors are responsible for maintaining regular contact with their mentee. Program evaluation includes surveys completed by both mentors at the beginning and end of each year. Written feedback is also solicited from the mentees.

I found the Northern Illinois University New Faculty Mentoring Program Web site to be particularly thorough and informative (Northern Illinois University, n.d.), with detailed lists of goals for both mentors and mentees, suggested mentoring activities, descriptions of the process, "The 10 Commandments of Mentoring," and a list of useful links. The Web site describes this program as "voluntary" and "not meant to be a substitute for existing mentoring programs at the department or college levels but can be a supplement to those programs" (Northern Illinois University, n.d.).

A number of higher education institutions offer mentoring programs specifically for women and minorities (Gibson, 2006; Thomas, 2005; Wasburn, 2007). As Luna and Cullen (1995) have documented, effective mentoring emphasizes the importance of people within the educational environment by acknowledging and helping to reconcile individual perspectives and situations. Mentoring programs can serve to empower women and minorities to become leaders, ultimately benefiting both individual faculty members and the institution as a whole.

Exemplary Junior Faculty Mentoring Programs (Thomas, 2005) for the Yale University Women Faculty Forum presents the results of a review of junior faculty mentoring programs at seventeen of Yale's peer institutions. Ultimately, five programs were identified as being exemplary: Emory University, Passages Program; University of California San Diego, Faculty Mentoring Program; Stanford Medical School, Faculty Mentoring; University of Wisconsin, Women Faculty Mentoring Program; and University of Oregon, Women Faculty Resource Network.

Among these five programs, two were designed particularly for women, one was particularly for medical faculty, and one was originally designed for women but was eventually expanded to include all junior faculty. Although each of these programs was unique and tailored to the needs of a particular population and academic setting, they had many commonalities:

- Structured process and procedures
- A formal process for matching mentors with mentees

- o Regular meetings between mentor and mentee
- o Formal goal setting
- o Formal group meetings for specific training
- o Informal group meetings for socialization and information exchange
- o Detailed guidelines defining the roles of mentor and mentee
- o A comprehensive Web site providing easy access to information
- o Provision for changing mentors if the relationship does not work

Putting Research into Practice: Reflections on a Pilot Program

At my university, our department has had a long-standing tradition of mentoring, with the department head assisting in pairing each new faculty member with a more experienced faculty member to assist with professional development and help the new faculty member become a productive departmental citizen. When I joined our faculty as a new department head in 2007, with several new faculty nearing the time for their tenure or promotion vote, as well as several faculty searches in progress, I quickly became aware of our acute need for a more formalized mentoring process. We looked to the literature and models of successful practice and were also fortunate to be able to build on some excellent recommendations from a faculty committee. Opportunities for faculty input were an important part of this process as our mentoring policy was developed over several months.

Our departmental mentoring program begins with the new faculty member and the department head working together to select three tenured faculty members for nomination to serve on a mentoring committee (based on research interests, as well as balancing faculty workloads and teaching responsibilities). The final mentoring committee is based on mutual agreement by the department head, the faculty member, and the committee members, with the understanding that a "no-fault" policy remains in place in which the mentoring committee members may choose to step down or may be replaced if that is deemed in the best interest of the candidate or the committee member as the process moves forward. The mentoring committee works directly with the new faculty member in important professional development activities such as preparing for annual job performance reviews and developing the promotion and tenure dossier.

In practice, making changes to the mentoring committee has presented some serious challenges that we have not yet resolved. Although the option to request a change in mentoring committee members is clearly available as a matter of policy, this may be difficult to achieve in reality because a candidate may not wish to acknowledge formally (and perhaps exacerbate) any disagreements that may have emerged with a member of the mentoring committee. A change in mentoring committee membership is rather straightforward and nonconfrontational when it is necessitated by differences in research interests or other mutually acknowledged professional or practical reasons, such as scheduling conflicts or a mentoring committee member being off campus for sabbatical. However, when some perceived political or personal conflict between the candidate and an assigned mentor may be at play, the candidate may be placed in a no-win situation in which the option of keeping the disagreeable faculty member on the mentoring committee may seem to hold no worse consequences than exacerbating already strained professional relations by formally requesting a change of committee. Thankfully, these situations have been rare, but we have not yet succeeded in developing a policy that genuinely functions as "no fault" when serious conflicts arise between the candidate and an assigned mentor.

This pilot mentoring program is not presented as a model, but rather as an example of a practical application of the literature; only time will tell if our mentoring program has been effective (as gauged by the success of our new faculty). Certainly it is likely that as we learn through experience, our faculty will revisit our policies and consider making some adjustments. Although we have not yet conducted a formal evaluation of our program, preliminary observations seem consistent with the literature. Our new faculty report that the mentoring program is generally beneficial and that they feel well informed about protocol and policies within our department and college. These observations are similar to Mullen and Hutinger's (2008) findings that most participants (both mentors and mentees) believed that they had benefited from a formal mentoring program.

We are also observing considerable variation among mentee-mentor teams in the level of both perceived and observed success. One important factor appears to be the mentee's role in the process. The most successful mentoring teams seem to be those in which the mentee assumes a very active role (for example, frequently contacting mentors, initiating meetings, submitting unsolicited materials to the mentors for review), while teams in which the mentee assumes a more passive role (for example, waiting for the mentor to take the initiative to schedule all meetings, request copies of articles or the CV) do not appear to be as successful. As observed in the literature, the most effective mentoring relationships appear to be those in which participants actively engage in a two-way process with clearly defined expectations for both mentor and mentee (Mullen & Hutinger, 2008; Thorndyke, Gusic, & Milner, 2008).

Conclusion

Engaging in formal mentoring can be time-consuming, but the potential benefits far outweigh the costs. The prospect of senior faculty working together to support the professional development of our new faculty colleagues represents a proactive approach—a much more efficient use of time and effort in comparison to the grueling and emotionally draining prospect of dealing with a new faculty member who flounders because he or she has not been prepared to function as an effective citizen within the culture of the department and the campus. Increased professional expectations brought about through digital technology (distance courses, e-mail), budget issues (limited funding, increased pressure on faculty to generate external funding), and other factors are contributing to an increasingly complex working environment for all faculty, but new faculty are particularly vulnerable (Mullen & Hutinger, 2008). Investing time and effort in a formal, structured mentoring program can ultimately increase productivity for all and may contribute to a more collegial and pleasant departmental culture.

REFERENCES

Conciecao-Runlee, S. (2001). *A phenomenological study of college faculty experiences derived from teaching in a computer-mediated environment when there is an absence of physical presence.* Paper presented at the Annual Meeting of the Adult Education Research Conference, Lansing, MI. (ED481589)

Donnelly, R., & McSweeney, F. (2011). From humble beginnings: Evolving mentoring within professional development for academic staff. *Professional Development in Education, 37*(2), 259–274.

Driscoll, L. G., Parkes, L. A., Tilley-Lubbs, G. A., Brill, J. M., & Bannister, V.R.P. (2009, February). Navigating the lonely sea: Peer mentoring and collaboration among aspiring women scholars. *Mentoring and Tutoring: Partnership in Learning, 17*(1), 5–21.

Finkelstein, M. J., Frances, C., Jewett, F. I., & Scholz, B. W. (2000). *Dollars, distance, and online education: The new economics of college teaching and learning.* Washington, DC: American Council on Education, Oryx Press.

Gibson, S. K. (2006). Mentoring of women faculty: The role of organizational politics and culture. *Innovative Higher Education, 31*(1), 63–79. doi:10.1007/s10755-006-9007-7.

Hansman, C. A. (2009). Ethical issues in mentoring adults in higher education. In E. J. Burge (Ed.), *New directions for adult and continuing education: No. 123. Negotiating ethical practice in adult education* (pp. 53–63). San Francisco, CA: Jossey-Bass.

Harnish, D., & Wild, L. A. (1994). Mentoring strategies for faculty development. *Studies in Higher Education, 19*(2), 191–202.

Kansas State University College of Education. (n.d.) *Faculty mentoring program.* Retrieved from http://coe.ksu.edu/about/govern/mentoring.htm

Leslie, K., Lingard, L., & Whyte, S. (2005). Junior faculty experiences with informal mentoring. *Medical Teacher, 27*(8), 693–698.

Luna, G., & Cullen, D. L. (1995). *Empowering the faculty: Mentoring redirected and renewed.* ASHE-ERIC Higher Education Report series 95–3 (Volume 24–3).

Mandernach, B. J. (2006, August). Confessions of a faculty telecommuter: The freedom paradox. *Online Classroom,* 3–8.

Mentor. (2010). *Wikipedia.* Retrieved from http://en.wikipedia.org/wiki/Mentor

Mullen, C. A. (2006). *Mentoring guide for new and experienced faculty in education.* Retrieved from http://www.coedu.usf.edu/main/faculty/documents/MentoringBooklet07_08.pdf

Mullen, C. A., & Forbes, S. A. (2000). Untenured faculty: Issues of transition, adjustment and mentorship. *Mentoring and Tutoring, 8*(1), 31–46.

Mullen, C. A., & Hutinger, J. L. (2008). At the tipping point? Role of formal faculty mentoring in changing university research cultures. *Journal of In-Service Education, 34*(2), 181–204.

Northern Illinois University. (N.d.). *New faculty mentoring program.* Retrieved from http://www.niu.edu/facdev/services/newfacmentoring.shtml

Orr, R., Williams, M. R., & Pennington, K. (2009). Institutional efforts to support faculty in online teaching. *Innovative Higher Education, 34,* 257–268.

Roberts, A. (2000). Mentoring revisited: A phenomenological reading of the literature. *Mentoring and Tutoring, 8*(2), 145–166.

Savage, H. E., Karp, R. S., & Logue, R. (2004, Winter). Faculty mentorship at colleges and universities. *College Teaching, 52*(1), 21–24.

Schneider, A. (1997, June 13). Empty tables at faculty club worry some academics. *Chronicle of Higher Education,* A12.

Selby, J. W., & Calhoun, L. G. (1998). Mentoring programs for new faculty: Unintended consequences? *Teaching of Psychology, 25*(3), 210–211.

Simpson, C. M. (2010). *Examining the relationship between institutional mission and faculty reward for teaching via distance. Online Journal of Distance Learning Administration, 13*(1), 1–13.

Sorcinelli, M. D. (2000). *Principles of good practice: Supporting early-career faculty: Guidance for deans, department chairs, and other academic leaders.* Washington, DC: American Association for Higher Education.

Thomas, R. (2005). *Exemplary junior faculty mentoring programs.* Retrieved from http://www.yale.edu/wff/pdf/ExemplaryJuniory%20Faculty%20MentoringPrograms.pdf

Thorndyke, L. E., Gusic, M. E., & Milner, R. J. (2008). Functional mentoring: A practical approach with multilevel outcomes. *Journal of Continuing Education in the Health Professions, 28*(3), 157–164.

Trower, C. A., & Gallagher, A. (2008, November 4). Why collegiality matters. *Chronicle of Higher Education,* A50–A51.

Tysome, T. (2007, January 26). The common room shapes ideas. *Times Higher Education Supplement,* p. 9.

University of Iowa College of Engineering. (N.d.). *Faculty mentor program.* Retrieved from http://www.engineering.uiowa.edu/faculty-staff/mentor-program.php

Wasburn, M. H. (2007). Mentoring women faculty: An instrumental case study of strategic collaboration. *Mentoring and Tutoring, 15*(1), 57–72.

8

TOUGH-LOVE CONSULTING

USING A PROVOCATIVE CONSULTATION STYLE TO EFFECT CHANGE

Allison P. Boye, Suzanne Tapp,
Texas Tech University

WHILE IT *is important for faculty developers to build trust in consultation relationships, many of us find ourselves in challenging situations. With what we call the provocative consultation approach, the faculty developer adopts a more direct role and attempts to address perceived challenges in a frank discussion. This chapter uses three case studies—one focusing on a graduate student, one a pretenured faculty member, and one a multidisciplinary course—to discuss how faculty developers can effect change in difficult consultations through use of a more confrontational style.*

Conventional wisdom suggests that it is crucial to establish trust and warmth in a consultation relationship between a faculty developer and instructor, creating an environment that fosters growth and focuses on goals and new ideas without defensiveness or threat. Yet as faculty developers, many of us find ourselves in situations in which we need to challenge or push, perhaps even to the point of discomfort. Some faculty members may struggle with issues of social intelligence, as Rosier observes (2011), while others may be apathetic about confronting known problems, and it can be difficult for faculty developers to address these touchy situations. However, the call endures for faculty developers to persist as advocates for change (Fletcher & Patrick, 1998), stepping beyond traditional roles to become change agents through individual consultation (Zahorski, 1993).

This chapter discusses how faculty developers can observe that call to action as we consider the impact of consultation style for initiating pedagogical transformation and the results of employing a more confrontational style. With what we informally call the "tough love" or "provocative" consultation approach, the faculty developer takes on a more direct role and attempts to bring up perceived challenges in a frank discussion. We examine what happens when consultants adopt a consultation method that may be outside their comfort zones to effect change with graduate students, faculty members, or even departments reluctant to recognize negative attitudes, consistently poor student feedback, or problematic communication patterns and social skills.

Resistance to Faculty Development

Both new and experienced faculty developers know that resistance to faculty development is an ongoing obstacle, and the literature verifies this dynamic (Hodges, 2006; Lucas, 2001; Smith & Smith, 2001; Turner & Boice, 1986). Turner and Boice (1986), for instance, observe that faculty often struggle to assimilate suggestions for change, perhaps appearing inflexible and unappreciative; they suggest that resistant faculty sometimes perceive faculty development as implying incompetence or remediation. Hodges (2006) adds that fear—such as fear of loss of control or content, of embarrassment, or of failure—is also a major factor in faculty resistance to development and change.

DiPietro and Huston (2009) offer a model of compounding factors that can help or complicate the course of consultations, identifying two main categories: qualities of the instructor and institutional or departmental factors. They identify issues such as personal problems, cultural differences, or a generally resistant attitude on the part of the instructor, and departmental or institutional politics, which can all work in some way to create what they call "entangled consultations," or those that are "layered with complexity" and "extend far beyond pedagogical questions" (p. 8).

Undoubtedly these factors that DiPietro and Huston identified are crucial to recognize when entering into difficult consultations. However, based on our own experiences as faculty developers, we believe that there are additional factors to include on the list, which we address here. Regarding instructor qualities, one important element to consider is lack of social intelligence, which Rosier (2011) describes as the ability to "understand what another person feels and act effectively and

Figure 8.1. Compounding Factors with an Impact on Consultations.

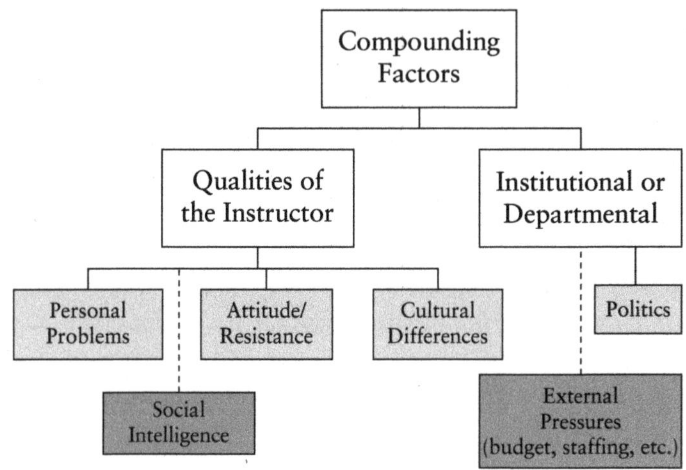

Source: *Adapted from DiPietro and Huston (2009).*

appropriately based on that understanding" (p. 75). Whereas she explores it as a factor related to teaching, our experiences also suggest that it can affect the consultation process.

Beyond departmental or institutional politics, other pressures external to the instructor can complicate the consultation process. For instance, we have seen how budget or staffing concerns, or even time constraints and burgeoning departmental administrative responsibilities, can affect the ability to enact curricular change or remain open to the consultation process. (See Figure 8.1.) Indeed, many factors that can lead to resistance and impede the progress of a consultation, and multiple philosophies or styles, can inform the consultation approach.

Other Consultation Models

Several scholars have worked to identify consultation models that can help us as faculty developers define our own styles. Building on work from the fields of education, psychology, organizational behavior, and medicine, Brinko (1997) identified five consultation styles or patterns commonly shared by faculty developers:

- *Product model.* The consultant is seen as the expert, and the faculty member, or client, is the seeker of that expertise. The client identifies the problem (for example, students are not reading their assigned materials), and the consultant produces a solution (for example, the instructor can give students formative quizzes at the start of class for accountability).

- *Prescription model.* In this model, often seen in doctor-patient relationships, the consultant serves as the identifier or diagnoser of problems, while the client is the unquestioning receiver.
- *Collaborative or process model.* A partnership is formed with the consultant operating as the "catalyst" or "facilitator of change" and the client as the content expert. Many faculty developers identify with this model.
- *Affiliative model.* In this less commonly used model, the consultant serves in a combined role as instructional and psychological counselor, working with the client toward professional and personal growth.
- *Confrontational model.* The consultant plays the role of challenger, particularly in situations in which he or she realizes that confrontation is necessary before real change can occur.

Little and Palmer (2011) describe a collaborative consultation strategy that combines careful listening, asking thoughtful questions, and encouraging action. In this expanded collaborative framework, consultants help to move instructors from one point to another or act as coaches, perhaps most powerfully by careful consideration of questions. Little and Palmer encourage faculty developers to focus on the difficult task of speaker-focused or deep listening and suggest the use of questions such as, "Which of your values are you honoring in this situation?" and "In what ways are you stuck?" The third component they recommend takes the questioning further by focusing on action. For example, consultants might pose questions such as, "What first steps will you take?" and, "How you will know that you are making progress toward these goals?"

In their article on "entangled consultations," DiPietro and Huston (2009) suggest employing the collaborative approach for tricky situations, and surely the work of Little and Palmer (2011) offers excellent supplementation to the collaborative model with their extended use of thought-provoking questions and careful listening. Our model builds on their identification of these complications in consultations by suggesting further steps to help us reflect on the "Now what?" conundrum we face when dealing with difficult consultations.

Difficult Consultations: Three Case Studies

Using three case studies, we explain and explore our approach and how it has worked for us in consultations. Permission was obtained from all participants, and for purposes of anonymity, the names and identifying details for each case study have been changed.

Our first case involves Dr. Jones, a third-year faculty member who had not involved himself with our teaching and learning center aside from attendance at a few scattered workshops. A large, loud man, he is an intimidating presence in the classroom. He came to our center for consultation, but we later realized he was really just checking off a to-do list given to him after a rocky third-year evaluation from his tenure and promotion committee. Although Dr. Jones's self-perception is that he is one of the best teachers at the university, it became clear when we observed him that his overbearing ways have worn out their welcome with students and perhaps even his colleagues.

Our second case involves Jessica, a bright, third-year doctoral student. She expresses great interest in teaching and is familiar with some of the best practices and educational literature. However, her teaching evaluations remained low despite her hard work, and she came to us for assistance. As we got to know her, we realized that Jessica struggles with her social awareness and her ability to interpret and stay in tune with others' feelings and perceptions. These social problems were taking a toll not only on her relationship with her undergraduate students, but also with her department faculty and graduate student colleagues and were also complicating the consultation process.

Our third case involves our work with a large, multidisciplinary course taught in one department in the College of Agriculture but required for students in another, vastly different department (from the College of Human Sciences). Consultants at our center had worked with several graduate student instructors from this course over several years, witnessing the same recurring problems but with little to no improvement or progress. Many of the problems that course instructors faced involved the palpable tension between the two departmental cultures. The course remained in control of the faculty member who designed and continues to oversee the course.

Our Model

We have found that a more direct approach is often called for in certain complicated consultation situations, whether it is an instructor in denial about the success of his class or a teaching assistant (TA) who does not seem to hear the feedback from her students and advisers. In these situations, we have begun implementing what we call the "provocative approach," which at its core involves having direct and assertive conversations. It is a consultation style that is perhaps slightly new and uncomfortable for many faculty developers, but it has foundations in the counseling literature and can be quite effective. The steps a faculty developer might consider in this model can be remembered using the mnemonic phrase, "Don't Ever Call Sally A Loose Cannon":

Describe

Evidence

Cut in and call them out

Straightforward

Ask questions

Listen, language, like-minded

Compromise

The D in Don't stands for *describe the situation and explain the consequences.* A common approach used to initiate discussion in a consultation is to ask the faculty member a series of simple but telling questions such as, "Was this a typical day?" "What usually happens in your classes?" and, perhaps most important, "What did you notice?" This is an opportunity for the faculty member to direct the conversation, and indeed, what he or she shares often reveals his or her comfort levels and openness to the consultation process. For example, when Dr. Jones met with the consultant and reflected on a recent class observation, he noted that he saw nothing of concern and thought it had been a great example of his teaching. Yet the consultant had noticed patterns of verbal dominance on the part of the teacher with minimal participation from students. These potential discrepancies alert the faculty developer and may be the first sign that the consultation could prove to be complicated. Asking simple, reflective questions also helps the faculty developer gain context for understanding the particular challenges facing the instructor and build a frame of reference, particularly if this is the first observation.

The E in Ever suggests that we *explain the evidence, data, and research.* Data and evidence play an important role in our consultation practices. We begin every teaching observation by creating a time line or factual record of the class and take extensive notes on the teaching techniques used, organization of content, student participation, and student behaviors such as attentiveness, note taking, and displays of distraction such as texting. We count the number of student questions, record the wait time, and pay attention to displays of teacher immediacy such as facial expressions and nonverbal communication. This time line often proves to be a significant conversation starter in our consultations as we ask the instructor to review the time line and comment. Often this data conversation opens the door to deeper reflection, particularly when led by the consultant through questions such as, "I noticed that students seemed to get restless after about twenty minutes. What do you think was going on? Did you see it?" Little and Palmer (2011) suggest that finding neutral ways to incorporate data into a consultation and combining this information with careful questions can help instructors hypothesize and reflect on their actions and student behavior.

For instance, when we realized that the graduate student instructors of the third case study were not sharing student feedback with the faculty members in charge, and consequently faced similar problems from year to year, we felt that being more direct with those with authority over the course and presenting them with the actual information on what we saw would make greater strides toward influencing change. Cook (2001) affirms the power of empirical data in reaching consensus and encouraging curricular reform. After receiving the permission of the graduate student instructors, we called a meeting with the course's faculty adviser and the relevant department chair from the College of Human Sciences to share the prevalent patterns of student feedback collected over the years. Once presented with the data demonstrating the ongoing problems with the course, the faculty members were much readier to consider possible change.

Another hallmark of our consultation practices is to provide feedback steeped in teaching and learning research. We work hard to connect any comments we might make to established literature. We also try to make sure that the instructor leaves us with some kind of resource in hand, perhaps an article from the scholarship of teaching and learning literature or a link to a resource found on a teaching and learning Web site. Calling attention to the rich body of teaching and learning literature gives us credibility, even as we establish roles in collaborative consultations in which the faculty members are seen as experts of their discipline and the faculty developers play the role of facilitator (Brinko, 1997). With some faculty members and instructors, this extra step has built trust that paves the way for more difficult conversations later.

The C in Call encourages faculty developers to *cut in and call instructors out when needed.* Little and Palmer (2011) remind us that the difficulty and value of deep listening can be easily underestimated. It is all too easy to fall into a passive listening role or focus on our next statement or rebuttal, but we strive to maintain a speaker-focused or deep listening mode. Faculty developers operating in this mode, paying attention to what the speaker is communicating verbally and nonverbally, may find that they occasionally need to interrupt and confront their clients. For example, as the consultant worked in consultation with Jessica, the very bright but somewhat socially challenged graduate student, she realized after some time that she needed to work harder to intervene in the moment and help her identify patterns of behavior. In this case, the consultant's role during confrontation should be one of puzzlement versus hostility (Hill, 2009). Perhaps the greatest challenge for faculty developers is finding the right strategies and words so that our clients do not feel attacked. Hill suggests that we adopt a quizzical, "What do you think?" attitude as we collaboratively work to talk through and clarify behaviors. During a discussion with Jessica about a frustrating classroom dynamic, the consultant interrupted her and said, "May I stop you for a moment? I noticed that you have been talking a little louder and faster, and your voice is higher. What do you think is going on? What are you feeling right now?" With this collegial confrontation and encouragement to examine herself, perhaps we can persuade her to see a new perspective.

The S in Sally reminds us to *be straightforward and communicate directly, even though it is difficult.* This element is perhaps the most challenging part of the approach for many faculty developers, especially those more accustomed to the give-and-take style of the favored collaborative approach. Many of us are trained in using qualifiers or softened language in our feedback, and we strive to demonstrate great respect for the vulnerability of the instructors who are seeking consultation. However, in our experience, directness need not undermine that respect and is frequently required in various forms to reach instructors who might be aggressive, inept at reading social cues, or generally resistant or in denial.

For faculty developers who struggle with assertive communication, the field of counseling psychology offers some useful strategies. Stephen Cook (2009) advises those attempting to communicate assertively to start with "I feel" statements because others cannot argue with personal emotions. Counseling literature also suggests making those direct statements about thoughts, feelings, and needs in a kind but firm fashion. Wood (2010) writes that "people who are assertive appear to be very confident because of their body language. . . . They maintain good posture and stand a little straighter . . . their voices are relaxed, clear, and loud enough to be understood. And their eyes maintain regular contact with the other person" (p. 141).

For example, we found it to be more effective to communicate directly with Jessica because she was not adept at reading between the lines, and her listening skills were not strong. In stressful situations, her voice often became louder and shrill, and she would interrupt those around her, despite their clear exasperation with her behavior. Instead of letting her dominate group discussions or talk over others attempting to share student feedback with her, we tried pointing out her behavior patterns during consultation, saying things like, "Jessica, I feel that you are not listening when you interrupt and raise your voice." Since Jessica lacked the self-awareness to recognize this behavior, our directness proved to be quite beneficial for her, and she began to work on monitoring her listening behaviors and volume.

The **A** stands for *ask questions about instructors' assumptions, perceptions, and practices.* Brinko (1997) and Little and Palmer (2011) discuss the value in presenting an instructor with questions about his or her assumptions and practices in the classroom, and the counseling literature (Hill, 2009; Wood, 2010) similarly discusses the occasional need to challenge clients by questioning discrepancies in their actions and beliefs. Instructor-focused, thought-provoking questions can help encourage instructors to reflect on their teaching and thereby promote change. Perhaps an instructor does not truly know why he has made certain decisions in the classroom, or perhaps she has not considered the implications or the inconsistencies in her actions. Dr. Jones, for instance, was surprised when asked about his discussions in class regarding current events. He claimed to value student participation and in fact asked many questions of his students to solicit their ideas. However, when the consultant pointed out and literally counted the number of rapid-fire questions he asked, he was surprised to see that students were literally left no time to respond.

Little and Palmer (2011) offer many useful examples of probing or challenging questions that can assist consultants in working with instructors to identify attitudes and point out potential discrepancies. Questions such as, "What do you think is really going on?" "Why does it matter to you?" and "What is another perspective you could have about this?" are simple yet effective in helping an instructor cull out underlying beliefs and potentially faulty assumptions that might be creating conflicts both in and outside of the classroom.

The **L** in Loose encourages consultants to *listen closely and mirror an instructor's language,* as well as exercise empathy and courtesy. While directness and assertiveness are undeniably important, so is using our own social intelligence skills by demonstrating empathy, deep listening, and taking cues from the instructor. Remaining sensitive to the instructor's needs and staying in tune with his or her individual personality can be especially powerful in difficult consultations. For instance, when working with the aggressive and brisk Dr. Jones, the consultant realized that "speaking his language" and using his own words would have the most impact. Therefore, in the consultation, when he said, "So I just need to shut up," she responded in kind by saying, "Yes, I think you need to shut up." Those words meant something to him, and it was a light bulb moment.

Conversely, when working with Jessica, a more sensitive young woman, we were sure to acknowledge her strong desire to see her students succeed as we tried to help her recognize the disconnect she had with them. We would never say "shut up" to Jessica, because she would never use those words and would find them insulting. We might instead show respect for her efforts and knowledge by saying something like, "You know how important it is to have a good relationship with your students," and then direct her toward the feedback that highlights the disconnect. And similarly, we knew that by offering years of quantitative and qualitative data based on self-generated student feedback, we would be speaking the language of the faculty in charge of the large, science-based, interdisciplinary course.

Social work literature provides some examples of leads for empathic responses that we can use in the consultation process. Rohdieck (2007) suggests starting with questions such as, "Could it be that you are feeling . . . ," "What I'm hearing is . . . ," or "To me, it's almost like you're saying . . ." It is important to have a rich vocabulary and consider the power of words that we use. In all three of the case stories, the use of empathy and like-mindedness softened the potential awkwardness and directness of the other questions we were asking and the issues we were raising.

Finally, the **C** in Cannon reminds us to be willing to *compromise and negotiate as needed, even asking the instructor for alternative solutions when necessary.* The counseling literature similarly advises "turning the tables" and turning the problem over to the instructor or "client" (Linehan, 1993). If the instructor is struggling with the idea of making changes, it can be beneficial to be flexible and ask, "How do you think it would be best to approach this problem?" As Hodges (2006) suggests, perhaps fear is an issue, and finding answers or solutions that are simple, minimally intrusive, or "doable on a small scale with a good chance of success," especially those solutions an instructor devises, can offer greater chance for openness to change (p. 131).

In the multidisciplinary course, for example, we worked with the faculty members to devise just a few simple changes as a beginning. Rather than suggesting wide-scale curricular revision, we started with suggesting smaller classes that divided the majors and nonmajors and offering a section of the course on campus that was physically more accessible to the nonmajors. These solutions were not threatening and emanated from the instructors themselves, and while they were perhaps not going to solve all of the problems of the course, they were a reasonable starting point and more easily implemented.

Evaluating Effectiveness

Development and progress take time. When developers adopt a more direct consultation style, one might wonder what happens to the trajectory of the consultation relationship. The outcomes of the three case studies highlighted here provide insight into the merit of this provocative consultation approach.

In the case of Dr. Jones, we realize that we have just begun a relationship with him. He is certainly intimidating, but our institution invested in him by bringing him in as a new faculty member, and everyone loses when the tenure process goes awry. We want to see him connect with students and with his colleagues, and after following up with him about his experiences with our consultation services, he said:

> After talking to you I started paying more attention to what I was doing in class and started to make conscious decisions to get more from the students. I found the think-pair-share, and the reframing of my questions in class (going from "Any questions" to "What questions do you think my prior class asked about this") has increased class participation [personal communication, October 12, 2011].

Although Dr. Jones's comments could be easily dismissed, we interpret them as small steps and movement in a positive direction. In fact, Dr. Jones invited us back into his classroom to continue our observations and interview his students about their learning. Clearly the direct approach did not impede our relationship with him and helped him begin to make some important realizations about his teaching.

Jessica also experienced positive growth as a result of this provocative consultation approach. One of her faculty advisers communicated to us that the increased directness with Jessica "helped them get along" and worked to improve their relationship (personal communication, October 18, 2011). Another of Jessica's advisers noted that our work with her "took a huge weight off of her shoulders" because she was "at a loss" about how to communicate with her (personal communication,

October 18, 2011). Both mentors felt confident guiding her in discipline-specific matters but struggled with knowing how to approach her egocentrism, awkward discussion patterns, and misunderstanding of social cues (Rosier, 2011). Jessica had an "aha" moment midway through our work with her during a painful conversation about her social intelligence; she revealed that although others had pointed out her awkwardness, they never explained that awkwardness directly or helped her devise tangible strategies for more effective communication and interpreting social cues. Perhaps Jessica's most important strength, and one that might make her unique among others struggling with social intelligence, was her eventual recognition of her problem and desire to change.

Our direct approach also seemed to be the key in making a difference with the interdisciplinary course. After a meeting with key faculty from both departments and a review of the data, these faculty members grew excited and even began looking into potential new classrooms on campus for the following semester. Unfortunately, departmental compounding factors (DiPietro & Huston, 2009) got in the way during a difficult year. The course adviser became department chair and faced an overwhelming number of new responsibilities. The economy also went sour, and budgets were cut, leaving no room to pay a second instructor to teach the course or to pay one instructor to teach a second section. Both departments still communicate interest in implementing those basic changes, but it is clear that it will take some time (personal communication, September 21, 2011). Ultimately our direct approach instigated conversations about the course that we hope will continue.

Conclusion

The practice of consulting with faculty is undoubtedly complicated, especially when individual personalities and issues beyond the classroom come into play. It would be nice if consultations always went smoothly, or if we could use the same approach with everyone, but that is not the case. It is important to note that the provocative approach might be inappropriate for sensitive or timid instructors, or those who might be facing a mountain of other difficult circumstances. Furthermore, consultants could modify this approach to meet individual needs or even change consultation methods, adopting a more or less direct approach as a relationship develops and layers are revealed.

We do not claim to have all the answers for dealing with every difficult situation, but we think that this practice of occasionally stepping out of our comfort zones and adopting a more direct style when needed might at least fill in another piece of the puzzle. This might mean pointing out inappropriate behaviors, presenting convincing data, or simply asking thought-provoking, frank questions. Faculty developers know that one size does not fit all when it comes to consultations. The provocative approach can offer one more option for advancing the consulting relationship.

REFERENCES

Brinko, K. (1997). The interactions of teaching improvement. In K. Brinko & R. Menges (Eds.), *Practically speaking* (pp. 3–8). Stillwater, OK: New Forums Press.

Cook, C. (2001). The role of a teaching center in curricular reform. In D. Lieberman & C. Wehlburg (Eds.), *To improve the academy: Resources for faculty, instructional, and organizational development, Vol. 19* (pp. 217–230). San Francisco, CA: Jossey-Bass/Anker.

Cook, S. W. (2009). *Communicating assertively.* Lubbock: Texas Tech University, Department of Psychology.

DiPietro, M., & Huston, T. (2009). A theory and framework for navigating entangled consultations: Using case studies to find common ground. *Journal on Centers for Teaching and Learning, 1,* 7–37.

Fletcher, J., & Patrick, S. (1998). Not just workshops anymore: The role of faculty development in reframing academic priorities. *International Journal for Academic Development, 3*(1), 39–46.

Hill, C. E. (2009). *Helping skills: Facilitating exploration, insight, and action* (3rd ed.). Washington, DC: American Psychological Association.

Hodges, L. (2006). Preparing faculty for pedagogical change: Helping faculty deal with fear. In S. Chadwick-Blossey & D. R. Robertson (Eds.), *To improve the academy: Resources for faculty, instructional, and organizational development, Vol. 24* (pp. 121–134). San Francisco, CA: Jossey-Bass/Anker.

Linehan, M. (1993). *Skills training manual for treating borderline personality disorder.* New York, NY: Guilford Press.

Little, D., & Palmer, M. S. (2011). A coaching-based framework for individual consultations. In J. Miller & J. Groccia (Eds.), *To improve the academy: Resources for faculty, instructional, and organizational development, Vol. 29* (pp. 102–115), San Francisco, CA: Jossey-Bass/Anker.

Lucas, A. F. (2001). Reaching the unreachable: Improving the teaching of poor teachers. In K. H. Gillespie, L. R. Hilsen, & E. C. Wadsworth (Eds.), *A guide to faculty development: Practical advice, examples, and resources* (pp. 167–179). San Francisco, CA: Jossey-Bass/Anker.

Rohdieck, S. (2007). *Using the helping process to strengthen our consultation skills.* Paper presented at the 31st annual meeting of the Professional and Organizational Development Network in Higher Education, Portland, OR.

Rosier, T. (2011). There was something missing: A case study of a faculty member's social intelligence development. In J. Miller & J. Groccia (Eds.), *To improve the academy: Resources for faculty, instructional, and organizational development, Vol. 29* (pp. 74–88). San Francisco, CA: Jossey-Bass/Anker.

Smith, J., & Smith, S. L. (2001). Promoting active learning in preparing future faculty. In K. Lewis & J. P. Lunde (Eds.), *Face to face: A sourcebook of individual consultation techniques for faculty/instructional developers* (pp. 313–329). Stillwater, OK: New Forums Press.

Turner, J., & Boice, R. (1986). Coping with resistance to faculty development. In M. Svinicki, J. Kurfiss, & J. Stone (Eds.), *To improve the academy: Resources for faculty, instructional, and organizational development, Vol. 5* (pp. 26–36). San Francisco, CA: Jossey-Bass/Anker.

Wood, J. C. (2010). *The cognitive behavioral therapy workbook for personality disorders.* Oakland, CA: New Harbinger Publications.

Zahorski, K. (1993). Taking the lead: Faculty development as institutional change agent. In D. Wright & J. Lunde (Eds.), *To improve the academy: Resources for faculty, instructional, and organizational development, Vol. 12* (pp. 227–245). San Francisco, CA: Jossey-Bass/Anker.

9

RESEARCHING THE IMPACT OF EDUCATIONAL DEVELOPMENT

BASIS FOR INFORMED PRACTICE

Nancy Van Note Chism
Indiana University-Purdue University Indiana

Matthew Holley, Cameron J. Harris
Indiana University

In this review of 138 studies on the impact of educational development practices, we discuss the idea of impact and summarize previous studies of this topic. We then present an overview of findings on impact from current studies of typical educational development activities: workshops, formal courses, communities of practice, consultation, mentoring, and awards and grants programs. We conclude that although the studies vary in quality, the sheer volume of results offers guidance for development practice.

Calls to improve the assessment of the impact of educational development have permeated the literature on this topic from early studies, such as Hoyt and Howard (1978), to the present (Stes, Min-Leliveld, Gijbels, & Van Petegem (2010). Advice to new centers emphasizes the collection of information on effectiveness for improvement as well as accountability. The literature on educational development stresses the scholarship of practice, the serious study of educational development work that can establish credibility, and sound warrants for specific development approaches (Baume, 2002).

Nearly fifty years after the formal establishment of educational development centers in North America, these calls continue, yet the consensus among developers is that documentation of impact is still lacking (Weimer, 2007).

The Idea of Impact in Educational Development

Educational developers and training specialists more generally have suggested several levels at which the impact of their work might be assessed. The most cited of these is Kirkpatrick (1998), who, along with Guskey (2000), listed four levels that can be adapted for this context: satisfaction of the participant, learning, application, and results on the organization and its mission. Chism and Szabo (1998) listed similar levels but included a focus on the learner rather than the organization: immediate satisfaction of the participant, change in teaching beliefs or knowledge, change in teaching behaviors, and change in student learning. Smith (2004) added a focus on the career trajectory, suggesting that impact can occur at the level of the individual participants, their careers, their students' experiences, and the effect on the teacher's department and the institution.

More comprehensive lists that build on the work of these researchers have been provided by three overviews. Kreber and Brook (2001) asserted that impact can be assessed at six levels: (1) participants' perceptions and satisfaction with the intervention, (2) their beliefs about teaching and learning, (3) their teaching performance, (4) students' perceptions of participants' teaching performance, (5) students' learning, and (6) the culture of the institution. Steinert et al. (2006) developed six similar levels, adding a separate category for changes in teacher knowledge and skills to this list, and not dividing students' perceptions and learning. Finally, Stes et al. (2010), working from Steinert et al.'s (2006) framework, eliminated the satisfaction level and added four levels of learning change for teachers (attitudes, conceptions, knowledge, and skills), three levels for student impact (perceptions, study approaches, and learning outcomes), and levels for teacher behavior change and institutional impact.

Such frameworks are important in conceptualizing studies; these advances in their development are important steps for the study of impact. Overviews of the findings and methods used in the literature on impact have also continued to accrue, a development that has helped to describe patterns that are useful for practitioners and researchers alike.

Past Overviews of the Impact Literature

Overviews of educational impact activity and findings span over thirty years and have become substantially more detailed with time. Chism and

Szabo (1998) found support for the belief that the attention of most educational development assessment efforts is at the level of participant satisfaction rather than impact on actions or thinking, and that measurement of impact at the level of the learner or the overall organization is quite rare and complicated. Using similar categories to the Chism and Szabo study, Hines (2009) found that the same situation continues to exist. These studies follow general reviews in the literature (Hoyt & Howard, 1978; Levinson-Rose & Menges, 1981; Weimer & Lenze, 1991), as well as overviews of activity in certain spheres (see, for example, Schönwetter & Nazarko, 2009, on activities for new faculty) that concluded that rigorous evaluation of faculty development programs is rare. In a summary review, McKinney (2002) listed the main overall patterns from these studies: they document high levels of satisfaction, elevated levels of collaboration and community, and conceptual change in teachers associated with interventions. She finds that few studies measure student perceptions and calls for more systematic research.

Three more recent studies looked at trends in current literature, all from different perspectives. In the first, Bamber (2008) examined a selection of studies evaluating the results of academic development programs. She focused explicitly on how theory was used and on the stance of the evaluation. She concluded that large-scale studies (cross-institutional, systematic) offer political advantages and the opportunity to use statistical techniques designed for large populations, but that small-scale studies, conducted in local settings with research designs that probe depth and supply detail, are especially useful. While emphasizing that evaluation is a complex and uncertain activity, she offered hope that patterns emerging from locally designed and theory-based studies will offer important insights for practice.

Kucsera and Svinicki (2010) applied five standards of rigorous research to their examination of 750 studies that appeared in seven leading journals from 1997 to 2001. They excluded certain types of studies that did not meet seven criteria, such as focus on teaching and learning, about faculty, activity initiated by faculty developer, and containing a description of methods, which eliminated all but ten studies. On the basis of this review, the authors agreed with prior surveys of the literature, finding that rigor is lacking; they issued a general call for more rigorous work, stating that qualitative in-depth approaches are needed.

Steinert et al. (2006), examined fifty-three papers that explored results of educational development interventions for faculty in medicine and presented detailed summaries of eight exemplary studies. The studies generally found beneficial effects from educational development activities, citing changes in teachers' attitudes, knowledge, skills, and behaviors, as reported by teachers and their students. They found that few studies focused on the levels of student learning or organizational impact and that the strongest results were associated with interventions that included experiential learning activities in educational development interventions, used a variety of pedagogical approaches and good instructional design in interventions, provided frequent feedback, and created a positive social context for the faculty learners.

The extensive reviews by Stes et al. (2010) were based on an initial eighty sources identified through using teaching development descriptors in the ERIC database in 2008. After applying criteria for inclusion, such as postsecondary context, intentional initiative, focus on impact, and empirical data, they selected thirty-six studies for further review on the basis of a scan of the abstracts. All of the studies, except one that was inconclusive, found positive effects on at least one of the areas of impact that they studied, although several could not identify an impact on all of those areas. The authors concluded that designs from 2000 to the present do not differ significantly from earlier ones. They acknowledged the challenges of studying impact and suggest that future research focus more on actual behavioral outcome measures instead of self-reported outcomes, stating that mixed-methods studies, quasi-experimental designs, and use of standard instruments would improve the quality of future research.

Despite this critical history of past findings, the volume of studies that have looked at the impact of various common faculty development approaches, often within the context of a single case, continues to grow. The overview of these studies that follows presents findings by type of intervention, with the goal of informing those in practice settings of the potential efficacy of choices they make in allocating their efforts and resources. Our review thus differs from other recent ones that have focused more on methodological issues with the literature than on implications for practice.

Methods

To provide an overview of the findings of existing research studies, we searched literature from 2000 to the present in the following international publications: *To Improve the Academy, International Journal for Academic Development, Journal of Faculty Development* (and its predecessor, *Journal of Staff, Program, and Organizational Development*), *Journal of Graduate Teaching Assistant Development, College Teaching,* and *International Journal of Teaching and Learning in Higher Education.* We also examined the results produced through a search of popular databases in education and reference lists in the articles that were originally found. We kept information on most sources in a Zotero database, with the exception of some that were contextual in nature. We used these criteria for identifying articles

- *About a developer-led activity: Developer* is defined as one who leads an activity designed to support or improve the practice of another.
- *About teaching:* Can be about instructional strategies, design work, curriculum development or other aspects.
- *Aimed at anyone who teaches:* Can be graduate students or full-time or part-time faculty.
- *About any disciplinary context or from any country.*
- *Within a higher education context* (as opposed to staff development in K–12 schools or corporate settings).

We coded each piece by type of intervention, target of intervention, disciplinary (or general) context, and the researcher's method to study impact. We wrote a summary of each study, included the abstract (where available), and attached a PDF (when further reference would be needed). The three team members coded several pieces together to establish consistency of coding at the start of the process.

In this way, we compiled information on 138 studies in our database. Table 9.1 displays the type of interventions studied and the methods used to study them. We did not attempt to select studies based on perceived quality or specific criteria for the type of research methods that were used, although we eliminated studies that did not detail the use of any data collection methods that warranted their claims. Our results, then, are descriptive of a broad cross-section of impact evaluation.

Results

In the following sections, we present highlights of the results, focusing only on one or two exemplary studies in each section. We intentionally chose examples from across disciplines and methods used to show variety, as well as examples that depicted representative outcomes across the range of studies on a given intervention. An annotated bibliography with full information on all the studies, including the structural change category that was omitted here due to space constraints, is available on the POD Network's Wikipodia page. The results are presented here by type of intervention. General statements about a specific type of intervention

Table 9.1 Intervention Studied and Method of Analysis Used in Research.

Type of Development Activity	Number of Studies	Method of Analysis	Number of Studies
Workshops	62	Debrief or informal interview	11
Workshop series	13	Document analysis (for example, syllabi)	45
Institutes (eleven) or shorter (thirty-eight)	49	Interview	30
Course	20	Observation	19
Communities of practice	29	Scores on standard instruments	26
Faculty learning community	17	Survey	75
Project	12	External evaluation	3
Consultation	18	Other	6
With professional consultant	5		
With peer	8		
Involving student evaluations	5		
Grants and awards	7		
Structural change	6		
Mentor	4		
Other	3		
Total	149[a]		215[a]

[a]*Total unique studies: 138. Some studies included more than one intervention or method.*

carry the caveat that the statement holds true only for implementations that are well designed and well executed.

Workshops

In general, workshops are used to elevate the visibility of professional development units or activities or to interest faculty in more intensive interventions. Workshops are also used in combination with other instructional development approaches, such as coaching, in which faculty members attend an initial workshop to introduce them to a concept and then receive follow-up coaching to implement the approach. However, in this section, we review studies of workshops as the major approach being studied. In our presentation of the sixty-two studies we examined, we differentiate institutes of one day or more (eleven), shorter workshops (thirty-eight), and workshops in a series (thirteen).

INSTITUTES OF ONE DAY OR MORE. Workshops delivered over the course of one day or more on a focused topic or theme have been shown to have positive effects on teaching attitudes and changes in teaching practices. For example, through a follow-up e-mail survey, Kahn and Pred (2001) found that forty-six of the fifty participants in a one-day institute on using instructional technology reported that they were using technology effectively in their teaching four months later. The faculty members were also more motivated to seek further development.

In addition to campus-based institutes, we found a growing literature on institutes sponsored by professional associations and organizations (Walstad & Salemi, 2011, for example, report on a program funded by the National Science Foundation).

SHORTER WORKSHOPS. For many teaching centers, workshops on various topics are often offered in short, one-time offerings. In a one-hour workshop teaching a specific skill (for example, the one-minute preceptor technique in medical clinical teaching), Furney et al. (2001) found that residents who were taught the technique reported changes in their behavior and appreciation for the strategy on a follow-up survey. Students of the residents showed improvements in their skills and greater motivation to do outside reading compared with students of control-group residents.

Assuming quality is high, there appear to be moderate improvements in demonstrated teaching behaviors as the length of the workshop increases. For example, a four-hour workshop for medical faculty on using more interactive classroom approaches found through surveys and videotapes of participants and a control group of nonparticipants that participants both reported and were observed using more interactive techniques that increased student participation (Nasmith & Steinert, 2001).

WORKSHOPS IN A SERIES. A growing number of studies examine the effectiveness of workshop series, in which participants attend multiple workshops over time, often based on their personalized needs. Such series that blend elements of traditional workshops with communities of practice have been shown to be both highly relevant and contribute to changes in faculty practice. For example, Ho, Watkins, and Kelly (2001) charted the growth over time of participants in four-session college teacher conceptual change courses against a control group, finding that perceptions of teaching, teaching behaviors, and students' approaches to study all changed favorably in the treatment group (see also Ho, 2000).

Formal Courses in Teaching

Formal courses on teaching offered to faculty members over a term are quite common in the United Kingdom and countries modeled on its system, where faculty who seek promotion are often required to document completion of these courses. In North America, weeklong institutes or a sequence of full-day sessions over a period of time are more likely to be the format of choice. In general, research on the use of these extended experiences on teaching usually finds that they influence teachers' thinking about teaching but concludes that documenting effects on student learning is difficult.

There are some exceptions. Gibbs and Coffey (2000) studied the effects of teaching development courses that aimed at developing more student-centered approaches, finding effects on students' learning. Lawson, Fazey, and Clancy (2007) found positive change in teachers' beliefs and approaches and students' approaches to studying following a teaching development course. Stes (2008) found that a 140-hour course in general teaching methods had significant positive effects on how teachers approached their work, but did not find definitive evidence that students learned better in the classes of teachers who took the course. She estimated that the way that a course is taught influences only about 6 percent of the outcome, given the importance of student motivation, time on task, and other learner factors.

Although these studies vary in the interventions they studied and their results, they suggest that longer, more intensive learning experiences have beneficial effects on faculty teaching beliefs and behaviors, which sometimes can be linked to enhanced student learning. With the exception of those working in countries where formal courses are mandatory for promotion, developers do not often have this format available to them since faculty are unwilling to invest extended time in formal learning about teaching. A more realistic approach that may lead to similar impacts would be to support meetings of a cohort over time, a format exemplified by various types of communities of practice.

Communities of Practice

In our literature base, we found twenty-nine faculty communities of practice, defined here as groupings of a cohort of faculty members engaged in dialogue about teaching for a semester or more. These are organized around a variety of topics and may involve several elements, such as course revision or inquiry projects, as well as regular discussion among participants. Communities of practice can be formally designated as faculty learning communities (Cox, 2003) or teaching and learning circles (Erklenz-Watts, Westbay, & Lynd-Balta, 2006) or can simply be general series of project- or dialogue-based meetings. Commitment of time and mutual reinforcement of learning among participants are key features of these interventions. Generally writers in the literature have found positive effects on teaching development associated with communities of practice. The combination of facilitated peer exchange, sharing of questions and solutions, and task-oriented nature of the regular gatherings is found to advance teaching knowledge and behaviors.

In sum, research on communities of practice has blossomed over the last decade, perhaps because such sustained interventions provide a more practical context for collecting data and the promise of more recognizable impact accruing from the time invested by the participants. Although there is great variation among these types of activities, the studies document solid gains for participants; some even are able to trace these to impacts on student learning.

The examples that follow highlight studies of general and specialized communities of practice.

GENERAL COMMUNITIES OF PRACTICE. Many communities of practice focus on conceptual change. Qualters (2009) evaluated Dialogues, a sustained program that engaged thirty-one participants at two institutions in examining their assumptions about teaching together. Through analysis of transcripts and notes of meetings and participant survey results, she concluded that participants were better able to think about the assumptions behind their practice and made plans for or enacted change in their teaching.

PROJECT-BASED COMMUNITIES. Other communities of practice are project based, often involving course redesign. O'Meara (2005) collected pre-, during-, and postprogram self-ratings; interviewed faculty; and observed meetings of a program for early-career science and technology faculty that spanned an academic year in which participants attended sixteen dinner seminars and completed a course redesign project. She found gains in the impact of the program on teaching careers (commitment, satisfaction, teaching skills), participants' understanding of how students learn, and their understanding and use of assessment. She concluded that the project component of the program was crucial for participants' self-knowledge and their understanding of how their actions influenced student learning, a finding that Gusic et al. (2010) strongly endorse within the context of medical education.

SCHOLARSHIP OF TEACHING AND LEARNING COMMUNITIES. Scholarship of teaching and learning is often the focus of communities of practice. In her analysis of a year-long program in which eight faculty members were engaged in a scholarship of teaching and learning (SoTL) program, Schroeder (2005) used products of faculty scholarship to document "transformational learning" of the participants. Their ability to articulate assumptions, reflect critically, and take action to implement new practices was associated with participation in the program.

Mentoring

Although there is a considerable literature base about mentoring in general, we found only four studies of educational development devoted solely to its impact. Three of these centered on increasing technological skills through mentoring by a more experienced colleague. In one study of a more general and common use of mentoring, Miller and Thurston (2009) examined the impact of a new faculty mentoring program over the course of nine years of operation through formative annual surveys, summative surveys at the fifth and ninth years, and interviews with administrators. Based on responses from a group of twenty-nine mentors and twenty-three mentees, the authors found that 55 percent of the respondents said that the program aided their transition, while 27 percent said that the program influenced their teaching and research and 34 percent said that the mentoring influenced their ability to publish and present their research.

Across the studies, authors found that successful mentoring programs are those in which mentees had flexibility in shaping both the topics and ways in which they interacted with mentors. They often cited reciprocal benefits for mentor and those mentored, which involved increased confidence, improvements in specific targeted teaching skills, and richer conceptualization of learning.

Consultation

Piccinin (1999) and Piccinin and Moore (2002) found that instructional consultation helped improve the student ratings of younger faculty within a year and older faculty within one to three years. Their findings echo the results of major meta-analyses of consultation with feedback such as Cohen (1980) and Menges and Brinko (1986). We encountered only eighteen studies of consultation in our search, and several of these involved other interventions as well.

Although studies of the beneficial effects of consultation and feedback have focused primarily on discussions of student ratings, some literature on consultation in general also documents resulting changes. McShannon and Hynes (2005) reported on a semester-long program for engineering and science faculty that involved weekly classroom observations and discussions with a consultant. Their results are based on sixty-two faculty who participated during one semester during the five years of the program that were studied. In addition to finding that the faculty reported greater use of active learning methods and increases in student learning, the authors found small increases in the number of students receiving grades of A, B, and C, as well as gains in the numbers of students remaining in science and technology programs.

In addition to these examples of consultation with an educational developer, the literature documents positive effects of consultation with a peer. For example, Bell and Mladenovic (2008) found that peer observers were able to help faculty improve their recognition of strengths and weaknesses and develop motivation to make changes. They used results of the observations, a survey, and focus group data to evaluate the effectiveness of the program.

In general, these studies of the effects of consultation suggest that talking with an expert or a knowledgeable peer about a particular teaching context is associated with changes in teaching knowledge and behaviors when the consultation is done skillfully. The literature supports the case that those who establish a consulting relationship with faculty members are likely to be able to support their transition to successful implementation of teaching change.

Awards and Grant Programs

The most common extrinsic rewards educational developers use in promoting faculty change are awards and grants. Studies of faculty awards programs as a developmental approach have largely failed to identify much impact beyond the general reinforcement of the institution's value for teaching. Chism and Szabo (1997) were not able to locate studies documenting that awards either prompted award recipients to further their own growth or encouraged others to make improvements in order to gain the awards. Chism (2006) analyzed existing awards programs and found that very few had established criteria or systematic review processes. In a community college context, Peterson (2005) found "ambivalent attitudes, even hostility and anger, toward the formalized nomination process for awards as well as the way in which awards are disseminated" (p. 157).

Less is known about the impact of grants on faculty change. Seven of the 138 studies reviewed used grants as the primary intervention. Common results described grant programs used with other types of interventions, such as instructional coaching coupled with course releases. For example, Morris and Fry's (2006) study of a small grants program tied to SoTL found that recipients reported growth in their understandings of practice. They cited the opportunity to reflect on and develop new teaching skills and expertise, their development of partnerships, and interactions with peers on teaching and learning issues as most beneficial.

The impact of the studies reviewed generally showed both short-term and continuing improvement in teaching practices and reflective thinking. However, the combination of grants with other strategies makes it difficult to determine their effectiveness alone. For example, Cox (2003) found that small stipends or grants associated with faculty learning communities were an important motivator. In all of the studies examined for this review, the connection with the support offered along with the grant was highlighted over the monetary incentive itself.

In sum, the literature suggests that grants may be an initial motivator, inspiring some faculty to engage in teaching development activities, but support associated with the grant might be more important. Strong beneficial effects of awards without accompanying development programs have not been extensively documented on either those who receive them, their peers, or the culture of the institution.

Discussion

Based on this review of the literature on the impact of educational development, we offer several observations:

- Studies are increasing in quantity. A disproportionate number (one-third) of the studies we coded have been published in the past two years. The 138 we examined are those that were readily retrievable; we believe that there are many more not available in online databases. We found that most published studies describing interventions now have an assessment section. In addition, we found growth in the documentation of faculty development efforts in discipline-specific areas, such as medicine and science, technology, engineering, and mathematics fields.

- Studies are assessing other levels of outcomes beyond participant satisfaction. Although most focus on knowledge change, many assess changes in teacher behavior, and some are attempting to explore student learning changes tied to these teacher behavioral changes. Studies of institutional impact are still infrequent.
- The methods used in studies vary widely. While survey research and self-reported data are still the prevailing mode, quasi-experimental design is frequently employed (often in medical education), and qualitative methods such as observation, interview, and analysis of documents are on the upswing.
- Authors of the overwhelming majority of the studies report specific, effective results; some are not able to demonstrate clear outcomes. There are few studies of failures.
- The presence of increased detail regarding context and program design of assessed activities is enhancing opportunities for developers to judge the transferability of results to their own settings.

Questions of quality pervade reviews of research on educational development impact. First, there is the quality of the research itself. Across the studies, we encountered research that was well described and methodologically sophisticated; there were also studies that were less detailed in their descriptions and used more informal methods. A second issue is the quality of the intervention itself. In this collection of published articles, we read descriptions of interventions and how they were designed and delivered, but we do not know whether the workshop facilitator was skilled, whether the faculty attended all sessions of the course or learning community, whether the consultant was experienced or new, and a host of other factors that may have affected the quality of the intervention that was assessed. In most cases, contextual factors are described, but analysis often does not test whether different outcomes were found for participants by gender, discipline, or other variable. Most studies are of interventions located at only one institution and were performed by researchers associated with the unit in which the program was located,

Finally, all of the studies found positive results on at least some dimension of impact that were explored.

Conclusion

Despite these limitations, the body of accrued literature on impact is now substantial enough to reveal patterns that can provide guidance for decision making within educational development programs, as well as providing support for the efficacy of development practice. Believing that the establishment of a systematic scholarship is essential for the field of educational development, we are heartened by this exploration of the literature on impact and urge that this line of research continue. We also call for increased efforts, such as postings to Wikipodia, that will enable the educational development community to collaborate in collecting and analyzing studies in ways that make them easily accessible for use in practice and further study.

REFERENCES

Bamber, V. (2008). Evaluating lecturer development programmes: Received wisdom or self-knowledge? *International Journal for Academic Development*, *13*, 107–116. doi:10.1080/13601440802076541.

Baume, D. (2002). Scholarship, academic development and the future. *International Journal for Academic Development*, *7*(2), 109–112.

Bell, A., & Mladenovic, R. (2008). The benefits of peer observation of teaching for tutor development. *Higher Education: The International Journal of Higher Education and Educational Planning*, *55*(6), 735–752.

Chism, N. (2006). Teaching awards: What do they award? *Journal of Higher Education*, *77*(4), 589–617.

Chism, N., & Szabo, B. (1997). Teaching awards: Assessing their impact. In D. DeZure (Ed.), *To improve the academy: Resources for faculty, instructional, and organizational development, Vol. 16* (pp. 181–199). San Francisco, CA: Jossey-Bass/Anker.

Chism, N., & Szabo, B. (1998). How faculty development programs evaluate their services. *Journal of Staff, Program, and Organization Development*, *15*(2), 55–62.

Cohen, P. (1980). Effectiveness of student rating feedback on the improvement of instruction: A meta-analysis of findings. *Research in Higher Education*, *13*, 321–341.

Cox, M. D. (2003). Proven faculty development tools that foster the scholarship of teaching in faculty learning communities. In C. Wehlburg &

S. Chadwick-Blossey (Eds.), *To improve the academy: Resources for faculty, instructional, and organizational development, Vol. 21* (pp. 109–142). San Francisco, CA: Jossey-Bass/Anker.

Erklenz-Watts, M., Westbay, T., & Lynd-Balta, E. (2006). An alternative professional development program: Lessons learned. *College Teaching, 54*, 275–280. doi:10.3200/CTCH.54.3.275–280.

Furney, S. L., Orsini, A. N., Orsetti, K. E., Stern, D. T., Gruppen, L. D., & Irby, D. M. (2001). Teaching the one-minute preceptor: A randomized controlled trial. *Journal of General Internal Medicine, 16*(9), 620–624.

Gibbs, G., & Coffey, M. (2000). Training to teach in higher education: A research agenda. *Teacher Development, 4*(2), 31–44.

Gusic, M. E., Milner, R. J., Tisdell, E. J., Taylor, E. W., Quillen, D. A., & Thorndyke, L. E. (2010). The essential value of projects in faculty development. *Academic Medicine, 85*(9), 1484–1491. doi:10.1097/ACM.0b013e3181eb4d17.

Guskey, T. R. (2000). *Evaluating professional development.* Thousand Oaks, CA: Sage.

Hines, S. R. (2009). Investigating faculty development program assessment practices: What's being done and how can it be improved? *Journal of Faculty Development, 23*(3), 5–19.

Ho, A. (2000). A conceptual change approach to staff development: A model for program design. *International Journal for Academic Development, 5*(1), 30–41.

Ho, A., Watkins, D., & Kelly, M. (2001). The conceptual change approach to improving teaching and learning: An evaluation of a Hong Kong staff development programme. *Higher Education*, 42, 143–169.

Hoyt, D. P., & Howard, G. S. (1978). The evaluation of faculty development programs. *Research in Higher Education, 8*, 25–38.

Kahn, J., & Pred, R. (2001). Evaluation of a faculty development model for technology use in higher education for late adopters. *Computers in Schools, 18*(4), 127–150.

Kirkpatrick, D. (1998). *Evaluating training programs: The four levels* (2nd ed.). San Francisco, CA: Berrett-Koehler.

Kreber, C., & Brook, P. (2001). Impact evaluation of educational development programmes. *International Journal for Academic Development*, 6(2), 96–108.

Kucsera, J. V., & Svinicki, M. (2010). Rigorous evaluations of faculty development programs. *Journal of Faculty Development, 24*(2) 5–18.

Lawson, R. J., Fazey, J. A., & Clancy, D. M. (2007). The impact of a teaching in higher education scheme on new lecturer's personal epistemologies and approaches to teaching. In C. Rust (Ed.), *Improving student learning through teaching*. Oxford, UK: Oxford Centre for Staff Development.

Levinson-Rose, J., & Menges, R. J. (1981). Improving college teaching: A critical review of research. *Review of Educational Research*, *5*(3), 403–434.

McKinney, K. (2002). Instructional development: Relationships to teaching and learning in higher education. In D. Lieberman & C. Wehlburg (Eds.), *To improve the academy: Resources for faculty, instructional, and organizational development, Vol. 20* (pp. 225–237). San Francisco, CA: Jossey-Bass/Anker.

McShannon, J., & Hynes, P. (2005). Student achievement and retention: Can professional development programs help faculty GRASP it? *Journal of Faculty Development*, *20*(2), 87–93.

Menges, R., & Brinko, K. (1986, April). *Effects of student evaluation feedback: A meta-analysis of higher education.* Paper presented at the annual meeting of the American Educational Research Association, Washington, DC.

Miller, T. N., & Thurston, L. P. (2009). Mentoring junior professors: History and evaluation of a nine-year model. *Journal of Faculty Development*, *23*(2), 35–40.

Morris, C., & Fry, H. (2006). Enhancing educational research and development activity through small grant schemes: A case study. *International Journal for Academic Development, 11*(1), 43–56. doi:10.1080/13601440600579001.

Nasmith, L., & Steinert, Y. (2001). The evaluation of a workshop to promote interactive lecturing. *Teaching and Learning in Medicine*, *13*(1), 43–48.

O'Meara, K. (2005). The courage to be experimental: How one faculty learning community influenced faculty teaching careers, understanding of how students learn, and assessment. *Journal of Faculty Development*, *20*(3), 153–160.

Peterson, C. (2005). Is the thrill gone? An investigation of faculty vitality within the context of a community college. In S. Chadwick-Blossey & D. R. Robertson (Eds.), *To improve the academy: Resources for faculty, instructional, and organizational development, Vol. 23* (pp. 144–161). San Francisco, CA: Jossey-Bass/Anker.

Piccinin, S. (1999). How individual consultation affects teaching. In C. Knapper & S. Piccinin (Eds.), *New directions in teaching and learning: No. 79. Using consultants to improve teaching* (pp. 71–84). San Francisco, CA: Jossey-Bass.

Piccinin, S., & Moore, J. P. (2002). The impact of individual consultation on the teaching of younger versus older faculty. *International Journal for Academic Development*, 7(2), 123–135.

Qualters, D. M. (2009). Creating a pathway for teacher change. *Journal of Faculty Development*, *23*(1), 5–13.

Schönwetter, D. J., & Nazarko, O. (2009). Investing in our next generation: Overview of short courses, and teaching and mentoring programs for newly-hired faculty in Canadian universities (part 2). *Journal of Faculty Development, 23*(1), 54–63.

Schroeder, C. (2005). Evidence of the transformational dimensions of the scholarship of teaching and learning: Faculty development through the eyes of SOTL scholars. In S. Chadwick-Blossey & D. R. Robertson (Eds.), *To improve the academy: Resources for faculty, instructional, and organizational development, Vol. 23* (pp. 47–71). San Francisco, CA: Jossey-Bass/Anker.

Smith, H. J. (2004). The impact of staff development programmes and activities. In D. Baume & P. Kahn (Eds.), *Enhancing staff and educational development* (pp. 96–117). Oxford, UK: Routledge-Falmer.

Steinert, Y., Mann, K., Centeno, A., Dolmans, D., Spencer, J., Gelula, M., & Prideaux, D. (2006). A systematic review of faculty development initiatives designed to improve teaching effectiveness in medical evaluation: BEME Guide No. 8. *Medical Teacher, 28*(6), 497–526.

Stes, A. (2008). *The impact of instructional development in higher education: Effects on teachers and students.* (Doctoral dissertation.) Antwerp: University of Antwerp.

Stes, A., Min-Leliveld, M., Gijbels, D., & Van Petegem, P. (2010). The impact of instructional development in higher education: The state-of-the-art of the research. *Educational Research Review*, 5, 25–49. doi:10.1016/j.edurev.2009.07.001.

Walstad, W. B., & Salemi, M. K. (2011). Results from a faculty development program in teaching economics. *Journal of Economic Education*, 42, 283–293.

Weimer, M. (2007). Intriguing connections but not with the past. *International Journal for Academic Development, 12*(1), 5–8.

Weimer, M., & Lenze, L. F. (1991). Instructional interventions: A review of the literature on efforts to improve instruction. In J. C. Smart (Ed.), *Higher education: Handbook of theory and research* (Vol. 7, pp. 294–333). New York: Agathon Press.

PART FOUR

PRACTICING INNOVATIVE TEACHING AND LEARNING

10

EXAMINING EFFECTIVE FACULTY PRACTICE

TEACHING CLARITY AND STUDENT ENGAGEMENT

Allison BrckaLorenz, Tony Ribera,
Jillian Kinzie, Eddie R. Cole
Indiana University

This study explores the frequency of student exposure to teaching-clarity behaviors and the extent to which these behaviors relate to student engagement, deep approaches to learning, and students' self-reports of gains in college. Researchers found that students exposed to more clear teaching behaviors, such as explaining course goals and requirements, had positive relationships with all of these outcomes. There were particularly strong relationships between students' exposure to clear teaching behaviors and their sense of campus support and self-reports of gains.

Improving the quality of learning in undergraduate education is a national imperative. Regional accreditation agencies have placed greater demands on institutions to provide evidence of student learning and effective teaching. Institutions must also demonstrate that this evidence is being used to make improvements in the quality of student learning. At the core of any agenda to improve undergraduate education is an emphasis on effective teaching practices. As colleges and universities shift to a learning-centered paradigm, a growing emphasis is being placed on understanding which teaching practices are effective in promoting student learning (Barr & Tagg, 1995). There are varying ideas on what constitutes effective teaching; however, one that is often referenced when discussing the characteristics of effective teaching is teaching clarity (Feldman, 1989; Hativa, Barak, & Simhi, 2001; Sherman, Armistead, Fowler, Barksdale, & Reif, 1987).

Teaching clarity has been defined as "a cluster of teaching behaviors that result in learners' gaining knowledge or understanding of a topic" (Cruickshank & Kennedy, 1986, p. 43) and as "the ability of the teacher to provide instruction, expositional or otherwise, which helps students come to a clear understanding of material" (Metcalf, 1992, p. 275).

For this study, we draw from Ginsberg's (2007) work by defining teaching clarity as a teaching method where faculty demonstrate a level of transparency in their approach to instruction and goal setting in an effort to help students better understand expectations and comprehend subject matter. This includes activities such as providing examples and summarizing key points of lectures (Chesebro & McCroskey, 2001; Myers & Knox, 2001). Unfortunately, little is known about the extent to which students are exposed to specific teaching clarity-behaviors and the relationship to other important elements of an undergraduate education, such as student engagement, deep learning, and self-reported gains.

Literature Review

Research suggests that student engagement in educationally purposeful activities is a predictor of student learning (Astin, 1993; Kuh, 2003; Kuh, Cruce, Shoup, Kinzie, & Gonyea, 2008; Pace, 1980; Pascarella & Terenzini, 1991). Undergraduate students report higher levels of student engagement and learning at colleges and universities where faculty engage in effective educational practices (Umbach & Wawrzynksi, 2005). This supports the research of Kuh, Nelson, Laird, and Umbach (2004) who concluded, "Almost across the board, students at institutions where faculty emphasize a range of effective educational practices reported making more progress since starting college on various dimensions of student learning and personal development" (p. 28).

Providing an overview of studies on undergraduate education, Pascarella and Terenzini (2005) position teaching clarity as an effective educational practice by highlighting the positive relationship between teaching clarity and student learning and achievement. Students who report higher levels of teaching-clarity and organization experiences tend to grow more on a wide variety of student outcomes, including moral reasoning, leadership, openness to diversity and challenge, and positive attitudes toward literacy. Similarly, students who reported lower levels of these experiences are less likely to grow on these outcomes (Wabash National Study of Liberal Arts Education, n.d.).

Based on a comprehensive review of the research, Pascarella (2006) concluded that student perceptions of instructional practice, such as teaching clarity, had moderate correlations with various measures of course learning, including grades and final examination performance. Studies have identified a relationship between teaching clarity and student comprehension of material (for example, Chesebro & McCroskey, 2001; Myers & Knox, 2001), greater satisfaction and achievement (Hativa, 1998), and motivation (Ginsberg, 2007). Also, student perceptions of instructor behaviors, such as explanation of course goals and assignments, have been positively associated with general measures of cognitive growth in the first year of college (Pascarella, Edison, Nora, Hagedorn, & Braxton, 1996). In general, students struggle to comprehend material and express dissatisfaction with courses when the instructor lacks clarity (Hativa, 1998).

Although teaching clarity is generally promoted as an effective teaching practice, we know little about how widely students are exposed to this practice in undergraduate education. In addition, little research has been done to link teaching clarity to other forms of effective educational practice such as student-faculty interaction or active and collaborative learning. This study explores the frequency of student exposure to teaching-clarity behaviors and the extent to which these behaviors relate to student engagement, deep learning, and self-reported gains in college. Three research questions guided this study:

1. What teaching-clarity behaviors are students exposed to most and least frequently?
2. What is the relationship between teaching clarity and student engagement?
3. How does teaching clarity relate to deep learning and students' reports of gains in college?

Methodology

Undergraduate students from a variety of higher education institutions were surveyed using the National Survey of Student Engagement (NSSE).

Data Source and Sample

The data for this analysis come from the 2010 administration of the NSSE. NSSE was designed by a team of assessment experts to measure student behaviors and the time and energy students invest in activities linked to learning and personal development (Hayek & Kuh, 2004; Kuh, 2001a, 2001b). More specifically, NSSE asks students how often they engage in various effective educational practices, as well as

Table 10.1. Student and Institution Characteristics.

		First-Year Students (%)	Seniors (%)
Student characteristics			
Female		65	66
Transfer student		12	55
Full-time enrollment		91	73
Fraternity or sorority member		7	11
Student-athlete		11	5
Living on campus		65	18
First generation		49	56
Traditional age		88	48
Race or ethnicity	African American/black	15	12
	Asian/Pacific Islander	7	5
	Caucasian/white	54	57
	Hispanic/Latino	13	14
	Other	7	6
Primary major field	Arts and humanities	12	11
	Biological sciences	9	5
	Business	16	22
	Education	9	10
	Engineering	6	4
	Physical science	4	3
	Professional	13	12
	Social science	12	13
Grades	Mostly A's	39	51
	Mostly B's	47	43
	Mostly C's	13	6
Institution characteristics			
Control	Public	45	49
Carnegie classification	Doctoral	19	17
	Master's	49	49
	Baccalaureate	31	34

their perceptions of their college environment and various gains while in college. The teaching-clarity item set was adapted from the Wabash National Study (www.liberalarts.wabash.edu/study-overview/) and has been tested in the study's research (see Pascarella, Salisbury, & Blaich, 2009). The sample for the current study consists of 8,102 (41 percent) first-year students and 11,761 (59 percent) senior students from thirty-eight colleges and universities. (For additional information about student demographics and characteristics see Table 10.1.)

Variables

Several scales and collections of items were examined in this study, as well as various student-level demographics and institution-level characteristics. The teaching-clarity scale (Table 10.2) was created using the additional items about teaching clarity that were administered at the end of the NSSE. These items asked students how often their instructors behaved in various ways such as giving clear explanations of assignments or making abstract ideas and theories understandable.

The remaining scales and benchmarks used in this study were created using items from the core NSSE survey. Student engagement was measured with individual engagement items from the core NSSE survey, as well as four of NSSE's benchmarks of effective educational practice: Level of Academic Challenge, Active and Collaborative Learning, Student-Faculty Interaction, and Supportive Campus Environment. These

Table 10.2. Component Items and Reliability Coefficients for the Teaching-Clarity Scale.

In your experience during the current school year, about how often did your instructors do each of the following? (never, sometimes, often, very often)

- Gave clear explanations of assignments
- Used examples or illustrations to explain difficult points
- Reviewed and summarized course material effectively
- Made abstract ideas and theories understandable
- Gave assignments that helped you learn the course material
- Presented course material in an organized way
- Came to class well prepared
- Used class time effectively
- Explained course goals and requirements clearly

Note: *Teaching clarity: Cronbach's alpha =.93 for first-year students and .94 for seniors.*

benchmarks, broad measures critical to student learning and development, are intended to provide feedback on institutional performance and investigate actionable solutions for improvement.

Deep learning and students' self-reported gains in college were measured with scales created from the NSSE survey. Deep learning was assessed with the scales Higher Order Learning, Integrative Learning, and Reflective Learning. Deep approaches to learning get at a deep understanding of an issue, not just the surface knowledge, and a reflection on the relationships between pieces of information. Students' self-reports of gains were measured using the scales Gains in Practical Competence, Gains in General Education, and Gains in Personal and Social Development. These scales explore the degree to which students report having made gains in a variety of competency areas as a result of their undergraduate education. (See nsse.iub.edu for the component items and reliability coefficients of the scales and NSSE's benchmarks of effective educational practice used in this study.)

Analysis

For all research questions, data from first-year and senior students were analyzed separately in order to present distinct results reflective of the first-year and senior experience in college. To answer the first research question, items on frequencies of teaching clarity were examined. Pearson's *r* correlations were used to answer the second research question in order to relate the teaching-clarity scale with four of NSSE's benchmarks of effective educational practice and individual engagement items.

Evidence for the third research question was gathered using a series of multivariate ordinary least squares regressions to determine the relationship between students' reports of teaching clarity and the measures of deep learning and student-reported gains. With the teaching-clarity scale as an independent variable, each measure of deep learning and student-reported gains was analyzed as a dependent variable with its own model controlling for gender, transfer status, enrollment status, fraternity or sorority membership, athletic participation, race or ethnicity, primary major field, grades, first-generation status, age, institutional control, and institutional Carnegie classification.

Findings

For both first-year (FY) and senior students (SR), the most frequently (students responded "often" or "very often") observed teaching-clarity behaviors were instructors' coming to class well prepared (FY: 91.1

percent, SR: 90.8 percent) and instructors' explaining course goals and requirements clearly (FY: 87 percent, SR: 89.2 percent). The least often observed teaching-clarity behaviors were instructors' reviewing and summarizing course material effectively (FY: 80.3 percent, SR: 83.5 percent) and instructors' making abstract ideas and theories understandable (FY: 75.9 percent, SR: 79 percent).

For both first-years and seniors, the teaching-clarity scale had significant ($p < .001$), positive relationships with NSSE's benchmarks of effective educational practice. For first-year and senior students, the strongest relationship was found between teaching clarity and Supportive Campus Environment (FY: $r = .537$, SR: $r = .553$), followed by Academic Challenge (FY: $r = .397$, SR: $r = .364$). Although seniors still had small, positive relationships between teaching clarity and Student-Faculty Interaction (SFI) ($r = .287$) and Active and Collaborative Learning (ACL) ($r = .200$), these relationships were stronger for first-year students (SFI: $r = .301$, ACL: $r = .276$). These findings suggest that teaching-clarity behaviors may be particularly important for the development of first-year students' relationships with their faculty and classmates.

Individual items on the NSSE survey also had significant ($p < .001$), positive relationships with the teaching-clarity scale. For both first-years and seniors, the items with the highest correlations with the teaching-clarity scale were about students' ratings of their relationships with faculty members (FY: $r = .478$, SR: $r = .515$), of their institution's emphasis on providing the support they need to succeed academically (FY: $r = .473$, SR: $r = .517$), and of their entire educational experience at their institution (FY: $r = .507$, SR: $r = .525$). These findings support the idea that teaching clarity contributes to students' relationships with faculty members and contributes to their overall satisfaction with their college experience.

Controlling for a wide variety of student-level characteristics, regressions indicated significant, positive relationships between teaching clarity and all subscales of deep learning and student-reported gains. Because all continuous independent and dependent variables were standardized before being entered in the models, the unstandardized coefficients can be interpreted as effect sizes. The magnitude of these effect sizes is reflected in Table 10.3. All coefficients were statistically significant and ranged between a small to medium relationship (+) to a large relationship (++++). For both first-years and seniors, the teaching-clarity scale had the strongest relationships with student-reported gains in college, specifically between teaching clarity and student-reported Gains in Practical Competence and Gains in General Education. Again for both

Table 10.3. Relationship Between Teaching Clarity and Deep Learning and Gains.

	Integrative Learning	Higher-Order Thinking	Reflective Learning	Gains in Practical Competence	Gains in Personal and Social Development	Gains in General Education
First-years	++	++	+	++++	+++	++++
Seniors	++	++	+	++++	+++	++++

Note: *Key for unstandardized beta:* + > .2; ++ > .3; +++ > .4; ++++ > .5.

classes, there were slightly stronger relationships between the teaching-clarity scale and the Integrative Learning scale and the Higher Order Thinking scale than with the Reflective Learning scale. These results further support the notion that teaching clarity is strongly related to important outcomes such as students' perceptions of gains and deep approaches to learning.

Implications, Limitations, and Next Steps

This study adds to research demonstrating that faculty who are perceived by students to be well prepared for class and design assignments that students consider clear and meaningful have consistently positive effects on student engagement and desired educational gains. The strength of the relationship between teaching clarity and the four NSSE benchmarks for first-year students suggests the need to emphasize the value of teaching clarity, particularly among faculty teaching first-year courses. In general, as all institutions are challenged to improve student learning and success, it is essential to focus on expanding students' exposure to practices that can make a significant difference in engagement and learning. Greater instructional clarity helps students understand expectations for the course and better identify with the instructor, and it can also promote the kinds of deep learning and educational gains desired for all students.

The findings from this study have specific implications for faculty development. Generally all of the clarity behaviors were frequently observed by most students, but it is worth noting deficiencies; for example, a quarter of first-year students rarely find that their instructors are making abstract ideas and theories understandable. These results suggest that faculty developers should expand their awareness of the value of teaching clarity for improving student engagement and the quality of learning. Results could also be promoted to foster a broader understanding among faculty, administrators, and students of the importance of teaching clarity and to expand investment in ensuring an emphasis of teaching clarity. For example, as part of their ongoing classroom evaluation, faculty could be encouraged to assess teaching clarity at the midpoint of a course for formative feedback. Development workshops could also be conducted in which faculty members share effective approaches to ensuring teaching clarity. In programs to prepare future faculty, emphases on teaching clarity can even be added to training in order to enrich the pedagogical techniques of tomorrow's professors.

This study reflects an initial exploration of teaching clarity and student engagement, presenting a one-dimensional picture of teaching clarity. To provide a more comprehensive picture, the researchers have begun exploring faculty perceptions of the importance of teaching-clarity behaviors and the relationship between teaching clarity and other effective educational practices using data from the 2011 administration of the Faculty Survey of Student Engagement. Further examination of clarity perceptions and behaviors from both students and faculty will add valuable information about teaching practices in different fields.

As colleges and universities strive to improve undergraduate education and are challenged to enact a culture that assesses teaching quality based on the impact on student learning, it is important to emphasize the value of measurable practices like students' perceptions of teaching clarity. Past research has shown that teaching clarity is important for student learning, motivation, and achievement. The positive relationships between teaching clarity and learning and engagement shown here continue to support the position that teaching clarity is valuable and should be promoted as a goal in faculty development.

REFERENCES

Astin, A. W. (1993). *What matters in college? Four critical years revisited.* San Francisco, CA: Jossey-Bass.

Barr, R. B., & Tagg, J. (1995). From teaching to learning: A new paradigm for undergraduate education. *Change, 27*(6), 13–25.

Chesebro, J. L., & McCroskey, J. C. (2001). The relationship of teacher clarity and immediacy with student state receiver apprehension, affect and cognitive learning. *Communication Education, 50*(1), 59–68.

Cruickshank, D. R., & Kennedy, J. J. (1986). Teaching clarity. *Teaching and Teacher Education,* 2(1), 43–47.

Feldman, K. A. (1989). The association between student ratings of specific instructional dimensions and student achievement: Refining and extending the synthesis of data from multisection validity studies. *Research in Higher Education, 30,* 583–645.

Ginsberg, S. M. (2007). Teacher transparency: What students can see from faculty communication. *Journal of Cognitive Affective Learning,* 4(1), 13–24.

Hativa, N. (1998). Lack of clarity in university teaching: A case study. *Higher Education, 36*(3), 353–381.

Hativa, N., Barak, R., & Simhi, E. (2001). Exemplary university teachers: Knowledge and beliefs regarding effective teaching dimensions and strategies. *Journal of Higher Education,* 72(6), 699–729.

Hayek, J., & Kuh, G. (2004, March–April). Principles for assessing student engagement in the first year of college. *Assessment Update, 16*(2), 11–13.

Kuh, G. D. (2001a). Assessing what really matters to student learning: Inside the National Survey of Student Engagement. *Change, 33*(3), 10–17, 66.

Kuh, G. D. (2001b). *The National Survey of Student Engagement: Conceptual framework and overview of psychometric properties.* Bloomington: Indiana University, Center for Postsecondary Research.

Kuh, G. D. (2003). What we're learning about student engagement from NSSE. *Change, 35*(2), 24–32.

Kuh, G. D., Cruce, T., Shoup, R., Kinzie, J., & Gonyea, R. M. (2008). Unmasking the effects of student engagement on college grades and persistence. *Journal of Higher Education, 79,* 540–563.

Kuh, G. D., Nelson Laird, T. F., & Umbach, P. D. (2004). Aligning faculty and student behavior: Realizing the promise of expectations. *Liberal Education, 90*(4), 24–31.

Metcalf, K. K. (1992). The effects of a guided training experience on the instructional clarity of pre-service teachers. *Teaching and Teacher Education, 8*(3), 275–286.

Myers, S. A., & Knox, R. L. (2001). The relationship between college student information-seeking behaviors and perceived instructor verbal behaviors. *Communication Education, 50*(4), 343–356.

Pace, C. R. (1980). Measuring the quality of student effort. *Current Issues in Higher Education, 2,* 10–16.

Pascarella, E. T. (2006). How college affects students: Ten directions for future research. *Journal of College Student Development, 47,* 508–520.

Pascarella, E., Edison, M., Nora, A., Hagedorn, L., & Braxton, J. (1996). Effects of teacher organization/preparation and teacher skill/clarity on general cognitive skills in college. *Journal of College Student Development, 37,* 7–19.

Pascarella, E. T., Salisbury, M. H., & Blaich, C. F. (2009, November). *Exposure to effective instruction and college student persistence: A multi-institutional replication and extension.* Paper presented at the annual conference of the Association for Study of Higher Education, Vancouver, BC, Canada.

Pascarella, E. T., & Terenzini, P. T. (1991). *How college affects students: Findings and insights from twenty years of research.* San Francisco, CA: Jossey-Bass.

Pascarella, E. T., & Terenzini, P. T. (2005). *How college affects students: A third decade of research* (Vol. 2). San Francisco, CA: Jossey-Bass.

Sherman, T. M., Armistead, L. P., Fowler, F., Barksdale, M. A., & Reif, G. (1987). The quest for excellence in university teaching. *Journal of Higher Education, 58*(1), 66–84.

Umbach, P. D., & Wawrzynski, M. R. (2005). Faculty do matter: The role of college faculty in student learning and engagement. *Research in Higher Education, 46*(2), 153–184.

Wabash National Study of Liberal Arts Education. (N.d.). *High-impact practices and experiences from the Wabash National Study*. Retrieved from http://www.liberalarts.wabash.edu/storage/High-Impact_Practices_Summary06.01.09.pdf

11

MILLENNIAL STUDENTS

INSIGHTS FROM GENERATIONAL THEORY AND LEARNING SCIENCE

Michele DiPietro
Kennesaw State University

Recent theory and research suggest that the current generation of students, labeled millennials, is unique in formative experiences, beliefs, attitudes, and goals. This chapter goes beyond the "Gameboy-in-the-crib" characterization of today's students by examining societal trends that have shaped them and connects these findings to insights from the learning sciences. This analysis uncovers how these students' experiences affect their readiness for college and attitudes about learning. The chapter argues that the current sociocultural context leaves students ill equipped for certain cognitive functions, particularly metacognitive awareness and progress toward mature stages of intellectual development, and it suggests strategies to support the development of those functions.

Do students on campus seem different from those ten to fifteen years ago, or did you just grow old? Every generation is, of course, different from the previous one, but many in higher education, those who write for the popular press, and even corporate America agree that something is unique about this cohort of students, a change so profound to be a "discontinuity" or even a "singularity" (Prensky, 2001). Some decry this change, some celebrate it, and others try to offer tips to deal with it. In fact, the millennial generation has spawned an industry of consultants who help institutions understand, teach, and manage these young adults. A simple Google search on "understanding millennials" yields almost 2 million Web pages. Many of these pieces highlight the ubiquitous presence of technology in millennials' lives and their multitasking habits, concluding with how higher education needs to be more responsive to this reality.

Among the most influential perspectives, we find the somewhat pessimistic one of Twenge (2007), who describes a generation victim of the self-esteem movement and, as a result, narcissistic, self-centered, entitled, disrespectful, and depressed when it realizes not all its wishes are attainable. Similarly, Bauerlein (2008) argues that the ubiquity and immediacy of technology have made this generation dumb and underachieving. In his view, social networking sites have made teenagers self-centered and uninterested in anything that does not immediately concern them. These sites invite expressive writing, which promotes transmission of information but not necessarily learning or critical thinking. Finally, he adds that text messaging, with its blasé attitude about spelling and punctuation, has promoted poor writing by normalizing illiteracy. Prensky (2001), who coined the terms *digital immigrants* and *digital natives* to refer to those born, respectively, before and after the computer and Internet revolution, goes on to state, "It is very likely that *our students' brains have physically changed*—and are different from ours [emphasis in the original]" (p. 1) and that therefore teaching must change, specifically incorporating more technology.

Although neuroscience has refuted Prensky's claim (brains do not evolve in such short time spans), this meme has spread in the popular press (a Google search for "millennial brains have evolved" yields 4 million pages discussing this idea). Others have highlighted the generational shift as a cultural one, often taking a humorous approach to sensitize faculty to this change. Since 1998, Beloit College has been issuing its "Beloit College Mindset List" (Beloit College, 2011). Started as a reminder for faculty not to use outdated references, it has chronicled the evolving generational gap between students and faculty. For instance, for traditional students in the class of 2015, born in 1993, the Communist Party has never been the official political party in Russia, altar girls have never been a big deal, and no state has ever failed to observe Martin Luther King Jr. Day. These and other items are stark reminders that compared to professors in their fifties, the racial, gender, and political landscape is radically different for this generation.

Finally, writers like Howe and Strauss (1992), who coined the term *millennial,* have celebrated this generation as the next great generation and the cultural heir to the GI generation (born 1901 to 1924). The strategies they suggest involve capitalizing on the social and hyperconnected nature of millennials, for instance, by rebranding college as a bonding experience.

While technology, multitasking, and social connectedness are certainly facets of the millennial experience, two crucial pieces are often absent from such conversations. The first is an in-depth look at the cultural, societal, parental, and educational trends that have helped shape millennial students into the beings we see on our campuses. While Howe and Strauss's "Seven Core Traits of Millennials" (2000) are often cited, they are not mentioned in the context of their broader generational theory that explains those traits.

The second is a serious connection of these considerations to the insights from learning science. For instance, what impact have these trends had on the development of students' metacognitive skills? How does this translate into readiness for learning? What does learning science tell us about crafting pedagogical strategies that are both proven to be effective and likely to be well received by millennials? Other than the false claims about the evolution of the millennial brain, learning research is seldom invoked in these conversations.

This chapter aims to bridge these two gaps and is divided into three sections. The first section reviews Howe and Strauss's (1992) generational theory. The second section examines their seven core traits of millennials, with particular attention to the social trends that generated them (Howe & Strauss, 2000; Strauss & Howe, 2003). The third section reviews seven principles of learning (Ambrose, Bridges, DiPietro, Lovett, & Norman, 2010); ties them to generational traits, especially in relation to intellectual development, metacognitive awareness, and epistemological beliefs; and draws implications for learning and pedagogical strategies.

Generational Theory

Beyond classifying the traits of a given cohort, generational theory tries to build a framework to predict how current generations emerge from previous ones. If the parents had certain generational traits, what can we expect of their children?

Generational theories usually rely on the "pendulum" idea, postulating that generations alternate by swinging back and forth along a character axis as they challenge and react to the previous generation's values

(Marías, 1976). Howe and Strauss (1992) theorize a reoccurring cycle of four states: the swing to one side, the coming down to the middle from that side, the upswing to the opposite side, and again the coming back to the middle, but from the opposite side. In their theory, a generational cycle encompasses four generations and two social moments. They define a generation as "a special cohort-group whose length approximately matches that of a basic phase of a life, or about 22 years" (p. 34). What distinguishes a generation from the next is its peer personality, which they define as "a generational persona recognized and determined by common age location, beliefs and behaviors, and perceived membership in a common generation" (p. 64). From this definition, we see that a generation lasts about twenty years, and it gives rise to the next one when the people born after that no longer share the same broad cultural traits or peer personality. For instance, we can immediately evoke certain traits associated with people raised during the Great Depression (such as thriftiness) or with baby boomers (such as their emphasis on self-exploration, often drug mediated). The trait does not have to be shared by all members of a generation to define its personality. Not everybody in the 1960s used drugs, but people were aware that was the cultural trend.

Some generations (the upswings of the pendulum) herald social moments, "era[s], typically lasting about a decade, when people perceive that historical events are radically altering their social environment" (Howe & Strauss, 1992, p. 71). The 1960s were one such moment, an era of inner-oriented spiritual awakening that changed the social landscape by focusing on finding oneself, importing and spreading Eastern spirituality, and eventually launching the self-esteem movement. In Howe and Strauss's (1992) theory, we are living through the latter stages of another social moment, this time an outer-oriented secular crisis brought about by 9/11 and the Iraq war.

The decade following 9/11 has redefined what it means to be an American, a citizen, a patriot, across the political spectrum. Compare this with the Gulf War in the 1990s, which did not have such a pervasive effect because the social conditions were not there yet. Rather remarkably, Howe and Strauss predicted in 1992 that we would reenter a social moment in the next decade based on their historical analysis of the previous generational cycles. Not all generations herald social moments. Those that do are said to be dominant, and they alternate with recessive generations. Recessive generations can behave in two alternating ways. Adaptive generations follow a secular crisis and simply adopt, expand, and consolidate the previous generation's values. The stereotypical image of the housewife in the 1950s, with her ever-growing menagerie of household appliances, exemplifies one such generation (aptly named the silent generation). Reactive generations follow a spiritual awakening, and they rebel against the previous generation's values, but without offering a viable substitute. The jaded Generation X is a typical example of a reactive generation.

Millennial Theory

The last generational cycle started with the GI generation (born 1901 to 1924), followed by the silent generation (born 1925 to 1942), the boomers (born 1943 to 1960), and Generation X (1960 to 1981). Millennials (born 1982 to 2004) start a new cycle, heralded by the secular crisis. Therefore, the first key to understand this generation is that it plays a role in history analogous to the GI generation—the civic-oriented generation who built modern America.

Usually each generation begets the next: for example, GIs begat silents, and silents begat boomers. Boomers delayed having children in favor of self-exploration. As a result, Generation X is one of the smallest generations. When Xers began getting married and having children—millennial children—boomers were now ready to settle down and have children. As a result, millennials are parented by both preceding generations. This is significant because boomers, being older, are more socially established than Xers, in the sense that they controlled institutions such as school boards while millennials were growing up, and therefore have been the dominant generation in terms of setting standards for how millennials have been raised.

As a caveat, this generational theory has been criticized as unwarranted overgeneralization. Many of the traits easily map onto children from comfortable and privileged backgrounds. Howe and Strauss's research (1992) has maintained that the traits are confirmed across different social and racial/ethnic groups, keeping in mind that the outer manifestations might vary according to wealth. However, Howe and Strauss posit that the only group for which those traits do not characterize the generational culture is very rural families.

With these ideas in mind, Howe and Strauss have identified the following seven core traits of millennials.

Millennials Are Special

Prevalent societal attitudes from the 1970s often considered children a hindrance. For instance, only 55 percent of college freshmen in 1974 declared that "raising a family" was an "essential or very important life goal." Through the 1980s and 1990s, this trend reversed itself, with that same percentage rising to 78 percent in 1998 (Higher Education Research Institute, 1998). Family income increased and family size decreased, so that more resources were concentrated on fewer children. As Howe and Strauss pointed out, fertility programs skyrocketed through the same period, with the result that those babies were literally special because of the investment of time, financial resources, and emotional energy in them. Children became fashionable, as evidenced by celebrities who have publicly appeared pregnant on the covers of magazines or taking their children to the Oscars. Las Vegas rebranded itself as a family place rather than a sexcapade paradise. A new market segment dedicated to kids exploded, with blockbuster teen movies and teen pop stars.

Hillary Clinton's *It Takes a Village* (1996) ensconced child rearing as the foundation of society. Meanwhile, President Clinton coined the term *kinderpolitics*, referring to the strategic practice of tying legislation to the benefit of children in order to get it passed. The first cohort of millennials was born in 1982, which means they were the high school graduating class of 2000, the very beginning of the new millennium. They grew up in the school system to cries of, "You are the future!" in ways that other cohorts before them had not.

Millennials Are Protected

A consequence of having special offspring is that parents must act to protect them. In fact, this is a recurring trait in this generational theory. The first generation in the cycle (or the hero generation, as the theory calls it) is raised in an uncertain and insecure world by pessimistic parents. As Gen Xers came of age and entered the adult world, divorce, crime, sexually transmitted infections (including HIV/AIDS), drug and alcohol use, and teen suicides all increased (National Center for Health Statistics, 1999; Bureau of Justice Statistics, 1999).

It is no wonder that, with this backdrop, parents took on an unprecedented protective role characterized by "Baby on Board" stickers, padded playgrounds, flame-retardant pajamas, child car seats, childproofed dwellings, Amber Alerts, Megan's law, stranger danger campaigns—the list goes on and on. Things once deemed healthy, like playing outside in the sun and riding bikes, are now regarded dangerous without essentials such as sunblock and bike helmets. The genesis of helicopter parents, hovering over their child, must be traced to the early years, or even pregnancy.

Millennials Are Team Oriented

This is the linchpin of the whole theory. The first generation in the cycle is civic and outer oriented. It looks at the failures and hypocrisies of previous generations and decides to join together, roll up its sleeves, and get to work. The way this gets instantiated with millennials is that they are team oriented. As examples of this orientation, consider that they have been brought up with organized play dates. They grew up watching *Barney* on television and internalizing his upbeat message of unconditional love and solving problems together. They are used to school uniforms, which promote group spirit over individualistic self-expression. The rules of the Massachusetts Youth Soccer Association specify that less skilled players will get more playing time than in the past and that parents will cheer for all the players at a game (Jacobi, 1998). Millennials also prefer group outings to one-on-one dates, often arranged through sites like www.datingingroups.com, and they have identified selfishness as the major cause of the country's problems (Roper Starch Worldwide, 1998). This trait is often translated into a pedagogical strategy of using group work whenever possible in hopes that it will increase student motivation through familiarity, but the linkage does not necessarily follow by itself.

Millennials Are Trusting Optimists

According to this position, millennials are trusting in two ways. First, they are trusting of societal institutions. Even when they do not agree with specific rules, they trust that such institutions are necessary and value them. This theory was formulated before the wave of scandals that rocked many institutions, from the Catholic church to government and corporate America, so this aspect can be criticized. Second, and more important, millennials are trusting of themselves and confident about the power of their generation. This is a direct product of the self-esteem movement. Whereas the previous generation looked to the established power elite to find answers to many of the difficult questions facing the nation, millennials see their role as instrumental in solving social and political problems. Involvement in programs like the Peace Corps, Teach for America, and Habitat for Humanity rose dramatically in the millennial years, according to those associations' Web sites. Similarly, involvement in politics increased from previous generations with the 2008 presidential election, with many parents reporting they were influenced in their voting decisions by their millennial children, most notably Caroline

Kennedy, daughter of President Kennedy, who was convinced to endorse President Obama by her millennial daughter (Newsweek, 2008).

Millennials Are Conventional

Compared to previous generations that rebelled to the tune of sex, drugs, and rock 'n' roll, millennials are comfortable with their parents' values. Even when they disagree with them, they understand that the general parental framework is in their best interests. Most relevant to this discussion, millennials have been brought up with zero-tolerance policies in schools (first instituted in Cincinnati in 1991), with behavioral standards about touching, language, and dress that are clearly articulated and strictly enforced. School behavior that would not have been noticed in the early 1980s may now result in suspensions, and what was punishable behavior then may now result in expulsion. Because one of the defining moments of the generation was the Columbine massacre, students appreciate the safety and order brought on by these rules even at the expense of fun, spontaneity, and imagination.

Millennials Are Achieving

This trait is a direct result of educational experiences focused on standardized achievement, especially following federal programs like No Child Left Behind and Race to the Top. Given the emphasis these programs place on standardized test scores, this generation has internalized the value of achievement and results over the learning process itself. This generation has also achieved remarkable feats in its teenage years compared to previous generations. For instance, millennial teenagers have bested adults in prestigious science talent searches (Business Wire, 1999). This obsessive fixation on performance is its own anxiety-producing curse. Rather than being treated as a learning opportunity, failure—or even mere mediocrity—is met with tutoring, coaching, and special instruction, with the result that many students arrive at college without having experienced serious failure.

Millennials Are Pressured

Millennials are achieving, but they are also pressured to achieve. Perfectionist helicopter parents place high expectations on their children. Each level of schooling is a high-stakes gateway to the next one. Good grades are paramount to get into good schools and then good colleges. SAT scores, and even extracurricular activities, are crucial. This translates into highly scheduled and planned lives, with little free time. Tellingly, although this generation is generally healthier than previous ones, stress and anxiety are major health challenges for millennials (National Center for Health Statistics, 1999).

Learning Theory

The question for educators who want to be culturally responsive in their teaching is: how do these generational traits influence learning, readiness for the mental demands of college, and attitudes toward knowledge and performance? In order to answer that question, it is helpful to review the major findings from learning research. In their review of the past fifty years of research into learning, Ambrose et al. (2010) synthesize and organize the major findings in the field into seven interrelated principles. Considered in relation to the seven generational traits of millennials, these seven principles highlight learning issues and suggest educational strategies for both teachers and faculty developers.

Students' Prior Knowledge Can Help or Hinder Learning

Students possess a wealth of prior knowledge and experiences that they bring to bear on new learning experiences, consciously or not, for better or for worse. This repertoire shapes the assessments students make of their learning activities: which ones are boring, interesting, relevant, fun, busywork, memorable, and so on. Of course, millennials' mindscape is different from that of previous generations, as the Beloit list demonstrates, and this gap can cause some activities to fizzle.

STRATEGIES

- Educate yourself about the millennial mind-set and frame of reference.
- Activate students' prior knowledge as it becomes relevant to the educational task.
- Engage the material through multiple modalities whenever appropriate (such as text, videos, and personal narratives).
- Judiciously use technology to increase familiarity and relevance.

How Students Organize Knowledge Influences How They Learn and Apply What They Know

This principle highlights the limitations of our information processing system. In order to retain new knowledge, students need to connect to knowledge already stored in the brain. Unfortunately, the deep processing necessary for deep learning does not occur naturally for students: attention wanes in lectures after fifteen minutes; working memory capacity is limited; students tend to make much fewer connections than experts do, and the ones they make tend to be based on superficial features that do not facilitate problem solving and other applications of knowledge (Bligh, 2000; Chi, Feltovich, & Glaser, 1981). While these limitations have been observed with Xers and boomers first, they sometimes are pinned onto millennials, as if attention spans have somehow shrunk in the past twenty to forty years (Oblinger & Oblinger, 2006).

STRATEGIES

- Alternate lecture, discussion, video clips, and other instruction every fifteen minutes or so to hold attention.
- Use compare-and-contrast exercises, analogies, and student-generated examples to enable more mental connections.
- Use clickers to check quickly if students are building a good knowledge organization.
- Explicitly teach students how to process material with the underlying principles in mind, using key words, heuristics, and guiding questions, for example.

Students' Motivation Determines, Directs, and Sustains What They Do to Learn

Motivation determines behavior, so it is important to unpack the motivations that trigger behaviors conducive to learning. Generally people expend more effort in learning situations where they can clearly see the connection between the task and something they value and expect to be successful at the task (Wigfield & Eccles, 2000).

Because of the focus on and the pressure to achieve, reinforced by current educational practices focused on standardized tests, the cultural value for this generation is shifting to performance and credentialing rather than learning, with the consequence that educators face reduced intrinsic motivation and increased instrumental (extrinsic) motivation. Furthermore, the pressure to achieve fosters a much narrower definition of success. Far from learning opportunities, mistakes are instead viewed as personal failures and something to avoid at all costs, with obvious implications for cheating as well as risk taking, innovating, and experimenting with new ideas or approaches.

STRATEGIES

- Model how you deal with problems, difficulties, or challenges.
- If risk taking and creativity are desired, make them explicit learning objectives, and construct a grading scale that allows for them.
- Discuss the formative value of failure explicitly.

To Develop Mastery, Students Must Acquire Component Skills, Practice Integrating Them, and Know When to Apply What They Have Learned

Learning complex skills such as writing, coding, and painting requires practice at various levels. Each individual subskill must be mastered, put together with the others, and applied appropriately. None of this is surprising, but research findings highlight a potential problem for millennials. Studies have shown that, other than experts who have automated skills to the point that they require minimal cognitive processing, people's performance tends to degrade when they are asked to do more than one task at a time because the integration of different skills and activities is particularly taxing of our cognitive capacities (Wickens, 1991). This runs counter to the millennial cultural ideal of multitasking. Students are used to it and value it, but it does not necessarily mean that they are good at it.

STRATEGIES

- Share with students the research on multitasking.
- Discuss the value of working in distraction-free environments (for example, without Facebook).
- When students complain about grades, include study habits in the conversation.

Goal-Directed Practice Coupled with Targeted Feedback Enhances the Quality of Students' Learning

The best practice opportunities are designed with specific, measurable goals in mind that enable learners to receive frequent, timely, and constructive feedback highlighting points of strengths, areas to improve, and concrete steps to incorporate in future practice in an iterative fashion (Ericsson, Krampe, & Tescher-Romer, 2003).

Conventional wisdom claims that millennial students crave constant feedback, and indeed those special, achieving millennials are used to frequent feedback. Unfortunately, the kind of constructive feedback necessary for learning is often different from the positive reinforcement to which some of them are culturally habituated. Constructive feedback must highlight areas for improvement in addition to offering praise. Furthermore, developmental and motivational psychologists point out that what is praised matters, and compare praising the student's ability to praising the productive effort a student put in that leads to the desired final result. The latter builds productive habits, while the former promotes a self-image that must be continually sustained, with the result that students culturally pressured to do well always may disengage from tasks they consider too challenging (Kamins & Dweck, 1999).

STRATEGIES

- Praise the solid effort behind a student's good performance. In cases of poor performance, bring the conversation back to the kind of effort put into the task.
- Sandwich negative feedback between positive, and give concrete steps students can take next.
- Double-check that the student understands your feedback and does not overlook the negative parts of it.

Students' Current Level of Development Interacts with the Social, Emotional, and Intellectual Climate of the Course to Influence Learning

Learners are always developing and facing specific developmental challenges in each stage of life. In particular, traditional college-age students are developing intellectually. They usually enter college with conceptions of knowledge that are black and white, with teachers having right answers that must be memorized and regurgitated on the test. These students have to move toward conceptions of knowledge where they can compare competing theories on the basis of evidence supporting them and on the consequences of committing to a certain approach (Perry, 1968). These developmental challenges play out in the social environment of the classroom.

Developmental considerations apply to all generations. Every generation of students faces the developmental challenge to adopt a more sophisticated epistemology. Unfortunately, standardized testing procedures that have become routine with millennials foster discomfort with uncertainty and ambiguity rather than movement toward embracing complexity.

One of the cornerstones of further developmental achievements, according to Chickering and Reisser (1993), is the development of confidence, or the sense that an individual can successfully deal with challenges that come her way. On the surface, millennials' cultural optimism looks like this confidence, but the close relationship that protected, sheltered millennial students have with their helicopter parents might mean that for some, this confidence is not grounded in an ability to handle challenges. Helicopter parents may actually delay development of student ability to deal with challenges or difficulties, solve problems, manage time, and make decisions, all of which have negative effects on learning and performance.

STRATEGIES

- Resist a single right answer when multiple answers are appropriate, but make uncertainty safe.
- Demonstrate that personal opinion alone is insufficient, and probe for evidence.
- Identify and challenge inaccurate beliefs about knowledge.
- Set expectations about the instructor's role in the learning process, not as the dispenser of truth but as a facilitator of learning.
- Use the Family Educational Rights and Privacy Act to manage parental interference if it arises. Leverage parental concern into a collaborative partnership to develop independent adults.
- Direct students to institutional resources on broader life skills such as time management and conflict resolution.

To Become Self-Directed Learners, Students Must Learn to Monitor and Adjust Their Approaches to Learning

A strategic awareness of oneself as a learner is just as important as the notions and skills to be learned. In fact, learners have not really taken responsibility for their own learning until they have internalized these strategic habits: making sense of the task ahead of them, examining their own strengths and weaknesses in relation to it, coming up with a good plan, monitoring their own strategies, and reflecting and adjusting as needed when those strategies do not work as planned, possibly starting the cycle over. Moving along the cycle is facilitated by certain beliefs about learning, such as learning is gradual rather than quick or that the mind is like a muscle: it develops with exercise rather than a fixed intellectual ability (Zimmerman, 2001).

Unfortunately, fact-driven educational experiences in high school provide millennials little opportunity to practice higher-level cognitive functions such as planning, monitoring, reflecting, and adjusting as needed. In addition, an honest strategic assessment of one's own strength and weaknesses, necessary for self-directed in learning but hard to do accurately (Dunning, 2005), might be impeded by millennials' cultural optimism and their multitasking history. Millennials are used to working on homework while texting and doing other activities, and this strategy has often been effective in high school, leading them to think they are successful multitaskers. But when the intellectual demands of homework increase in college, their optimistic assumption is likely to prove inadequate.

STRATEGIES

- Give assignments that focus on strategies, planning, or methods of preparation rather than implementation.
- Provide checklists, rubrics, or other heuristics to monitor progress.
- Provide opportunities for guided self-assessment.
- Provide opportunities for guided reflection.

Conclusion

The seven principles of learning apply to all generations: they characterize the constant, common elements of learning rather than the individual differences. However, the cultural traits of each generation influence areas of strength and weakness. For instance, because of the social moment they heralded, boomers emphasized questioning assumptions and finding personal meaning rather then adherence to a specified truth and memorization and regurgitation pedagogies, a facet of the seventh principle of intellectual development. Because this was not part of the traditional values of teaching, it led to conflict with teachers who espoused traditional ways of thinking about teaching.

In this sense, the challenges of teaching millennials are simply the most recent instantiation of this generational dialectic. When millennials become faculty and teach the next generation, that transition will bring its own unique issues. The good news is that viewed through the lens of learning science, the task of teaching millennials becomes more manageable. The sample strategies set out in this chapter are the kind of learning-centered strategies that faculty development has long been advocating. Faculty developers are well equipped to support educators to make teaching more generationally responsive without falling into overgeneralizations and sensationalistic perspectives about current students.

REFERENCES

Ambrose, S., Bridges, M., DiPietro, M., Lovett, M., & Norman, M. (2010). *How learning works: Seven research-based principles for smart teaching.* San Francisco, CA: Jossey-Bass.

Bauerlein, M. (2008). *The dumbest generation: How the digital age stupefies young Americans and jeopardizes our future (or, don't trust anyone under 30).* New York, NY: Tarcher/Penguin.

Beloit College (2011). *The mindset list.* Retrieved from http://www.beloit.edu/mindset/

Bligh, D. (2000). *What's the use of lectures?* San Francisco, CA: Jossey-Bass.

Bureau of Justice Statistics. (1999). *National Crime Victimization Survey.* Washington, DC: Federal Bureau of Investigation.

Business Wire. (1999, March 8). *Fourteen-year-old high school senior from Colorado wins top honors in the Intel science talent search.* Retrieved from http://findarticles.co/p/articles/mi_m0EIN/is_1999_March_9/ai_54047811

Chi, M.T.H., Feltovich, P. J., & Glaser, R. (1981). Categorization and representation of physics problems by experts and novices. *Cognitive Science, 5,* 121–152.

Chickering, A., & Reisser, L. (1993). *Education and identity* (2nd ed.). San Francisco, CA: Jossey-Bass.

Clinton, H. R. (1996). *It takes a village.* New York, NY: Simon & Schuster.

Dunning, D. (2005). *Self-insight: Roadblocks and detours on the path to knowing thyself.* New York, NY: Taylor & Francis.

Ericsson, K. A., Krampe, R. T., & Tescher-Romer, C. (2003). *The role of deliberate practice in the acquisition of expert performance. Psychological Review, 100,* 363–406.

Higher Education Research Institute. (1998). *CIRP Freshman Survey.* Los Angeles: UCLA.

Howe, N., and Strauss, W. (1992). *Generations: The history of America's future, 1584 to 2069.* New York, NY: HarperCollins.

Howe, N., & Strauss, W. (2000). *Millennials rising: The next Great Generation.* New York, NY: Vintage Books.

Jacobi, J. (1998, June 2). PC police are spoiling it for kids who play soccer. *Boston Globe*, p. A19.

Kamins, M., & Dweck, C. (1999). Person versus process praise and criticism: Implications for contingent self-worth and coping. *Developmental Psychology, 35*(3), 835–847.

Marías, J. (1976). *Generations: A historical method.* Auburn: University of Alabama Press.

National Center for Health Statistics. (1999). *National Vital Statistics Report.* Atlanta, GA: Centers for Disease Control.

Newsweek. (2008, January 30). *Why Caroline backed Obama.* Retrieved from http://www.newsweek.com/2008/01/29/why-caroline-backed-obama.html

Oblinger, D., & Oblinger, J. (Eds.). (2006). *Educating the Net generation.* Washington, DC: EDUCAUSE. Retrieved from www.educause.edu/educatingthenetgen/

Perry, W. (1968). *Forms of intellectual and ethical development in the college years: A scheme.* New York, NY: Holt.

Prensky, M. (2001). *Digital natives, digital immigrants. On the Horizon, 9*(5), 1–6.

Roper Starch Worldwide. (1998). *The PRIMEDIA/Roper national youth opinion survey.* Harrison, NY: Author.

Strauss, W., & Howe, N. (2003). *Millennials go to college: Strategies for a new generation on campus.* Washington, DC: American Association of Collegiate Registrars.

Twenge, J. (2007). *Generation me: Why today's young Americans are more confident, assertive, entitled—and more miserable than ever before.* New York, NY: Free Press.

Wickens, C. D. (1991). Processing resources and attention. In D. L. Damos (Ed.), *Multiple task performance* (pp. 3–34). London: Taylor & Francis.

Wigfield, A., & Eccles, J. (2000) Expectancy-value theory of achievement motivation. *Contemporary Educational Psychology, 25*, 68–81.

Zimmerman, B. J. (2001) Theories of self-regulated learning and academic achievement: An overview and analysis. In B. J. Zimmerman & D. H. Schunk (Eds.), *Self-regulated learning and academic achievement* (2nd ed., pp. 1–38). Mahwah, NJ: Erlbaum.

12

CONTEMPLATIVE PEDAGOGY

THE SPECIAL ROLE OF TEACHING AND LEARNING CENTERS

Daniel Barbezat
Amherst College and Contemplative Mind in Society

Allison Pingree
Harvard University

We provide an overview of the definition, intention, and benefits from contemplative exercises, showing how these practices can build and sustain attention, deepen understanding of the material presented, support and increase connection and interrelatedness, and inspire inquiry and insight. Following that, we provide approaches to fostering these of sorts of practices through university teaching and learning centers. We also provide a cautionary note on possible problems with this approach. We hope that these descriptions will stimulate interest and inquiry into contemplative/introspective exercises and enable further investigation and discovery.

In our courses, we try to teach our students to be independent thinkers. We endeavor to teach the whole person, with an intention to go beyond the mere transference of facts and theories. While concentrating on these holistic goals, we also want to challenge and develop students' analytical problem-solving skills, as well as provide careful explanations of complicated material. We want to create the opportunity for our students to engage with material so that they recognize and apply its relevance to their own lives, deeply feeling and experiencing themselves within their education. In other words, while fostering their knowledge base and analytical abilities, we want to present material in a way that supports students in having their own agency so that the material is not simply a set of intellectual hoops for them to jump through but active opportunities for them to find meaning and personal and intellectual development.

This is no easy task. Focusing on our students' agency does not mean that our courses should or even could be equal collaborations. No matter what we do to create such an environment, we remain their leaders and teachers. We are the architects of the syllabi and make informed evaluations of their work. Negotiating this divide—wanting to engage with students rather than talk at them, while knowing that we remain their teachers—is an extremely difficult but worthwhile process. In traversing these two poles, we often err on the side of rigid structure. In much of formal education, we stress the abstract and conceptual; indeed, learning requires this powerful form of thinking. However, we have often stressed this form of learning to the exclusion of personal reflection and integration. It is understandable how this happens; developing careful discursive, analytical thought is certainly one of the hallmarks of a good education. However, creative, synthetic thinking requires more than this; it requires a sort of holistic engagement and attention that is especially fostered by students' finding themselves in the material. The one aspect of their learning for which students are sovereign is the awareness of their experience and their own thoughts and reactions to the material covered in the course.

This concentration on outcomes and narrow information handling has it costs. In her book *Mindfulness* (1989), Ellen Langer writes that perhaps one of the reasons that we become "mindless" is the form of our early education. "From kindergarten on," she writes, "the focus of schooling is usually goals rather than on the process by which they are achieved. This single-minded pursuit of one outcome or another, from tying shoelaces to getting into college, makes it difficult to have a mindful attitude toward life. Questions of 'Can I?' or 'What if I can't do it?' are likely to predominate, creating an anxious preoccupation with success or failure rather than on drawing on the child's natural, exuberant desire to explore" (pp. 33–34). Indeed, the history of educational reform is full of examples of the responses to the heavy costs of this sort of concentration.

These responses have formed a rich tradition of integrative and experiential education that has developed over time in many ways.

Researchers and educators have pursued the objective of creating learning environments that are rich and deeply focused on the relationship of the student to what she or he is learning, as well as the interrelatedness of personal relationships to the rest of the world. We have found that contemplative practices respond powerfully to these challenges. These practices can provide an environment that is inclusive of the increasing diversity of our students and a modality that is particularly effectively presented to campuses through teaching and learning centers (TLCs). While the specific structures of contemplative practices vary greatly, at the heart of them all is a sincere intent to integrate students' own rich experience into their learning. As B. Alan Wallace (2007) points out, *contemplation* is derived from the Greek word *theoria*. It refers to a "total devotion to revealing, clarifying and making manifest the nature of reality" (p. 1). By leading our students through introspective exercises, the reality they are revealing is their own internal experience of the material covered in our courses.

To be sure, others have thought about this more expansive approach to teaching. For example, the famous work of John Dewey and Jean Piaget and the radical reframing of education by Paolo Freire all have experiential components at the heart of their systems (Dewey, 1986; Freire, 1970; Piaget, 1973). In fact, whole educational systems have been built around experience. For example, the experiential learning theory system of Daniel Kolb posits two sets of related inquiries: concrete experience and abstract conceptualization, on the one hand, and reflective observation and active experimentation on the other. Indeed, the advocates of the integrative education movement, influenced by the systems of thinkers like Ken Wilbur and Sri Auronbindo, call for the active attention on combining domains of experience and knowing into learning (see, for example, Awbrey, 2006). Thus, our focus on contemplative and introspective practices is not unknown in academia; what distinguishes the experience and integration discussed here is that "experience" is focused on students' introspection and their cultivation of awareness of themselves and their relationship to others. The exercises are relatively simple and mainly conducted in their own minds, relating directly to their personal experience discovered through attention and awareness, yet these private investigations yield increased empathy with others and a deeper sense of connection around them (Birnie, Speca, & Carlson, 2010).

Formally legitimizing their experiences changes students' relationship to the material being covered. In much of formal education, students are actively dissuaded from finding themselves in what they are studying. All too often, students nervously ask whether they may use "I" in their papers. A direct inquiry brought about through their introspection validates and deepens their understanding of both themselves and the material covered. In this way, students not only more richly understand the material, but they retain it more effectively since they have a personal context in which to frame it. There need not be direct, clumsy questions about how the material students are learning fits "into the real world" or is in some way relevant to their lives. The presentation of the material can be approached in a manner in which students can directly see its impact on their lives; they themselves discover the fit. This builds capacity, deepens understanding, generates compassion, and initiates an inquiry into their human nature.

Remarkably, these exercises can be used effectively throughout the curriculum: in sciences, like physics, chemistry, and neuroscience; in social sciences, like sociology, economics, history, and psychology; in humanities such as art history, English, and philosophy; and in professional schools like nursing, social work, architecture, business, law, and medicine. Their exact use changes from discipline to discipline, but as we shall see, the diverse practices are deeply connected. TLCs, with their transdisciplinary connections throughout higher education, are perfect vehicles for disseminating information about these practices and helping to create working groups of interested faculty. In addition, once the contemplative practices are introduced, the centers are uniquely placed to gather and analyze data on student outcomes from these practices.

In this chapter, we provide an overview of the definition, intention, and benefits from contemplative exercises. Following that, we provide approaches to fostering these sorts of practices through university teaching and learning centers, as well as cautionary notes on using these practices. We hope that these descriptions will stimulate interest and inquiry into contemplative and introspective exercises and enable further discovery.

Introspective and Contemplative Practices

Contemplative pedagogy uses forms of introspection and reflection allowing students the opportunity to focus internally and find more of themselves in their courses. The types of contemplation are varied, from guided introspective exercises to open-ended *lectio divina* ("divine reading") to simple moments of quiet, as are the ways in which the practices are integrated into classrooms. There is no easy way to summarize all the types of practices available. However, what unites them all is a focus on personal connection and awareness, leading to some insight.

As an introduction, we can present an overview using Figure 12.1, the tree of contemplative practices presented by the Center for Contemplative Mind in Society. This is not an exhaustive summary, but it does give an excellent overview of the basic categories of practices and types of practice within each.

Figure 12.1. The Tree of Contemplative Practices.

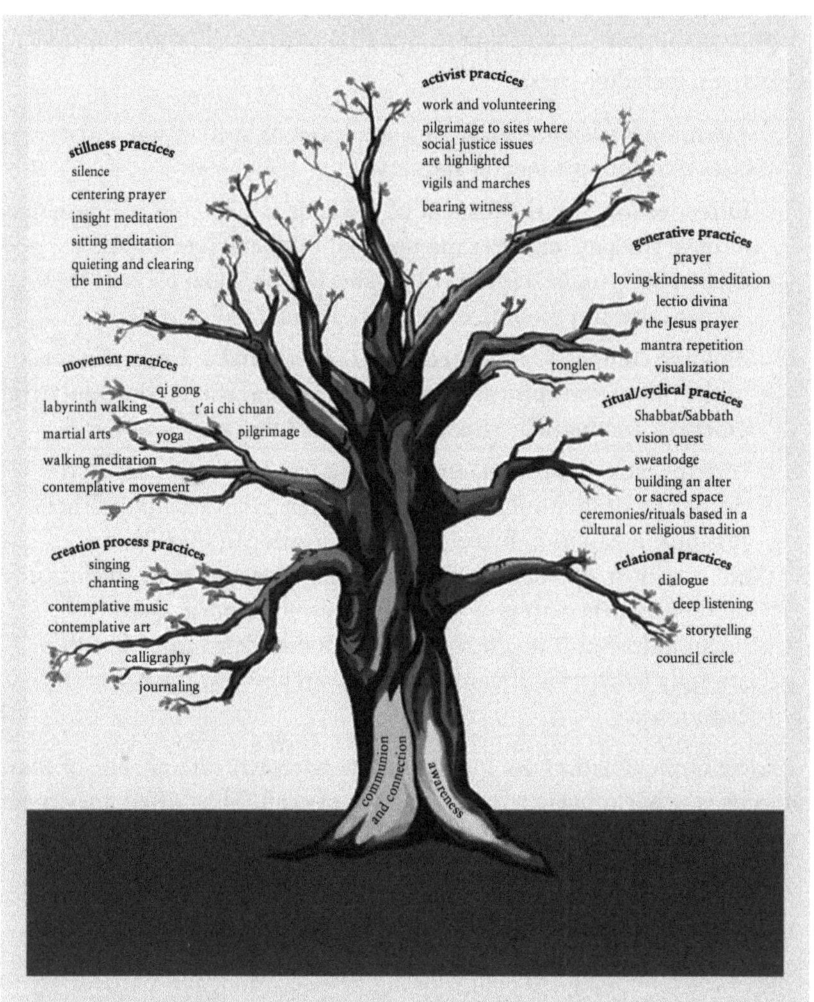

Reprinted by permission of The Center for Contemplative Practices (www.contemplativemind.org).

Of course, practices from different categories can also be combined; for example, meditation can be combined with freewriting or journaling, or a movement exercise can be combined with the intentions of activist activities. The exact form of the practices introduced depends on the context, intent, and capabilities of the facilitator. You might already be familiar with practices that combine some form of personal reflection or contemplation that are not listed on the tree. We do not intend the illustration to be exhaustive; rather, we hope that it may demonstrate the wide variation in practice and perhaps give you new ideas about practices that you might want to learn and introduce.

Classroom introspective and contemplative exercises have a variety of objectives, including these:

- Attention building, mainly through focusing meditation and exercises that support mental stability.
- Introspection into the content of the course. Exercises are designed to have students discover the material in themselves and thus deepen their understanding of it. This is a personal form of the deeper critical reasoning in more traditional pedagogy.
- Building compassion, connection to others, and a deepening sense of the moral and spiritual aspect of their education (contemplative practices are uniquely situated to support this sort of inquiry).
- Perhaps most important, an invitation to begin an inquiry into the nature of their minds, selves, and their relationship to others. A simple meditation focusing on the breath can quickly lead to an inquiry as to where these intervening thoughts come from, an inquiry into the nature of our self-determination, and so forth. It can indeed be a profound moment for students to realize they are fully in control of neither their awareness nor their overall experience.

Some of the practices are focused rather narrowly on only one of these objectives, while others are combinations of each. Most often, they focus on one, but on reflection, they naturally open into the others.

Attention and Analytical Problem Solving

One of the more vaunted claims of higher education, and particularly of liberal arts colleges, is that we teach students "how to think." But what does this actually mean? Surely our students can think, so in what sense do they need to be taught to think? This response could mean that we aid them in developing their analytical problem-solving skills and their ability to creatively integrate different aspects of situations. Certainly one of the aspects of contemplative exercises is to develop these skills.

A key element in solving any problem is attention. Focus is clearly required in any multistage problem. Anyone who has ever attempted to solve complex problems knows the intense concentration and attention it requires. Contemplative exercises, many of them directly aimed at cultivating attention, hone this skill. Many neuroscience studies have documented the increase in attention skills from meditation practice. (For an overview, see Raffone & Srinivasan, 2010.) Of course, concentration is developed by any concerted effort. Musicians, dancers, and athletes, for example, all acquire high levels of concentration. However, problem solving also often requires thinking about a problem from various angles, so while attention is important, so is the ability to let go of a direction that is not working while focusing on (but not clinging to) another. Thus, a clear but not rigid attention is required to solve more open-ended insight problems, which require a moment of discovery.

Insight problems require thinking in different ways. Suppose you were to be asked to describe how to throw a ball so that it would travel a short distance, come to a complete stop, and then reverse itself. You are not allowed to bounce it off any surface or tie anything to it. As long as you think of the ball moving horizontally, you will not be able to describe the motion. Being keenly aware of the directions, however, you note that nothing in the problem states in which direction the ball should go. With this realization, you can think outside the constraint of throwing a ball as you normally do. In fact, if you think about how objects suspend for a moment when thrown up, you realize that throwing the ball up in the air would cause it to rise, stop, and then reverse. Psychologists M. Murray and R. Byrne (2005) argue that in order to solve these sorts of problems, people must have the capacity to hold different alternatives, along with the ability to switch their attention between alternative possibilities. These abilities are especially refined and honed by contemplative practices.

Logical analytical modes of thinking are just one aspect of our broad abilities. For many years, it was taken for granted that each person had a given level of intelligence, often referred to as the index *g* that simply determined cognitive ability. Teachers could support students in living up to the potential of their given level of intelligence, but essentially the die was cast. This view has come under serious criticism for a variety of reasons. First, the notion that some single metric can capture a meaningful notion of intelligence does not seem possible. As Howard Gardner, Robert

Sternberg, David Perkins, and others have argued, humans have different aspects of intelligence, most prominently captured by Gardner's (2004) idea of multiple intelligences. Second, whatever the intelligence might be, the notion that it is fixed within very tight bounds for all time has also shown to be incorrect. Stephen Jay Gould, in *The Mismeasurement of Man* (1996), argues convincingly that such a static metric does not capture how our abilities change over time. Indeed, in its rather conservative review of this issue, the task force designated by the American Psychological Association concluded that "a given person's intellectual performance will vary on different occasions, in different domains" (p. 77).

Robert Sternberg's *Beyond IQ: A Triarchic Theory of Human Intelligence* (1985) divides intelligence into three areas: analytical, creative, and practical. The analytical aspect is supported through contemplative exercises through the stabilization of the mind and the increased ability to focus that it supports. Logical problem solving involves clear, focused linear thinking, requiring the ability to concentrate and not be driven off-track by any distraction. Yet it also requires being open to inspiration and intuition. Creative aspects of problem solving are more synthetic, requiring the awareness of many possible solution avenues. Complex problems demand being able to see outside the constraints of strong initial attempts or useful heuristics that do not solve the actual, current problem. Founder of analytical philosophy Alfred North Whitehead famously pronounced, "Fools act on imagination without knowledge; pedants act on knowledge without imagination. The task of a university is to weld together imagination and experience" (1929, p. 93). Being aware of when to use a quick rule and when not to use such a rule is the first step in solving complex problems. Beyond that, learning not only how to focus but on what to focus is the essence of effective problem solving.

Deeper Understanding

Beyond cognitive skills, contemplative and introspective exercises can deepen students' understanding of the material presented. A practice like *lectio divina*, for example, provides students the opportunity to sink into their experience of reading, a rare chance given the amount of reading they are daily assigned. In chemistry courses, for example, Michelle Francl of Bryn Mawr College allows students an extended time simply beholding the figures of electron wave functions prior to discussing them. Students are given the chance to realize the impact of the words or graphs for themselves and can better understand the material from a clearer sense of their own experience. Students report that they can see the regular, successive amplitude changes themselves and thus have a deeper connection to Bohr's correspondence principle that mathematically defines these changes.

No longer are these texts or figures something abstract or foreign to students; they are allowed the time to discern first what they see in them prior to examining them thoroughly in the course. In my economics classes, I (D.B.) provide students with the opportunity to experience directly the assumptions of the abstract models they are studying. Rather than give them only the definition and explanation of the Easterlin paradox or the relative income hypothesis, students are given a chance to examine their personal responses to exercises that have them experience and reflect on relative gains or losses and how they actually select to whom they compare themselves. In this way, they come to realize the importance of context and choice in matters of positional changes and have a deeper understanding of the theoretical literature. Carefully designed practices presented with care can locate the students directly in their own learning like no other practice we know, allowing students direct access to the material, which makes it more meaningful and understandable.

Connection

This third area—emotional regulation and intra- and interpersonal connection—is especially relevant for the application of contemplative exercises. Each student brings her or his own approach to the material, and it is often difficult to discern just how to reach students and how to treat them fairly because of this. In *Frames of Mind* (2004), Howard Gardner goes beyond logical-mathematical and linguistic modes of knowing and discusses others, like spatial, musical, kinesthetic, and "interpersonal" and "intrapersonal" intelligences. These last two are essential forms for anyone who must navigate personal meaning and the connection to others.

In a related vein, Daniel Goleman has written about his idea of emotional intelligence, and both Antonio Damasio (2000) and R. B. Zajonc (1980) have shown the central aspect of emotion in the process of decision making. Regardless of the nuances between these views, an increasing amount of evidence has shown that emotional awareness and regulation are essential for well-being and positive decision making. A whole host of teaching and learning methods has been developed out of these ideas, with various forms of teaching presentations and assessments designed to work with students' varying abilities. Mary Helen Immordino-Yang of the University of California's Rossier School of

Education has shown that contemplative exercises that focus on compassion and social connectivity are especially effective in this regard (see, for example, Immordino-Yang & Damasio, 2008).

Practical problems and their solutions require personal involvement and what Sternberg calls "action-oriented knowledge, acquired without the direct help from others, that allows individuals to achieve goals they personally value" (Neisser et al., 1996, p. 79). In our experience, contemplative practices can be especially powerful in supporting this sort of inquiry. Students directly engage with experienced aspects of what they are learning through the exercises and thereby glean meaning in a very practical manner. While all sorts of experiential learning have this quality, contemplative exercises have the special attribute that students do not need to leave the classroom to complete them and can replicate them easily on their own. The point here is not whether this is actually a specific form of intelligence but that broad problem solving requires this sort of thinking.

Personal Meaning

So while these three practices can hone attention, stimulate a deeper understanding of the material, and develop social connectivity, they also allow students to explore personal meaning, which might be the least well defined yet perhaps the most important. As noted in a study on spirituality in higher education conducted by Alexander and Helen Austin at UCLA's Higher Education Research Institute, students yearn for support in their search for personal meaning:

> More than two-thirds (69%) consider it "essential" or "very important" that their college enhance their self-understanding and a similar proportion (67%) rate highly the role they want their college to play in developing their personal values. Nearly half (48%) also say it is "essential" or "very important" that colleges encourage their personal expression of spirituality [Parker & Zajonc, 2010, p. 117].

Although our students might call for it, we know that we are on thin ice in the area of morality and spirituality within the classroom. It is not without reason that professors are skeptical about the introduction of personal questions of spirituality and moral meaning in their teaching. Although we certainly agree that caution is appropriate, we also believe that we can support students in examining these issues for themselves. Because of the deeply personal nature of the exercises, they provide a framework for our students to begin to open to their own sense of meaning—first to the material we are covering in the class and then to a broader and deeper sense of how their learning fits into the fabric of their lives. Meditation and introspection provide effective means for our students to become aware of their emotions and reactions, while at the same time helping clarify what is personally most important to them. For effective decision making, both of these qualities must be developed.

While we provide information and help students modify behavior, we do very little to help them discover and develop their deepest purpose. How can they decide without examining what truly matters to them? It is no wonder that students are calling out for this opportunity. It does not require much to engender this form of inquiry. For example, a simple exercise in which students are asked to focus on their breath can stimulate significant insights. When students realize that although they are committed to focusing on their breath and yet they somehow wind up thinking about this or that, they start to question the nature of their thinking. In what sense are these rising thoughts theirs? This quite naturally leads them to thinking about their wanting. If their thinking seems to come out of nowhere and does not seem to really be theirs, then if their desires arise in a similar fashion, are they really their desires? What sense does it make, then, to attempt to satisfy these wants even though they arise like the thoughts, seemingly from nowhere? These questions provide an opportunity for students to think deeply about the fundamental premise of economics: that consumers achieve well-being by attempting to satisfy their wants. This inquiry is initiated from within, from a personal insight, and so has far greater valence than a prompt from someone else.

The Role of Teaching and Learning Centers

Given the strong impact of contemplative practices on learning, TLCs can play an important role in supporting such practices. Dedicated to enhancing student learning on their campuses, TLCs provide key support across the curriculum and coordinate teaching and research networks across entire institutions. Thus, contemplative pedagogy programs have been developed successfully by and through TLCs, often in the form of faculty working groups. In addition to providing infrastructure, TLCs can offer clarity and legitimacy to forms of instruction and learning that might be regarded with skepticism if individual faculty members promoted them. Isolated practitioners or even separated small groups using contemplative pedagogy can find it very hard to coordinate across campuses and convince deans or curriculum review boards to approve courses. The unique position of TLCs thus enables them to foster interdisciplinary coordination and work to overcome hostility or misunderstandings of these sorts of practices. Finally, TLCs often have the resources to study the impact of contemplative practices. Evaluative research on contemplative practices is currently underdeveloped and is needed to provide better outcome measures to legitimate teaching methods and test whether all types of students are equally benefiting from these practices.

In order to capitalize on the strengths of TLCs, the Center for Contemplative Mind in Society is hosting an initiative exploring ways in which college and university TLCs can introduce and support contemplative pedagogy within courses on their respective campuses. Over the past year, representatives of the center have been meeting with TLCs and giving workshops and lectures in order to showcase contemplative pedagogy. In September 2011, it hosted a planning workshop with a dozen leaders of TLCs and the leadership of POD. The center hopes to increase its consultation with TLCs across the country and develop a strategic plan that could include seed grants for curricular initiatives, increased inter- and intracampus networking, and collaboration and consultation to demonstrate and explain the role of contemplative practices in teaching.

Already several centers have developed programs incorporating contemplative practices. The Teaching Resource Center at the University of Virginia, the University of Colorado, and Vanderbilt University, for example, all have established resources. Vanderbilt's Center for Teaching's innovations over the past few years include a contemplative pedagogy working group, comprising faculty and graduate students from across the university; a Web-based teaching guide on contemplative pedagogy (http://cft.vanderbilt.edu/teaching-guides/teaching-activities/contemplative-pedagogy/); and a video, *Fostering Attention*, highlighting the ways in which Vanderbilt faculty have integrated contemplative practices into their classrooms (http://youtube/wqRGJhW5wZE). We hope that increasing collaboration can extend and deepen the use of these practices across higher education and see the key role that TLCs can play in this process.

Cautionary Tales

William James (1890) recognized both the appeal and problem of an integrated, contemplative pedagogy:

> Whether the attention come by grace of genius or by dint of will, the longer one does attend to a topic the more mastery of it one has. And the faculty of voluntarily bringing back a wandering attention,

> over and over again, is the very root of judgment, character and will. No one is *compos sui* if he has it not. An education which should improve this faculty would be the education *par excellence* [p. 424].

James focuses here on only on attention, describing its benefits as making us perceive, conceive, distinguish, remember, and react better than we would otherwise. James has been seen as a champion of the use of contemplative practices. However, he was always the careful thinker and cautions against excessive optimism. He continues: "But it is easier to define this ideal than to give practical directions for bring it about." He does not see introspection as a panacea, and neither do we. James continues to caution against the idea that focused awareness and introspection can cure problems in observation and insight:

> But, since the rest of this volume will be little more than a collection of illustrations of the difficulty of discovering by direct introspection exactly what our feelings and their relations are, we need not anticipate our own future details, but just state our general conclusion that *introspection is difficult and fallible; and that the difficulty is simply that of all observation of whatever kind* [italics in original; p. 424].

While contemplative exercises provide another means for students to explore themselves and the material of our courses, they are by no means perfect or intended to replace other powerful means of teaching. Rather, they are powerful complements to instruction across the curriculum.

Because of the subtle difficulties of the practices, teachers wanting to employ them must have experience with them. These are not modes that can easily be taught in a single workshop; without a committed sense of what it is actually like to engage in these types of exercises, instructors will not be able to guide or respond to them. Their introduction and support should be accompanied by resources for faculty to engage in the practices themselves prior to presenting them to students. In addition, since these types of practices are often mistaken for religious practices, care must be given to ensure the greatest inclusive environment. Providing a bit of background to let students know that these practices are known across cultures all over the world allows access to students from all backgrounds. In addition, it is essential that students know that they do not need to adopt any particular beliefs in order to engage in the exercises; the practices are done more in the spirit of lab exercises, allowing students to experience the material and gain insight without any doctrinal position required. Finally, students come to our classrooms from many backgrounds. It is important that the practices be framed so that we foster inclusion. Sometimes, though, this can be easily overlooked. For example, students who have felt silenced in their lives might bristle at the command to close their eyes and be silent; framing silence by an introduction emphasizing that the exercise allows more of the students to be fully engaged in the classroom. Learning about our students' backgrounds is important as we introduce the practices because we can easily alienate students without any intention or awareness of doing so.

Conclusion

Contemplative and introspective modes of learning have been an exciting development over the past decade. Placing students in the heart of their education fosters a rich environment for learning and provides the opportunity for students to foster attention, deepen their understanding of their studies, engender richer relationships with themselves and others, and stimulate profound inquiries into the nature of themselves and the world around them. We see that this important work can be greatly fostered by the work of teaching and learning centers and look forward to continued progress and cooperation in the future.

RESOURCES

Awbrey, S. M. (2006). *Integrative learning and action: A call to wholeness.* New York, NY: Peter Lang.

Birnie, K., Speca, M., & Carlson, L. E. (2010). Exploring self-compassion and empathy in the context of mindfulness-based stress reduction (MBSR). *Stress and Health, 26*(5), 359–371. doi:10.1002/smi.1305

Damasio, A. (2000). *Descartes' error: Emotion, reason and the human brain.* New York, NY: Penguin Books.

Dewey, J. (1986). Experience and education. *Educational Forum, 50*(3), 241–252. doi:10.1080/00131728609335764.

Freire, P. (1970). *Pedagogy of the oppressed.* New York, NY: Continuum.

Gardner, H. (2004). *Frames of mind: The theory of multiple intelligences.* New York, NY: Basic Books.

Gould, S. J. (1996). *The mismeasurement of man.* New York, NY: Norton.

Immordino-Yang, M. H., & Damasio, A. (2008). We feel, therefore we learn: The relevance of affective and social neuroscience to education. In M. H. Immordino-Yang (Ed.), *The Jossey-Bass reader on the brain and learning* (pp. 183–198). San Francisco, CA: Jossey-Bass.

James, W. (1890). *The principles of psychology.* New York, NY: Holt.

Langer, E. J. (1989). *Mindfulness.* Cambridge, MA: Da Capo Press.

Murray, M., & Byrne, R. (2005, July). Attention and working memory in insight problem solving. In *Proceedings of the Cognitive Science Society* (pp. 1571–1575). Austin, TX: Cognitive Science Society.

Neisser, U., Boodoo, G., Bouchard, T. J., Boykin, A. W., Brody, N., Ceci, S. J., . . . Urbina, S. Intelligence: Knowns and unknowns. *American Psychologist, 51*(2), 77–101.

Parker, P., & Zajonc, A. (2010). *The heart of higher education: A call to renewal.* San Francisco, CA: Jossey-Bass.

Piaget, J. (1973). *To understand is to invent: The future of education.* New York, NY: Grossman.

Raffone, A., & Srinivasan, N. (2010). The exploration of meditation in the neuroscience of attention and consciousness. *Cognitive Processing, 11*(1), 1–7.

Sternberg, R. J. (1985). *Beyond IQ: A triarchic theory of human intelligence.* Cambridge UK: Cambridge University Press.

Wallace, B. A. (2007). *Contemplative science: Where Buddhism and neuroscience converge.* New York, NY: Columbia University Press.

Whitehead, A. N. (1929). *The aims of education.* New York, NY: Free Press.

Zajonc, R. B. (1980). Feeling and thinking: Preferences need no inferences. *American Psychologist, 35*(2), 151–175.

PART FIVE

ASSESSING STUDENT LEARNING

13

A COMPARISON OF FACULTY AND STUDENT PERSPECTIVES ON COURSE EVALUATION TERMINOLOGY

Carol Lauer
Rollins College

Students completed a questionnaire on the meanings of several terms commonly used in narrative course evaluation forms, and instructors completed a similar form asking them what they believed students meant by these same words. Both groups produced complex and multifaceted definitions for the terms "not fair," "professional," "not organized," "challenging," and "not respectful." Instructors were frequently incorrect in inferring common student definitions. If instructors misjudge students' meanings, how useful are evaluation forms for evaluative or developmental purposes? Faculty peer review of class meetings and course materials can help provide the necessary filter for interpreting evaluation comments.

o

I once believed that narrative comments on course evaluation forms were straightforward and useful. Then I had the opportunity, as a department chair and as a member of a collegewide tenure and evaluation committee, to read literally thousands of course evaluations for faculty at all stages of their careers.

At the same time, I examined syllabi and other course materials for the faculty under review and attended a sampling of their classes. I quickly discovered that narrative comments on student evaluations forms were far from straightforward and could not be easily connected with course materials and my class observations. Because student course evaluations are frequently used for evaluative and developmental purposes, this would appear unwise without some decoding process if they are as cryptic as my experience suggests.

While a great deal of research has been done on the problems of the numerical rating systems in course evaluations (Benton & Cashin, 2012; Gray & Bergmann, 2003; Laube, Massoni, Sprague, & Ferber, 2007; Pounder, 2007), a dearth of information exists on how to interpret student comments. This study examined what students at a single institution meant when they used several commonly seen terms in narrative sections of evaluation forms and what faculty believed students meant by these terms.

The Literature on Limitations of Student Course Evaluations

Most institutions use evaluations with numbered scales (Laube et al., 2007) since the ratings are easily summarized and compared. This practice continues to grow despite studies that show ratings can be biased by a variety of factors that have nothing to do with good classroom practices and resultant student achievement (Gray & Bergmann, 2003; Pounder, 2007).

Pounder (2007) summarized a wide range of studies demonstrating that class size, age, experience, and gender of instructors have an impact on numeric scores on course evaluations. Since instructors have no control over any of these factors, they provide few useful insights for developmental or evaluative purposes. Evaluations may even punish instructors for policies that other faculty would view as appropriate and even exemplary. For example, instructors whom students view as giving too much work and grading harshly are rated lower than their less demanding peers (Laube et al., 2007). The literature also documents a host of seemingly random effects that can influence evaluation results. When expected grades were low, students gave lower ratings to female instructors than to male instructors (Laube et al., 2007). Faculty who bring food to class are rated higher than those who do not (Pounder 2007). Better-looking instructors get higher ratings (Gray & Bergmann, 2003). Faculty in the arts and humanities are rated as more effective teachers than those in more quantitative fields like economics, math, and physics (Pounder, 2007).

Other findings bring into question the seriousness with which students fill out their evaluations. Beyers (2008) argued that students pick a number they feel represents their instructor's level of achievement and use it repeatedly regardless of the question posed. Beyers based this conclusion on observations in large lecture halls packed with students filling out course evaluation forms. He also conducted a personal experiment where he returned every class assignment at the class meeting immediately following its submission, and yet only five of his thirty-nine students give him the highest numerical rating for "returned materials promptly." Rating instructors is clearly not a straightforward enterprise. Benton and Cashin's (2012) summary of forty years of research on student ratings is also revealing in the number of disagreements and alternative hypotheses presented. They suggest the use of "multiple sources of information" and the careful interpretation of results (p. 13).

Although these studies focus on numbered scale evaluations, my own reading of course evaluation forms suggests that similar biases affect narrative comments. For example, arts and humanities professors are more likely to receive superlative comments on their forms than are instructors in other disciplines, and the descriptors used for female faculty are likely to be different and, under some circumstances, more negative than those used for males. While the existing literature can help faculty and their evaluators deconstruct student comments in the light of these likely biases, what about the issue of the terms used to describe instructors? Can we assume they have a set of standard meanings that students and instructors share? Could faculty be misinterpreting these terms?

The Study

Methods

My institution uses a narrative evaluation form as well as a numerical ratings scheme for student course evaluations. The narrative form includes open-ended questions like: "What, if anything, could have been changed about this course to improve your learning experience?" "What were the major strengths and weaknesses of the instructor?" An initial review of the comments on forms for several hundred classes and close to seventy instructors, along with reviews of syllabi, other course materials, and classroom visits, suggested that some commonly used terms must have more than one meaning. An instructor with a syllabus that includes few specifics and a nonstructured approach to classroom discussions might be labeled as disorganized, but so might an instructor with a clear and detailed syllabus and a highly structured classroom. An instructor who uses a detailed rubric for grading might be called unfair in grading practices.

The study presented here examined whether a set of commonly used terms means different things to different students and whether a single term could have multiple meanings for a student. A second line of inquiry was whether faculty accurately predicted student meanings for this set of terms and if they saw these terms as having single or multiple meanings. Finally examined are faculty and student agreement between and among them about whether the attributes described are important.

Research Design

A set of five common terms was culled from narrative comments on student course evaluations for use in a survey of students and faculty at a medium-sized liberal arts college: *not fair, professional, not organized, challenging,* and *not respectful.* Students used these terms frequently, yet interpreting what they meant continually challenged the collegewide tenure and promotion committee. Questionnaires about the meanings of the terms were developed for a nonrandom sample of students and faculty and were approved by the college's institutional review board. The questionnaires are reproduced in Exhibits 13.1 and 13.2. Both negative and positive terms were presented to avoid the appearance of bias toward a particular view of evaluation comments.

Exhibit 13.1. Student Questionnaire.

Year: Please circle one Freshman Sophomore Junior Senior
Gender: Please circle one Male Female
Major:
What do the following phrases from course evaluation forms mean to you? The instructor is: Not fair Professional Not organized Challenging Not respectful
Are any of these critical to the success of a course? If so, which ones?

13.2. Faculty Questionnaire.

Rank: Please circle one Instructor   Assistant Professor   Associate Professor   Full Professor
Gender: Please circle one Male   Female
Division: Please circle one Arts   Humanities   Social Sciences   Science and Mathematics
What do the following phrases from course evaluation forms mean to you? That is, what do you think students are trying to convey when they use these phrases. The instructor is: Not fair Professional Not organized Challenging Not respectful
Are any of these critical to the success of a course? If so, which ones?

Student questionnaires were handed out during spring semester so that all students had had some experience filling out the college's standard course evaluation forms during the fall. Seven instructors representing a variety of disciplines and all four undergraduate divisions (Arts, Humanities, Science and Mathematics, and Social Sciences) handed out and collected the anonymous forms during their own class sessions. The courses involved from first year to senior level. Faculty questionnaires, which were also anonymous, were passed out during several faculty meetings and collected by the end of the meetings. These meetings included faculty representing all undergraduate divisions and departments.

Of the 185 students who completed the questionnaire, 68 percent were female and 32 percent were male; 32 percent of them were first-year students, 20 percent sophomores, 20 percent juniors, 23 percent seniors, and the rest were of unknown status. They were majors in every undergraduate division.

The 45 faculty members who responded were 53 percent female and 44 percent male, with the rest not reporting gender. They represented every rank, with 9 percent of them holding the rank of instructor, 35 percent assistant professor, 27 percent associate professor, and 29 percent full professor. The rest did not indicate rank. Respondents came from all four undergraduate divisions.

Data Analysis

I did all coding. The open-ended portions of the questionnaires were coded for key word phrases (Bernard, 2011). The coding process at this level was frequently straightforward since many respondents used the same terminology. A single request for a definition on the questionnaire frequently produced multiple phrases in response, and each was coded independently so that one answer might generate several entries for the coding book. Once all the questionnaires had been coded, key word phrases were collapsed into broader thematic categories using an open coding system. That is, the themes emerged from the data (Bernard, 2011).

To preserve the diversity of answers, thematic categories were kept fairly narrow. For example, "plays favorites," one of the themes listed for the term *unfair,* was mentioned in 59 of the 119 student responses in this category. The variant phrase "unequal treatment of students" appeared 15 times, and "biased toward certain students" appeared 7 times. Since all these phrases concerned differential treatment of students, they were considered part of a single theme. However, not all coding was this simple. The theme "formal" that emerged for the term *professional* included "serious," "businesslike," "a balance between friendly and authoritarian," and "designated adult." Although no single phrase dominated in the responses, all definitions focused on a particular way of behaving in a classroom.

Results

As Table 13.1 demonstrates, students and faculty listed multiple definitions for the terms presented. Both groups generated the most multifaceted definitions for the terms *professional, not organized,* and *not respectful* despite the fact that *organized* and *respectful* are defined on the numerical ratings portion of the standard course evaluation forms used by every class. Examining the diversity of definitions for each term provided insight into agreements and misunderstandings within and between faculty and student groups.

Table 13.2 presents results for the term *not fair.* In Tables 13.2 through 13.7 the heading "number" refers to the total number of times a particular definition category or theme was listed, and "percentage" converts this number into a percentage of the total number of definitions listed. For all tables, only categories that included at least 5 percent of the key word phrases recorded are listed. For the term *not fair,* most student responses fit into four themes. Almost half of the students used the term to mean that the professor has favorites in the class whom he or she treats in a

Table 13.1. Survey Results.

	Students			Faculty		
Term	Number of Responses	Number of Respondents	Average Number of Responses per Individual	Number of Responses	Number of Respondents	Average Number of Responses per Individual
Not fair	260	177	1.5	63	44	1.4
Professional	360	174	2.1	81	43	1.9
Not organized	353	176	2	80	39	2.1
Challenging	255	177	1.4	68	44	1.5
Not respectful	312	167	1.9	78	39	2.0

Table 13.2. What *Not Fair* Means to Students.

	Students		Faculty	
Comments	Number	Percentage	Number	Percentage
Plays favorites	119	45.8	20	31.7
Grading problematic	58	2.3	31	49.2
Work is too hard	33	12.7	0	0
Will not "work with you" on problems	32	12.3	0	0
Other	18	6.9	12	19.0
Total	260	100	63	100

manner that privileges them. Another 35 percent saw the term as meaning a course that is overly difficult, which could refer to harsh grading, unclear grading, or demanding course content. These two themes are broken out in Table 13.2. The other prominent category focused on a professor's willingness to bend the rules on request. This could mean letting a student redo an assignment, allowing extra time for assignments, or allowing a student to skip an assignment when family concerns or other work interfered—for example, "Does not try to work around any problems you may have with an assignment or something." The irony is that instructors are "not fair" if they do or do not make exceptions for students. Faculty thought students usually used the term to mean one of two things: grading problematically (usually too harsh) or favoritism. No one listed hard work or an unwillingness to bend the rules to accommodate a particular student's needs as a possible student definition.

Results for the term *professional* appear in Table 13.3. Much less agreement than for *not fair* existed on what this term meant for both faculty and student groups. No definition rose above the 10 percent mark for students, and ten terms had a frequency of over 5 percent. The definitions listed focus on a wide range of items, from being knowledgeable and formal in class to being on time and wearing, literally, a suit. The formal comportment category, for example, includes "uptight," "air of dignity," "knows the difference between inside and outside of class behavior," and "remains the designated adult in class." Ironically, given the lack of consensus on meanings that Table 13.3 demonstrates, this is one of the attributes that students found most critical for the success of a class, as will be discussed in reference to Table 13.7.

Table 13.3. What *Professional* Means to Students.

	Students		Faculty	
Comments	Number	Percentage	Number	Percentage
Knowledgeable	37	10.3	7	8.6
Formal comportment	35	9.7	11	13.6
Timely and efficient	31	8.6	10	12.3
Organized	29	8.1	6	7.4
Calm and polite (includes language)	29	8.1	5	6.2
Fair and unbiased	28	7.8	2	2.5
Prepared	26	7.2	5	6.2
Not too friendly with students	24	6.7	5	6.2
Controls classroom	23	6.4	0	0
Respects students	22	6.1	4	4.9
Dresses formally (suit)	16	4.4	10	12.3
Other	60	16.6	16	19.8
Total	360	100	81	100

For faculty, two definitions, "formal comportment" and "timely and efficient," rose above the 10 percent level, and eight had frequencies higher than 5 percent. Faculty, like students, presented many definitions for the term *professional*, and they often appear at frequencies similar to those found in the data from students. The primary exception is that instructors believed students were much more focused on how faculty members dress than students actually reported they were.

This term has many responses (seventy-six) coded as "other," which illustrates the breadth of answers that may make up this category. Ten students said it meant "helpful." Another six defined it as "available." Singular student responses included "updates Blackboard with grades," "lectures," and, "unattached." Faculty responses included "doesn't forget things," "strict," and "traditional."

Table 13.4 provides data for *not organized*. Students' responses produced nine categories that included 5 percent or more of the definitions, but faculty responses fit mostly into only three of these popular categories. For students, the most common definitions were that faculty members are not prepared, do not have a clear plan for the class period, or are slow to return graded tests or assignments. Many comments, however, concerned changing syllabi, losing papers, and forgetting things like assignment due dates.

Table 13.4. What *Not Organized* Means to Students.

	Students		Faculty	
Comments	Number	Percentage	Number	Percentage
Not prepared	61	17.3	10	12.5
No apparent daily plan	53	15.0	4	5.0
Grades slowly	45	12.7	4	5.0
Changes or does not follow syllabus	40	11.3	23	28.8
Forgetful	31	8.8	2	2.5
Loses things	29	8.2	2	2.5
Late	28	7.9	4	5.0
Unclear syllabi, assignments	25	7.1	5	6.3
Goes off topic	1	—	7	8.8
Other	41	11.6	19	23.8
Total	353	100	80	100

Only two faculty members, however, mentioned knowledge of due dates on their questionnaires. For faculty respondents, who had only four categories above the 5 percent mark, close to 30 percent of responses were about changing or not following the syllabus. They believed that students used this term to describe someone who gets off topic in class, but only 1 of 353 student phrases about organization focused on this concern. Only four faculty (5 percent of responses) mentioned daily plans as associated with organization in student minds (as opposed to 15 percent for students), and slow grading appeared only forty times (5 percent) in eighty key word phrases versus representing 12.7 percent of student responses.

While the "other" category for this term is not as large (sixty responses) as that for *professional*, the variety of responses demonstrates how idiosyncratic answers could be. Six students responded with some version of "is messy": "disheveled," "disorderly office," and "disorderly course materials." "Ditsy with PowerPoints" is an example of a particularly opaque comment. Faculty members also recorded singular responses: "a normal human," "not obsessive," "shy," and "self-deprecating."

Students and faculty had much more unified views of the term *challenging*, as is evident in Table 13.5. For students, six categories rose above the 5 percent mark, but four of these could be collapsed into the broad theme of "hard work," which constitutes 57.3 percent of all the

Table 13.5. What *Challenging* Means to Students.

	Students		Faculty	
Comments	Number	Percentage	Number	Percentage
Thinking required	4	21.2	5	7.3
Hard work combined	146	57.3	31	45.6
Hard work	51	20.0	18	26.5
Lots of work	39	1.35	8	11.8
Hard but reasonable	31	12.2	5	7.3
Too hard	25	9.8	0	0
Hard grader	18	7.1	17	25.0
Engaging	15	5.9	3	4.4
Other	22	8.6	12	17.6
Total	255	100	68	100

responses. I separated out the subcategories since over 20 percent of these were surprising, to me at least, in that students felt the need to qualify the kind of hard work to be "hard but not too hard" (12.2 percent) or to say that challenging was not a good thing (9.8 percent) since it meant that the work was too hard.

For faculty, five categories were above the 5 percent mark, but 45.6 percent could be placed in the "hard work" category. Faculty members, unlike students, never understood "challenging" to be a negative attribute meaning "too hard." Faculty were also almost four times more likely than students to include a reference to hard grading in their list of definitions. They were three times less likely than students to make a reference to critical thinking in their list. This may mean that many faculty are unaware of the importance of critical thinking to students.

Finally, the results for the term *not respectful* are shown in Table 13.6. Student responses are clustered in five categories and faculty in three. Students' top category focused on instructors not listening to them or taking them seriously. The comment "treats us like children" or "like an inferior species" came up repeatedly (seven times). "Criticizes student ideas" was also part of this set of responses and constituted thirteen of the ninety-eight comments included in this grouping. The next most frequently listed definitions were "embarrasses students" or "demeans students" and was "rude to students." These categories are listed separately but may well be all about the same set of behaviors. Since the word *rude*

Table 13.6. What *Not Respectful* Means to Students.

	Students		Faculty	
Comments	Number	Percentage	Number	Percentage
Does not listen to or does not take students seriously	91	31.4	23	29.5
Embarrasses or demeans students	49	15.7	18	23.1
Rude to students	48	15.4	8	10.3
Not understanding of student problems	34	10.9	5	6.4
Discriminates against certain students	24	7.7	1	1.3
Other	49	15.7	23	29.5
Total	312	100	78	100

was usually listed with no qualifiers, it was hard to do more than guess as to its meaning. "Not being understanding of student problems" came up here (10.9 percent) and also as a definition for the term "fair."

The top three categories for faculty members' sense of what students meant by "not respectful" mirrored those of the students. However, 14 percent (eleven) of faculty responses mentioned criticizing student ideas as a definition for this term, making this definition more than three times more frequent than in the student responses. For faculty 29.5 percent of all responses fell into the "other" category, meaning they could not be easily grouped. Included were comments like "blunt," "does not call students by name," and "does not act maternal," which are not mirrored on the student list.

The final question posed to both students and faculty was whether any of these terms were about attributes critical to the success of a course. Few students (five) or faculty (three) thought the terms were unimportant, while fifty-three (28.5 percent) students and eleven (24.4 percent) faculty thought all were important. As Table 13.7 shows, for students, the most critical categories were "professional," "not organized," and "challenging." "Professional" and "not organized" also had the most definitions listed by students. Combining votes for the individual category with those for the "all" category generated these percentages. For example, the 118 student votes for "professional" include 65 separate votes for "professional" and 53 votes for the "all" category, which, of course, includes "professional."

Table 13.7. Attributes Considered Critical for Course Success.

	Students		Faculty	
Comments	Number	Percentage	Number	Percentage
Professional	118	21.00	17	14.8
Organized	116	20.6	24	20.9
Challenging	114	20.3	27	23.5
Fair	106	8.9	16	13.9
Respectful	95	16.9	19	16.5
None of these	5	0.9	3	2.6
Left blank	8	1.4	9	7.8
Total	562	100	115	100

Faculty thought the most critical attributes for course success had to do with organizing and challenging students. They did not follow the students' pattern of more definitions for the terms they felt most important. They did agree with students on "organized" and "challenging" as the most important of the attributes under consideration.

Discussion

The results of this study show that faculty and students do not have synonymous definitions of a set of terms that are common on narrative course evaluation forms. For all the terms, multiple definitions, whose meanings may or may not overlap, were generated by both faculty and student samples. Faculty members believed students had many definitions for these terms (and students did); faculty sometimes accurately identified student definitions but frequently did not. In actuality, faculty and students definitions were frequently at odds and can be quite idiosyncratic. It might be that while no consensus on meaning emerged, it is because these are not considered important terms. It could even be that their lack of significance led to the multiplicity of definitions. That is, they were characteristics that people had not given much thought to explaining.

Both groups, however, saw at least some of these terms as representing characteristics critical to course success. It is therefore particularly unfortunate that the terms are so opaque. As noted, two of the most critical categories for students were "professional" and "not organized," and yet these also had the most diverse definitions. Perhaps they are considered so important because they encompass so many attributes.

Instructors have the job of reading these forms and trying to figure out how to improve their teaching based on the comments—not easy to do since the meanings are so inconsistent. Many instructors thought that students labeled them as disorganized because they changed their syllabi over the course of a semester, when student comments were really about returning graded papers promptly. The problem can be even worse in evaluations based on numeric rating scales since the narrative comments sometimes include qualifying descriptions or examples that help faculty decipher meanings, something that rating scales never do. Clearly faculty in this small sample had not been well educated by such contextualizing student comments because they frequently misunderstood what students meant by the basic terms surveyed.

Beyond instructors, administrators and evaluation committees at the college under review use narrative descriptions for developmental and evaluative purposes. This study suggests how problematic that can be and has implications for the similar use of numeric scales. My own experience, and that of my colleagues on our collegewide evaluation committee, indicates a great deal of confusion in trying to match what we observed about instructors with what we read in comments. We eventually learned that without class visits, we could not attempt any assessment of an instructor's work as a teacher.

A single example may prove instructive. I read the evaluations of a candidate who was clearly liked and respected by students but was frequently labeled by them as disorganized. The individual had carefully designed Web sites for courses and clearly took great care with syllabi and other course materials. The instructor was plainly confused about what the comments about organization could mean. I attended a class meeting and quickly realized that while the professor was organized on the macrolevel, he was not on the microlevel. He brought in the wrong memory stick, for example, apologized profusely, and returned to an office to fetch the appropriate one. Since the office was only a few steps away, the class still started on time. The instructor mentioned forgetting things several times, but if not for the instructor's self-deprecating comments, I would never have noticed anything was amiss without having attended the class and, without this direct classroom experience, could not have helped the instructor understand the comments on evaluations. I learned to decipher student assessment of this instructor as meaning, "This is someone who does an excellent job, but has some organization issues, albeit minor ones."

In this case I came to agree with the students, but understanding what students meant by the terms surveyed in this study suggests that students sometimes define excellence in teaching in ways with which most faculty could not agree. Some of the higher-frequency definitions of terms that students label as critical for course success are reasonable: be prepared, grade promptly, have students work hard (although not too hard) with some critical thinking involved. Other frequent comments, however, fit with a customer satisfaction model for evaluations but are not helpful for improving teaching (for example, "Willing to let things slide when we have time management problems" as a definition of *fairness*).

Even some definitions that may appear reasonable at first glance, like "has no apparent daily plan" for "not organized," can reflect lack of understanding of a discipline. The instructor could have an unapparent daily plan, as in philosophy classes I observed where the "plan" is for student commentary on the readings to shape the focus of the discussion, with many alternatives possible and equally enriching. An instructor who follows this approach might be labeled "not organized" but is actually "alternatively organized." Without some lexicon of what terms might mean to students and visits to classroom, evaluators are not likely to be able to make these distinctions. Narrative course evaluation questions would be much more useful to evaluators and instructors if they asked for specific examples and not just general statements. This might help direct teaching energies toward changing patterns that need to be changed and not toward changing what are already good practices that simply need to be explained to students.

Finally, faculty and students did not entirely agree on what is critical for course success. More students than faculty, for example, thought that being "professional" and "fair" were important. If, however, faculty and students do not agree between or among themselves as to what these terms mean, how can instructors or evaluators use comments about them for any useful purpose? While almost everyone in the sample thought at least two of the terms (or all of them) surveyed represented something critical to course success, no consensus emerged about what is absolutely critical. For students the highest numbers were for "professional" and "organized" at 21 percent of responses and for faculty "challenging" with 23.5 percent of responses.

Many students' comments about the positive attributes of instructors fit into the theme of "student centered" abstracted by Onwuegbuzie et al. (2007) from a survey of over nine hundred students at a midsize public university. "Professional" also emerged as one of the metathemes uncovered by this study of student perceptions of effective teachers (Onwuegbuzie et al., 2007). While this suggests that the survey focused on some widely held student beliefs, unless faculty can decode these from evaluation forms, they provide little help for instructors in setting priorities. In sum, without peer review of class meetings and course materials, and requests for clarifying information, especially examples, on course evaluation forms, comments are likely to be misinterpreted, and instructors are likely to spend time and energy trying to fix the wrong problems or nonexistent problems. Student comments, however, could be a rich source of information for faculty development if peer reviewers would educate faculty members about their complex nature.

Conclusion

The results of this study are clearly preliminary since they used a sample of students and faculty from a single institution. Yet while the idiosyncrasies of the definitions provided may represent campus culture, it would certainly be useful to check on the study's applicability to other campuses. Unless institutions do extensive training in the vocabulary of evaluations, it seems unlikely that the broad findings are unique to a single location.

These findings suggest that narrative comments on course evaluations can have many meanings to students and to faculty, and not necessarily the same meanings. Given this, their use without contextualizing information can lead to inaccurate evaluations and misplaced faculty efforts. To address this problem on the campus studied, a pilot project on an informed peer review process, organized by the campus's Institute for Effective Teaching, will include the discussion of the intended meanings of student course evaluation responses. Peer reviewers will attend classes of several faculty volunteers, examine course evaluations, and help faculty members interpret the meaning of student responses based on these classroom observations. While the bureaucracy required to change the evaluation of teaching procedures makes reform a slow process, we hope that this pilot project will facilitate such changes and lead to training faculty in deciphering intended student meanings.

REFERENCES

Benton, S. L., & Cashin, W. E. (2012). *Student ratings of teaching: A summary of research and literature.* (IDEA Paper No. 50). Manhattan: Kansas State University, Center for Faculty Evaluation and Development.

Bernard, H. R. (2011). *Research methods in anthropology* (5th ed.). Lanham, MD: Altamira Press.

Beyers, C. (2008). The hermeneutics of student evaluations. *College Teaching, 56*(2), 102–106.

Gray, M., & Bergmann, B. R. (2003). Student teaching evaluations: Inaccurate, demeaning, misused. *Academe, 89*(5), 44–46.

Laube, H., Massoni, K. Sprague, J., & Ferber, A. L. (2007). The impact of gender on the evaluation of teaching: What we know and what we can do. *NWSA Journal, 19*(3), 87–104.

Onwuegbuzie, A. J., Witcher, A. E. Collins K. M. T., Filer, J. D., Wiedmaier, C. D., & Moore, C. W. (2007). Students' perceptions of characteristics of effective college teachers: A validity study of a teaching evaluation form using a mixed-methods analysis. *American Educational Research Journal, 44*(1), 113–160.

Pounder, J. S. (2007). Is student evaluation of teaching worthwhile? An analytical framework for answering the question. *Quality Assurance in Education, 15*(2), 178–191.

14

TIME TO RAISE QUESTIONS ABOUT STUDENT RATINGS

Linda B. Nilson
Clemson University

Students have changed a great deal in the past few decades, but has the validity of student ratings correspondingly changed with them? Drawing on recent research conducted on students, this chapter examines the relationship between student ratings and student learning, the biases found in these ratings, and their factual accuracy and apparent truthfulness. It also addresses why findings of early and recent studies differ, what information student ratings now provide, and how institutions and faculty have consolidated the effects on ratings that today's students initiated.

o

The bulk of research on validity of student ratings and their contaminating biases was conducted in the 1970s and 1980s, when a very different generation of students filled classrooms. Dozens of publications on the millennial generation document how much students have changed since then (for example, Bauerlein, 2008; Lancaster & Stillman, 2003; Nathan, 2005; Pryor, Hurtado, DeAngelo, Palucki Blake, & Tran, 2011; Singleton-Jackson, Jackson, & Reinhardt, 2010; Twenge, 2007). They tell us that today's students under thirty years old devalue academics and reflection; feel entitled to higher education, high grades, top-quality customer service (as they define it); and attend college for primarily instrumental reasons—that is, not for the sake of learning but for the credential that will get them a job.

Furthermore, given that almost half of these students easily graduated from high school with an A-average, they come to college with an inflated estimation of their abilities and knowledge. They "earned" these A's with little effort; in fact, nearly two-thirds of entering freshmen in 2009 devoted less than six hours a week to their homework as seniors in high school—a proportion of entering freshmen that has been increasing steadily since 1987 (Pryor et al., 2011). Being so unaccustomed to working hard and practicing persistence in their learning, these students do not study much more in college (Babcock & Marks, 2010; Pryor et al., 2011). Besides, they do not think they should have to because, in their fixed intelligence mind-set, they are "smart." Aside from misrepresenting the way the brain actually works, this mind-set interferes with learning by inducing students to avoid challenges, give up easily, ignore criticism, and value high grades above mastery (Dweck, 2006). Yet, achievable challenge, time on task, and high expectations of performance are associated with greater student learning.

Given the values, beliefs, and behaviors of today's students, it is time to raise questions about the validity of student ratings—specifically to reexamine the key assumptions and older literature. Fortunately, new research studies are available, and this chapter synthesizes their findings to identify what these ratings are really measuring.

What Validity Means for Student Ratings

The validity of student ratings as indicators of teaching effectiveness has rested on two findings and one assumption.

The first of the two findings is the moderately strong positive relationship between student ratings and student learning and achievement. Cohen (1981, p. 281) stated it very clearly: "It [teaching effectiveness] can be further operationalized as the amount students learn in a particular course. . . . If student ratings are to have any utility in evaluating teaching, they must show at least a moderately strong relationship to this index." His meta-analysis found correlations between global rating items and learning, as measured by an external exam, of between .44 and .47. Meta-analyses by Marsh (1984) and Feldman (1989) synthesized comparable results and found a few slightly higher correlations between certain criterion-specific items and learning. These two literature reviews made convincing cases by focusing on studies of multisection courses with common syllabi and exams. Together, these three meta-analyses provided the justification for using student ratings as a proxy for student learning in faculty reviews.

The second finding is the minimal effect of rating biases due to extraneous variables. Cashin's (1995) meta-analysis identified a short list of biases: students' prior interest in the course subject matter, their expected grades, the level of course, the academic field, the purpose of ratings, the instructor's presence or absence while students filled out rating forms, and the anonymity of the ratings. But none of these except students' prior interest had notable effects, and the correlation between expected grades and ratings was largely mediated by student learning and motivation. In addition, a whole host of variables had no significant impact on ratings: students' gender, age, level, grade point average, and personality; instructor's gender, age, teaching experience, race, personality, and research productivity; class size; time of day of class meetings; and time in the semester that students filled out the rating forms. Cashin maintained that the effects of instructor rank and expressiveness were not biasing because they were related to learning. Although the findings varied some across studies, Hoyt (1997) estimated that biases accounted for only between 5 and 25 percent of the variance in rating items.

The assumption was the presumed honesty of students when filling out rating forms. So strong was this assumption that it attracted little research until the 1990s.

Recent Findings on Student Ratings

The research that substantiates the validity of student ratings is hardly recent. In fact, the main validity argument—the relationship of student ratings to learning—rests on the oldest data. All three of the key meta-analyses cited above were based on data collected in the 1970s, well over thirty years ago, and published on or before 1980. Feldman's later publications on the subject (1997, 1998, 2007) drew from the same aging data set. Cashin's (1995) literature review contained no studies published after 1994. Perhaps the time factor would not matter if the education-relevant values, attitudes, and behaviors of the raters had not changed, but they have, and quite radically. This is why only the most recent studies will answer the questions raised.

Are Student Ratings Still Related to Learning?

No. In fact, the relationship may be negative. Recent research has shifted the measure of learning from students' exam performance at the end of the course to their performance (grade) in follow-up courses. This latter measurement taps longer-lasting learning, which is presumably deeper learning. While student ratings on multiple items (global and criterion-specific) and students' grades were positively correlated in the base course, this was not the case in follow-up courses, according to studies conducted at the U.S. Air Force Academy and Duke University (Carrell & West, 2010; Johnson, 2003). Ratings of the base course instructor and students' grades in follow-up courses were negatively correlated. In other words, the more effective introductory instructors—those who best prepared their students for advanced courses in the discipline—received lower ratings. In another study, this one conducted at Ohio State, student ratings on multiple items bore no statistically significant relationship to learning once grades, which did correlate with ratings, were controlled (Weinberg, Hashimoto, & Fleisher, 2009). In fact, in his recent meta-analysis, Clayson (2009) could not locate a single study documenting a positive relationship between student learning and student ratings that was published after 1990. A study at the University of California, Riverside, uncovered a weak relationship between student ratings and learning (Marks, Fairris, & Beleche, 2010), but the learning measured was not of the long-term type. Rather it was based on students' scores on a high-stakes final exam administered across multiple sections.

Might ratings be related to students' perceived learning? Indeed, two of the studies that found no relationship between objective measures of student learning and student ratings did find a positive one between students' perceived learning and their ratings (Johnson, 2003; Weinberg et al., 2009). But perceived learning is no substitute for actual learning. Weinberg et al. (2009) did not find any relationship between the two. Nor did the Wabash Study (Bowman, 2011), which encompasses seventeen institutions. Bowman examined how accurately students' perceived learning progress mirrored their actual progress on several longitudinal assessments—a series of objective tests, the Collegiate Assessment of Academic Proficiency focusing on critical and analytical reasoning, and the Defining Issues Test-2 assessing moral reasoning—and he reported no significant relationships. In fact, quite a few studies have found that students tend to overestimate their knowledge and abilities, except possibly the best students (Bell & Volckmann, 2011; Kruger & Dunning, 1999, 2002; Longhurst & Norton, 1997; Miller & Geraci, 2011).

Are Student Ratings More Biased Than in the Past?

Yes. Research published in the past decade confirms and adds to Cashin's short list of biases. The newest contaminants include well over a dozen variables extraneous to learning and largely beyond faculty control: instructor's charisma (Shevlin, Banyard, Davies, & Griffiths, 2000), physical attractiveness (Hamermesh & Parker, 2005), personality (congeniality, confidence, optimism, and enthusiasm, estimated by studies cited in Clayson, 2011, to explain 50 to 75 percent of the variance in student ratings), age (McPherson & Jewell, 2007; Zabaleta, 2007), rank (Isley & Singh, 2007; McPherson & Jewell, 2007), gender in the sciences and engineering (Potvin, Harazi, Tai, & Sadler, 2009; Superson, 1999); membership in a disadvantaged racial group (McPherson & Jewell, 2007) and Asian accent (Gravois, 2005); the length of class meeting, in that longer meetings lower ratings (Isley & Singh, 2007; McPherson & Jewell, 2007); the timing of the ratings, in that collecting the data shortly before tests and due dates of major assignments and after returning graded work depresses ratings (Hall & Fitzgerald, 1995); class size (McPherson & Jewell, 2007; Wines & Lau, 2006); the number of rows in the classroom (Wines & Lau, 2006); other aspects of the classroom, the quality of the curriculum, and the functionality of the room's technology (Nowell, Gale, & Handley, 2010); and the students' perceived or anticipated grade in the course (Clayson, Frost, & Sheffet, 2006; Isley & Singh, 2007; McPherson & Jewell, 2007; Wines & Lau, 2006; Zabaleta, 2007).

Regarding the last bias, the recent studies do not attribute the relationship between expected grade and ratings to greater student learning or motivation, as have Cashin (1995) and others. To the contrary, student scores on items tapping course rigor, challenge of the content, and required student effort—all presumably related to learning—vary negatively with instructor ratings (Centra, 2003; Steiner, Holley, Gerdes, & Campbell, 2006; Weinberg, Fleisher, & Hashimoto, 2007; others cited in Clayson, 2009). Clayson (2011) hypothesized six possible explanations for the grade-ratings correlation: teaching effectiveness/learning, student motivation, grade attribution, prior student and instructor characteristics, grading leniency, and reciprocity. His prior research (Clayson et al., 2006) led him to endorse the reciprocity theory over the others. It posits that a student's evaluation of an instructor simply reflects what the student sees to be the instructor's evaluation of her. In other words, students give what they see themselves receiving. In addition, the correlation between expected grade and ratings has increased over the past few decades; it used to be .10 to .30 but is now .45 to .50 (Clayson, 2011). So what Cashin (1995) dismissed as a mild bias has become a major predictor of student ratings.

All of these findings—those documenting more and stronger biases and those suggesting that rigor, challenge, and required effort lower student ratings—add to the evidence that learning and ratings are either uncorrelated or negatively correlated.

Are Student Ratings Honest?

We have assumed that students generally are telling the truth, as they see it, when they fill out the rating forms. Yet many of us have also found factual inaccuracies in our own student ratings and written comments and, as faculty developers, have counseled other instructors who have. We have said and heard protests like these: "But I've *never* been late to class!" "But I returned all the papers and exams within a week!" "But I followed the syllabus faithfully!"

Surprisingly few studies have addressed this problem. Stanfel (1995) quizzed his students on their knowledge of his evaluation procedures in his course, and all of them correctly described the procedures. In addition, whenever he returned graded work, he asked them to sign a document stating that they had received their graded work at the first possible opportunity. Yet on the end-of-semester rating forms, only 3 percent of his students "strongly agreed" with the item, "The instructor explains clearly to students how they are evaluated," and 64 percent "disagreed" or "strongly disagreed." In response to the item, "Tests and written assignments are graded and returned in a reasonable period of time," only 3 percent "strongly agreed" while over 46 percent "disagreed" or "strongly disagreed." In a similar study, Sproule (2002) diligently returned all graded work for one of his classes the very next class meeting during the entire semester, but only half of his students' responses to the relevant rating item reflected this.

Were these misrepresentations of the truth due to students' forgetting, misunderstanding, or lying? Clayson and Haley (2011) surveyed students about their honesty in their ratings and written comments, and the disturbing results confirmed Stanfel's and Spoule's worst suspicions: about one-third of the students confessed to "stretching the truth," 56 percent said they knew peers who had, and 20 percent admitted to lying in their comments. Moreover, half the students did not think that what they did constituted a kind of cheating.

While few in number, Stanfel's, Sproule's, and Clayson and Haley's studies cast doubt on the validity of all student responses on rating forms. When added to the recent research documenting serious biases in the ratings and a disconnect between student learning and the ratings, they lead us to conclude that student ratings lack content validity and all three kinds of construct validity—convergent, discriminant, and divergent (Clayson, 2011).

Older Studies in Perspective

How did the studies of student ratings conducted in the 1970s and 1980s obtain the results that they did? Of course, they examined only short-term learning using end-of-course final exams. But Marks et al. (2010) did as well and found only a weak association between learning and ratings. Most likely the explanation lies with the respondents, because the early ones had very different values, attitudes, and behaviors from today's students. This earlier student generation attended college more for learning-focused and life-enhancement reasons than for good jobs. In 1967, 86 percent of freshmen said they were attending to develop a meaningful philosophy of life (Hong, 2004). Today about as high a proportion say "to get a better job," and less than 40 percent care about developing a meaningful philosophy of life (Pryor et al., 2011).

In the past, what students wanted out of college more closely matched the mission of higher education—liberal arts education, in particular. In addition, the K–12 system in the United States apparently operated more effectively, as its students scored high on reading and math in international tests. Entering college students either had or had to quickly acquire solid, independent study skills and habits, or institutions flunked them out. (High freshman attrition rates were points of pride for some universities.) It seems that these students realized that their learning was their responsibility. What they did not glean from the lectures, they had to learn on their own or seek help from faculty or teaching assistants. (Few, if any, academic assistance centers existed then.) Given their reasons for attending college and their educational experience, these students probably expected rigor, valued challenge, and gave higher ratings to professors from whom they learned the most. Maybe a combination of student learning and motivation did mediate the relationship between grades and ratings at the time.

In addition, institutions did not see themselves operating within the customer-seller model. They functioned more within the client-professional model, exemplified by the patient-physician or the client-attorney relationship. It is an unequal pairing in that both parties agree that the professional has expertise that the client needs to draw on. While clients want professionals to display caring and warmth, what they most want—and are paying for—is well-informed advice and appropriate follow-up action. For example, a patient expects to receive appropriate testing, an accurate diagnosis, proper treatment, and, if possible, restoration to health. In the lawyer's office, a client wants an expert assessment of her situation, followed by legal actions that promote and protect her best interests. Being a reasonable patient or client entails accepting bad news, taking prescribed actions, and enduring side effects, sacrifices, or costs if they serve her longer-term, rational interests.

When faculty assumed the role of professional, student clients came to college respecting their expertise and not anticipating a democratic, empowering classroom experience. While they no doubt valued an instructor's caring, warmth, and ability to motivate them, they expected her to have up-to-date knowledge and skills and hoped that she could convey them effectively. They might have had to work very hard, accept critical feedback, and deal with some low grades to get through their learning process, but these were par for the course. While this description of the professor-student relationship reflects the pure client-professional model, it may accurately represent the norms of the time.

Institutional and Faculty Responses to Today's Students

Nuhfer (2010) interprets student ratings on global items as reflections of student affect toward an instructor and valid measures of student satisfaction with the instructor and course experience. This makes sense given how strongly instructor personality and expected grade influence these ratings. Today's students want an instructor they can relate to, who is expressive and energetic, and who cares about and empathizes with them (Chonko, 2004; Clayson, 2011; Kelley, Conant, & Smart, 1991; La Lopa, 2011; Walsh & Maffei, 1994). If an instructor's ability to project such a persona motivated students to learn more, then ratings and learning would be positively related, but we have already established that they are not. Students also want the good grades that they were accustomed to getting before college (Pryor et al., 2011) and to preserve their positive self-concept. Thus, they accordingly reward faculty who give them high grades with high ratings.

In general, colleges and universities have come to view themselves as sellers in the market economy, competing to attract students and striving to retain them. In this marketplace model, student satisfaction means customer satisfaction, whether the customer is the student or her parents or both. (If a dependent student is unhappy about something, the parents typically know about it and share that unhappiness, and they often contact the instructor or administrators to get satisfaction.) According to Kirp (2005), colleges and universities have dutifully responded to what their prospective and current customers want, upgrading residence halls, building recreational facilities, improving student services, and making academics more "palatable" to the general public. Although no definitive study shows that institutions have dumbed down their curricula, Babcock and Marks (2011) uncover evidence that the standards of effort that they set for students have dropped precipitously since 1961, and students have allocated their out-of-class time toward social and leisure activities. At the same time, colleges and universities have allowed considerable grade inflation over the past thirty years (Johnson 2003; Rojstaczer, 2009). They have also placed increasing importance on student ratings in hiring, retaining, and promoting faculty—in particular, the global ratings that Nuhfer interprets as an affective satisfaction measure.

The institutional response to market pressures has changed faculty incentives and, in turn, faculty behavior (Sperber, 2005). To keep up their student ratings, instructors have generally graded more leniently than in the past (thus, grade inflation) and have reduced course workloads (Johnson, 2003; Sperber, 2005). Some even may have learned to practice the social immediacies that make students feel cared for and respected. Williams and Ceci (1997) demonstrated that faculty could raise their ratings just by learning to act more enthusiastic, but how many instructors have adopted this strategy is unknown. (Interestingly, Ceci's enhanced ratings did not result in better student performance on the final exam.) Conversely, upholding high standards seems to yield no institutional rewards and can result in lower student ratings and the accompanying career consequences (Babcock & Marks, 2011).

In view of institutional responses to the values, attitudes, and behaviors of today's students, followed by faculty responses to the resulting new incentives, the diminishing validity of student ratings is due to changes not only in students but also in colleges and universities and their faculties. Students may have initiated the trend, but they have received a great deal of cooperation. To reverse the trend, institutions would have to be willing to sacrifice student satisfaction for greater learning and accept the possibility of higher attrition. They would also have to deemphasize (if not eliminate) student ratings in faculty reviews and rely largely on well-informed peer review and measures of student learning. Instructors would then be free to challenge students more and work them harder without fearing that falling student ratings would derail their academic career. Faculty would also have the discretion to fail indifferent and poorly performing students without parental interference or administrative sanction. As a result, students might learn more in college than they currently do, and some of those who failed might return to college later, ready to work and learn.

The current accreditation system is not designed to increase rigor and counterbalance the power of student ratings. Accrediting agencies require institutions to develop and assess student learning outcomes, but they do not require that all graduating students achieve those outcomes at the target level. All they do demand is that institutions try new strategies that promise to improve the results. So far, these strategies have left a lot to be desired.

Conclusion

Many colleges and universities go through cycles with their student rating forms, every several years reexamining the items they settled on at the end of the previous cycle. They often look to faculty developers to provide the scholarship and guidance to improve these forms and decide how they should be used. Developers typically recommend adding evidence of teaching effectiveness beyond student ratings, such as peer review of course materials, well-informed classroom observations, and pre- and posttests of learning (Arreola, 2007; Stark-Wroblewski, Ahlering, & Brill, 2007). Still, the primacy of student ratings persists. It is ironic that these ratings have acquired increasing importance in tenure, promotion, and reappointment decisions over the same time period that their validity has waned. The question never raised is whether we should use these ratings in faculty reviews at all (faculty private use is not problematic). It is time to initiate the discussion.

The academy has to decide what "teaching effectiveness" really means. If it means student learning, as Cashin (1988) defined it, then institutions should assess it using measures that reflect learning, not student ratings. These ratings belong in the faculty review process only to the extent that faculty and administrators regard student/customer satisfaction as an important goal unto itself, even though it has nothing to do with and can actually work against student learning. Deciding the fate of instructors based in whole or in part on their student ratings is an institution's choice, but it should inform its faculty explicitly that they are being assessed on student satisfaction, independent of learning, if that is the case.

REFERENCES

Arreola, R. A. (2007). *Developing a comprehensive faculty evaluation system.* San Francisco, CA: Jossey-Bass/Anker.

Babcock, P., & Marks, M. (2010, August). *Leisure College, USA: The decline in student study time.* (American Enterprise Institute for Public Policy Research, No. 7). Retrieved from http://www.aei.org/outlook/100980

Babcock, P. S., & Marks, M. (2011). The falling time cost of college: Evidence from a half century of time use data. *Review of Economics and Statistics, 93,* 468–478.

Bauerlein, M. (2008). *The dumbest generation: How the digital age stupefies young American and jeopardizes our future.* New York, NY: Tarcher/Penguin.

Bell, P., & Volckmann, D. (2011). Knowledge surveys in general chemistry: Confidence, overconfidence, and performance. *Journal of Chemical Education, 88*(11), 1469–1476.

Bowman, N. A. (2011, April 11). *The validity of college seniors' self-reported gains as a proxy for longitudinal growth.* Paper presented at the annual meetings of the American Educational Research Association, New Orleans, LA.

Carrell, S. E., & West, J. E. (2010). Does professor quality matter? Evidence from random assignment of students to professors. *Journal of Political Economy, 118*(3), 409–432.

Cashin, W. E. (1995) *Student ratings of teaching: The research revisited.* (IDEA Paper No. 32). Manhattan: Center for Faculty Development and Evaluation, Kansas State University.

Cashin, W. E. (1988). *Student ratings of teaching: A summary of the research* (IDEA Paper No. 20.). Manhattan, KS: Kansas State University, Center for Faculty Evaluation and Development.

Centra, J. A. (2003). Will teachers receive higher student evaluations by giving higher grades and less coursework? *Research in Higher Education, 44,* 495–518.

Chonko, L. B. (2004). If it walks like a duck...: Concerns about quackery in marketing education. *Journal of Marketing Education, 26,* 4–16.

Clayson, D. E. (2009). Student evaluations of teaching: Are they related to what students learn? A meta-analysis and review of the literature. *Journal of Marketing Education, 31*(1), 16–30. Retrieved from http://jmd.sagepub.com/content/31/1/16.full.pdf+html

Clayson, D. E. (2011). *A multi-disciplined review of the student teacher evaluation process.* Retrieved from http://business.uni.edu/clayson/Ext/SETSummary2011.doc

Clayson, D. E., Frost, T. E., & Sheffet, M. J. (2006). Grades and the student evaluation of instruction: A test of the reciprocity effect. *Academy of Management Learning and Education, 5*(1), 52–65.

Clayson, D. E., & Haley, D. A. (2011). Are students telling us the truth? A critical look at the student evaluation of teaching. *Marketing Education Review, 21,* 101–112.

Cohen, P. A. (1981). Student ratings of instruction and student achievement: A meta-analysis of multisection validity studies. *Review of Educational Research, 51,* 281–309.

Dweck, C. (2006). *Mindset: The new psychology of success.* New York, NY: Random House.

Feldman, K. A. (1989). The association between student ratings of specific instructional dimensions and student achievement: Refining and extending the synthesis of data from multisection validity studies. *Research in Higher Education, 30,* 583–645.

Feldman, K. A. (1997). Identifying exemplary teachers and teaching: Evidence from student ratings. In R. P. Perry & J. C. Smart (Eds.), *Effective teaching in higher education: Research and practice* (pp. 368–395). New York, NY: Agathon Press.

Feldman, K. A. (1998). Identifying exemplary teachers and teaching: evidence from student ratings. In K. A. Feldman & M. B. Paulsen (Eds.), *Teaching and learning in the college classroom* (2nd ed., pp. 391–414). New York, NY: Simon & Schuster.

Feldman, K. A. (2007). Identifying exemplary teachers and teaching: evidence from student ratings. In R. P. Perry & J. C. Smart (Eds.), *The scholarship of teaching and learning in higher education: An evidence-based approach* (pp. 93–129). New York, NY: Springer.

Gravois, J. (2005, April 8). Teach impediment: When the students can't understand the instructor, who is to blame? *Chronicle of Higher Education.* Retrieved from http://chronicle.com/article/Teach-Impediment/33613/

Hall, C., & Fitzerald, C. (1995). Student summative evaluation of teaching: Coder of practice. *Assessment and Evaluation in Higher Education, 20*(3), 307–311.

Hamermesh, D. S., & Parker, A. M. (2005). Beauty in the classroom: Professorial pulchritude and putative pedagogical productivity. *Economics of Education Review, 24,* 369–376.

Hong, P. Y. (2004, January 26). Money top goal of college freshmen. *Los Angeles Times.* Retrieved from http://articles.latimes.com/2004/jan/26/local/me-survey26

Hoover, E. (2009, October 11). The millennial muddle. *Chronicle of Higher Education.* Retrieved from http://chronicle.com/article/The-Millennial-Muddle-How/48772/

Hoyt, D. P. (1997). *Studies of the impact of extraneous variables.* Manhattan: IDEA Center, Center for Faculty Development and Evaluation, Kansas State University. Retrieved from http://www.bus.lsu.edu/accounting/faculty/lcrumbley/idea.html

Isley, P., & Singh, H. (2007). Does faculty rank influence student teaching evaluations? Implications for assessing instructor effectiveness. *Business Education Digest, 16,* 47–59.

Johnson, V. E. (2003). *Grade inflation: A crisis in higher education.* New York, NY: Springer.

Kelley, C. A., Conant, J. S., & Smart, D. T. (1991). Master teaching revisited: Pursuing excellence from the students' perspective. *Journal of Marketing Education, 13,* 1–10.

Kirp, D. L. (2005). This little student went to market. In R. H. Hersch & J. Merrow (Eds.), *Declining by degree: Higher education at risk* (pp. 113–130). New York, NY: Palgrave Macmillan.

Kruger, J., & Dunning, D. (1999). Unskilled and unaware of it: How difficulties in recognizing one's own incompetence lead to inflated self-assessments. *Journal of Personality and Social Psychology, 77,* 1121–1134.

Kruger, J., & Dunning, D. (2002). Unskilled and unaware—but why? *Journal of Personality and Social Psychology, 82*(2), 189–192.

La Lopa, J. M. (2011). Student reflection on quality teaching and how to assess it in higher education. *Journal of Culinary Science and Technology, 9*(4), 282–292.

Lancaster, L. C., & Stillman, D. (2003). *When generations collide: Who they are. Why they clash. How to solve the generation puzzle at work.* New York, NY: HarperCollins.

Longhurst, N., & Norton, L. S. (1997). Self-assessment in coursework essays. *Studies in Educational Evaluation, 23*(4), 319–330.

Marks, M., Fairris, D., & Beleche, T. (2010, June 3). *Do course evaluations reflect student learning? Evidence from a pre-test/post-test setting.* Riverside: Department of Economics, University of California, Riverside. Retrieved from http://faculty.ucr.edu/~mmarks/Papers/marks2010course.pdf

Marsh, H. W. (1984). Students' evaluations of university teaching: Dimensionality, reliability, validity, potential biases, and utility. *Journal of Educational Psychology, 76,* 707–754.

McPherson, M. A., & Jewell, R. T. (2007). Leveling the playing field: Should student evaluation scores be adjusted? *Social Science Quarterly, 88*(3), 868–881.

Miller, T. M., & Geraci, L. (2011, January 24). Unskilled but aware: Reinterpreting overconfidence in low-performing students. *Journal of Experimental Psychology: Learning, Memory, and Cognition.* doi:10.1037/a0021802.

Nathan, R. (2005). *My freshman year. What a professor learned by becoming a student.* Ithaca, NY: Cornell University Press.

Nowell, C., Gale, L. R., & Handley, B. (2010). Assessing faculty performance using student evaluations of teaching in an uncontrolled setting. *Assessment and Evaluation in Higher Education, 35*(4), 463–475.

Nuhfer, E. B. (2010). *A fractal thinker looks at student ratings.* Retrieved from http://profcamp.tripod.com/fractalevals10.pdf

Potvin, G., Hazari, Z., Tai, R. H., & Sadler, P. (2009). Unraveling bias from student evaluations of their high-school teachers. *Science Education, 93*(5), 827–845. Retrieved from http://onlinelibrary.wiley.com/doi/10.1002/sce.20332/pdf

Pryor, J. H., Hurtado, S., DeAngelo, L., Palucki Blake, L., & Tran, S. (2011). *The American freshman: National norms fall 2010.* Los Angeles, CA: Higher Education Research Institute, UCLA.

Rojstaczer, S. (2009). *GradeInflation.com: Grade inflation at American colleges and universities.* Retrieved from http://gradeinflation.com/

Shevlin, M., Banyard, P., Davies, M., & Griffiths, M. (2000). The validity of student evaluation of teaching in higher education: Love me, love my lectures? *Assessment and Evaluation in Higher Education, 25,* 397–405.

Singleton-Jackson, J. A., Jackson, D. L., & Reinhardt, J. (2010). Students as consumers of knowledge: Are they buying what we're selling? *Innovative Higher Education, 35*(5), 343–358.

Sperber, M. (2005). How undergraduate education became college lite—and a personal apology. In R. H. Hersch & J. Merrow (Eds.), *Declining by degree: Higher education at risk* (pp. 131–144). New York, NY: Palgrave Macmillan.

Sproule, R. (2002). The underdetermination of instructor performance by data from the student evaluation of teaching. *Economics of Education Review, 21,* 287–295.

Stanfel, L. E. (1995). Measuring the accuracy of student evaluations of teaching. *Journal of Instructional Psychology,* 22(2), 117–125.

Stark-Wroblewski, K., Ahlering, R. F., & Brill, F. M. (2007). Toward a more comprehensive approach to evaluating teaching effectiveness: Supplementing student evaluations of teaching with pre-post learning measures. *Assessment and Evaluation in Higher Education,* 44(5), 539–556. Retrieved from http://www.tandfonline.com/doi/pdf/10.1080/02602930600898536

Steiner, S., Holley, L. C., Gerdes, K., & Campbell, H. E. (2006). Evaluating teaching: Listening to students while acknowledging bias. *Journal of Social Work Education, 42,* 355–376.

Superson, A. M. (1999). Sexism in the classroom: The role of gender stereotypes in the evaluation of female faculty. *APA Newsletter on Feminism and Philosophy,* 99(1), 46–51.

Twenge, J. M. (2007). *Generation me: Why today's young Americans are more confident, assertive, entitled and more miserable than ever before.* New York, NY: Free Press.

Walsh, D. J., & Maffei, M. J. (1994). Never in a class by themselves: An examination of behaviors affecting the student-professor relationship. *Journal of Excellence in College Teaching, 5*(2), 23–49.

Weinberg, B. A., Fleisher, B. M., & Hashimoto, M. (2007). *Evaluating methods of evaluating instruction: The case of higher education.* (NBER Working Paper No. 12844). Retrieved from http://www.nber.org/papers/w12844.

Weinberg, B. A., Hashimoto, M., & Fleisher, B. M. (2009). Evaluating teaching in higher education. *Journal of Economic Education, 40*(3), 227–261.

Williams, W. M., & Ceci, S. J. (1997, September/October). How'm I doing? Problems with student ratings of instructors and courses. *Change, 29*(5), 13–23.

Wines, W. A., & Lau, T. J. (2006). Observations on the folly of using student evaluations of college teaching for faculty evaluation, pay, and retention decisions and its implications for academic freedom. *William and Mary Journal of Women and the Law, 13*(1). Retrieved from http://scholarship.law.wm.edu/cgi/viewcontent.cgi?article=1089&context=wmjowl

Zabaleta, F. (2007). The use and misuse of student evaluations of teaching. *Teaching in Higher Education, 12*(1), 55–76.

15

USING SMALL GROUP INDIVIDUAL DIAGNOSIS TO IMPROVE ONLINE INSTRUCTION

Jennifer H. Herman, Melissa Langridge
Niagara University

As online education grows, so does the need for professional development for faculty teaching online courses. This chapter explains how a faculty development technique, small group individual diagnosis, was adapted to the online environment. This technique provides faculty with anonymous midsemester feedback from students regarding the quality of the course. The timing and nature of this feedback is the impetus for a teaching consultation with a trained facilitator. In this study, surprising challenges emerged when the technique was adapted to the online environment. Faculty perceptions of the success of the online diagnoses are shared.

Over the past several years, online education has been growing rapidly in higher education. According to the results of a 2010 national survey administered by the Sloan Consortium and the Babson Survey Research Group of over twenty-five hundred accredited higher education institutions in the United States, "almost 4.6 million students were taking at least one online course during the fall 2008 term; a nearly 17 percent increase over the number reported the previous year." This means that "more than one in four higher education students now take at least one course online" (Allen & Seaman, 2010, p. 1). Palloff and Pratt (2003) report that according to the National Center for Education Statistics, about 60 percent of students take an online course during their college career.

With at least one-fourth of all American college students enrolled in an online course, and with these numbers continuing to increase, the need for faculty development supporting online course design and delivery is greater than ever before. However, "nearly one-fifth (19 percent) of all institutions do not provide any training (even informal mentoring) for their faculty teaching online courses" (Allen & Seaman, 2010, p. 11). Even among those institutions that provide professional development support for faculty making the transition to the online environment, over 30 percent of faculty surveyed perceived their institution's support for online course development as "below average" (Seaman, 2009).

With a lack of professional development for online instruction at some institutions and with poor faculty perceptions of the quality of existing programs at others, there is clearly a need to investigate the effectiveness of how existing techniques can be adapted for professional development for online instruction.

Small Group Individual Diagnosis: Development and Previous Evidence of Success

Small group individual diagnosis (SGID) is a faculty development technique designed to provide instructors with midsemester feedback from students about the quality of their instruction. The SGID process, originally developed by D. Joseph Clark at the University of Washington's Biology Learning Resource Center, was adapted from Melnik and Allen's clinical model at the University of Massachusetts (Clark & Bekey, 1979; Bergquist & Phillips, 1977). Since its inception, the SGID process has been known by a number of names, including "group interviews" (Braskamp, Ory, & Pieper, 1981). It has been altered to meet the needs of specific institutional contexts, but the basic process of the technique typically contains several common elements.

During an SGID, a facilitator elicits feedback directly from students in the classroom. Typically conducted about halfway through the semester, this process is designed to help faculty strengthen their teaching during the remainder of the semester by providing them with anonymous, candid feedback on the course's strengths and weaknesses. This carefully constructed process consists of several steps. First, the instructor meets with the facilitator to review the SGID process and schedules about thirty minutes of class time in which the SGID will take place. Next, on the day of the SGID, the instructor introduces the facilitator to the class, explains the purpose of the process, and leaves the room. The facilitator then divides the students into small groups; each group of students must come to a consensus about what they like about a course, what they do not like, and what suggestions they have for improving it (Coffman, 1998; Wulff, Staton-Spicer, Hess, & Nyquist, 1985). This information is then shared with the other students and with the facilitator. In some cases, the facilitator initiates a discussion about the results and asks the entire class to come to a consensus about the course's strengths and weaknesses. After the session, the facilitator meets with the instructor in an individual teaching consultation to discuss the results as well as ways to improve the course. Finally, the instructor responds to the students' feedback during the next class session (Wulff et al., 1985).

Some studies have been conducted on the effectiveness of SGID as a classroom-based evaluation technique. Seldin (1988) found that the SGID process opened the lines of communication between faculty and students. Creed (1997) reported that students who participated in the process felt that their voices had been heard, that the process brings back into the group those with extremely divergent views, and that "because an SGID provides more reflective feedback, the information is qualitatively different than that gotten in end-of-the-semester ratings." Seldin (1993) suggests that if course evaluations are to be used to improve instruction, they should be given within a semester so that instructors have a chance to adjust their teaching.

One of the strengths of SGID is the follow-up teaching consultation to discuss the results of the process. According to McKeachie and Kaplan (1996), consultation with an expert is an important factor in determining the amount of improvement that a teacher makes. Redmond (1982) explains several other factors of the SGID process that have an impact on faculty development. Since the instructor receives feedback from students around midterm, students have a genuine opportunity to evaluate the effect of their feedback and the receptivity and responsiveness of the instructor. Chen and Hoshower (2003) found that students generally consider the improvement of course content and format, thus creating an improvement in teaching as one of the most important outcomes of teaching evaluations. The major benefit SGID provides to students is the opportunity to compare views, which is not accomplished with traditional paper-and-pencil evaluations at the end of the semester (Redmond, 1982). Also, students participating in an SGID can impose their own priorities and values, as well as provide constructive suggestions on how to handle current problems (Schein & Bennis, 1965). Finally, small group research (Tubbs, 1997) generally supports the contention that using small group discussion for organizational decision making will result in more active acceptance of changes (Redmond, 1982).

Impetus for the Study

Because SGID has been an effective technique to improve instruction, as demonstrated through the literature and our own experiences in implementing this technique in traditional classroom-based courses, there was a growing interest—and need—to adapt this technique for online education. Also, since faculty prefer individual consultations with faculty development staff as the mode of training for learning to teach online (Kinuthia, 2005; Carroll, 1993; Gilbert, 1995), there was reason to suspect that individual consultations as part of the online SGID process would also be perceived positively by faculty. The purpose of this study was to evaluate faculty members' perceptions of the effectiveness of SGID as a development tool when adapted to online instruction.

Only one other study analyzed the use of SGID when modified for distance or online education. Sherry and Burke (1995) evaluated the effectiveness of interactive television courses through online computer-mediated communication. The results of the study support the success of its translation to the online forum, stating meaningful communication from all participants. The courses in this study included those facilitated by video and two-way audio. This study builds on the previous findings by Sherry and Burke by investigating the application of SGID to contemporary, Internet-based courses that use course management software and other technologies that were not available during the 1995 study.

However, Millis and Vasquez (2010–2011) contend that quick course diagnosis is more efficient and effective than the SGID. Although the tools are quite similar, the use of SGID in online courses blends elements of each. According to Millis and Vasquez, conducting the SGID in Blackboard's virtual classroom is similar to the collaborative brainstorming activity, or roundtable, data collection. Instant message chat supports rapid-fire comments that furthers idea development within the group. The transcribed activity is then saved to a file in order to avoid error that may occur in documenting the SGID in the traditional classroom. Furthermore, Millis and Vasquez argue that SGIDs take up too much class time. One of the major reasons students enroll in an online course is the ability to complete assignments asynchronously (Richardson & Swan, 2003; Drennan, Kennedy, & Pisarski, 2005; Watson & Rutledge, 2005). Conducting the

SGID online avoids classroom disruption considering there are no set class times.

Framework and Methodology

In her 2004 article, "Using a Framework to Engage Faculty in Instructional Technologies," Nancy Chism outlines a conceptual framework that faculty developers can use to "better estimate the potential effectiveness of various strategies" (p. 39) for teaching faculty how to use technology effectively for instruction. Chism's framework describes faculty learning as a cycle consisting of four repeating steps: planning, acting, observing, and reflecting on their teaching. Two components of her framework are key to evaluating the potential effectiveness of a faculty development program. First, Chism explains that transformative experiences within this cycle tend to occur when faculty recognize a problematic situation. In other words, when faculty realize that an aspect of their teaching is not working effectively, this is often the catalyst for change. Next, Chism recommends specific developmental approaches for each of the four phases of this cycle: if a faculty development program addresses the specific needs of the faculty in each of these phases, the program is more likely to be successful. This framework will be helpful to analyze whether the application of SGID to online classes has the potential to be effective according to Chism's framework.

The study began by recruiting and preparing SGID facilitators as well as faculty participants. First, facilitators were selected: one was a staff member in the institution's faculty development office; the other was a reference librarian who was also a member of an institution-wide faculty learning community focused on online education. Facilitators were selected based on two criteria. One was that they had to have experience with online education or at least a strong familiarity with research related to online education. For this reason, members of the faculty learning community, who all were familiar with the literature on online learning and demonstrated proficiency with educational technologies, were invited to apply. The other criterion for selection was that the facilitator could not be from the same college as the participant. The motivation for this criterion was to prevent possible bias and ensure confidentiality. For this study, a research librarian with expertise in technology and facilitation was selected to avoid potential intradepartmental conflicts.

Facilitators were provided with an informational packet that included detailed directions concerning their role in the process. The facilitators collaborated during all phases of the project to ensure that the process was consistent. Next, the sixteen instructors who were teaching online courses during the upcoming semester were invited to participate in the project; seven of the sixteen volunteered. The instructors who chose to participate selected one of their classes for the online SGID and asked the students to participate; participation was not mandatory or tied to the students' course grades. The courses in the study encompassed five disciplines (education, philosophy, business, English, and computer science) and both undergraduate and graduate students.

Data were collected from participating faculty members through surveys and semistructured interviews. First, instructors completed an online needs assessment survey about their previous experience with online instruction, their current online course, their expectations for the SGID process, and their future goals and needs for professional growth related to online education. They were then matched with a facilitator; they met with the facilitator to review the process and select a date for the SGID to take place. Instructions were sent to students, who were told to log on to the course management system's online chat feature at a designated day and time. In many cases, multiple sessions were arranged in order to accommodate conflicts with student schedules. During the online session, the facilitator asked students to discuss the three most positive aspects of the course, as well as the three aspects of the course that needed the most improvement. The facilitator summarized results of the chat, eliminating student names and identifying information to ensure anonymity. After the SGID, faculty reviewed these results with the SGID facilitator in a teaching consultation. The facilitator then interviewed the faculty member about the SGID process; this interview was recorded on video.

The surveys and interviews gathered information about faculty participants' previous experience with online instruction and their challenges and expectations related to online instruction. These data provided valuable contextual information that assisted facilitators in both conducting the SGID and assisting the faculty member during the subsequent teaching consultations.

Participants

All participants completed an online background survey that provided valuable information about their experiences with online instruction. Five of the participating instructors were full time, and two were part time. Among the full-time faculty, all were tenure track; three were posttenure

Table 15.1. Profile of Participating Instructors.

Participant Number	Discipline	Number of Courses Previously Taught Online	Rank
1	Education	10	Associate professor (full time)
2	Education	4	Associate professor (full time)
3	Commerce	3	Assistant professor (full time)
4	Education	3	Lecturer (part time)
5	Computer and information sciences	2	Professor (full time)
6	English	2	Assistant professor (full time)
7	Philosophy	1	Lecturer (part time)

and two were pretenure. Participants varied in their previous experience with online instruction. (See Table 15.1.)

The background survey revealed that one instructor had taught a blended course, which includes at least one face-to-face class meeting; the others taught completely online, asynchronous courses. Three participants had previous professional development related to online instruction. The average class size was twenty-six students, and only three instructors had used Blackboard's chat feature, the tool used to conduct the SGID. Six instructors indicated that they were participating in the SGID because they were hoping to improve or refine their current course, two were planning to increase the number of online courses they were teaching, and four indicated that they were interested in continued professional development for online instruction.

Results

The purpose of this study was to evaluate faculty members' perceptions of the effectiveness of SGID as a faculty development tool when adapted to online instruction. The researchers identified five indicators to measure whether the use of SGID was effective and perceived positively by faculty participants:

1. The faculty member indicated that he or she personally benefited from the experience or felt that the experience would be helpful to others.
2. The faculty member found the feedback to be helpful for understanding either students' learning or whether the current course design was successful.
3. The faculty member was able to plan course improvements based on data gathered during the SGID.
4. The faculty member identified the need for or expressed interest in additional professional development as a result of participation in the SGID.
5. The faculty member felt that taking the time to participate in an SGID was beneficial; he or she would participate in the process again in a future class.

These indicators were identified through the researchers' perceptions of markers of a successful faculty development program; these perceptions were founded in experience with faculty development, as well as locally identified benchmarks at their institution.

The interview results below are presented by success indicator. Faculty interviews, which were conducted after the SGIDs took place, demonstrate that participating faculty perceived that SGID is a successful and useful tool for professional development and a beneficial vehicle for student feedback when applied to the online environment. Faculty responses for each of the success indicators appear below; responses were generally evenly distributed among the participants.

1. *The faculty member perceived that he or she personally benefited from the experience or felt that the experience would be helpful to others.* Faculty members found the SGID to be "extremely helpful." One participant explained, "What I expected, what I hoped for, was to get some real evaluation back from my students. Students are afraid to tell a professor exactly what they want." Many noted that the SGID was a vehicle to give them timely, accurate, and in-depth feedback about the course. One participant explained,

> [SGID] is the only feedback that [we] get other than the course evaluations. And with online classes, it's an online course evaluation, therefore, they can opt to do it or not. It's not like there's a piece of paper

> in front of you on the desk and someone is waiting to take it away. In a lot of cases, what I have found is that everybody who hated the class complained in the evaluations. . . . At least in this case, you have pros and cons. Something like this is very helpful for an online class. It gives a more balanced perspective to the instructor.

Faculty also explained that they benefited because they learned more about their students as online learners. One faculty participant explained, "I guess [SGID] gives me a different view of how students work." Another explained that "many of the students were not familiar with online learning" and were "reticent in terms of what to expect" from the online course. She had "taken for granted" that the students were familiar with the required technology. Another participant felt that the process made her "more aware of how to approach online learning" and recommended that instructors "who are not really sure for whatever reason how their students are feeling about the course" participate in the process.

Instructors also felt that they benefited from SGID because it validated their current practices or bolstered their confidence. Once faculty member remarked, "It really told me that I'm on the right path." Another person said, "Before, I was fumbling in the dark. I think the feedback is useful, especially for online classes, because we don't get feedback otherwise. Although online teaching is so convenient and effective, I need positive reinforcement too." Another professor explained, "At the end, I got a few indications on their reflection papers that they really liked the papers rather than just the text. Other than that, I had no clue. I haven't seen the official evaluations on the course. I think it went okay, everybody seemed happy, but this is nice to know that you interfaced with them, and they were saying positive things."

2. *The faculty member found the feedback to be helpful for either understanding students' learning or understanding whether the current course design was successful.* Each of the participants found student feedback to be helpful because it "validated the remarks that students made" in previous semesters' course evaluations. One person explained that "there were some consistent remarks that I sort of suspected but that are confirmed." Another faculty participant felt that "there's nothing really new here . . . [but] some of these remarks confirm things that . . . have been noted in the past" and that he was "not surprised" by the students' comments.

Five of the participants noted that the students' comments were more positive and helpful than they had anticipated. One of these faculty members noted, "There were some good responses in terms of how I can make the course better next semester for the students. So I really appreciated the feedback that I received from the study and from the students." Another explained that student feedback "surprised her on the pro-side" and helped her to understand "the things that the students like about the course, [such as] the consistency of the course, the organization of the course, [and] the feedback that I give to them. Interestingly enough, they don't feel like they're treated like students, but that they're treated more like colleagues. I don't know what I'm doing that they feel that way, but it'd be interesting to find out." Overall, in some cases, the data served to confirm previous course feedback; in other cases, the data helped the instructors identify successful elements in their approach to online teaching.

3. *The faculty member is able to plan course improvements based on the data gathered during the SGID.* Each of the faculty participants planned on making improvements to their online courses based on the data gathered during the SGID. In each of the cases, the planned changes were the result of very specific student feedback. One faculty member planned to incorporate a live component to the course, either on-campus office hours or availability by Skype, after learning that her graduate students wanted to talk to her face-to-face. Another faculty member, who teaches a course that requires a twenty-hour service component, planned to reduce the number of hours to ten after learning that most of her students worked full time and had families to care for. However, she increased the number of text-based quizzes after discovering that they were surprisingly popular among the students and also "forced" the students to complete the required reading. A third faculty member planned to provide more technical support to help her students learn how to do voice-overs in PowerPoint for a class assignment. She is also going to improve the organization of online files so that her students will be able to find what they are looking for more easily. In each case, the changes are very specific improvements based on detailed student feedback.

4. *The faculty member identified the need or expressed interest in additional professional development as a result of participation in the SGID.* Two faculty participants, both of whom had taught at least three courses online, felt that they did not need any further professional development. One of them explained that she was already proficient in the technology; the other said, "I don't know that you really need training, other than knowing that the capability is there."

However, the less experienced faculty participants expressed a strong desire for continued support. One explained, "I have not read much literature—I probably haven't read any of the literature—on how to conduct an online class. I've been feeling my way, and I probably would benefit from the experience of other instructors." Another participant advocated for additional training:

> We need many more opportunities to continue learning about online instruction. There is so much technology out there that's upgraded daily. I don't want to become passé. I don't want to be working in a medieval century when the students know much more about it than I do and can do many more things. I think we need to know what's out there and how to incorporate that into online instruction. I also believe that we need to help new online instructors who are looking for support from experienced people. These results corroborate responses from the pre-SGID faculty survey. In general, participants who asked for more professional development were those who had less previous experience with online instruction.

5. *The faculty member felt that taking the time to participate in an SGID was beneficial and would participate in the process again in a future class.* All participants interviewed were interested in participating in an SGID again. Two faculty members mentioned a willingness to participate because of a lack of time commitment on their behalf. One said that he would participate again because he does not "see a reason not to." Another said that she would participate again because the SGID was "nothing that I had to worry about."

Five participants explained that they wanted "to hear more" from their students because they "got a lot of valuable feedback" and that if "there are ideas out there [from students] that could help, I should be open to them." One said that she would "absolutely" participate in order to find additional ways to be innovative and that she "love[s] the fact that I'm part of the study, I think it's a healthy experience for us all. We need to know how well we're doing, and I think that this is one excellent way that can give us that measure, that opportunity." Finally, one instructor explained, "I'm really grateful for the SGID. Otherwise, I just had nothing to go on."

Discussion

Faculty responses demonstrated a positive view of the online SGID process. Analyzed through Chism's conceptual framework, online SGID has demonstrated potential effectiveness as a faculty development approach for helping faculty learn how to teach online. Online SGID provides faculty with information about problems in a course: Chism argues that faculty recognition of problems in their teaching is often the impetus needed to spur faculty to change within the ongoing four-step learning cycle. As the results explained, the online SGID process resulted in faculty identifying areas for change within their courses, planning change, and expressing the desire for further participation in professional development. Feedback from students allowed faculty to identify and evaluate possible weaknesses in their course, as well as validate strong areas.

Chism also recommended specific developmental approaches for faculty in each of the four phases of the faculty learning cycle. She argues that faculty development programs should address the specific needs of the faculty in each of these phases to increase their chances for success. Chism explains that faculty in the reflecting phase benefit most from programs that help them reflect on the effectiveness of their current teaching practices, such as programs that provide them with information on their teaching or identify existing instructional needs. Online SGID provides this information, as well as the peer support that Chism recommends during this phase. Faculty in the planning phase benefit from additional ideas for teaching or information that helps evaluate the usefulness of ideas. Online SGID offers a space for this information sharing to take place during the teaching consultations that follow the online meetings with students. Faculty in the acting phase need support in implementing a teaching innovation, such as encouragement from a peer or instructional developer experienced in the approach. Relationships formed with the facilitator in the online SGID process can be extended to support faculty involved in this phase of the faculty learning cycle. Finally, faculty in the observing phase are searching for information about the effectiveness of a new approach; Chism specifically recommends "informal oral or written student reactions . . . or using a mid-semester course evaluation process" (p. 43) to provide faculty with this information. Online SGID as a faculty development tool clearly fits this need well and is potentially effective for faculty at any stage of Chism's faculty learning cycle.

Challenges and Opportunities

The faculty who participated in the online SGID process gained valuable insights into their own teaching, had a positive perception of the process, and expressed the desire for future participation in the online SGID program. Analysis of the adaptation of this faculty development technique to the online environment indicates that this strategy has the potential to be effective in helping faculty in any stage of Chism's faculty learning cycle. However, although the overall approach appeared to be successful, some logistical challenges arose that made implementation of the program more difficult. These challenges led to several insights and recommendations that other faculty developers can apply to minimize potential problems in implementing a similar program at their own institutions.

Student participation in these online SGIDs was lower than anticipated: whereas students in a traditional, classroom-based SGID are a captive audience, an online, synchronous SGID can make student participation more difficult. The lower participation could be primarily attributed to the terms of the institutional review board approval for this study, which required faculty not to offer rewards or require student participation in the process as part of the course grade. Without mandating participation in the process through extra credit, a participation grade, or other incentive, faculty developers conducting an online SGID can anticipate similar low student participation in the SGID. For asynchronous courses, it may also be helpful to offer more than one time for participation in the synchronous online discussion in order to accommodate conflicting student schedules.

Faculty resistance to participation in an online SGID was an unexpected challenge. Of the sixteen faculty invited to participate in the study, only seven accepted the offer; three of the faculty who opted not to participate noted specific reasons for their refusal. One was retiring at the end of the semester, and so the need to improve teaching for future courses was not necessary. However, the other two faculty members expressed anxiety about confidentiality. Although the facilitators provided faculty with assurances of complete confidentiality, including prepared confidentiality forms approved by the university's institutional review board, these faculty members remained anxious that negative student feedback would somehow be shared with their colleagues. Because both faculty were about to be reviewed for promotion, they declined participation. Their reaction demonstrates the need for professional development in online instruction: these faculty members—who consistently receive stellar reviews for their classroom teaching—lacked such confidence about the quality of their instruction online that they felt that student feedback had the potential to damage their professional reputations. Faculty developers implementing an online SGID program should be prepared with alternative ways to support faculty who are anxious about receiving feedback about their online teaching, such as private, confidential individual teaching consultations.

REFERENCES

Allen I. E., & Seaman, J. (2010). *Learning on demand: Online education in the United States, 2009*. Retrieved from http://www.sloan-c.org/publications/survey/pdf/learningondemand.pdf

Bergquist, W. H., & Philips, S. R. (1977). *A handbook for faculty development*. Washington, DC: Council for the Advancement of Small Colleges.

Braskamp, L. A., Ory, J. C., & Pieper, D. M. (1981). Student written comments: Dimensions of instructional quality. *Journal of Educational Psychology, 73*, 65–70.

Carroll, R. G. (1993). Implications of adult education theories for medical school faculty development programmes. *Medical Teacher 15*(2/3), 163–170.

Chen, Y., & Hoshower, L. B. (2003). Student evaluation of teaching effectiveness: An assessment of student perception and motivation. *Assessment and Evaluation in Higher Education, 28*(1), 71–88.

Chism, N. (2004). Using a framework to engage faculty in instructional technologies. *EDUCAUSE Quarterly, 2*, 39–45.

Clark, D. J., & Bekey, J. (1979). Use of small groups in instructional evaluation. *Journal of the Professional and Organizational Development Network in Higher Education, 1*, 87–95.

Coffman, S. J. (1998). Small group instructional evaluation across disciplines. *College Teaching, 46*(3), 106.

Creed, T. (1997). Small group instructional diagnosis. *National Teaching and Learning Forum, 6*(4). Retrieved from http://www.ntlf.com/html/pi/9705/sgid.htm

Drennan, J., Kennedy, J., & Pisarski, A. (2005). Factors affecting student attitudes toward flexible online learning in management education. *Journal of Educational Research, 98*(6), 331–338.

Gilbert, S. (1995). Teaching, learning and technology: The need for campuswide planning and faculty support services. *Change, 27*(2), 46–52.

Kinuthia, W. (2005). Planning faculty development for successful implementation of Web-based instruction. *Campus-Wide Information Systems, 22*(4), 189–200.

Millis, B. J., & Vasquez, J. (2010–2011). Down with the SGID! Long live the QCD! *Essays on Teaching Excellence Toward the Best in the Academy, 22*(4), 1–5.

McKeachie, W. J., & Kaplan, M. (1996, February). Persistent problems in evaluating college teaching. *AAHE Bulletin, 48*(6), 5–8.

Palloff, R. M., & Pratt, K. (2003). *The virtual student: A profile and guide to working with online learners*. San Francisco, CA: Jossey-Bass.

Richardson, J. C., & Swan, K. (2003). Examining social presence in online courses in relation to students' perceived learning and satisfaction. *Journal of Asynchronous Learning Networks, 7*(1), 68–88.

Redmond, M. V. (1982). *A process of midterm evaluation incorporating small group discussion of a course and its effect on student motivation.* Washington, DC: U.S. Department of Education Educational Resources Information Center.

Schein, E. H., & Bennis, W. G. (1965). *Personal and organizational change through group methods.* Hoboken, NJ: Wiley.

Seaman, J. (2009). *Online learning as a strategic asset. Volume II: The paradox of faculty voices: Views and experiences with online learning.* Washington, DC: Association of Public and Land-Grant Universities.

Seldin, P. (1988). Evaluating college teaching. In R. E. Young & K. E. Eble (Eds.), *New directions for teaching and learning: No. 33.* San Francisco, CA: Jossey-Bass.

Seldin, P. (1993, July 10). The use and abuse of student ratings of professors. *Chronicle of Higher Education.*

Sherry, A. C., & Burke, W. F. (1995). Applying an interactive evaluation model to interactive television. In *Proceedings of the 1995 Annual National Convention of the Association for Educational Communications and Technology (AECT).* Anaheim, CA.

Tubbs, S. L. (1997). *A systems approach to small group interaction* (6th ed.). New York, NY: McGraw-Hill.

Watson, S. W., & Rutledge, V. C. (2005). *Online course delivery and student satisfaction.* (ED490363)

Wulff, D. H., Staton-Spicer, A. Q., Hess, C. W., & Nyquist, J. D. (1985). The student perspective on evaluating teaching effectiveness. *ACA Bulletin, 53,* 39–47.

PART SIX

SETTING A CONTEXT FOR PROMOTING DIVERSITY

16

SUPPORTING INTERNATIONAL FACULTY

PERSPECTIVES OF A TIGER TEACHER WHO ADAPTED TO THE AMERICAN CLASSROOM, A COLLEAGUE, AND AN ADMINISTRATOR

Cuiting Li, Sterling K. Wall, Marty Loy, Kelly Schoonaert
University of Wisconsin–Stevens Point

This chapter is an account of a Chinese faculty member's experiences integrating into American higher education. Told from three points of view, her story emphasizes the importance of openness and willingness to talk about cultural issues.

o

International scholars contribute to campus diversity, awareness of global contexts, scientific improvement, and international expertise (see Altbach, 2005, 2006; Horn, Hendel, & Fry, 2007; Mamiseishvili, 2010; NAFSA, 2006; Stromquist, 2007). The number of international students and scholars is increasing rapidly in colleges and universities. The Institute of International Education reported 126,123 international scholars teaching or doing research in U.S. universities during the 2007–2008 academic year, 8 percent more than the prior year (Institute of International Education, 2008). The 2004 National Study of Postsecondary Faculty

(NSOPF: 04) survey found that 36.8 percent of foreign-born scholars in the United States were women.

However, it is not enough to recruit diverse faculty; ongoing communication and support must take place (Tuitt, Sagaria, & Turner, 2007). International scholars have been found to be more involved in research and have more publications but are less engaged in teaching and less satisfied with their jobs compared to American faculty (Corley & Sabharwal, 2007; Johnson & Regets, 1998; Levin & Stephen 1999; Mamiseishvili, 2010; Marvasti, 2005; Wells, 2007). Students continuously doubt and challenge the teaching quality of international faculty, which affects their teaching evaluation and promotion evaluation (Skachkova, 2007). Often international scholars excel in research functions but struggle in meeting teaching obligations (Mamiseishvili, 2010). Foreign-born teachers face many challenges, including language; accent; rejection by students; isolation; alienation; difficulty balancing teaching, scholarship, and service; lack of support; racism, prejudice; and bias (Essien, 2003; Jackson-Weaver, 2011; Mamiseishvili, 2010; Mayuzumi, 2008; Michaels, 2011; Skachkova, 2000). Different cultural backgrounds and unfamiliarity with U.S. cultural norms in teaching and learning play a key role in these challenges (Thomas & Johnson, 2004). Suggestions have been made to universities to help international faculty succeed in the teaching environment by, for example, pairing them with mentors, increasing institutional support, or trying to construct a friendlier environment (Fouad & Carter, 1992; Atkinson, Brown, Casas, & Zane, 1996; Moradi, & Neimeyer, 2005; Pololi, 2010; Sharon, 2011). It important for administrators to realize that developing strategies for diverse faculty requires understanding cultural identity at the individual level (Smith, 2009).

Toward that end, this chapter is a case study of discovery, perseverance, and uncovering subtle nuances that vastly changed the experiences of both student and teacher. This is a story of an articulate, passionate, competent professor of Chinese descent, Cuiting Li, and her experiences assimilating into a midsize university in upstate New York and then again at another university in the Midwest. The insights offered illustrate what is truly meant by "accepting cultural diversity."

This story is told from three perspectives: that of the foreign-born professor, Cuiting Li; her colleague, mentor, and friend, Sterling Wall; and her department chair, and now dean, Marty Loy. The story begins in China where Li was educated in the traditional Chinese way from elementary school, through middle and high school and then in the university. Like the recent media attention around Chinese "tiger mothers," one might say that in China, "tiger teachers" push students to the pinnacle of performance and are respected and loved because of their strict teaching methods (Chua, 2011).

Li's Perspective

Tiger Teachers

In China, I was taught by "tiger teachers" and thought they were very good teachers. Teachers had authority in everything, and students were not encouraged to question or disagree. If students did not do well on exams, teachers could yell at students and also at their parents. From elementary school, we were required to sit in class quietly—no moving, no talking, just listening and following teachers' directions. If someone couldn't concentrate on the teacher's lectures, the teacher would throw chalk at the student, often hitting the student's face. Sometimes the teacher would quietly go over to that unattentive student and pull him or her out of the seat suddenly. The student would be shocked and stand there red-faced as classmates stared, like a thief caught red-handed. Sometimes the teacher might call the student's name and ask him or her to answer a question. The student would stand there speechless, in front of classmates and the teacher because not being able to answer the teacher's questions was shameful.

I was not a good student in the early years (I was always distracted by pens, pencils, flies, trees, sunlight, or my own thoughts) so I experienced this treatment from several times a day in elementary school to a few times each semester in middle and high school. Nevertheless, I grew up happily, had great memories about my school years, and never complained about the teachers or hated them. On the contrary, I loved school and I loved the teachers because I went to one of the best universities with their help (I was in the top 1 percent of students in the area). I firmly believed that good teachers should hold high expectations for students and that this type of behavior was necessary and accepted as evidence of high functioning, even for professors.

Becoming a Professor

Li finished her formal education in China and taught three years in a traditional Chinese university before coming to the United States to get a master's degree and Ph.D. in human development and family studies from Auburn University. Li's first job teaching as an assistant professor in a state school in New York was another kind of acclimation beyond her experiences as a student in America. This acclimation to American culture and the expectations of an American educator now took her to the next level of challenge and became much more difficult.

Li's Perspective

LANGUAGE CHALLENGES. When I started teaching, I worked very hard to be a good professor. I spent over ten hours preparing for each one-hour class. I was very serious about the material, lectured for the entire class period, and sometimes kept students longer than the allotted time because I thought (according to my background) that was how you prove you are diligent and competent—a master of content. Nevertheless, my student evaluations were bad. Students complained the class was boring, unclear, stressful, and even threatening. Feeling insulted, hurt, frustrated, scared, and confused, I worked even harder—and got worse evaluations.

Finally I began to identify and address some of my challenges. The first basic challenge I faced was speaking fluent English. I started learning British English at age twelve in China. After I came to the United States, I spent a lot of effort mastering English by reading scholarly articles. When I started teaching, I had no problem communicating material in my professional field of expertise. However, I did not understand my students when they talked about their lives outside the classroom. Academic topics were easy to talk about; real life was not. As I became friends with colleagues, I felt more at ease asking questions so that I could understand my students' examples and lives. I have tried using humor, but that doesn't always work. Sometimes my students or colleagues didn't think I was funny because Chinese humor doesn't translate well. So in class I use funny pictures instead of jokes for entertainment.

Sometimes I still have difficulty with language. Once I came to school at about 11:00 A.M. to get ready to teach that afternoon. One of my colleagues asked me if I had slept late. I smiled proudly and said, "Yes!" I was puzzled by the look she gave me. It was not until a year and a half later that I learned from another colleague that in America, "sleeping late" means getting up late. In China, "sleeping late" means you went to sleep late. In fact, when I was asked that question, I had stayed up until 4:00 A.M. preparing for class. Colloquialisms can be challenging.

One of my colleagues has suggested to me that I should tell my students to ask for clarification if they do not understand something that I have said in class. Taking a moment early in the semester to state the obvious—that there might be some confusion due to language differences—and then to instruct students on what to do if they do not understand a word or idea allows students to ask in a way that does not make the student or me uncomfortable.

WORKLOAD AND TEACHING CHALLENGES. Sometimes I spend up to ten hours preparing for each lecture. In addition to understanding the material and planning how to teach it, I need to rehearse each sentence I want to say and learn the pronunciation of the words, especially if there is a specialized vocabulary. I used to write every sentence down and memorize them.

When I started teaching, I slept only five or six hours a night, even on the weekends, and had no leisure time. Few people understood why I was so busy and tired, including my best friends and my parents. I resented my teaching job for a long time. I no longer need as much preparation time, but it is still difficult to talk to anyone before class as I am making last-minute adjustments to my presentation.

I was surprised by some of the ways my colleagues conducted their classes, so different from my Chinese teachers. But over the years, I have changed my teaching, and I now use information from different sources besides the textbook—for example, news releases, videos, Web sites, magazines, and guest speakers. I also added online quizzes and surveys and the use of interactive activities where students can anonymously and electronically answer questions in class.

OUTSIDER STATUS. My students often still see me as an outsider. My colleagues shared with me the PowerPoints they were using in a different section of the same class I was teaching, and I used them, though with a few changes. But my students were angry about the grammatical mistakes I had made in my slides; they pointed out the mistakes immediately and criticized my English. But these errors were in the slides when I got them, and I was surprised that neither my colleagues nor their students had noticed these errors. In addition, students have complained that the wording in my exams was weird, or poor, yet these questions were taken from a publisher's test bank and had been selected by the American instructor who had preceded me. The students continued to complain even after I told them about this test bank. I remain extra conscious of my grammar when e-mailing students and colleagues.

A New Position: Starting Over

On the advice of graduate school friend and mentor, Sterling Wall, Li applied for a new position in Wisconsin that focused on increasing student exposure to diversity. Li accepted the offer, but that was just the start of the process of beginning a new job for both Li and her new employer.

The wait for a visa to get approval to transfer to a different university was about a year and a half. At that point, Li was already halfway through the green card application process (incurring expenses of about six thousand dollars, with each additional call to her lawyer paid from her own pocket) when she was offered the position, and she had already waited years for her application to be accepted. Li needed a green card to stay and work legally long term in the United States because a working visa allows only a six-year maximum in-country stay. If she could not get a green card within this period, she would have had to leave the country, permanently even if she had a job, because the working visa is directly connected to the job. If she changed jobs, she needed to restart the green card application process, which, for a Chinese citizen, is usually more than a five-year process. Therefore, changing jobs may have meant that she would not be able to get the green card within the required time frame.

Many delays kept the new position in limbo, and Li was very nervous about the effect that moving would have on her application. She worried, in fact, that she might have to start the green card process all over again. During that wait, she did not visit her family in China because she worried that she might not be allowed to reenter the United States with just the visa. She might also have lost the job and the right to work and stay in the United States if she did not obtain the visa in time.

During this time Li was in immigration limbo, she was unsure whether the job offer from Wisconsin would be rescinded or whether her New York employer would continue to employ her until her immigration status was clear. If that happened, she would have to return to China. But her department in Wisconsin covered her courses while she was waiting for all the paperwork to get sorted out, and finally things fell in place. She moved to Wisconsin, and the acclimation and adjustment process started all over again.

Li's Perspective on Academic Adjustment

I had gotten used to work in New York and made progress in teaching, and then I changed jobs. When I started teaching in Wisconsin, it was very frustrating: new courses, new students, new schedules, and even a new culture. I was back working day and night just to keep my head above water. My teaching evaluations and self-esteem were low, my frustration high, and I was depressed and lonely. It was very, very difficult.

My new university has a program called Teaching Partners, where faculty are paired with a mentor for a year to help them in their teaching. The mentor also meets periodically with the mentee's students, without the mentee there, to get their feedback about how the class is going. The mentor shares the results. I have finished the program, but I asked my mentor to come to my class several times last semester. His visits completely changed students' opinions of me! Each time he came to class, he told them that I was working hard to improve my teaching and that he was there to get their ideas on what I could improve. Through meeting with him and other colleagues, I made further progress addressing challenges to my teaching.

For example, I now go to class early to give students access to ask questions or chat. I used to believe good professors should not go to class early. In China, this never indicated a professor was proficient. There, if the professor was early, he or she waited outside the door until the appointed time, then entered and promptly began lecturing. It was an amazingly enlightening moment when, during a meeting with my department and personnel chairs, this cultural difference was brought to light.

I began trying some new class activities. I used to give students a list of questions to answer for each lecture so that they had to think instead of taking notes passively. I tried to engage students by calling on them individually by name to answer a question or give an example. I was frustrated that students never answered or raised their hands. Again, in another routine meeting, my department chair pointed out another cultural difference: our students are highly self-conscious and do not like to stand out. Dr. Wall, my mentor, suggested I use the think-pair-share method, where students first think about a question or concept and write briefly about it, then share answers with a partner. When I then asked questions, students were ready, willing, and able to share their answers since they had already discussed the topic with their classmates.

I began briefly introducing the content before I lectured. When I was growing up in China, I was taught to follow the teacher passively in class and was used to surprises, not knowing ahead of time what they might discuss. Again, thanks to my department chair, I learned that American students prefer to know the big picture first.

I tried to explain assignments in more detail. It turns out that my understanding of clarity is very different from that of my students. Many students like to envision the final product and feel uncomfortable if they are given too much latitude. Preparing students to accept more responsibility for envisioning a final product helps them accept that responsibility, and allowing them to participate in the development helps alleviate issues down the road.

I tried to be more encouraging and positive to students. I used to believe it was normal and good to be harsh and direct with students. Just as a Chinese person may say to a friend or family member, "You are fat; lose some weight," a Chinese teacher may tell a student, "You are wrong; do it again." Chinese professors are direct and to the point. They do not spend time worrying about students' reactions because harsh words mean teachers are just being honest, not offensive. Nevertheless, now that I frame feedback positively, the reactions from students are better.

These changes have helped me connect with students and improved my course evaluations. However, it does not mean that I have changed completely. I have become a bit more lenient with students, but I still find that I have had to rein in the amount of freedom students expect. My students had told me that during lectures, it was normal for students to talk, leave the room to go to the bathroom, text, or check e-mails. But I found that teaching a large-enrollment class became a huge challenge because students were distracted by their own and others' activities. Taking the advice of a colleague, I moved back to being stricter with classroom discipline once again. Now I have simple rules: no laptop, no cell phone ringing, and no talking—but I still smile. So returning to being the "Chinese tiger teacher" has made my teaching a big class more effective. Finding the median between both approaches, the Chinese and the American, is serving me well.

A Colleague's Perspective: Sterling Wall

Communicating Openly Helps Cross Culture Barriers

Sometimes when Li is co-teaching or working on a project with another faculty member who is higher ranking, older, or more senior, she often defers to that person, not offering many opinions and respecting the other's direction. To those of us in her department, it seemed baffling, and we wondered why she did not speak up. But we didn't say anything, so as not to be rude, and simply thought that she was not contributing. Later, however, Li confessed that she felt shut out because her colleagues did not acknowledge or bring up awkward issues. Once we all talked, however, we quickly were able to understand one another.

Especially noteworthy is that every time that Li has finally understood some of the underlying cultural differences, she immediately made changes. It was not for lack of desire and certainly not laziness. It is simply the very real difference between how she sees the world and how we do. Experiences we take for granted, she never had.

Promoting Her Positive Image to Students Helps Both

Last fall, before I began a guest lecture in Li's class, I told the students that they needed to know something about their instructor. I explained to them how hard she had worked at Auburn, day and night. I told them the funny story about how my wife and I taught her how to drive (we made her sit in the driver's seat and drive down the freeway with clenched fists around the wheel). I also told them about an e-mail that she had received last year when we had sent a mass announcement inviting them to study abroad for three weeks with her in China. A student had responded to her saying things like, "Aren't they the reason there is an overpopulation problem? Isn't that where SARS started? Aren't they taking all our jobs? Wouldn't it be better if they didn't exist? No, I don't want to go to China with you." Of course, Li was polite, as always, and had simply forwarded the e-mail to me asking, "Sterling, how should I respond to this?" My point to the class was that they have a hard-working person here, with a wealth of experience from a major country in the world, who is giving her very best efforts on their behalf. I then gave my lecture.

A couple of weeks later, Li showed me an e-mail from a different student, expressing gratitude for her hard work and lectures. Li was enormously pleased and happy. In fact, she told me that after my lecture, she could tell the difference in student attitudes toward her in that large class of three hundred. They were kinder, more respectful, and engaged.

An Administrator's Perspective: Marty Loy

One of a department chair's responsibility is to recruit, hire, and mentor new faculty who will help the department meet its mission. One of the goals of our department is to increase student exposure to all types of diversity. With Li, we had an opportunity to bring a Chinese citizen face-to-face with our students, and because she was interested in leading study-abroad programs and creating a student exchange with China, many of our students could be exposed to one of the most interesting cultures in the world.

Being Patient and Accepting Is Very Important

Another responsibility of a department chair is to provide the support necessary to help faculty lead successful, rewarding academic lives, which includes getting them over the often pressure-filled hurdle of tenure. This is what led me to work closely with Li in her new role within our university.

Cuiting Li is a ball of complexity—a mix of strength, confidence, and independence with naiveté, seemingly illogical behaviors to my

American sensitivities, and lack of "American common sense." I found her to be meek and charming, yet she was the toughest salary negotiator that I had ever encountered. She was a good thinker and accomplished scholar, yet she had difficulty understanding the financial aspect of buying a new house in America. She was so independent that she had left the security of her family in China, yet navigating the visa process confounded her. These dichotomies, as confusing as they were at the time, were, in hindsight, the result of simple differences of cultures. Being patient and accepting was very important when working with her because it was difficult to predict when language and culture barriers would arise.

Understanding Culture

Cultural differences created difficulties in her teaching too. It was hard work for me to understand Li's complexities, and her teaching evaluations were below average. She asked many questions, and because cultural differences would not allow her to fully accept the offered answers, sometimes she would ask the same question over and over again. Mentoring her took more of my time and energy than any other new faculty member had ever taken.

Our students, most of them from small town rural America, liked Li but struggled to understand her teaching. They said that she "made you feel horrible and embarrassed" or "appears rude and intimidating." By being direct with her feedback, Li was only trying to help, but they saw her comments as hurtful. By lecturing didactically, she was providing her students with an expert, which was surely something that they would appreciate, but they were more interested in each other's opinions than they were in hers. By coming to class a few minutes late, Li thought she was ensuring that her students had time to ready themselves for class. Instead, they felt that she was unapproachable and took the tardiness as a sign of being unorganized.

At first, it seemed to Li that the harder she worked, the worse her teaching evaluations became. I gave her Brookfield and Preskill's *Discussion as a Way of Teaching: Tools and Techniques for Democratic Classrooms* (2005), which I thought was a brilliant book, but it only confused her. I told her to smile more and be more personable to her students, but in light of her strict cultural behaviors, these suggestions confused her. I suggested that she just be herself when she taught, which of course caused her to accentuate all of those cultural differences that were already causing her trouble.

Enhancing Teaching

Over time, and with a great deal of hard work on her part and on the parts of her colleagues and students, teaching became easier for Li. She gained insights into how cultural differences between students and teachers affect student satisfaction and learning and began to understand her students better. Li had more and more "aha" moments when she became more confident and comfortable, and a better teacher.

It has also been hard work for her students. But I am certain that now they leave her classrooms not only understanding required content but with a much better understanding of the complexities of the world. Over time and with hard work, I too began to appreciate Li and her culture. She and I have become close friends through all of this, and that is exactly the type of ending that I hope all of our students have when they encounter her.

Summary of Success: Lessons Learned for Administrators and Colleagues

The experience of learning to teach in the United State is interesting in many people's eyes because there are so many moments of epiphany. However, it has been a painful experience for Cuiting Li. Similar to other scholars from foreign countries, she experienced many difficulties: different teaching style expectations, misinterpretation of the language, a heavy workload, alienation, and criticism caused by mistrust (Essien, 2003; Jackson-Weaver, 2011; Mamiseishvili, 2010; Mayuzumi, 2008; Michaels, 2011; Skachkova, 2000).

Support and caring from colleagues and administrators was a key to her success. She would not have succeeded had she been left struggling by herself. At the individual level, understanding the concerns and experiences of international faculty, providing mentorship involving coaching, political management, and emotional support, are very important (Atkinson et al., 1996; Jackson-Weaver, 2011). In Li's case, unconditional acceptance and the following support from colleagues and administrators played a significant role in her successful transition and adaptation to teaching in a U.S. university:

- Being open and accepting even when asking questions that her students found awkward such as why they go home on the weekend or why they missed class for a doctor's appointment
- Observing her behavior and style and giving suggestions to remove blind spots due to culture differences

- Addressing misunderstandings, frustration, or confusion openly
- Being patient, even when she asked the same questions over and over or when she did not immediately make alterations as suggested
- Creating a positive image of her in students' eyes, as colleagues stepped in to give her students a peek behind the scenes, helping them understand their foreign professor—her intentions, background, and that she had their best interests at heart
- Advocating for her when she was treated unfairly, even if she may not have even realized it
- Assisting her through ongoing discussion to clarify and frame her questions in a way that is understandable to all
- If possible, adapting her workload to compensate for these additional challenges

Li's experience is congruent with that of other studies and efforts supporting minority scholars. Many institutions are committed to achieving greater diversity. The Board of Ethnic Minority Affairs was founded in 1980, and the Commission on Ethnic Minority Recruitment, Retention, and Training was established in 1994 (American Psychological Association, 2003) to promote faculty diversity. At the institutional level, creating a supportive, inclusive, and collaborative environment; offering needed resources; providing fair treatment; holding realistic and balanced expectations; allotting reasonable teaching loads; and giving recognition are critical in recruiting and retaining minority faculties (Fouad & Carter, 1992; Helms, 2001; Moradi & Neimeyer, 2005; Olmedo, 1990; Pololi, 2010; Ridley, 1991; Sue, 2001). "Just having a safe person to ask cultural questions without fear of offending them would be extremely useful" to nonnative faculty members (Fredericks, 2011, p. 2).

REFERENCES

Altbach, P. G. (2005). Globalization and the university: Myths and realities in an unequal world. In National Education Association, *The NEA 2005 Almanac of Higher Education* (pp. 63–74). Washington, DC: Author.

Altbach, P. G. (2006). The internationalization of higher education: Motivations and realities. In National Education Association, *The NEA 2006 Almanac of Higher Education* (pp. 27–36). Washington, DC: Author.

American Psychological Association. (2003). Guidelines on multicultural education, training, research, practice, and organizational change for psychologists. *American Psychologist, 58,* 377–402.

Atkinson, D. R., Brown, M. T., Casas, J. M., & Zane, N.W.S. (1996). Achieving ethnic parity in counseling psychology. *Counseling Psychologist, 24,* 230–258.

Brookfield, S. D., & Preskill, S. (2005). *Discussion as a way of teaching: Tools and techniques for democratic classrooms* (2nd ed.). San Francisco, CA: Jossey-Bass.

Chua, A. (2011). *Battle hymn of the tiger mother.* New York, NY: Penguin.

Corley, E., & Sabharwal, M. (2007). Foreign-born academic scientists and engineers: producing more and getting less than their U.S.-born peers? *Research in Higher Education, 48*(8), 909–940.

Essien, V. (2003). Visible and invisible barriers to the incorporation of faculty of color in predominately white law schools. *Journal of Black Studies, 34,* 63–71.

Fouad, N. A., & Carter, R. T. (1992). Gender and racial issues for new counseling psychologists in academia. *Counseling Psychologist, 20,* 123–140.

Fredericks, S. (2011). Supporting non-native faculty members. *Tribal College Journal, 22,* 37–38.

Helms, R. (2001). NBPTS: The highest form of certification. *Kappa Delta Pi Record, 38*(1), 20–23.

Horn, A. S., Hendel, D. D., & Fry, G. W. (2007). Ranking the international dimension of top research universities in the United States. *Journal of Studies in International Education, 11*(3/4), 330–358.

Institute of International Education. (2008). *Open doors 2008: International scholars.* Retrieved from http://opendoors.iienetwork.org/?p=131567

Jackson-Weaver, K., (2011). Diversity and the future of the professoriate: A call to action. *Diverse: Issues in Higher Education, 27,* 27–27.

Johnson, J., & Regets, M. (1998, June 22). *International mobility of scientists and engineers to the United States—Brain drain or brain circulation?* Washington, DC: National Science Foundation.

Levin, S. G., & Stephen, P. E. (1999). Are the foreign born a source of strength for U.S. science? *Science, 285*(5431), 1213.

Mamiseishvili, K. (2010). Foreign-born women faculty work roles and productivity at research universities in the United States. *Higher Education, 60,* 139–156.

Marvasti, A. (2005). U.S. academic institutions and perceived effectiveness of foreign-born faculty. *Journal of Economic Issues, 39*(1), 151–176.

Mayuzumi, K. (2008). "In-between" Asia and the West: Asian women faculty in the transnational context. *Race, Ethnicity and Education,* 11(2), 167–182.

Michaels, W. B. (2011, Winter). The trouble with diversifying the faculty. *Liberal Education,* 14–19.

Moradi, B., & Neimeyer, G. J. (2005). Diversity in the ivory white tower: A longitudinal look at faculty race/ethnicity in counseling psychology academic training programs. *Counseling Psychologist, 33,* 655–675.

NAFSA: The Association of International Educators. (2006). *Restoring U.S. competitiveness for international students and scholars.* Retrieved from http://www.nafsa.org/uploadedFiles/NAFSA_Home/Resource_Library_Assets/Public_Policy/restoring_u.s.pdf?n=8823

Olmedo, E. L. (1990). Minority faculty development: Issues in retention and promotion. In G. Stricker, E. Davis-Russell, E. Bourg, E. Duran, W. R. Hammond, J. McHolland, . . . Vaughan, B. E. (Eds.), *Toward ethnic diversification in psychology education and training* (pp. 99–104). Washington, DC: American Psychological Association.

Pololi, L. (2010, September 4). A prescription for diversifying medical-school faculties. *Chronicle of Higher Education, 57,* 32–34.

Ridley, S. E. (1991). Faculty development and retraining: Some committee recommendations. In H. F. Myers, P. Wohlford, L. P. Guzman, & R. J. Echemendia (Eds.), *Ethnic minority perspectives on clinical training and services in psychology* (pp. 165–168). Washington, DC: American Psychological Association.

Skachkova, P. (2007). Academic careers of immigrant women professors in the U.S. *Higher Education, 53,* 697–738.

Smith, D. G. (2009). *Diversity's promise for higher education: Making it work.* Baltimore, MD: Johns Hopkins University Press.

Stromquist, N. P. (2007). Internationalization as a response to globalization: Radical shifts in university environments. *Higher Education, 53,* 81–105.

Sue, D. W. (2001). Surviving monoculturalism and racism: A personal and professional journey. In J. G. Ponterotto, J. M. Casas, L. A. Suzuki, & C. M. Alexander (Eds.), *Handbook of multicultural counseling* (2nd ed., pp. 45–54). Thousand Oaks, CA: Sage.

Thomas, J. M., & Johnson, B. J. (2004). Perspectives of international faculty members: Their experiences and stories. *Education and Society, 22*(3), 47–64.

Tuitt, F. A., Sagaria, M. A., & Turner C. S. (2007). Signals and strategies in hiring faculty of color. *Higher Education: Handbook of Theory and Research, 22,* 497–535.

Wells, R. (2007). International faculty in U.S. community colleges. In E. Valeau & R. L. Raby (Eds.), *New directions for community colleges, No. 138: International reform efforts and challenges in community colleges* (pp. 77–82). San Francisco, CA: Jossey-Bass.

17

UNDERSTANDING INTERSECTING PROCESSES

COMPLEX ECOLOGIES OF DIVERSITY, IDENTITY, TEACHING, AND LEARNING

Kristen A. Renn
Michigan State University

Teaching and learning take place within complex interactions of students, instructors, and environments. Within these environments, diversity and identity play a role in how individuals experience the learning context. This chapter describes an ecological model (Bronfenbrenner, 1979, 1993) and uses it to analyze how diversity and identities interact with the processes of teaching and learning. Examples from research with students of color and lesbian, gay, bisexual, and transgender students illustrate barriers to learning and opportunities to use diverse identities to engage students more effectively. The chapter ends with recommendations for improving the classroom climate for diverse learners.

o

Eleanor is a sophomore taking beginning Spanish. The professor believes in integrating student experiences into language learning. Students create scrapbooks of their families and friends and then learn vocabulary related to the images. Students begin dialogues: "*Esta es mi madre.*" "*Es que tu padre?*" "*Sí, estos dos son mis padres.*" This is my mother. Is this your father? Yes, these two are my parents. And then the instructor continues to question Eleanor. "How can these be your parents?" he says in Spanish. "They can't be your parents. They don't look like you." Eleanor barely understands the barrage of Spanish and is defenseless to respond. More than that, though, she is stunned by the accusation that her white mother and black father are not her parents.

Hoping to engage her first-year seminar in a debate about global climate change, an instructor goes for an easy division of students into teams. "Okay, everyone, we'll have guys on this side and ladies over here." For most students, the instructions are clear and simple. But for Caiden, who has been exploring gender identity, they are more complicated. Caiden identifies with neither the hypermasculine "guy" code of college life nor with the hyperfeminine "ladies." While everyone else shuffles to the "correct" side of the room, Caiden wonders what will happen if other students sense the hesitation or notice that Caiden does not belong on the side to which Caiden ultimately goes.

Jon's professor has invited students in an interdisciplinary seminar to write research papers on any topic they choose. Jon wants to write about the intersection of scientific research, activism, and politics related to the AIDS crisis. Jon identifies as gay, though he has not come out publicly at his small Christian college. He is worried that his professor will (correctly) assume that his interest in the history and politics of HIV research stems from his identity as a gay man. He is shocked when he gets back his topic statement from the professor with the comment, "This sounds terrific! I've got friends at the Centers for Disease Control who can help with this. I'll put you in touch." Working on the paper, Jon makes important connections with openly gay and lesbian scientists, one of whom hires him to work in her laboratory after graduation.

These three scenarios, all from participants in studies of mixed-race college students and lesbian, gay, bisexual, and transgender (LGBT) students (Renn, 2004, 2007), demonstrate the ways that identities enter the complex interactions that make up the processes of teaching and learning. Eleanor's and Caiden's experiences of alienation in the classroom occurred even when faculty were trying to use inclusive teaching strategies. Viewing the complexity of diversity, identities, teaching, and learning through a human or developmental ecology lens provides insight into the interactions among them and suggests ways to improve student learning.

Ecologies of Teaching and Learning

Human and developmental ecology theories parallel biological concepts of ecology in ways that are useful for examining complex person-environment interactions, such as those that occur in the teaching and learning processes. Four key concepts in ecology relate to teaching and learning in higher education. First, students and instructors are organisms operating within dynamic environments. These environments are natural (geography, climate, weather) and human-made (architecture, curriculum, organizations) (Moos, 1973; Strange & Banning, 2001). Second, organisms influence environments, and environments influence organisms. Specifically, students influence learning environments, and learning environments influence students (Bronfenbrenner, 1979; Strange & Banning, 2001). Third, different environmental niches favor organisms, including students, with particular traits (Renn & Arnold, 2003). One student might thrive at a community college, another at a liberal arts college, and a third at a comprehensive university. Finally, when an organism and its environment do not match well, one or both must adapt or be adapted lest the organism extinguish. In colleges and universities "extinction" means that students leave a course, a major, or an institution. Or a student may remain in place, extinguishing his or her learning. A learning ecology lens forms the foundation for understanding how educational environments influence individuals and outcomes.

Urie Bronfenbrenner's developmental ecology model provides a blueprint for this foundation (Bronfenbrenner, 1979, 1993). Bronfenbrenner created the model out of his work with young children. Renn and Arnold (2003) adapted it specifically for use in higher education. It has four key elements: person, process, context, and time. (Bronfenbrenner typically ordered them process-person-context-time; I present person first.)

Person

The person element of the model refers to the demographic and personal characteristics of the learner, including heritage, demographics, talents, and habits of mind. It also includes "developmentally instigative characteristics" (Bronfenbrenner, 1993, p. 11) that influence the individual's interactions with the environment.

Bronfenbrenner described four developmentally instigative characteristics. First are characteristics that invite or inhibit responses from the environment. For college students interacting with faculty, these characteristics might include physical appearance, confidence, manners, and language. The second group relates to selective responsivity, or the ways that students explore and react to their surroundings. Some students, for example, may seek out faculty in office hours and respond quickly to e-mail messages from a professor, while others do not. Structuring proclivities are the third category of characteristics. These are the ways that students engage in increasingly complex activities such as more difficult courses, independent research, and leadership activities, which are keys to their development and learning. The fourth category is directive beliefs, relating to the ways that individuals understand agency in relationship to the environment. Some students are active creators of their college experience, and others are more passive.

As a group, the developmentally instigative characteristics shape how an individual will experience the learning environment and how faculty and other students will react to him or her. These characteristics help explain why some students may seem easy to mentor, enjoyable to teach, and engaging to advise, while other students seem harder or less rewarding to engage. To illustrate, I will use a model student, Maria, whose story is a composite drawn from my research with students of color (Renn, 2004).

Maria is a first-generation Latina student who excelled in math and science in high school. She seeks out new academic challenges but is shy and holds back from social interactions with peers. In her first year, she had a campus job washing beakers for the chemistry department, and she has since been promoted to supervising other students and setting up equipment for multiple lab sections. The white male faculty member for whom Maria works nominated her for a summer research fellowship and offered to introduce her to faculty and graduate students in the department, including women and people of color. Maria likes being at the university but does not have many friends here. She lives in an apartment with a high school friend and prefers to go home on weekends to be with her family. All of these characteristics—demographic, identities, and tendency to seek some challenges while avoiding others—make up the person who is Maria.

Maria's story begins to show how the ecology model plays out in terms of ecological niches. She thrives in courses and her job in the lab because she seeks out challenges and demonstrates her maturity and responsibility. She has successfully integrated into her academic life and has attracted an academic mentor. She is surviving, though not thriving, in social niches, where her shyness holds her back. She is not very likely to attract a friendship group to provide additional social, academic, and personal support for her college journey.

The ecology model takes a value-neutral stance on niches, though educators may have ideas about which are more important for student success. Maria's differential integration into the overall college environment illustrates the concept of niches and personal characteristics. Some characteristics are highly favored in some niches (responsibility is highly valued in the work setting) but may not get students far in others (work-related responsibility is not always valued in the formation of friendship groups, for example). An outgoing student who seeks novel social situations might integrate easily into the peer culture but could be less successful in attracting an intellectual mentor.

Process

These interactions with other people and with the environment are the second part of the Bronfenbrenner model: process. To promote learning and development, interactions must be of increasing complexity and adequately supported (Renn & Arnold, 2003). Maria's inclination to challenge herself in more difficult course work promotes greater learning than if she plateaued with midrange courses. Similarly, the increased responsibility she assumes in her job provides opportunities for increased complexity of human interaction. Her so-called soft skills may be challenged, and she will have to learn more complex ways of interacting. Her decision to go home to her family and friends on weekends, however, does not necessarily call for increasing complexity, so she may not grow as much in those interactions. The process part of the model calls for increasing complexity and challenge in proximal settings, a familiar concept in constructivist learning theory (see King, 2009).

Context

Context is where learning and development occurs, and for college students, the settings are many and diverse. Bronfenbrenner (1979, 1993) named four levels of the context (see Figure 17.1). Microsystems are the immediate settings in which the individual interacts with the environment. Maria's microsystems include courses and lab sections, her campus job, her apartment mate, and family and friends at home. For other students, there might be a sports team, sorority or fraternity, Reserve Officer Training Corps, performing arts group, or faith community.

Interactions between and across microsystems create the mesosystem: a web of interactions that set a context of peer culture and learning expectations. These may be very consonant mesosystems, where a uniform message is reinforced, or dissonant mesosystems, in which the learner has to manage competing messages (as when a student-athlete gets one message from teammates and a different message from his instructors). As with the notion of niches, the model is neutral as to whether consonant or dissonant is better for learning. I maintain that dissonance does not stifle learning; rather, it challenges the learner in different ways.

Figure 17.1. Ecology of Teaching and Learning.

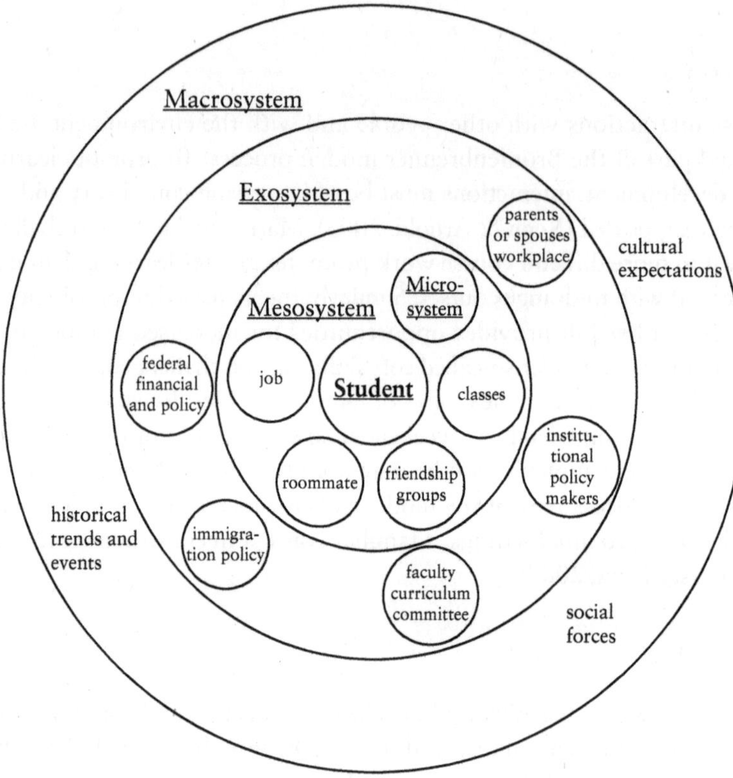

Source: *Renn & Arnold (2003). Reprinted by permission of The Ohio State University Press.*

The contexts in which teaching and learning occur are influenced by factors outside the immediate actors of faculty and students. Bronfenbrenner (1979, 1993) called these factors the exosystems: systems that affect development and learning but do not contain the individual. Maria's parents' workplaces are good examples. Maria is not in these contexts, but if one of her parents is laid off or gets a raise, it is likely to have an impact on Maria. She may have to work more, or she may be able to afford to study abroad. Faculty decisions about curriculum are exosystems because they do not contain the student but influence her or him; financial aid policy and immigration laws offer additional examples.

Exosystems are important contexts to consider, even though they are not directly in front of the learner.

Finally in the context element, the macrosystem contains the sociohistorical and cultural factors that influence learning. The fact that a woman is in science or a Latina is in chemistry is possible because of changes in the macrosystem over time that open society to diverse learners. Cultural values about family also influence Maria's educational decisions and options. The macrosystem represents the big picture context that influences learning.

Time

The last element of the model is time. Time accounts for large-scale historical events, such as the terrorist attacks on September 11, 2001, or the election of the first man of color as U.S. president, that influence individuals. Time also includes more personal events, like the timing of a sibling's birth or parents' divorce in the life span of the individual, that make a difference in his or her learning opportunities.

Diversity and Identity

With the four elements (person-process-context-time) of the ecology model in place, I turn now to the question of diversity and identity in the ecology of teaching and learning. Like other students, Maria brings her characteristics and characteristic ways of being in the world into the college context. Some niches in the context favor her characteristics, and others do not. Maria can adapt to fit the latter niches, or she can leave these niches. But ecology is not one-way: Maria also has influence on her environment. The way she interacts in class shapes the environment for faculty and other students, just as the way she does her work in the chemistry lab shapes that environment for others. The very fact that Maria is a visible Latina major in the sciences may alter how some younger students perceive their options and opportunities. The ecosystem is a dynamic place of mutual influence, construction, and reconstruction.

For instructors, this dynamic learning ecosystem is made more complex when dozens, if not hundreds, of individual students come together in the microsystem of a single class. There are as many different learning ecologies in a class as there are students. Faculty also bring their own ecosystems to the context. A class represents a shared microsystem for each student and instructor, but it is only one of many microsystems in each person's life. The ecological perspective may be useful in thinking about individuals, but it quickly seems overwhelming when considering using it to improve teaching and learning on the scale of real institutions. The model also offers a potential solution to the complexity: focusing on creating microsystems that favor, or at least tolerate, a wide range of characteristics that learners bring with them so that Eleanor, Caiden, Jon, or Maria can thrive. Creating such microsystems involves attending to the vital topics of diversity and identities, which are inherently part of the person element of the ecology model.

Campus diversity talk revolves around a common set of terms, with limited variation across institutions: sex, gender, race, ethnicity, sexual orientation, ability, social class, religion, and faith tradition. Less often considered are diversities of student status (part time or full time, straight from high school or nontraditional). Other groups include returning war veterans; students from urban, suburban, and rural areas; and in-state, out-of-state, and international students. For many people, these categories describe not just demographics but also identities.

Students exist within complex ecologies of interactions, identities, and development. The examples of Eleanor, Caiden, Jon, and Maria show how identities come with students into different microsystems, or proximal processes, and have the ability to enhance or erode the quality of learning that takes place. These examples are drawn from race, gender, and sexual orientation and point to the ways that identities can be felt, seen, and ascribed to others. Visible differences—skin color, a wheelchair, a veiled head, a gold cross necklace, a military tattoo—may indicate something about students, but it is unwise to assume too much about an individual's identity based on what is observable. Students may use clothing, jewelry, body art, or other means to signal their identities, but they may not identify strongly with the categories they seem to be displaying. There are also some identities that are not visible and are difficult to signal. Students may reveal these identities in a reflection paper, a class project, a conversation, or a Facebook profile.

A well-developed body of literature from psychology and sociology describes how individuals grow into different identities. Some of this research has made its way into the literature on college student development (see Torres, Jones, & Renn, 2009). For full-time students coming directly after high school, college can be a rich environment in which to explore identities. Students may encounter peers who are different, live in residence halls with people unlike those they have met before, and be on sports teams and student government with unfamiliar people. For adult students, commuters, and part-time students, the opportunities for interaction with diverse others on campus may be more limited. Where difference is nearly unavoidable, however, is in the learning context of classrooms, labs, and online courses. These are contexts in which to engage productively the intersecting processes of diversity, identity, teaching, and learning.

Barriers in the Ecosystem

Intersections in the teaching and learning ecology pose potential barriers to teaching and learning and also open opportunities that can be leveraged to increase learning. Barriers include obvious instances of discrimination and overt statements that seek to exclude or demean particular groups. It is increasingly rare in classrooms to hear overt racial slurs or deliberate put-downs of women. But the report *2010 State of Higher Education for LGBT People* (Rankin, Weber, Blumenfeld, & Frazer, 2010) showed that classrooms are commonly the site of verbal harassment or bullying of LGBT students. Student veterans report that some faculty and classmates conflate criticisms of war with criticisms of soldiers (Phillips, 2007), and students from poor families may be exposed to uninformed comments about "lazy" welfare recipients (Aries, 2008). Immigrant students and children of immigrants are at risk for hearing insensitive comments, which they may endure silently in a classroom where they keep their identity to themselves (see Schwartz, Donovan, & Guido-DiBrito, 2009). Some students' deeply held identities conflict with other students' identities: the classic example might be a religious fundamentalist and an LGBT student who has had a negative experience with organized religion. A lot can happen in a classroom that falls into a category I describe as outright hostility or an unwelcome climate. It is not hard to imagine how these statements and actions could interfere with the learning process.

As instructors, we have a duty to deal with these incidents when we are witnesses or when students tell us about them. Clear statements about the value of free speech in the context of respect for others, whether in the syllabus or given verbally, set a tone. Addressing instances immediately, either in class or privately afterward, also interrupts a hostile climate. Instructors themselves, of course, should refrain from consciously or thoughtlessly singling out groups for scorn. We must also educate and supervise teaching assistants appropriately.

Beyond outright hostility, there are also what Solórzano, Ceja, and Yosso (2000) called microaggressions—the more subtle everyday messages that accumulate in the micro- and mesosystems. Microaggressions include lowering expectations, tokenizing individuals, ignoring obvious discrimination, and tolerating or telling offensive jokes. They also include persistently surveilling students from one group, assuming that someone does not speak English, being surprised to meet someone from X background in Y major, refusing or forgetting to refer to a transgender student with the chosen pronoun, mixing up the names of the only two black or Asian or Native or female students in the class, or using readings that sustain stereotypes (for example, a textbook in which all nurses are female and all doctors are male). These examples cover a range that some people would classify as microaggressions and others as outright discrimination. My point is not to create a taxonomy, but to note the myriad everyday actions, images, and statements that batter against identities, and some of them happen in teaching and learning settings.

Faculty participate in and perpetuate some of these microaggressions, even when they think they are being progressive and inclusive in their teaching practices. Caiden's instructor was not trying to make a statement about a gender binary: she was trying to engage students in active learning and quickly divide students into groups. In all likelihood, she never knew the dilemma she created for Caiden and potentially others. Caiden's instructor could have accomplished her aims by using a more identity-neutral but equally quick scheme, like dividing by odd and even phone numbers.

The nature of teaching and learning ecologies means that there are multiple, intersecting ways to commit outright hostile acts and microaggressions. Indeed, active teaching and learning may be even riskier than lecturing from the textbook. The more interaction there is, the more the microsystems rub up against each other; the more students and instructors interact with one another in learning settings, the more likely it is that we will bump into identities in ways that may not be comfortable or welcoming. Eleanor's professor appeared to be welcoming students' families, and inherently their identities, into the learning process with the scrapbook assignment but was unprepared for the diversity of families that might come to class. He was not wrong to try to connect with students, but his limited sense of what families look like got in the way.

Opportunities in the Ecosystem

Just as there are risks of discrimination and microaggressions related to identities, there are opportunities to use identities to enhance learning through curriculum, assignments, classroom interactions, and out-of-class interactions. The positive response and follow-up Jon got from his professor is an example. I focus in this section on the ways that viewing students and diversity through an ecological lens may help promote learning.

Much of what people think of when they consider college teaching falls into the microsystem level of analysis: how to interact directly with students in the human-built context of classroom and online learning, lab sections, out-of-class interactions, and phone, text, and e-mail communication. Instructors signal through their words and actions the ways in which they are open to and affirming of diverse identities and the ways that they are, sometimes unconsciously, closed to and unwelcoming of some identities in their teaching and learning niches. Course readings, examples used in class to set up a math or science problem, methods for dividing students for group work: all of these are opportunities in the teaching ecology to create hospitable niches for diverse students to learn.

Microsystem interactions with students also become part of the mesosystem contexts of their lives. Here is where faculty can make a difference that extends beyond the immediate, proximal processes. In creating a space in which students can explore and experience diverse identities, faculty may extend an influence beyond the immediate academic interaction. The message, "You're okay here. Bring your whole self," may provide a refuge for a student whose other microsystems are sending a different message. Feeling safe to be who he or she is may be a buffer in an otherwise chilly context—a haven from dismissive or hostile attitudes that pervade other microsystems. For a student already in an overall supportive system of relationships and contexts, the "you're okay here" message may reinforce that support and signal that diversity is valuable and interesting. The message may be that one does not have to leave identity at the door to be an engineer or historian or lawyer; in fact, one may be a better engineer, historian, or lawyer by bringing one's identity and diversity to the table.

Faculty can create supportive and buffering niches by avoiding microaggressions, interrupting those that they witness, and thinking about how people from diverse identities will experience their invitation to bring identities into the learning process. Consider Eleanor's and Caiden's instructors' lack of understanding of students who identify outside racial categories and gender binaries, Jon's professor's support for research, and Maria's mentor in the chemistry lab. Throughout my data collection with LGBT and mixed-race students (see Renn, 2004, 2007), I have heard from students for whom one class, one professor, one assignment created breathing room to explore and express identity. I have also heard about the pervasive microaggressions that create a mesosystem that silences and makes identities invisible or unacceptable. Table 17.1 offers examples of positive and negative identity-based interactions between faculty and students in the micro- and mesosystems.

Faculty and faculty developers also play roles at the exosystem level in which they can enact policies, curricula, and programs that take advantage of identities and diversity to create enhanced learning ecologies for all students. Abundant research (Laird, Engberg, & Hurtado, 2005; Umbach & Kuh, 2006) indicates that so-called diversity requirements lead all students to have more civically engaged attitudes and to interact

Table 17.1. Examples of Negative and Positive Faculty Interactions with Student Diversity.

Discrimination and Microaggressions	Passive and Active Support
Instructor makes derogatory comments about an identity group or ignores such comments from students	Instructor publicly addresses negative comments, sets standards for civil discourse, and openly welcomes diverse identities
Instructor includes biased or negatively stereotyped course materials (readings, media)	Instructor includes positive portrayals of different identity groups in course materials (readings, media)
Instructor acts on the assumption that there are no invisible students and that everyone identifies the way he or she "looks" to others	Instructor expects that there are invisible differences among students and that those differences may make some students feel less welcome in the classroom; instructor makes clear to all students that he or she welcomes this unseen diversity and expects everyone to be respectful of it
Instructor asks students to speak for their group	Instructor invites all students to respond
Instructor discourages students from pursuing research or readings on identity-related topics	Instructor supports students in researching identity-related topics
Instructor limits mentoring to students from groups historically well represented in his or her academic discipline and from groups similar to the instructor's own	Instructor seeks out mentees from underrepresented groups; when mentoring students with identities different from their own, instructors use additional resources to provide role models and networks

with people who are different from themselves. Diversity requirements are most often developed and implemented in students' exosystems.

Another exosystem factor that has a trickle-down effect for students is the hiring, promotion, and tenure process. Attention to hiring diverse faculty creates opportunities for underrepresented students to see themselves in the faculty and for majority students to learn from and with people who are different from themselves. At a minimum, it is possible to prioritize hiring colleagues of any background who are committed to creating teaching and learning ecologies where all students can thrive. Faculty and organizational developers have an opportunity to bring attention to how decisions made in the exosystem of hiring, promotion, and tenure penetrate student learning experiences.

Finally, at the macrosystem level, faculty and faculty developers participate in the same larger sociocultural and historical context as do students. Students and faculty are immersed in a post-9/11 culture, and in the next decade most traditional-age students will have grown up predominantly or exclusively post-9/11. In Texas, California, and Michigan, they will not have known affirmative action in college admissions. Immigration and gay rights (military service, employment nondiscrimination, marriage equality) are critically important to individuals and are touchstones for divisive arguments. Student and faculty lives are saturated with technology and mobile connectivity. Acknowledging this larger context is critically important for instructors in creating learning ecologies where diverse students can thrive.

I do not believe that faculty can or should shelter students from the broader context, but I do believe that we have a duty to account for this larger context when we participate in learning organizations—our universities—that do not yet provide equitable access and opportunities.

Conclusion

My goal in presenting the ecology model is to provide a way to think about leveraging the power of the ecosystem to enhance teaching and learning through attention to diversity and identities. An ecosystem's frame can be useful in thinking about how instructors fit into the individual and collective learning ecologies of students and the ways that students from all backgrounds and identities bring assets and liabilities to the learning process. Identities seen and unseen, formed and forming, fluid and firmly held are at the core of individual student and faculty experiences, and ecologies challenge us to take them as seriously as we take our subject matter and other elements of our pedagogy. The stakes for teaching and learning are high. Eleanor, Caiden, Jon, and all the Marias, real and composite, are depending on us.

REFERENCES

Aries, E. (2008). *Race and class matters at an elite college.* Philadelphia, PA: Temple University Press.

Bronfenbrenner, U. (1979). *The ecology of human development: Experiments by nature and design.* Cambridge, MA: Harvard University Press.

Bronfenbrenner, U. (1993). The ecology of cognitive development: Research models and fugitive findings. In R. H. Wozniak & K. W. Fischer (Eds.), *Development in context: Acting and thinking in specific environments* (pp. 3–44). Mahwah, NJ: Erlbaum.

King, P. M. (2009). Principles of development and developmental change underlying theories of cognitive and moral development. *Journal of College Student Development, 50*(6), 597–620.

Laird, T.F.N., Engberg, M. E., & Hurtado, S. (2005). Modeling accentuation effects: Enrolling in a diversity course and the importance of social action engagement. *Journal of Higher Education, 76*(4), 448–476.

Moos, R. (1973). Conceptualizations of human environments. *American Psychologist, 28,* 652–665.

Phillips, S. (2007, February 16). Top guns on campus. *Times Higher Education.* Retrieved from http://www.timeshighereducation.co.uk/story.asp?storyCode=207842§ioncode=26

Rankin, S., Weber, G., Blumenfeld, W., & Frazer, S. (2010). *2010 state of higher education for lesbian, gay, bisexual and transgender people.* Charlotte, NC: Campus Pride.

Renn, K. A. (2004). *Mixed race college students: The ecology of race, identity, and community.* Albany: State University of New York Press.

Renn, K. A. (2007). LGBT student leaders and queer activists: Identities of lesbian, gay, bisexual, transgender, and queer-identified college student leaders and activists. *Journal of College Student Development, 48*(3), 311–330.

Renn, K. A., & Arnold, K. D. (2003). Reconceptualizing research on peer culture. *Journal of Higher Education, 74,* 261–291.

Schwartz, J. L., Donovan, J., & Guido-DiBrito, F. (2009). Stories of social class: Self-identified Mexican male college students crack the silence. *Journal of College Student Development, 50*(1), 50–66.

Solórzano, D., Ceja, M., & Yosso, T. (2000). Critical race theory, racial microaggessions, and campus racial climate: The experiences of African American college students. *Journal of Negro Education* 69(1/2), 60–73.

Strange, C. C., & Banning, J. H. (2001). *Educating by design: Creating campus learning environments that work.* San Francisco, CA: Jossey-Bass.

Torres, V., Jones, S. R., & Renn, K. A. (2009). Identity development theories in student affairs: Origins, current status, and new approaches. *Journal of College Student Development, 50*(6), 577–596.

Umbach, P. D., & Kuh, G. D. (2006). Student experiences with diversity at liberal arts colleges: Another claim for distinctiveness. *Journal of Higher Education, 77*(1), 169–192.

18

ORGANIZATIONAL STRATEGIES FOR FOSTERING FACULTY RACIAL INCLUSION

Dannielle Joy Davis
Alabama State University

Edward J. Brantmeier
James Madison University

Roben Torosyan
Fairfield University

Hyacinth E. Findlay
Alabama State University

> If you have come to help, you are wasting your time. If you have come because your liberation is bound in mine, then let us walk together.
>
> —Lilla Watson, Australian Aboriginal educator

Drawing on autoethnographic narrative reflections, this article explores the experiences of members of the Professional and Organizational Development Network in Higher Education and the HBCU Faculty Development Network during the organizations' first joint conference. Using the theory of professional interaction as a framework, we seek to understand how effectively the organizations manifested their interest in increased racial inclusion and collaboration.

o

Research suggests that fostering a culture of involvement within organizations provides many benefits, including reduced costs, efficiency, professional development, engagement (Oppermann, 1998), and networking. In particular, joint conferences can save time for participants while promoting learning across race and institutional types.

In an effort to "create, collaborate, and engage," the Professional and Organizational Development Network in Higher Education (POD) and the HBCU Faculty Development Network (HBCUFDN) held a joint conference. POD president Phyllis Dawkins's long-term affiliation with the HBCUFDN prompted the collaboration. This chapter explores the effectiveness of the organizations' joint conference using an autoethnographic approach.

Theoretical Framework

The theory of professional interaction (Davis, Boyer, & Russell, 2011) serves as the framework for this study (Figure 18.1). While the work from which it emerged was centered within the context of faculty mentor and protégé relationships, elements of the same model may inform interaction in the conference environment.

The theory suggests that professional interaction of mentors and junior faculty yields differing outcomes depending on the frequency and type of professional interaction (for example, e-mail versus face-to-face meetings). The degree and frequency of professional interaction are influenced by workload or availability to meet, as well as whether the workplace is perceived as fostering integration or isolation. The type of professional interaction one engages in reflects whether one has mentors or allies and the resulting collegial relationships. These in turn influence the protégés' overall experiences. Key experiences noted by participants of Davis's original study on faculty mentoring (from which the featured theory derived) included the degree of collegiality of mentors and coworkers, the quality and quantity of career-enhancing information, the degree of satisfaction, and perceptions of campus climate. The concept of professional interaction, coupled with the concepts of degree, frequency, and interaction will serve as the lens for this work.

Figure 18.1. Theory of Professional Interaction.

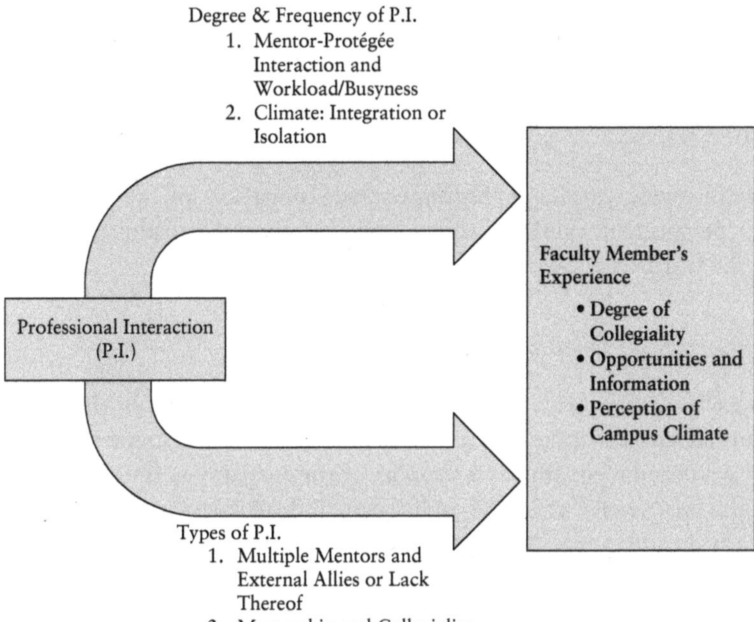

Source: *Davis, Boyer, and Russell (2011). Reprinted by permission of Administrative Issues Journal.*

Methods

Employing a narrative, autoethnographic approach, this study uses journaling, reflection, participant observation, and document analysis. Thematic analysis revealed emerging themes, which we discuss as they relate to the featured theoretical framework.

Participants

The featured participants offer a purposeful sample to evaluate the effectiveness of the POD-HBCU joint conference in promoting inclusion and professional interaction across race. Each author participated in the conference. Two of the authors are African American female faculty members from historically black colleges and universities (HBCU). The other two authors are white males, one of Middle Eastern descent, who hold both faculty and administrative roles at predominantly white institutions (PWIs). In terms of age, three contributors are members of Generation X, and one is a member of the baby boom generation.

Experiences

The following comments highlight the experiences of the authors and their perspectives on the effectiveness of promoting racial inclusion during the featured conference event.

Perspective 1: Deepening Our Liberation

I am white, male, and heterosexual. I have benefited from these social identities and the multiple layers of institutionalized systems of privilege and structural inequality as a member of the academy in the United States for the past twelve years. My whiteness and maleness have afforded me unearned entitlements (McIntosh, 1989) in various situations: a layer of trust that might not have existed if I was a person of color, a nod of approval by other white males for simply entering the room, and immediate solidarity in conversations about football or baseball and other male-dominated sports. These are just surface examples.

Hiring practices, evaluation, promotion, and how cultural capital operates in the academy are other institutionalized forms of unearned privilege I have received based on my race and gender. These entitlements were bestowed on me based on social identities that I did not choose. In other words, societal constructs operating in daily life serve to reinforce the power and privilege of those who benefit from the fact that these social constructs and related power structures exist. On the flip side, racial, gender, and sexually oriented "others" experience oppression, sometimes overt, sometimes covert, based on these social identities. Both the oppressed and the oppressor are dehumanized (Freire, 1973) amid such social realities.

As a critical multicultural educator for the past six years and intercultural educator for the past twelve years in several major research universities in the United States, I have had to do much deconstruction of my own identity while modeling that it is acceptable to deconstruct one's identity to understand how power, privilege, and oppression operate—what I call a pedagogy of vulnerability. Having worked mostly in teacher education for the past ten years, the majority of my students have been white and female, a demographic that matches national trends. The pedagogy of vulnerability that I model when doing a privileged and underprivileged audit, similar to the activity Johnson (2006) described, opens space for critical engagement in examining how social identities operate in schools to privilege some at the exclusion of others—part of my definition of structural violence.

As a new faculty developer, this was my first year attending the POD conference. I was delighted to find out that it was cosponsored by both POD and HBCUFDN, given my dedication to racial inclusion, equality, and equity based on my work in critical multicultural education. It was also appealing to me that the conference was held in Atlanta, a city rich with African American history, featuring the Martin Luther King Jr. National Historic Site, a place I have wanted to understand more since visiting the National Civil Rights Museum in Memphis. Given the history of open racial segregation in the South and of the silent racism of the North where I grew up, I anticipated palpable racial tension in Atlanta—the kind I experienced as a white male living and working in inner-city St. Louis for two years. Yet I also expected that racial tension to be different at a conference with academics.

My observations and experience of the joint conference were mostly positive. The plenary by James A. Anderson gave me insight into thinking like a chancellor and what solid, transparent leadership can do for a university. I overheard a few conference attendees disagreeing with some of the main messages conveyed by other speakers at the conference. My session, "Experiential White Privilege: Teaching for Social Justice Beyond Student Resistance," was well attended by over twenty colleagues, mostly white and female. Rich dialogue surrounding systems of privilege and power and the promise and pitfalls of experiential activities for bringing those systems to consciousness at predominantly white institutions filled the room. Yet one person who was African American indicated being tired of such activities based on experiences being the only person of color in classrooms at PWIs.

When I tallied my business cards on return, I received more cards from other white faculty developers. When I reflect on substantive conversations I had at the actual conference, most were with other white males. When observing lunchroom seating behaviors and tables for Jody Lynn Merriday's provocative and engaging jazz performance on Saturday evening, I noticed self-segregation according to race. I wondered if topical themes at various tables around various conference themes would have promoted more racial integration and inclusion rather than the sitting by familiar people.

Did this joint conference promote the racial inclusion desired? Racial inclusion is a long-term project given the history of deculturalization, displacement, enslavement, marginalization, and exploitation experienced by Native Americans, African Americans, Latinos, and Asian Americans in our country (Spring, 2010). No one could rightly expect one joint conference to change that history of institutionalized and social racism. One must hold a true commitment to these issues if we are to disrupt the institutionalized policy and practice of deculturalization embedded in schooling systems—systems historically established to serve the dominant, elite groups of people and their interests in societies around the world.

If we are to establish deep racial inclusion in the United States, premised by reconciliation and efforts toward a sustainable peace, we must be in it for the long haul (Kohl & Kohl, 1990). The three pillars that sustain white dominance—the assumption of rightness, the luxury of ignorance, and the legacy of privilege (Johnson, 2006)—are deeply engrained in the hegemonic collective conscious, commonsense notions of social realities (Buttigeig, 1992), as well as institutional, social, and civilization structures of inequality (Scheurich & Young, 1997). Dominance paradigms are formidable obstacles to overcome and operate along multiple social identities, including race, class, gender, sexual orientation, religion, geographic origin, and language. According to Allport's (1954) contact hypothesis, groups must have equal status, common goals, and shared forging of norms in order to improve relationships among various groups.

I am sure much thought was invested in the organization of this year's POD-HBCU conference. I wonder if these conceptually simple yet complex practices were consciously embedded in the organizational process. Did we achieve the goals of racial inclusion toward diversity affirmation? We surely took important first steps. As mentioned previously, I am a white male who has benefited from structural inequality and systems of privilege, yet I can identify with exclusion experiences by historically marginalized groups. Johnson (2006) described the paradox of privilege as the experience of not necessarily feeling privileged, yet benefiting from how social identities operate within wider spheres of society and how cultural power operates therein. I am a first-generation college graduate and come from rather humble farming roots with a low socioeconomic background. With that said, I stand in solidarity with other historically marginalized groups of people whose liberation is bound in mine.

If we are to rehumanize the academy by adding diverse voices and bringing equity to a system that has benefited elite groups throughout history, we must recognize deep division and the nested historical contexts that created that division. We must also work toward common ground, civil rights, and human rights for all people on our planet because our liberation is bound together.

Perspective 2: Steps Toward Promoting Inclusion

I am a new member of POD and have worked at an HBCU for about a year and a half. During the first presidential session at the POD-HBCU conference, I felt honored to witness organizational history as Phyllis Dawkins, a black female, served as leader at the first joint conference between the two organizations. Dawkins used Wordle to share participant ideas for how the two organizations might collaborate. Some suggestions included joint publications, conference presentations, and learning opportunities. These would move future joint conferences to greater integration.

However, determining racial integration at the conference sessions was challenging, as race is not an indicator of one's institutional affiliation (for example, whites work at HBCUs and vice versa). Few African Americans attended the sessions I participated in with the exception of the session, "Experiential White Privilege: Teaching for Social Justice Beyond Student Resistance," and a roundtable on creating rubrics. Only one African American attended my session on faculty writing groups. I noted this observation in the absence of ascriptive diversity in the following journal entries:

> In most of today's session's, again either I was the only person of African descent in the room or there was one lone "other." Sometimes the other lone minority was Asian or appeared Latino. Is the conference integrated or are we simply holding two separate conferences in the same building?
>
> Today I held my session on faculty writing groups. The session was marked as a POD-HBCU session. To my surprise, only two minorities filled a room of over thirty individuals. One was an African American woman and the other was an Asian woman. I am surprised that the turnout was not more diverse.

It is challenging to learn from each other with little genuine engagement. This suggests a need for more meaningful interracial interaction for future joint conferences.

POD does a good job of promoting inclusion through its diversity travel awards. The award is presented at a ceremony where recipients meet various members of POD. I found this to be a welcoming introduction to the organization. However, I find commitment to promoting organizational inclusion an avenue for more diverse participation. A potential POD-HBCU network committee might not only work on joint conferences but develop other joint activities such as cosponsored teleconferences for members or publications.

Perspective 3: Becoming More Mindful About Inclusion—Making the Professional Personal

After eighteen years of living in New York City, my family and I moved and "went suburban." We drive a car, keep up a home and garden, and enjoy the lush trees of Connecticut. But at the 2011 POD-HBCU joint conference, I realized how badly I missed interacting with more visibly diverse people. During sessions and conversations, I saw no more attention to racial inclusion than in my seven previous years of POD conferences. I also saw my own role in a series of racial microincidents, the need for me to keep learning how to be a better ally if I am to facilitate the professional development of others, and pathways that might make such work on ourselves more likely at joint conferences in the future.

JUMPY REACTIONS TO RACE. When I showed up to volunteer at POD's registration desk, I was pointed to a door to let myself in behind the desk. I walked over to a black woman sitting near it to introduce myself before walking past her. A couple of white folks behind the desk quickly spoke up. "Oh no . . . not there! There . . . ," pointing me to the door past her and adding, "That's for the HBCUs." My white colleagues may well have thought I was lost and confused. But I wanted to acknowledge this lone black woman before I walked by her to join them. Later the speed of their reaction struck me when I said good-bye to the same black woman. She smiled at me kindly and looked me in the eye knowingly. I said to her, "That was funny earlier about the door," and she chuckled with me.

One way to view this and other race-related episodes is to work on cultivating the mindfulness of my reactions, particularly emotional responses. A recent review of research on mindfulness (Hölzel et al., 2011) shows that "emotional regulation" includes reappraisal of one's reactions and exposure, or deliberately staying with whatever reaction presents itself to eventually change it. That often means going toward discomfort, such as wondering whether I should be more sensitive to racial differences, should see beyond them, or both. Most fascinating, however, is the possibility of extinction, in which I work not to remove my initial reaction but to either develop a new memory or reconsolidate the old memory with new contextual associations (Hölzel et al., 2011). That is, I reappraise my racial reactions, add a new memory of pride, at noticing the black woman and deliberately trying to interact or even simply make eye contact. At the same time, I may help myself attain a race-blind equal-mindedness as I learn to approach people the same way no matter their race. Then, when some people of color do not respond well to my approach, I can reconsolidate my old memory of that being race-derived with a new memory of that simply being a personality difference.

RACE OR PERSONALITY? Throughout the conference, I oscillated between wondering whether my actions were racist and feeling good that I acted as an ally. I gave myself credit for not just gravitating toward sameness, whether sameness of personality or race. For example, I made extra efforts to acknowledge a wide variety of people: from food service staff to colleagues of either conference. I enjoyed doing so. Mind you, this is where my sensitivity to personality differences can be my undoing, as I often think I am open and like to share personally. But I am often not as open, ironically, to when the other might prefer to simply stick to business or be more private. I struggle to respect that personality difference, although it is quite reasonable to prefer more formality or less personal sharing. I often ascribe the difference to a racial difference when it is just as likely simply a personality difference.

To take another example, in the fitness center, a black male using weights gave me a nod, a relative rarity generally among lifters or even gym users generally in my experience. I liked the personal acknowledgment from a person of color. I often do not get that acknowledgment from white colleagues. But again, might the difference have been more to his simply being more friendly, regardless of his race?

A term used by diversity scholars, *intersectionality*, captures some of the interplay of many dimensions of my experience (Banks, Iuzzini, & Pliner, 2011; Collins, 1998; Ouellett, 2011). While much diversity research usefully focuses on "single aspects of social identity" (Ouellett, 2011, p. 5), such as race, class, or gender alone, a more integrative "intersectional" analysis aims to "acknowledge the powerful interplay of the *many* aspects of social identity" (p. 5). I have multiple identities that influence me. First, I was born in Istanbul to the children of Armenian genocide survivors. I was bullied weekly throughout grade school for having a different name, dressing differently, and generally not fitting in. So I have long felt an affinity for what it is like to be marginalized on multiple fronts, while at the same time enjoying the privileges of "passing" as white in many contexts.

HOW DO WE PROMOTE BETTER INCLUSION? I would like to think I use plenty of inclusive practices in my courses on the philosophy of education and environmental justice, between my use of discussion, displaying student comments on screen, and continuing exchanges online outside class. However, in one midsemester assessment, my students asked me to rely on dialogue less heavily, offer more directive guidance, and suggest conceptual connections rather than rely so heavily on the connections they make. This challenges me to stretch beyond my own comfort zone and, ironically, forces me to get beyond a false dichotomy I hold in my mind: I keep assuming that for me to direct the connections would not get them to think, because they would hear it from me rather than generate the ideas themselves. But perhaps I can both offer ideas and invite dialogue, making connections myself and inviting theirs. Another way to practice inclusion, then, is to vary teaching modes and, ideally, even include student critique in one's changes.

Changing the mode of not just our teaching but the meeting structures at a future joint conference could directly promote inclusion of different backgrounds and learning styles. Prework could help too, such as if a plenary provided an overview of powerful insights about racial inclusion conversations. For instance, people often understandably fear inclusion conversations will come down to either, "Who me? I'm not racist," or "Darn, I'm so racist." But when those feelings arise, we can move from dichotomous "either racist or not" thinking to seeing race as a continuum that includes not just actions but thoughts. In one of the most helpful readings I have found on race, Heinze (2008) shows that our students experience a similar struggle, and it helps if we ask questions that let people reframe their prior assumptions themselves.

Several sessions into a course on multicultural psychology, Heinze showed students a film depicting a white male expressing "tacitly racist thoughts which elicited much disdain among the men of color in the group" (p. 5). After discussing it, he asked his students, "What is racism?" Responses reflected typical images of white supremacists. He then asked "if only behavior defines a racist" (p. 5). After most students answered no, he drew a continuum of responses (see Figure 18.2). He then asked students whether they thought the male in the film

Figure 18.2. Racism as a Continuum: Emphasis on Thoughts as Well as Behaviors.

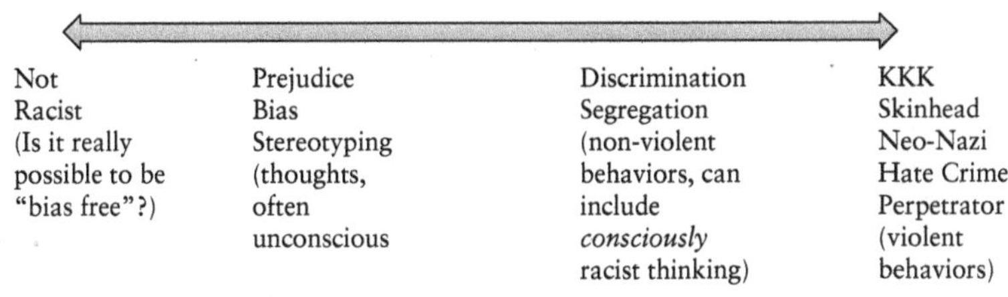

Source: *Heinze (2008). Reprinted by permission of Ramapo College of New Orleans.*

"perceived himself to be on the racism continuum both before and after the group experience captured in the film" (p. 5). In using such a continuum, Heinze exposed students "to a non-dualistic/dichotomous way of thinking" (p. 5). I teach exactly such relational worldviews myself, yet I fall prey to my own dichotomous labels regarding race repeatedly.

Using a future joint conference for such conversations could help people "develop emotional comfort in dealing with race and racism," one of eight key ways Sue (2010) recommends for educators "to become effective facilitators of difficult dialogues." He argues:

> Attaining comfort means practice outside of the classroom [and] lived experience in interacting with people or groups different from the teacher. It requires experience in dialoguing with people who differ from the teacher in terms of race, culture, and ethnicity. It ultimately means the teacher must be proactive in placing himself or herself in "uncomfortable" and new situations" [pp. 251–252].

For instance, if every plenary or keynote included the briefest interactive moment, people could be asked to write privately, then pair and share at tables on questions like, "How has the joint conference helped you understand inclusion in your practice?" and, "What would help you develop your practice regarding inclusion even more?" The more frequently participants discuss personal assumptions, the more we might explore how such thoughts bear on our practice in faculty development. I know that writing this narrative has helped me—despite the fact that my need to learn and change continues to grow.

Perspective 4: Engage and Collaborate

The joint conference was a collaborative endeavor signifying a commitment to diversity and recognizing the central role that it plays in faculty, professional, and organizational development. I believe the conference was successful in promoting diversity and engagement.

While racial diversity was evident in terms of the attendance of Caucasians, African Americans, and Asian Americans, it was also present in terms of international perspectives, as well as institutional size. Participants from large PWIs attended sessions given by faculty from comparatively small HBCUs and vice versa. These afforded interaction among a diverse group of people, enriching the overall experience and adding depth to presentations and to the conference. However, at shared meals, attendees self-segregated by organizational membership. POD members outnumbered HBCUFDN members by seven to one. So although the segregation was often by color, it may have been a matter of organizational affiliation. Joint presentations demonstrated that both groups can collaborate and work well together. POD member Saundra McGuire, nationally known for her work in metacognition and the improvement of student learning, joined with Michael Wilson of Dillard University, the main presenter. In his presentation, he integrated metacognitive learning strategies with cultural and generationally specific learning strategies in an African world studies course. This presentation demonstrated diversity in several ways: gender, age, university size, and expertise. Among the audience in many presentations by POD members were many HBCUFDN members. Business cards and e-mail addresses were shared to continue discussions, share resources, and develop collaborations.

ENGAGE. What was clear is the commitment of both groups to develop faculty who will serve students more effectively and will engage students so that permanent learning may occur. I was able to engage with colleagues from various colleges and share insights with them as well as gain insights from them.

COLLABORATE. From my observation, several members of the HBCUFDN are POD members. I would like to see POD members from PWIs have dual membership also. In this way, the connections begun at this conference would widen to form a stronger network or bridge between the two organizations. The benefits of continued joint conferences between POD and the HBCU Network abound. They include quality research, joint publications, the opportunities for shared resources, grantsmanship, opportunities to continue sharing innovative ideas on teaching and faculty development, and the development of a diverse group of scholars in professional development. Such collaboration would lead to improved cross-racial and cross-cultural understanding, thus breaking down racial and cultural stereotypes that exist in higher education.

Findings

This work suggests that hierarchical relationships centered on majority helping minority groups may result in further racial divides. Yet understanding how our liberation is bound together in a common struggle to actualize our humanity for both the oppressed and the oppressor is pivotal to rehumanizing the academy and academic organizations seeking to promote change. Of particular interest is the difference in participant observations related to their views of cross-race interaction. Three of the four authors noted the limited racial inclusion experienced and observed during the conference. Examples include a white male's comment on mainly receiving business cards from other whites and a black female's observation of few black and brown faces at sessions she attended. Such findings point to the need to seek more effective means of promoting cross-race professional collaborations. The low levels of racial integration and engagement witnessed by three of the authors suggests a limited degree of cross-racial professional interaction during the joint conference. And this influenced the frequency and degree of interaction as indicated by the three authors' observation of instances of racial isolation or low cross-race integration, lack of racial engagement, limited cross-race opportunities for collegiality, and information sharing for white male participants of this study.

The primary theme that emerged relating to practice centered on fostering greater racial integration for conference participants. Effective employment of this suggestion promises to improve the level of cross-race professional interaction. Transferring professional benefits of conferences into actual practice must be considered (Bredeson & Scribner, 2000). In particular, racial inclusion efforts need to be strategic to be effective during future joint ventures. These may involve cross-race networking, semistructured exchange, critical discussion, and collaborative problem solving (Dailey-Hebert, Donnelli, & Mandernach, 2010). Future work in this area might compare the findings of this study to conference survey data and interview participants of both organizations.

Implications

The findings of this work point to the importance of continued inquiry into the area of racial inclusion in higher education for faculty and hold implications at both micro- and macrolevels. While this work focused on two organizations' efforts to promote racial inclusion through a joint conference, similar efforts might be made on individual campuses using cross-institutional research and teaching collaboration. Such inclusive initiatives may center on race, gender, or institutional types (for example, PWI and minority-serving institution partnerships). An example of this is the National Center for Professional and Research Ethics, a collaboration between the University of Illinois at Urbana-Champaign and Howard University. Promoting such inclusion in academic work promises to yield greater cross-group understanding and intellectual innovation.

REFERENCES

Allport, G. W. (1954). *The nature of prejudice.* Cambridge, MA: Perseus Books.

Banks, C. A., Iuzzini, J., & Pliner, S. M. (2011). Intersection identities and the work of faculty development. In J. E. Miller & J. E. Groccia (Eds.), *To improve the academy: Resources for faculty, instructional, and organizational development, Vol. 29* (pp. 132–144). San Francisco, CA: Jossey-Bass/Anker.

Bredeson, P. V., & Scribner, J. P. (2000). A statewide professional development conference: Useful strategy for learning or inefficient use of resources? *Education Policy Analysis Archives, 8*(13), 1–14.

Buttigeig, J. (Ed). (1992). *Antonio Gramsci prison notebooks.* New York, NY: Columbia University Press.

Collins, P. H. (1998). *Fighting words: Black women and the search for justice.* Minneapolis: University of Minnesota Press.

Dailey-Hebert, A. D., Donnelli, E., & Mandernach, B. J. (2010). Access to success: A new mentoring model for women in academia. In L. B. Nilson & J. E. Miller. (Eds.), *To improve the academy: Resources for faculty, instructional, and organizational development, Vol. 28* (pp. 327–340). San Francisco, CA: Jossey-Bass/Anker.

Davis, D. J., Boyer, P., & Russell, I. (2011). Mentoring postsecondary faculty: A theory building case study and implications for institutional policy. *Administrative Issues Journal, 1*(1), 37–46.

Freire, P. (1973). *Pedagogy of the oppressed. Hagerstown, MN: Harper and Row.* Johnson, A. G. (2006). Privilege, power, and difference. New York, NY: McGraw-Hill.

Kohl, J., & Kohl, H. (1990). *The long haul: An autobiography.* New York, NY: Teachers College Press.

Heinze, P. (2008). Let's talk about race, baby: How a white professor teaches white students about white privilege and racism. *Multicultural Education, 16,* 1.

Hölzel, B. K., Lazar, S. W., Gard, T., Schuman-Olivier, Z., Vago, D. R., & Ott, U. (2011). How does mindfulness meditation work? Proposing mechanisms of action from a conceptual and neural perspective. *Perspectives on Psychological Science, 6*(6), 537–559.

McIntosh, P. (1989, July/August). White privilege: Unpacking the invisible knapsack. *Peace and Freedom,* 8–10.

Oppermann, M. (1998). Association involvement and convention participation. *Journal of Hospitality and Tourism Research, 21*(3), 17–30.

Ouellett, M. L. (Ed.). (2011). *Editor's notes. New directions for teaching and learning: No. 125. An integrative analysis approach to diversity in the college classroom* (pp. 1–7). San Francisco, CA: Jossey-Bass.

Scheurich, J. J., & Young, W. D. (1997). Coloring epistemologies: Are our research epistemologies racially based? *Educational Researcher, 26*(4), 4–16.

Spring, J. (2010). *Deculturalization and the struggle for equality: A brief history of the education of the education of dominated cultures in the United States* (6th ed.). New York, NY: McGraw-Hill.

Sue, D. W. (2010). *Microaggressions in everyday life: Race, gender, and sexual orientation.* Hoboken, NJ: Wiley.

PART SEVEN

INTEGRATING TECHNOLOGY INTO TEACHING, LEARNING, AND FACULTY DEVELOPMENT

19

PLEASE READ WHILE TEXTING AND DRIVING

C. Edward Watson
Virginia Tech

Krista P. Terry
Appalachian State University

Peter E. Doolittle
Virginia Tech

Over the past decade, an argument has been made and perpetuated regarding changes in the learning profile of today's students that includes new multitasking abilities. The belief in these skills has led some to encourage pedagogies that require multitasking. This chapter considers the lineage of the multitasking narrative, examines empirical research associated with multitasking, and charts a path forward for faculty, students, and developers to improve learning.

Faculty developers typically encourage instructors to engage in the process of learner analysis as they develop or revise learning modules, courses, or curriculum (Gustafson & Branch, 1997). However, as faculty seek to learn more about their students, especially at the undergraduate level, they discover a pervasive thread in the literature speaking to generational cohort conceptions of learners, those often called millennials (or Net Geners, Generation Y, and digital natives). Howe and Strauss (2000), researchers focusing on generation-based conceptions across various facets of society, define millennials as those born after 1982. Regardless of disciplinary focus, compelling accounts of learner characteristics said to be unique to millennial students have emerged over the past ten years and permeate popular narratives regarding teaching, learning, and performance.

Key among the millennials' traits often linked to education and educational settings is the idea of today's students as multitaskers. Multitasking, a term originally referring to a computer system performing two or more tasks concurrently, now also commonly refers to individuals who engage in multiple activities as once. It is often said that "multitasking is a way of life for this generation" (McGlynn, 2005, p. 20). However, a number of questions emerge for those who reflect on this assumption within higher education. Specifically, how accurate is this generalization? What do we really know about the human capacity for multitasking? How well can students multitask? Given the answers to these questions, what are the implications of what we know for faculty development and faculty practice?

The Making of a Myth

When one considers the breadth of research regarding learning, it is truly astonishing how quickly beliefs about student multitasking have spread over the past decade. The foundation for these beliefs is that students are tabulae rasae who have been nurtured and shaped by digital technologies (Pletka, 2007). Diverse areas in the literature echo that same sentiment. For example, an article on faculty development in *Nurse Educator* reported that "millennials have grown up in an environment that is enhanced by multiple forms of media so they have become adept at multitasking" (Mangold, 2007, p. 22). *Hispanic Outlook in Higher Education* warned about student attention spans due to their multitasking strengths (McGlynn, 2005). Papers published in *Innovate: Journal of Online Education* discuss these strengths and describe habitual student multitasking as a notable characteristic of their learning style (Barnes, Marateo, & Ferris, 2007; Sontag, 2009). Some have gone as far as to develop a new teaching paradigm predicated specifically on the belief that all students now possess these capabilities (Simon, 2005).

Certainly the popular media have played a role in perpetuating this conception of today's students. *Time* provided an in-depth discussion of what it termed the "multitasking generation" (Wallis, 2006), the *Chronicle of Higher Education* reported on multitasking characteristics of students (Carlson, 2005), and these perceptions have been echoed in other mass media contexts (Aratani, 2007; Oser, 2005). Most youth culture multitasking narratives ultimately reference the same small set of articles, and the commonality in this collection is the belief that technology has changed students' cognitive capacities.

Although never fulfilled as dramatically as described, there is a long history of predictions that stated technology would revolutionize learning and education in astonishing ways (see Saettler, 1968). It was predicted that radios would one day be present in every classroom, movies would replace books, and even B. F. Skinner suggested that the future would produce teaching machines that would double how much students could learn in a given time period (Seidensticker, 2006). More recently, Harel (1991) suggested that technological, constructivist-based activities could be the major leading factors in learning and cognitive development once such activities became widely available. This forecast was made the same year that the World Wide Web was launched and seemed to set the stage for the connections many would make regarding changes in student learning as a result of technology.

Throughout the 1990s, student behaviors associated with the Web and a variety of electronic devices were increasingly observable, and Tapscott (1998), a social software business executive, was among the first to chronicle them. Thoughtful, though often anecdotal, his book speaks of multitasking and the impact it may be having on student attention spans. In 2000, Jason Frand, then director of computing and information services in the Anderson School of Management at UCLA, shared his observations regarding an emerging information age mind-set, which, he said, "only a small number of students" possessed at that time (Frand, 2000, p. 16). A key characteristic of this emerging mind-set was the "multitasking way of life" (p. 18). He predicted the number of students possessing this mind-set would increase over time. However, no data collection or analysis was performed to empirically support either his current perception of students or his prediction for the future. The following year, Marc Prensky, a video game developer, coined the term *digital native* (2001). Without any data or research to support his statements, he offered confident observations about students, including how "digital natives accustomed to the twitch-speed, multitasking, random-access, graphics-first, active, connected, fun, fantasy, quick-payoff world of their video games, MTV, and Internet are bored by most of today's education, well meaning as it may be" (p. 5).

Tapscott, Frand, and Prensky comprise the core set of common citations typically found across the students-as-multitaskers literature; however, it is important to note that none of these citations are supported by qualitative or quantitative research or data. Think pieces such as these often serve a key purpose in the development of scholarship as they posit foundations for hypotheses and research questions that are then vetted through empirical research. Interestingly, it appears these observations and predictions transitioned to facts about students simply through multiple citations. Frand's own qualifications regarding the small number of students possessing multitasking capacities did not follow in other citations. Diana Oblinger in *EDUCAUSE Review*, citing Frand, attributed multitasking to "students who have grown up with technology" (2003, p. 40). While Frand's initial supposition was questionable and in need of validation, Oblinger's new framing offered a generalization that applied to most college students—a significant and oft-cited leap forward for the multitasker mythology.

In the early to mid-2000s, addressing issues associated with educating the millennials became a priority for EDUCAUSE, a nonprofit group whose mission is "to advance higher education by promoting the intelligent use of information technology" through teaching, learning, research, advocacy, and faculty development (EDUCAUSE, 2010). *EDUCAUSE Quarterly* published Dede's "Planning for Neomillennial Learning Styles" during this time (2005a). Multitasking is accepted as an authentic student trait in his narrative, and his discussion moves beyond descriptions of millennials to explore appropriate pedagogies for multitaskers. Technology is married to instruction throughout, and the following guiding observation is made: "Whether multitasking results in a superficial, easily distracted style of gaining information or a sophisticated form of synthesizing new insights depends on the ways in which this learning strategy is used" (p. 7). That same year, Dede (2005b) provided his own predictions regarding how the emergence of this new learning style might influence higher education. In it, he specifically cited a cognition dimension where learners would be moving away from "sequential assimilation of linear information stream" toward "multitasking among disparate experiences and information sources" (p. 15.18). Dede states that a variety of changes in technology and student populations, including their burgeoning multitasking abilities, ultimate necessitate shifts in faculty development that may involve faculty unlearning "unconscious beliefs, assumptions, and values about the nature of teaching, learning, and the academy" (p. 15.16).

These quotations are taken from *Educating the Net Generation*, a freely available online edited book self-published by EDUCAUSE. Multitasking is a recursive theme across multiple chapters of this text, and the Tapscott, Frand, and Prensky viewpoints are either echoed or are foundational to the discussion. One chapter's conclusion begins, "The net generation possesses sophisticated technological adaptability and a remarkable capacity to incorporate multitasking into day-to-day academic activities" (Hartman, Moskal, & Dziuban, 2005, p. 6.11). Unfortunately, there are few or even no reliable and valid data to support this claim that millennial students effectively multitask on a daily basis. These types of claims within the multitasking narrative tend to be supported by anecdotal evidence, self-report surveys, and misconceptions of what multitasking is. There is a need to move beyond reporting multitasking anecdotes and self-reports to examining and acting on multitasking in a rigorous, research-based manner.

Ultimately a great deal of inquiry is missing from this multitasking discussion, and while new books continue to tout students' multitasking and technological prowess (Jackson, 2008; Palfrey & Gasser, 2008; Tapscott, 2009), it is premature to suggest that faculty should unlearn their beliefs about teaching and learning. This is also not to say that there is a void associated with multitasking research; rather, this research has yet to be connected to the current narrative. It is this research that lays bare the mythology surrounding multitasking—students of the millennial generation are effective multitaskers—that threatens to lead higher education teaching and learning astray.

What Research Tells Us About Multitasking

Given that the literature addressing millennial students posits, without reference to scientific evidence, multitasking as a core attribute, it is essential to take a step back and examine the literature on multitasking so as to inform the discussion. It should be noted that over the past century of research, different terms have been used—*dual-task performance, split attention, divided attention,* and *multitasking*—to describe addressing an individual's ability to process and act on two or more streams of information, stimuli, or tasks. In this chapter, we use *multitasking* to describe what researchers may have originally termed *dual-task performance* or *split attention.*

The research on multitasking is extensive (see Charron & Koechlin, 2010; Fitts & Simon, 1952; Stager & Zufelt, 1972; Tombu et al., 2011); however, the results are notably consistent: when individuals perform a secondary task (such as studying for a test) during the performance of a primary task (such as watching a movie), the secondary task performance is degraded (Pashler, 1994). This degradation of performance is based on two attentional bottlenecks: the encoding bottleneck and the response selection bottleneck (Dux & Marois, 2009; Tombu & Jolicoeur, 2003).

The encoding bottleneck occurs when an individual attempts to encode into working memory a second task (or information set) while already processing a (first) task. The attention necessary to encode the first task hinders, or obstructs, the individual's ability to attend to and encode a second task. The response selection bottleneck occurs when an individual is asked to respond to two separate tasks. The attention necessary to select and implement the first response hinders, or obstructs, the individual's ability to attend to and select the second response. Thus, the more attentional resources a set of multiple tasks requires, the poorer the overall performance (especially of the subsequent tasks) will be.

Early discussions of multitasking began with philosophical observations—"the greater the number of objects to which our consciousness is simultaneously extended, the smaller is the intensity with which it is able to consider each" (Hamilton, Mansel, & Veitch, 1861, p. 164)—followed by behavioral observations that attention may be focused in two places at once (Angell & Moore, 1896; Hylan, 1903). These discussions developed into attempts to measure the degree to which an individual could attend to only a single task (clearness) or multiple tasks (vagueness). Geissler (1909) had participants attend to either a single task, marking a circle among distracters, or a dual task, marking a circle among distracters while simultaneously spelling challenging words or reciting lines of poetry. Following both the single and dual tasks, participants introspectively rated their "clearness" in attending, that is, their ability to focus their attention on the primary task. Geissler found that clearness was highly correlated with task type, such that single tasks were rated as being attended to more clearly than dual tasks. This focus on clearness, as a measure of attentional fidelity, then progressed to the use of reaction time. Cassel and Dallenbach (1918) used reaction time as an indicator of attention and determined that intermittent attentional distractions (a second attentional focus) led to decreases in reaction time performance. These early studies of attention and multitasking expanded over the following decades into discrete dual-task studies.

These dual-task studies resulted in a broad conclusion that "basic limits in doing two or more things at once seem to be a fundamental aspect of human performance" (Johnson & Proctor, 2004, p. 190). These studies typically required individuals to attend to and respond to a primary task (saying "high" or "low" on hearing a high- or low-pitched tone), while simultaneously attending to and responding to a secondary task (tapping a blue or white button on seeing a square on a screen that is either blue or white). The results of primary-secondary multitasking studies indicate that when the two tasks occur simultaneously, responding to the second task is significantly impaired; but if the onset of the secondary task is delayed, such that the primary task occurs and then the secondary task occurs, the magnitude of the impairment relative to responding to the second task is decreased (Broadbent, 1965; Ostry, Moray, & Marks, 1976; Pashler, 1993; Smith, 1967; Welford, 1952). One caveat to this reliable finding is that which task is considered "primary" is not always clear and is subject to the goals and decision making of the individual (Ruthruff, Pashler, & Hazeltine, 2003). For example, in studies of driving (Levy, Pashler, & Boer, 2006; Strayer & Johnston, 2001) where an individual is completing a second task (using a cell phone, texting, selecting a song from an MP3 player, adjusting the radio), driving performance is reliably impaired through, for example, reduced reaction time, failure to see stop lights, or poor steering control. While it might be assumed that driving would be the primary task during driving, it is evident that when individuals choose to text while driving, creating and sending the text becomes the primary task.

More recently, new methods for examining multitasking, beyond behavioral performance, have emerged that shine additional light on the effects of multitasking on learning and performance. Ophir, Nass, and Wagner (2009) compared heavy media multitaskers (HMM: individuals who tend to use several different media simultaneously) and light media multitaskers (LMM) on several measures of cognitive control. They determined that "heavy media multitaskers are distracted by the multiple streams of media they are consuming or, alternatively, that those who infrequently multitask are more effective at volitionally allocating their attention in the face of distractions" (p. 3). Ophir et al. indicate that it is unclear if this breadth bias, casting a wide but shallow net on information rather than a more narrowly focused net, represents a persistent individual difference or a learner strategy.

In addition to this cognitive approach, new technology is being employed to identify the regions of the brain that are activated under multitasking conditions and the structural limitations that exist when an individual attempts to perform multiple tasks at once. One such study (Charron & Koechlin, 2010), using functional magnetic resonance imaging (fMRI), employed a standard cognitive task of backward letter matching and emulated single- and dual-task conditions to discern which areas of participants' brains were activated during both the single- and dual-task performance scenarios. Their findings indicate that while frontal lobes work concurrently under single-task conditions, they divide during dual-task conditions, with one lobe supporting one task and the other supporting the second task. This supports a capacity-limit theory and indicates that this capacity limit "places a severe constraint bearing upon human higher cognition and may clarify several limitations in human decision-making and reasoning abilities" (p. 363). In addition, they hypothesized, and then affirmed, that given the split in resources tested during dual-task performances, "the frontal function is unable to accurately drive more than two concurrent tasks at one time" (p. 363).

These behavioral, cognitive, and neurological studies provide evidence that individuals can multitask (focus on two tasks simultaneously) but that multitasking leads to impaired cognition and performance. Can individuals multitask? Yes. Can students of the millennial generation multitask effectively? No.

So what does multitasking look like in the real world? Several studies related to laptop use during lectures have reported that the more students attempt to multitask during lectures, the more their academic performance is negatively affected (Fried, 2008; Kraushaar & Novak, 2006; Wood et al., 2012). In addition, a survey that asked students to report on their instant messaging (IM) activities found that students who reported IMing or doing other similar multitasking activities while doing homework reported a higher level of academic impairment than those who did not (Junco & Cotten, 2011). IMing has also been significantly related to higher levels of academic distractibility for academic tasks (Levine, Waite, & Bowman, 2007), which would infer that a degradation of performance would follow suit.

Although some evidence exists that practice may lessen the impact of the performance-limiting bottleneck (Dux et al., 2009; Schumacher et al., 2001), questions remain as to how extensive practicing needs to be to do so, what types of tasks (for example, motor versus cognitive tasks) can be susceptible to enhanced performance (Hiraga, Garry, Carson, & Summers, 2009), and to what extent the bottleneck can be completely eliminated (Van Selst, Ruthruff, & Johnston, 1999). The lingering questions about conditions under which multitasking may be able to be achieved do little to negate the well-established body of literature that speaks to definite limitations, and resultant consequences, of attempting to divide attention between more than one task at a time. This brings into question the claims that the millennial generation, just by virtue of having access to more technology and more information sources, is de facto adept at performing multiple tasks at once.

Conclusions and Recommendations

The writings of Tapscott (1998), Frand (2000), and Prensky (2001) gave voice to the notion of students as effective and efficient multitaskers. This multitasking meme was fed and nourished by subsequent authors

(McGlynn, 2005; Sontag, 2009; Wallis, 2006) such that myth became legend and legend became truth: students are multitaskers. The evidentiary truth about multitasking is in the empirical studies described above: humans lack the cognitive, behavioral, and neurological structures necessary to multitask effectively. Specifically, as we begin to engage two tasks simultaneously, the quality of the performance of the two tasks is reduced, and attempting three tasks simultaneously is chaotic. If multitasking, regardless of modern convention, is more myth than reality, how should faculty, administrators, and students respond?

The following five recommendations, based on what we empirically know regarding multitasking, provide guidance for addressing multitasking in academic life:

1. *Students and faculty need to be conscious of multitasking: what it is, when it occurs, and what the ramifications are.* The beginning point of dealing with multitasking is an awareness of what multitasking is and the impact it has on cognitive and behavioral performance. Ultimately this would require that students gain a better understanding of their own metacognition and that teachers gain a better understanding of students' metacognitive awareness and control. Metacognitive awareness represents one's recognition of one's own knowledge and skills and when to apply that knowledge and skill. Metacognitive control represents one's ability to plan a course of action (cognitive or physical), monitor the progress of that action, and evaluate the results of that action. Students rarely are taught these basic mechanics of learning; however, a first-year experience or a student orientation with a component on learning could provide students with information regarding the nature of multitasking, the outcomes of multitasking, and strategies for dealing with multitasking. Faculty members often have little understanding of these concepts as well; thus, these concepts could be incorporated and revisited in appropriate faculty development events.

2. *Students need to self-regulate in creating nonmultitasking environments in which to learn and perform.* The process of self-creating nonmultitasking learning environments builds off the first recommendation that students are self-aware of the ill effects of multitasking. Once students are self-aware of multitasking, they can begin the process of controlling it. This control, or self-regulation, would include (1) observing oneself in various situations in order to become more aware of when one tends to multitask; (2) avoiding multitasking distractions in class (such as Facebook, texting, talking, and reading) and not bringing potential distractions to class (a computer, cell phone, newspaper, magazine, and

so on); and (3) avoiding multitasking distractions when studying, completing course projects, and other out-of-class activities (Zimmerman, Bonner, & Kovach, 1996).

3. *Teachers should provide students with scaffolding in circumstances where multitasking is likely to occur.* As students engage in the processes of becoming aware of multitasking and learning to control it, teachers must also play an active part in recognizing and mediating multitasking. Multitasking represents an overload of an individual's working memory capacity—processing and storage. One avenue for ameliorating that overload is to provide students with scaffolds, from copies of diagrams and graphs to be discussed in class, to directions and pictures for completing procedures, to instructional strategies that foster simple to complex learning. Reiser (2004), in examining technologically based scaffolding within educationally relevant technological tools and activities, decomposes scaffolding into the subcomponents of structuring and problematizing, where *structuring* refers to simplifying complex cognitive tasks in order to make the task more tractable, and *problematizing* refers to directing learners' attention toward complex issues or characteristics of the task that might otherwise be overlooked. It is important to note that while Reiser's structuring is designed to simplify a task, problematizing is designed to make sure that learners engage in the complexity within that simplified task, "to guide the learner into facing complexity in the domain that will be productive for learning" (p. 288).

4. *Teachers should foster automaticity to reduce the effects of multitasking.* Students' ability to multitask effectively increases when the tasks to be completed are automated; thus, teachers should provide students with opportunities to engage in, experience, and practice tasks to foster automaticity and expect that advanced students (seniors and graduate students) will be able to multitask somewhat better than novice students (first-year students). In addition, given that seniors and graduate students should have greater experience with certain knowledge and skills, these students should be able to multitask more effectively based on more automated knowledge and skills (Dux et al., 2009).

5. *Teachers should focus on using instructional strategies that have been demonstrated to be effective and not technology for technology's sake.* Teaching is the creation of environments in which students learn. A central lever point of effective instructional environments is instructional strategies. The implementation of these instructional strategies should be with forethought and with the goals of achieving instructional outcomes at the forefront. A plethora of research (see Bruning, Schraw, & Norby, 2011)

delineates effective instructional strategies (such as cooperative learning, problem-based learning, and storytelling) from ineffective instructional strategies (such as learning style alignment and unguided discovery learning). Another corpus of research (see Jonassen, 1996; Mayer, 2005) clarifies how technology may be used to effectively foster student learning. The key to this strategy-technology relationship is to appreciate the supporting role that technology plays in fostering learning, while focusing on the overarching instructional strategies that frame the instruction.

Faculty developers must play a role in helping faculty become aware of the research and mythologies surrounding millennial students and should certainly take care to avoid perpetuating these narratives. Furthermore, faculty developers should promote instructional strategies and technologies that primarily foster learning and are not designed to take advantage of students' nonexistent multitasking abilities. Recognizing the ease with which students can engage in distracting course activities due to technology, the five recommendations for faculty and students should be seen as an outline of a curriculum for a faculty development event targeting those who are struggling with millennial conceptions of students in their courses. Only through active counterengagement with the multitasking mythology can practices that ultimately diminish the learning of our students be changed.

REFERENCES

Angell, J., & Moore, A. (1896). Studies from the psychological laboratory of the University of Chicago: 1. Reaction-time: A study in attention and habit. *Psychological Review, 3,* 245–258.

Aratani, L. (2007, February 26). Teens can multitask, but what are the costs? *Washington Post.* Retrieved from http://www.washingtonpost.com/wp-dyn/content/article/2007/02/25/AR2007022501600.html

Barnes, K., Marateo, R. C., & Ferris, S. P. (2007). Teaching and learning with the Net generation. *Innovate: Journal of Online Education, 3*(4). Retrieved from http://www.innovateonline.info/pdf/vol3_issue4/Teaching_and_Learning_with_the_Net_Generation.pdf

Broadbent, D. (1965) Techniques in the study of short-term memory. *Acta Psychologica, 24*(3), 220–273.

Bruning, R., Schraw, G., & Norby, M. (2011). *Cognitive psychology and instruction.* Boston, MA: Pearson.

Carlson, S. (2005, October 7). The Net generation goes to college. *Chronicle of Higher Education.* Retrieved from http://chronicle.com/article/The-Net-Generation-Goes-to/12307

Cassel, E., & Dallenbach, K. (1918). An objective measure of attributive clearness. *American Journal of Psychology, 29*(2), 204–207.

Charron, S., & Koechlin, E. (2010). Divided representation of concurrent goals in the human frontal lobes. *Science, 328*(5976), 360–363. doi:10.1126/science.1183614.

Dede, C. (2005a). Planning for neomillennial learning styles. *Educause Quarterly, 28*(1), 7–12.

Dede, C. (2005b). Planning for neomillennial learning styles: Implications for investments in technology and faculty. In D. G. Oblinger & J. L. Oblinger (Eds.), *Educating the net generation* (pp. 15.1-15.22). Retrieved from http://www.educause.edu/educatingthenetgen

Dux, P., & Marois, R. (2009). The attentional blink: A review of data and theory. *Attention, Perception, and Psychophysics, 71*(8), 1683–1700.

Dux, P., Tombu, M., Harrison, S., Rogers, B., Tong, F., & Marois, R. (2009). Training improves multitasking performance by increasing the speed of information processing in human prefrontal cortex. *Neuron, 63,* 127–138.

EDUCAUSE. (2010). *About EDUCAUSE.* Retrieved from http://www.educause.edu/about

Fitts, P., & Simon, S. (1952). Some relations between stimulus patterns and performance in a continuous dual-pursuit task. *Journal of Experimental Psychology, 43*(6), 428–436.

Frand, J. L. (2000). The information age mindset: Changes in students and implications for higher education. *Educause Review, 35*(5), 15–24.

Fried, C. (2008). In-class laptop use and its effects on student learning. *Computers and Education, 50*(3), 906–914. doi:10.1016/j.compedu.2006.09.006.

Geissler, L. (1909). The measurement of attention. *American Journal of Psychology, 20*(4), 473–529.

Gustafson, K., & Branch, R. M. (1997). *Instructional design models.* Syracuse, NY: ERIC Clearinghouse on Information and Technology.

Hamilton, W., Mansel, H., & Veitch, J. (1861). *Lectures on metaphysics and logic.* Edinburgh, UK: William Blackwood & Sons.

Harel, I. (1991). *Children designers: Interdisciplinary constructions for learning and knowing mathematics in a computer-rich school.* Norwood, NJ: Ablex.

Hartman, J., Moskal, P., & Dziuban, C. (2005). Preparing the academy of today for the learner of tomorrow. In D. G. Oblinger & J. L. Oblinger (Eds.), *Educating the Net generation* (pp. 6.1–6.15). Retrieved from http://www.educause.edu/educatingthenetgen

Hiraga, C. Y., Garry, M. I., Carson, R. G., & Summers, J. J. (2009). Dual-task interference: Attentional and neurophysiological influences. *Behavioural Brain Research, 205*(1), 10–18. doi:10.1016/j.bbr.2009.07.019.

Howe, N., & Strauss, W. (2000). *Millennials rising: The next great generation.* New York, NY: Vintage Books.

Hylan, J. (1903). The distribution of attention. *Psychological Review, 10*(4), 373–403.

Jackson, M. (2008). *Distracted: The erosion of attention and the coming dark age.* Amherst, NY: Prometheus Books.

Johnson, A., & Proctor, R. (2004). *Attention: Theory and practice.* Thousand Oaks, CA: Sage.

Jonassen, D. (Ed.). (1996). *Handbook of research for educational communications and technology.* New York, NY: Macmillan.

Junco, R., & Cotten, S. R. (2011). Perceived academic effects of instant messaging use. *Computers and Education, 56*(2), 370–378. doi:10.1016/j.compedu.2010.08.020.

Kraushaar, J. M., & Novak, D. C. (2006). Examining the effects of student multitasking with laptops during the lecture. *Journal of Information Systems Education, 21*(2), 241–252.

Levine, L. E., Waite, B. M., & Bowman, L. L. (2007). Electronic media use, reading, and academic distractibility in college youth. *Cyberpsychology and behavior, 10*(4), *560–566.* doi:10.1089/cpb.2007.9990

Levy, J., Pashler, H., & Boer, E. (2006). Central interference in driving: Is there any stopping the psychological refractory period? *Psychological Science, 17*(3), 228–235.

Mangold, K. (2007). Educating a new generation: Teaching baby boomer faculty about millennial students. *Nurse Educator, 32*(1), 21–23.

Mayer, R. (Ed.). (2005). *The Cambridge handbook of multimedia learning.* Cambridge, UK: Cambridge University Press.

McGlynn, A. P. (2005). Teaching millennials: Greater need for student-centered learning. *Hispanic Outlook in Higher Education, 16*(1), 19–20.

Oblinger, D. (2003). Boomers, Gen-Xers, & millennials: Understanding the new students. *Educause Review, 38*(4), 37–47.

Ophir, E., Nass, C., & Wagner, A. (2009). Cognitive control in media multitaskers. *Proceedings of the National Academy of Science, 106,* 15583–15587.

Oser, K. (2005). Kids cram more hours into media day. *Advertising Age, 76*(46), 31.

Ostry, D., Moray, N., & Marks, G. (1976). Attention, practice, and semantic targets. *Journal of Experimental Psychology: Human Perception and Performance,* 2(3), 326–336.

Palfrey, J., & Gasser, U. (2008). *Born digital: Understanding the first generation of digital natives.* New York, NY: Basic Books.

Pashler, H. (1993). Attentional limitations in doing two tasks at the same time. *Current Directions in Psychological Science, 1*(2), 44–48.

Pashler, H. (1994). Graded capacity-sharing in dual-task interference? *Journal of Experimental Psychology: Human Perception and Performance, 20*(2), 330–342.

Pletka, B. (2007). *Educating the Net generation: How to engage students in the 21st century.* Santa Monica, CA: Santa Monica Press.

Prensky, M. (2001). Digital natives, digital immigrants, part two: Do they really think differently? *On the Horizon, 9*(6), 1–6.

Reiser, B. (2004). Scaffolding complex learning: The mechanisms of structuring and problematizing student work. *Journal of the Learning Sciences, 13*(3), 273–304.

Ruthruff, E., Pashler, H., & Hazeltine, E. (2003). Dual-task interference with equal task emphasis: Graded capacity sharing or central postponement? *Psychonomic Society, 65*(5), 801–816.

Saettler, L. P. (1968). *A history of instructional technology.* New York, NY: McGraw-Hill.

Schumacher, E. H., Seymour, T. L., Glass, J. M., Fencsik, D. E., Lauber, E. J., Kieras, D. E., & Meyer, D. E. (2001). Virtually perfect time sharing in dual-task performance: Uncorking the central cognitive bottleneck. *Psychological Science, 12*(2), 101–108. Retrieved from http://www.ncbi.nlm.nih.gov/pubmed/11340917

Seidensticker, B. (2006). *Futurehype: The myths of technology change.* San Francisco, CA: Berrett-Koehler.

Simon, A. E. (2005). The new modus operandi: Techno tasking: Recognizing students' ability to use multiple technologies simultaneously presents a new paradigm. *School Administrator, 62*(4), 10–13.

Smith, M. (1967). Theories of the psychological refractory period. *Psychological Bulletin, 67,* 202–213.

Sontag, M. (2009). A learning theory for 21st-century students. *Innovate: Journal of Online Education, 5*(4). Retrieved from http://www.innovateonline.info/pdf/vol5_issue4/A_Learning_Theory_for_21st-Century_Students.pdf

Stager, P., & Zufelt, K. (1972). Dual-task method in determining load differences. *Journal of Experimental Psychology, 94*(1), 113–115.

Strayer, D. L., & Johnston, W. (2001). Driven to distraction: Dual-task studies of simulated driving and conversing on a cellular phone. *Psychological Science, 12*(6), 462–466.

Tapscott, D. (1998). *Growing up digital: The rise of the net generation.* New York, NY: McGraw-Hill.

Tapscott, D. (2009). *Grown up digital: How the Net generation is changing your world.* New York, NY: McGraw-Hill.

Tombu, M. N., Asplund, C. L., Dux, P. E., Godwin, D., Martin, J. W., & Marois, R. (2011). A unified attentional bottleneck in the human brain. *Proceedings of the National Academy of Sciences, 108*(33), 13426–13431.

Tombu, M. N., & Jolicoeur, P. (2003). A central capacity sharing model of dual task performance. *Journal of Experimental Psychology: Human Perception and Performance, 29*(1), 3–18.

Van Selst, M., Ruthruff, E., & Johnston, J. C. (1999). Can practice eliminate the psychological refractory period effect? *Journal of Experimental Psychology: Human Perception and Performance, 25,* 1268–1283.

Wallis, C. (2006, March 19). The multitasking generation. *Time,* 48–55.

Welford, A. (1952). The "psychological refractory period" and the review of high speed performance: A review and theory. *British Journal of Psychology, 43,* 2–19.

Wood, E., Zivcakova, L., Gentile, P., Archer, K., De Pasquale, D., & Nosko, A. (2012). Examining the impact of off-task multi-tasking with technology on real-time classroom learning. *Computers and Education,* 58(1), 365–374. doi:10.1016/j.compedu.2011.08.029

Zimmerman, B., Bonner, S., & Kovach, R. (1996). *Developing self-regulated learners: Beyond achievement to self-efficacy.* Washington, DC: American Psychological Association.

20

TWEETING #PODHBCU

CONTENT AND PROCESS OF THE 2011 POD HBCUFDN CONFERENCE TWITTER BACKCHANNEL

Mary C. Wright, Rachel K. Niemer
University of Michigan

Derek Bruff
Vanderbilt University

Katherine Valle
University of Michigan

This study analyzes the ways in which 2011 POD HBCUFDN Conference participants used Twitter to communicate about the annual meeting. Many messages mapped onto key faculty development priorities that were established in a prior large survey of faculty developers. However, important distinctions also arose, namely emphasis among tweeters on how faculty and students learn, faculty roles and rewards, and approaches to effectively engage in educational development work. We suggest that the conference backchannel served an important communicative function through development of social networks and resource sharing.

Social media have changed many facets of academic life, including attending and participating at conferences. In this chapter, we analyze messages, that is, tweets, posted to the microblogging service Twitter during the joint conference of the Professional and Organizational Development (POD) Network and the Historically Black Colleges and Universities Faculty Development Network (HBCUFDN) held in Atlanta, Georgia, October 26–30, 2011. In particular, themes of the tweets are compared to typical program offerings of educational development units as determined by the national survey of faculty developers reported in *Creating the Future of Faculty Development* (Sorcinelli, Austin, Eddy, & Beach, 2005). Comparing their survey data (collected ten years ago) and the 2011 Twitter content, we suggest potential new trends in educational development priorities. We also use findings about the identities of the participants in the conference backchannel, and how it was used, to make recommendations for enhancing communication within the faculty development community.

Microblogging is the act of sharing brief messages through a common Internet-based platform; the most commonly used platform is Twitter. Twitter allows users to post 140-character messages, known as tweets, which can be viewed by anyone visiting the user's Twitter profile. A Twitter user can also retweet another user's message, to share with others, making it possible for a tweet to spread very quickly through social networks. Often Twitter users (sometimes called tweeters) include URLs in tweets, linking to interesting Web sites and articles.

As scholarly communities have adopted social networking for professional purposes, conference organizers have begun using official hashtags (keywords preceded by the hash [#] symbol) in conference materials to facilitate the creation of a conference backchannel. A backchannel is "a line of communication created by people in an audience to connect with others inside or outside the room, with or without the knowledge of the speaker at the front of the room" (Atkinson, 2009, p. 17). Internet-connected mobile devices, such as laptops, smart phones, and tablets, have led to increasing use of Twitter and other platforms for backchannels at live events (Atkinson, 2009).

Previous research on conference backchannels has focused largely on the deduced intentions of posts (Ebner & Reinhardt, 2009; Ebner et al., 2010, Jacobs & McFarlane, 2005; McCarthy & Boyd, 2005; Ross, Terras, Warwick, & Welsh, 2011), the semantics of conference Twitter posts (Letierce, Passant, Decker, & Breslin, 2010; Weller, Dröge, & Puschmann, 2011), or the nature of the networks seen in the Twitter stream (Letierce et al., 2010). However, little research has investigated what the content of tweets suggests about the interests of those participating in a conference backchannel.

There has been more scholarship about the function, or process, of backchannels at conference settings. Before Twitter, McCarthy and Boyd (2005) analyzed messages posted to the Internet relay chat backchannels made available at a 2004 conference and found that most messages concerned the shared work of those at the conference, with other messages about logistics and social bonding. Informal interviews with backchannel participants indicated that some participants were concerned with the division of attention the front- and backchannels required, and some conference speakers "expressed dismay" (p. 1644) at attendees using laptops during talks. However, first-time attendees were particularly positive about the backchannel, indicating it provided them with a way to familiarize themselves with the conference and other participants.

Others have concluded that one key purpose of conference backchannels is to provide information to those not attending the meeting, although the extent of this function is a matter of debate. Ross et al. (2011) analyzed tweets from three digital humanities conferences held in 2009 and surveyed a subset of those who participated in the backchannels. They found that many of the tweets were intended for the benefit of people not physically present at the conference. In contrast, in an analysis of the EduCamp 2010 Hamburg Conference, others noted that the majority of tweets were not likely to be relevant to those absent because more context was necessary to understand their meaning (Ebner et al., 2010).

In sum, research on the use of conference backchannels suggests that Twitter may be an effective tool to build community, especially with newcomers and potentially with those not able to travel to a meeting. There has been little prior scholarship on the content of tweets. We build on this research to analyze the Twitter backchannel at the 2011 POD HBCUFDN Conference.

Who Were POD HBCUFDN Tweeters?

In 2011, the organizers of the POD HBCUFDN Conference took steps to encourage a productive Twitter backchannel, following the advice of Bruff (2011a). First, they designated #podhbcu as the hashtag for the event. Then, they recruited a "Twitter team": ten conference attendees who committed to tweet regularly during the conference in an effort to encourage other conference attendees to participate. Twitter team leader Derek Bruff recruited members from the POD Network's Electronic

Communications and Resources Committee and from his own followers on Twitter. In order to make participating in the conference backchannel more accessible for those not already using Twitter, a short YouTube video, "Twitter 101 for Conference Backchannels," was created and shared with the POD Network listserv, along with an invitation to participate in the backchannel at the conference (Bruff, 2011b).

A large number of tweets (1,320) were made during the week of the event, from 10:00 P.M. on October 23 to 11:08 P.M. on October 29, 2011. These tweets were made by 106 individuals, 14 percent of the number of official conference registrants. (However, not every tweeter was physically present at the conference.) Over half (54, or 51 percent) of the individuals posted just one or two messages. At the other end of the distribution, seven people had posted more than fifty times each.

Using Twitter profiles, Google, and university Web sites, titles and institutional affiliations were identified for all but two individuals who tweeted during this period. (Each of these unidentified individuals had just one tweet.) U.S. higher education institutions were classified according to the Carnegie Foundation for the Advancement of Teaching typology.

Among all of the Carnegie types, the largest percentage (44 percent) of tweets was written by individuals who work at research or doctorate-granting universities. (For a full breakdown of participants' affiliations, see Table 20.1.) This figure would suggest a substantial overrepresentation of a research institution perspective, given that doctoral/research universities comprise only 22 percent of teaching-learning development units in the United States (Kuhlenschmidt, 2011). However, given the comparisons made in this chapter to findings presented in *Creating the Future,* it is notable that an equivalent proportion (44 percent) of their respondents reported that they were employed in research and doctoral settings.

Among those working in higher education, all institutions were located in North America, which is surprising given greater moves toward internationalization of the POD Network and faculty development work generally (Lee, 2011; Van Note Chism, Gosling, & Sorcinelli, 2010). Five U.S institutions were historically black colleges and universities (HBCUs) and three were Hispanic-serving institutions, a low number given that the 2011 Conference was cosponsored by POD and the HBCUFDN Network. (As one tweet commented, "Seems like the #podhbcu Twitter backchannel is mostly populated from the POD side. Any HBCUers in the mix?")

Table 20.1. **Affiliation of 2011 POD Conference Tweeters, by Carnegie Classification or International Status.**

Institutional Classification	Percentage (Number) of Tweets	Percentage (Number) of Individuals	Percentage (Number) of Institutions
Associate	7.4% (98)	1.9% (2)	2.8% (2)
Baccalaureate	0.5% (7)	5.7% (6)	5.6% (4)
Master's colleges and universities	37.4% (494)	30.2% (32)	25.0% (18)
Doctorate-granting universities	1.2% (16)	4.7% (5)	6.9% (5)
Research universities	42.5% (561)	37.7% (40)	38.9% (28)
Special-focus institutions	4.6% (61)	2.8% (3)	2.8% (2)
Canadian universities	4.2% (56)	6.6% (7)	6.9% (5)
University in West Indies	0.1% (1)	0.9% (1)	1.4% (1)
Other (for example, publisher, K–12 organization)	1.8% (24)	7.5% (8)	9.7% (7)
Unidentified affiliation	0.2% (2)	1.9% (2)	—
Total	1320	106	72

Method

All tweets posted to #podhbcu were saved to one author's laptop, using the Archivist, an online tool to archive and export tweets. The coding framework took two stages: an analysis of the content of the tweets and a close examination of the communication patterns in the messages. Given that the key data used for this study were tweets, it is important to treat findings as a text-based representation of communication about the conference, not a representation of the conference sessions, which observational methods or an analysis of the conference program might generate.

Content Analysis

The content of the tweets was analyzed using a combination of deductive (Miles & Huberman, 1984) and grounded theory (inductive codes), with a broad conceptual lens (Charmaz, 1983, 1995; Glaser, 1987; Glaser & Strauss, 1967). Deductive codes were derived from the "portrait of key current issues that are being addressed through faculty development services" (Sorcinelli et al., 2005, p. 69), which document eight faculty development issues that educational developers reported were most important to address and were currently offered by their programs, as well as five areas that were important to address but not currently offered to an extensive degree.

These thirteen areas formed the key framing for the substantive coding of the Twitter feed in order to identify the ways that the 2011 POD HBCUFDN tweets mapped onto programmatic priorities of the field. Inductive coding found that an additional four thematic areas emerged from the tweets, illustrating other content that was discussed frequently in the messages. Some of these issues were similar to *Creating the Future* survey items but at that time, not reported as "important to offer." Table 20.2 offers sample topics for all seventeen areas, and illustrative tweets are provided in the text that follows.

One author coded all 1,320 tweets, using the full list of these substantive codes that can be found in Table 20.2. To check for interrater reliability, two other authors coded a subset (25 percent) of the tweets. The kappa statistic, a measure of interrater reliability, was 0.68 ($p < .001$), signifying substantial agreement (Vierra & Garret, 2005).

Process Analysis

The second type of coding focused on an analysis of how the Twitter feed functioned as a communication tool. This coding approach was solely deductive (Miles & Huberman, 1984), focusing on the following communicative functions:

- *Conference announcements.* These described POD Conference events, such as openings in excursions and availability of registration table staff.
- *General connections with colleagues and resources provided.* These tweets shared Web resources with others, as well as greetings to colleagues.
- *Dissemination of information around key events.* For the conference's plenary sessions and special invited talk, we applied

Table 20.2. **Content Codes from 2011 POD HBCUFDN Conference.**

	Sample Coding Topics	Number of Tweets Addressing Topic
Topics named as "important to offer" in *Creating the Future* (Sorcinelli et al., 2005)		
Integrating technology into traditional teaching and learning settings	E-portfolios, Blackboard	154
Changing faculty roles and rewards	Tenure, promotion, formative evaluation	69
Assessment of student learning	Learning outcomes, rubrics	54
Balancing multiple faculty roles	Writing groups, faculty time pressures	54
Teaching for student-centered learning	Learning-centered classroom	38
Active, inquiry-based or problem-based learning	Team-based leaning, problem-based learning	30
Multiculturalism and diversity related to teaching	Nontraditional students, students of color	16
Departmental leadership and management	Chair preparation, leadership development	14
New faculty development	Early-career faculty mentoring	13
Scholarship of teaching	Encouraging the scholarship of teaching and learning	12
Training and supporting part-time and adjunct faculty	Adjunct support	2
Interdisciplinary collaborations	Interdisciplinary, discipline	2
Writing across the curriculum	Interest in writing across the curriculum	1
Emergent themes		
Strategies for effective faculty development practice	Impact of faculty development programs, teaching center Web sites	187
Learning theory (student learning and faculty learning about teaching)	Visual thinking and learning, learning preferences	168

(*Continued*)

Table 20.2. (Continued)

	Sample Coding Topics	Number of Tweets Addressing Topic
Course, curriculum, and classroom design	Design of classroom spaces, goals	47
Future faculty, graduate students, and postdoctoral scholars	Certificate programs, teaching assistant training	17

focused codes to better understand how information was being transmitted. For tweets time-stamped during these three events, three codes were used: repetition of content related by the speaker; application or evaluation of content, in which the tweeter critically analyzed the information presented; and tweet not at all relevant to the presentation's content. For this focused coding, two authors (Niemer and Bruff) who had attended these events applied these codes, basing the analysis on their notes of the events and the texts.

Tweets fitting multiple themes could be coded with up to three codes, although given the brevity of tweets, only one code was applied to most messages. Retweets were coded for each time the message appeared in the Twitter feed. A possible drawback of this research is that we analyze only tweets labeled by #podhbcu. However, given the extensive number of messages with the #podhbcu hashtag, we suggest this to be a minor limitation. Another potential drawback is that we have no data on backchannel participants who read tweets but did not contribute to the backchannel.

Findings

After coding, findings from the study indicated patterns within both content and communication processes of the conference tweets.

Content Analysis

Of the 1,320 tweets, 776 (59 percent) addressed at least one content area as identified in the coding schema described. Looking first at the themes derived from *Creating the Future,* there were several similarities between the topics that resonated with the POD tweeters and the self-reported frequency of program offerings in the faculty development survey.

In the POD HBCUFDN Conference Twitter feed, the most frequently addressed topic was integration of technology into teaching and learning settings, with 154 occurrences (Table 20.2). This is not surprising, given the technology-based backchannel medium (Twitter). However, instructional technology also maps closely onto one of the most prominent service areas in *Creating the Future.* Indeed, the authors note, "The work of faculty developers is increasingly impacted by technology, not only as developers help faculty solve the challenges of integrating technology into teaching, but also as they integrate teaching technologies into the organizational structures of their institution" (Sorcinelli et al., 2005, pp. 77–78). Although tweets addressed numerous technologies, tools that were frequently mentioned included VoiceThread, cell phones (addressed in one of the keynotes), iPads, blogs, and e-portfolios.

In *Creating the Future,* the topic area that rated highest for both the most important issue to address and the one offered most broadly was student-centered learning, or "a range of classroom methods that shift the teacher's role from dispenser of information to facilitator of student learning" (p. 73). Although this theme arose in the Twitter feed through comments such as, "Let us adapt to our students' learning needs!" it did not appear to be as prominent as the faculty developer surveys would indicate (thirty-eight messages, Table 20.2). However, "course, curriculum classroom design," an inductive code that is similar to "teaching for student-centered learning," was also relatively frequently mentioned, with forty-seven tweets. For example, this tweet, while most directly addressing curricular and cocurricular alignment, also spotlights the need to engage in this process with a student-centered perspective: "Consider getting curricular & co-curr folks together to talk about their interactions w/students and how best 2 work together." In addition, assessment of student learning outcomes, a topic that also foregrounds the student in the learning process, had fifty-four occurrences. It is possible that many tweeters assumed the importance of student-centered learning in their comments without mentioning it explicitly.

A third similarity was the topic areas that were less frequently named in both studies. *Creating the Future* identifies the following issues as important to offer yet available to only a slight or moderate extent: training and supporting part-time and adjunct faculty, changing faculty roles and rewards, departmental leadership and management, balancing multiple faculty roles, interdisciplinary collaborations, writing across the curriculum, and the scholarship of teaching. In most cases these topics also occurred relatively infrequently in the POD HBCUFDN Twitter feed.

(The exceptions were two topics related to faculty roles, which were well represented in the backchannel and are discussed below.)

Although there are a number of similarities between the ideas expressed in the 2011 POD HBCUFDN Twitter feed and the survey findings in *Creating the Future,* there are also a number of important differences. We highlight these distinctions to suggest possible emergent priorities in the field of faculty development. In the Twitter feed, the most frequently represented idea was how to effectively engage in faculty development services, such as evaluation, strategies for publicity, and approaches to managing a teaching center (187 occurrences, Table 20.2). This topic was not presented in *Creating the Future,* given that study's focus on issues offered through programming, although related issues such as "support of institutional change priorities" and "unit and program evaluation" were reported to be unimportant and not extensively offered (Sorcinelli et al., 2005). Many tweets with this theme were posted during James Anderson's keynote, "Examining the Quality of Students' Education from an Organizational Perspective." However, the tweets also frequently addressed other conference sessions as well, such as creating strategic plans, measuring outcomes, and the use of e-portfolios and other online systems to document faculty development work.

A second key topic was theories of learning (168 messages), an issue not directly represented in Creating the Future (see Table 20.2). This code pertained to general discussions about how to best help students learn or assist faculty in their own learning. Tweets addressed ways to teach clarity, characteristics of millennial students, and beliefs about learning, such as the provocative post, "There are no such things as learning styles," which was tweeted or retweeted eight times. In addition, messages focused on changes in faculty beliefs about teaching, as well as motivational issues in faculty development, such as, "Don't try to persuade an instructor to not do something—just inform them of the consequences of what they are doing." A prominent portion of these posts were devoted to the topic of visual thinking and learning, the focus of several conference sessions. Indeed, of the sixty hashtags used in the Twitter feed (other than #PODHBCU), the most frequent tag was "#vizthink," with ninety-three occurrences.

Another key difference is the relative importance of communication about faculty roles and rewards in comparison with the survey study. Although named as important, services pertaining to faculty rewards and role balance were reported to be offered to a slight extent by survey respondents (Sorcinelli et al., 2005). In contrast, for conference tweets, these were among the most frequent themes, with sixty-nine occurrences for messages about faculty evaluation and rewards and an additional fifty-four about working with faculty to balance their multiple roles. In the former category, tweeters frequently addressed the evaluation of teaching for formative and summative purposes. For example, one attendee noted, "In ur faculty observation formative review indicate ur report should NOT be used for T&P. Could be used as argument for or against." Another tweeter queried, "At the centr of resistance 2 faculty development in higher education: reward system, how are faculty rewarded?" In turn, those tweeting about balancing multiple faculty roles frequently addressed educational development initiatives to address faculty stress, writing productivity, and myriad functions that faculty play in their academic positions, including as advisers and nurturers. The relative prominence of these themes is partially attributable to the conference program content, given the addresses by Claudette Williams, "The Role of the Faculty in the Twenty-First Century," and Robert Boice, "Creativity-Based Improvements for New Faculty as Teachers and Writers." However, it was also clear that the content of these sessions resonated with tweeters, and messages were found outside the time frame of these two large events.

In summary, there are many similarities in the key faculty development programmatic priorities documented by Sorcinelli et al. (2005): the importance of instructional technology and student-centered learning (and course, curriculum, and classroom planning based on this approach), as well as the lack of emphasis on ideas and programs addressing leadership, interdisciplinarity, writing across the curriculum, and the scholarship of teaching. This overlap is especially interesting given the differing modalities for data collection (a survey of all POD members versus tweets at the 2011 POD HBCUFDN Conference), as well as the ten-year span between these two studies.

In spite of the close alignment between the survey findings and the Twitter feed, there are also key differences that are important to highlight. Tweeters gave particular emphasis to communicating about how faculty and students learn, faculty roles and rewards, and approaches to effectively engaging in faculty development work. Although these topics were certainly forefronted in the large keynotes and invited presentations at the 2011 conference, it is significant that the ideas resonated enough with attendees that they were communicated to colleagues. One possible reason for the difference in findings is that the *Creating the Future* survey asked respondents about how these issues were addressed through services. It may be that such topics are not offered through programs but are instead important elements of the (usually implicit) foundation of our work as faculty developers. However, we also suggest that these three topics—how faculty and students learn, faculty roles and rewards, and effective faculty development practices—represent growing priorities in the field. Indeed, two related issues—faculty roles and student learning—were similarly defined by Sorcinelli et al. (2005) as "top challenges" that they indicated would have the potential to shape future priorities. Albeit directly representative of the focus of 106 conference attendees' tweets, it is also true that these themes are well represented in other recent overviews of faculty development work (Debowski, 2012; Gillespie & Robertson, 2010; Hines, 2011; Schroeder, 2010).

Process Analysis

We now turn to process issues, or how tweets were used as a communication mechanism. Of the 1,320 tweets, nearly 10 percent were devoted solely to making an announcement about a conference event, including both "curricular" (for example, keynote speakers scheduled for the day) and "cocurricular" elements (for example, morning yoga). (For a full breakdown of communicative function coding, see Table S-2 at http://tiny.cc/TWEETINGPODHBCU.) Slightly more frequently, POD conference tweeters passed along another attendee's message, indicated by the abbreviation "RT." Some of the most frequently retweeted ideas and resources were the winning video from the Create@POD contest, "How to Prank Your Boss Using Integrated Course Design" (Center for Excellence in Teaching and Learning, 2011), with five retweets, as well as the idea that the "visuals we use in presentations are a window into who we are. Think about relationship between function and aesthetic" (with four retweets).

However, most frequently, tweets were used to create social networks through both personal linkages and distribution of resources. Social connections were evident from the beginning of the Twitter feed, when conference attendees noted that they were "boarding the plane for #podhbcu." However, these connections were demonstrated throughout, as tweeters welcomed newcomers or noted that they were "inspired by this group." In addition, over two hundred messages offered functional enhancements to POD session content, such as links to recommended books, center Web sites, and, most frequently, resources on visual literacy. The social connections and sharing of resources fostered by the conference Twitter feed mirror the passing face-to-face conversations that occur at conferences. For example, in the limited time of an elevator ride, or in 140 characters in the case of Twitter, attendees can share a reference of interest, make plans for a future interaction, or present a brief reflection on what they have learned (Tufekci, 2001). This finding is consistent with other research: over half of Twitter users at conferences report using the tool to share resources or communicate with others (Reinhardt, Ebner, Beham, & Costa, 2009).

Most striking, the Twitter feed also helped create connections with those not able to travel to the annual meeting. To illustrate, one tweet noted, "Thanks to everyone at the #podhbcu conference who is contributing tweets and sharing links. Great for those of us unable to attend." Although conference backchannels are no substitute for attendance at a conference, as educational budgets limit conference travel further, they may become increasingly important for maintaining a sense of community and sharing resources.

A third way that the conference tweets were analyzed was through a focused coding of 187 tweets generated during the large, communal events, that is, the keynotes and invited talks. The key rationale for this focused coding was to better understand how attendees were processing the information generated at these events; coders for this piece of the analysis had attended these sessions and took notes on them. In 146 cases (78 percent of the tweets during this time frame), the tweets aligned with the content of the keynote, and these texts were coded for how the tweeters relayed the information. (For a full breakdown of keynote communicative function coding, see Table S-3 at http://tiny.cc/TWEETING PODHBCU.)

Over half (53 percent) of the tweets during keynotes involved dissemination of information similar to that given by the presenter. For example, during a keynote, a tweeter wrote, "Must have evidence, an assessment plan, willingness to present findings to public scrutiny," reflecting James Anderson's main points. Although we can only speculate, it may be that these summary tweets were intended for Twitter users not physically present at the conference—those following the backchannel from afar, as well as followers of those tweeting during the plenary events.

In the other cases (47 percent of the tweets), attendees evaluated or applied the presentation content, such as this participant who positively evaluated a session: "Loving the use of images in Dr. Williams talk." Others applied the keynote ideas to their own practice, such as an attendee who learned from the Anderson keynote that we need to "stop throwing away money on fragmented models, find what works best, do that." These evaluation- and application-oriented tweets suggest that the backchannel provides a useful medium for peer-to-peer interaction during keynote events that otherwise lack participant interaction.

In summary, the process codes indicate that the POD HBCUFDN Conference Twitter feed was a significant communicative tool. In addition to posting announcements about conference events, one of its most important roles was to foster social networks and the sharing of resources, including those who were not able to attend the annual meeting. Also, the focused coding of tweets generated during the large communal events indicated that the Twitter feed enabled participants to engage with the keynotes by disseminating and, to some extent, critically analyzing the content of those sessions.

Conclusion

This study analyzes the ways in which 2011 POD HBCUFDN Conference participants used Twitter to communicate about the annual meeting. Results show that most tweets mapped onto many key programmatic areas, as established in a prior large survey of faculty developers, but important distinctions also arose, particularly emphasis among tweeters on how faculty and students learn, faculty roles and rewards, and approaches to engage effectively in educational development work. We also found that the conference backchannel had important communicative functions for announcements, networking, connections with those not in attendance, and processing of information. Faculty developers seeking to use Twitter on their own campuses for events may wish to consult resources such as Bruff (2011a) and the Twitter feeds that many teaching centers now have (for a list of these, see http://Twitter.com/#!/UMich_CRLT/faculty-development).

The results of this study have implications for future POD Network conference programming and suggest growing areas of interest within the organization. How faculty and students learn, faculty roles and rewards, and effective faculty development practices all appeared frequently in tweets and are important to address in future POD conference sessions or publications. In addition, given our findings about the primarily replicative nature of tweets during the large, communal events at the conference, we would suggest that future keynote speakers more pointedly ask conference attendees to adapt and evaluate ideas for potential application and use and leverage the conference backchannel during their talks to foster more peer-to-peer learning.

Most significant, we find that Twitter builds community for POD, providing a lively backchannel in which audience members and nonattending participants can exchange views and ideas in real time. Given this richness, the use of the conference backchannel should be continued and developed further. Specifically, we recommend that participation in the POD Conference Twitter feed be encouraged across the organization in order to promote a greater diversity of tweeters. Two possible ways to accomplish this aim are to engage in more direct outreach to POD Network subcommittees and international educational development associations, as well as to more broadly publicize participation in the backchannel. As the conference backchannel grows, future research might examine historical trends, compare tweets with program content, or describe participant perceptions of backchannels.

REFERENCES

Atkinson, C. (2009). *The backchannel book: How audiences are using Twitter and social media and changing presentations forever.* Berkeley, CA: New Riders Press.

Bruff, D. (2011a, February 10). *Encouraging a conference backchannel on Twitter.* Retrieved from http://chronicle.com/blogs/profhacker/encouraging-a-conference-backchannel-on-Twitter/30612

Bruff, D. (2011b, October 6). *Twitter 101 for conference backchannels* [Video]. Retrieved from http://www.youtube.com/watch?v=aMy8RKkXEPQ

Center for Excellence in Teaching and Learning, Texas Wesleyan University. (2011). *How to prank your boss.* Video presentation at the annual meeting of the POD HBCU Networks, Atlanta, GA. Retrieved from http://www.youtube.com/watch?v=Re9PezLlhY0

Charmaz, K. (1983). The grounded theory method: An explanation and interpretation. In R. M. Emerson (Ed.), *Contemporary field research: A collection of readings* (pp. 109–126). New York, NY: Little, Brown.

Charmaz, K. (1995). Learning grounded theory. In J. Smith, R. Harré, & L. VanLangenhove (Eds.), *Rethinking methods in psychology* (pp. 27–49). Thousand Oaks, CA: Sage.

Debowski, S. (2012). Emergent shifts in faculty development: A reflective review. In J. E. Miller & J. E. Groccia (Eds.), *To improve the academy: Resources for faculty, instructional, and organizational development, Vol. 30* (pp. 306–322). San Francisco, CA: Jossey-Bass/Anker.

Ebner, M., Mulburger, H., Schaffert, S., Schiefner, M., Reinhardt, W., & Wheeler, S. (2010). Getting granular on Twitter: Tweets from a conference and their limited usefulness for non-participants. *IFIP Advances in Information and Communication Technology, 324,* 102–113. Retrieved from http://dx.doi.org/10.1007/978-3-642-15378-5_10

Ebner, M., & Reinhardt, W. (2009). Social networking in scientific conferences—Twitter as tool for strengthen a scientific community. In *Proceedings of the First International Workshop on Science*

(Vol. 2, pp. 1–8). Retrieved from http://telearn.noe-kaleidoscope.org/warehouse/Ebner_2009_TelSci2.0_(002197v1).pdf

Gillespie, K., & Robertson, D. L. (Eds.). (2010). *A guide to faculty development* (2nd ed.). San Francisco, CA: Jossey-Bass.

Glaser, B. (1987). *Theoretical sensitivity: Advances in methodology of grounded theory.* Mill Valley, CA: Sociology Press.

Glaser, B. G., & Strauss, A. L. (1967). *The discovery of grounded theory: Strategies for qualitative research.* New York, NY: Aldine De Gruyter.

Hines, S. R. (2011). *How mature teaching and learning centers evaluate their services.* In J. E. Miller & J. E. Groccia (Eds.), *To improve the academy: Resources for faculty, instructional, and organizational development, Vol. 30* (pp. 277–289). San Francisco, CA: Jossey-Bass/Anker.

Jacobs, N., & McFarlane, A. (2005). Conferences as learning communities: Some early lessons in using "back-channel" technologies at an academic conference—distributed intelligence or divided attention? *Journal of Computer Assisted Learning, 21,* 317–329.

Kuhlenschmidt, S. (2011). Distribution and penetration of teaching-learning development units in higher education: Implications for strategic planning and research. In J. E. Miller & J. E. Groccia (Eds.), *To improve the academy: Resources for faculty, instructional, and organizational development, Vol. 30* (pp. 274–287). San Francisco, CA: Jossey-Bass/Anker.

Lee, V. (2011). *Reflections on international engagement as educational developers in the United States.* In J. E. Miller & J. E. Groccia (Eds.), *To improve the academy: Resources for faculty, instructional, and organizational development, Vol. 30* (pp. 302–314). San Francisco, CA: Jossey-Bass/Anker.

Letierce, J., Passant, A., Decker, S., & Breslin, J. G. (2010, April). *Understanding how Twitter is used to spread scientific messages.* Presentation at the Web Science Conference, Raleigh, NC. Retrieved from http://journal.webscience.org/314/2/websci10_submission_79.pdf

McCarthy, J. F., & Boyd, D. M. (2005, April). *Digital backchannels in shared physical spaces: Experiences at an academic conference.* In *CHI '05: CHI '05 Extended Abstracts on Human Factors in Computing Systems.* New York, NY: Association for Computer Machinery.

Miles, M. B., & Huberman, A. M. (1984). *Qualitative data analysis: A sourcebook of new methods.* Thousand Oaks, CA: Sage.

Reinhardt, W., Ebner, M., Beham, G., & Costa, C. (2009). *How people are using Twitter during conferences.* In V. Hornung-Prähauser & M. Luckmann. (Eds.), *Creativity and innovation competencies on the Web: Proceedings of the Fifth EduMedia Conference* (pp. 145–156). Salzburg, Germany. Retrieved from http://www.scribd.com/fullscreen/17630303

Ross, C., Terras, M., Warwick, C., & Welsh, A. (2011). Enabled backchannel: Conference Twitter use by digital humanists. *Journal of Documentation, 67*(2), 214–237.

Schroeder, C., Ed. (2010). *Coming in from the margins: Faculty development's emerging organizational development role in institutional change.* Sterling, VA: Stylus.

Sorcinelli, M. D., Austin, A. E., Eddy, P. L., & Beach, A. L. (2005). *Creating the future of faculty development: Learning from the past, understanding the present.* San Francisco, CA: Jossey-Bass/Anker.

Tufekci, Z. (2001, May 19). Why Twitter's oral culture irritates Bill Keller (and why this is an important issue) [Web log comment]. Retrieved from: http://technosociology.org/?p=431

Van Note Chism, N., Gosling, D., & Sorcinelli, M. D. (2010). International faculty development: Pursuing our work with colleagues around the field. In K. J. Gillespie & D. L. Robertson (Eds.), *A guide to faculty development* (2nd ed., pp. 243–274). San Francisco, CA: Jossey-Bass.

Vierra, A. J., & Garrett, J. M. (2005). Understanding interobserver agreement: The kappa statistic. *Family Medicine, 37*(5), 360–363.

Weller, K., Dröge, E., & Puschmann, C. (2011, May). *Citation analysis in Twitter: Approaches for defining and measuring information flows within tweets during scientific conferences.* Presentation at the Eighth Extended Semantic Web Conference (ESWC 2011), Heraklion, Greece.

21

COLLABORATING WITH FACULTY TO DESIGN ACTIVE LEARNING WITH FLEXIBLE TECHNOLOGY

Beth A. Fisher, Kathryn G. Miller,
William E. Buhro, Deborah J. Frank, Regina F. Frey
Washington University in St. Louis

Collaboration among faculty and teaching center staff has produced in-class, active-learning methods that help students learn visualization, problem-solving, critical thinking, and communication skills as they develop disciplinary knowledge. These methods include instructor and student use of technology tools—or tools that are unobtrusive in the classroom, easy to integrate in coordination with "low-tech" tools, and adaptable to multiple pedagogical purposes. Preliminary evaluations suggest evidence of improved learning and high levels of student engagement. Our collaboration has produced insights into teaching and learning that are widely

We thank Hewlett-Packard for supporting this project with two Technology for Teaching Leadership grants (2005 and 2007). We also thank Elizabeth Peterson, Tra'Mel Harrell, Jon Baird, Greg Noelken, and Jason Crow for assistance with classroom technology and Carolyn Dufault, Bryn Lutes, and Michelle Repice for assistance with this chapter.

applicable, helping to make teaching innovation visible and to transform teaching into an act of scholarship.

o

Recent scholarship has demonstrated that incorporating active learning into the undergraduate classroom can improve student learning and engagement (Cooper, Cox, Nammouz, Case, & Stevens, 2008; Eberlein, et al., 2008; Gafney & Varma-Nelson, 2008; Hockings, DeAngelis, & Frey, 2008; Michael, 2006; Moog & Spencer, 2008; Prince, 2004; Yoder & Hochevar, 2005). However, instructors can be reluctant to incorporate active-learning methods. Reasons for this reluctance vary widely, but commonly include concern that incorporating active learning requires reducing the amount of content taught, lack of experience with planning and facilitating student-centered learning, and unfamiliarity with specific active-learning methods and tools (Bonwell & Eison, 1991; Michael, 2007; Prince, 2004; Weimer, 2002). Today's university students can also be reluctant to take on more active roles in the classroom, particularly in disciplines in which lecture is the primary instructional method (Bransford, Brown, & Cocking, 2000; Weimer, 2002).

Similarly, while faculty and students are increasingly using technology in the classroom, both groups remain uncertain as to whether technology improves student learning and engagement. For example, many instructors appreciate the convenience of using technology to disseminate information and communicate with students, but they are skeptical that technology can help students gain disciplinary knowledge (Zhu, 2008). Annual studies conducted since 2004 by the Educause Center for Applied Research have shown that undergraduates share with their instructors the perception that technology offers convenient tools for communicating and sharing information, but does not necessarily improve their learning or increase their engagement in courses (Dahlstrom, de Boor, Grunwald, & Vockley, 2011; Smith & Caruso, 2010). Students report that many of their instructors do not use technology effectively. However, they rate their instructors' effectiveness more highly when the use of technology "extend[s] learning beyond the classroom," gives them "control over [their] own learning," and "better prepare[s] [them] for the workforce" (Dahlstrom et al., 2011, p. 24).

A need clearly exists for institutional support for faculty who would like to incorporate active learning into their courses and are interested in exploring whether technological tools can facilitate in-class learning of disciplinary knowledge, as well as meaningful, transferable skills.

We have responded to this need by collaborating with faculty to design and implement active-learning methods in which instructors and students use flexible technology tools—those that are unobtrusive in the classroom, easy to integrate in coordination with low-tech tools, and adaptable for multiple pedagogical purposes. These tools include SMART Boards, tablet PCs, and a wireless network. Preliminary evaluation of course innovations suggests evidence of improved learning and high levels of student participation and satisfaction. Moreover, the process of working with these instructors has produced insights that teaching center staff have shared with faculty and graduate students from across the disciplines—and with a broader public through the Teaching Center's Web site. This process has also produced recommendations for faculty developers on how to collaborate with faculty to incorporate active learning with flexible technology. Finally, this process is helping to transform teaching into community property at our university (Shulman, 1993).

Consultation as Collaboration

The Teaching Center at Washington University combines two areas of expertise that are often housed in separate university offices: pedagogical development programs for faculty and graduate students and classroom technology services. The diverse expertise represented in our Teaching Center, combined with the expertise of faculty who are dedicated to improving teaching and learning, create fertile ground for the development of innovative and effective instructional methods.

The innovations described in this chapter originated in two series of faculty consultations—one with a professor of chemistry and one with a professor of biology. Each sought the advice of our center director, R. Frey, to redesign a course after realizing that there was a disconnect between what each wanted their students to learn and what their students were actually learning. Both professors consulted with Frey to understand this disconnect and to redesign their instructional methods to help students build the knowledge and skills that each saw as essential to the course in question. Initial consultations focused on articulating the course learning objectives and discussing the evidence that students were not obtaining those objectives. Subsequent discussions, occurring over multiple semesters, resulted in a gradual shift away from a traditional lecture format to a format that included multiple methods, including active learning with flexible technology tools.

Two Examples

In this section, we present a condensed account of each course redesign; more comprehensive descriptions of the active-learning methods employed in these two courses are available online (http://teachingcenter.wustl.edu/flexible-technology).

Solid-State and Materials Chemistry

This course for advanced undergraduates and beginning graduate students in chemistry and engineering has been taught since the late 1990s by W. E. Buhro. The course includes an overview of solid-state crystal structure and materials synthesis, and the course goals include teaching students how to visualize the structures of solid-state materials and understand the connection between a solid-state material's structure and its properties. In the sciences, as in many other disciplines, visualization skills are critical to building conceptual knowledge. In Solid-State and Materials Chemistry, the instructor and students use PowderCell, computer-modeling software, to generate and rotate digital images of solid-state structures. They also use this software to perform refinement exercises, in which they identify unknown materials by analyzing their structures (http://www.ccp14.ac.uk/ccp/web-mirrors/powdcell/a_v/v_1/powder/e_cell.html).

The integration of active learning and technology into Buhro's course took place in three phases. During the first phase, Buhro began demonstrating PowderCell on the SMART Board, and students were responsible for downloading and using the software outside class. Although PowderCell is easy to download and use, Buhro found that few students used the software outside class and instead used less effective methods to solve the homework problems. Concerned that the students' failure to use PowderCell hindered their development of visualization skills, Buhro consulted with Frey, who suggested that students learn to use PowderCell in class with laptops or tablet PCs. This innovation constituted the second phase. During the third phase, Buhro added in-class, problem-solving refinement exercises. Some students chose to work in pairs to complete the exercises; hence, a one-to-one student-laptop ratio was not necessary.

Buhro's use of the SMART Board worked in tandem with student use of the tablet PCs. Demonstrating how to use PowderCell on the SMART Board, rather than on a computer connected to a data projector, made it easier for the students to see—and to emulate—how Buhro was manipulating the software. Furthermore, because students were simultaneously watching Buhro and working on their own laptops or tablet PCs, they were able to put into practice the skills and procedures Buhro was demonstrating, in an atmosphere in which they could ask questions and continue to improve on their work. In addition, Buhro could assess student learning and make adjustments as needed.

Even as he integrated technology, Buhro continued to use the chalkboard to document the verbal explanations, formulas, and diagrams that he expected students to include in their notes. In addition, as he incorporated increasing amounts of active learning and technology, Buhro developed a more interactive teaching style, with frequent opportunities for questions and discussion. As they used PowderCell to perform the visualization and refinement exercises, his students actively took notes, asked and answered questions, and consulted with one another. Because tablet PCs are small, students were able to move easily between using the tablets and taking notes in their notebooks, just as Buhro moved easily between SMART Board and chalkboard.

Preliminary evaluation suggests that introduction of in-class, active-learning exercises using the SMART Board and tablet PCs in Solid-State and Materials Chemistry increased student learning, satisfaction, and participation. During the second phase (2006), when students used PowderCell in class, they were more likely to use PowderCell to complete out-of-class homework exercises. During the third phase (2007 and 2009), Buhro observed that adding in-class problem solving using the tablet PCs with the SMART Board led to improvements in homework scores (Figure 21.1).

Buhro also observed that students asked and answered questions more often when the tablet PCs were introduced in 2006. When he added in-class exercises in 2007, he observed that the increased student participation continued throughout the semester, even when tablet PCs were no longer used. Buhro postulates that using the tablets had an ice-breaker effect. When the students were learning to use PowderCell, they became comfortable asking about the technology. As a result, they were more likely later in the semester to ask questions about the chemical concepts.

End-of-semester surveys administered in 2006 and 2007 show that students perceived that using the tablet PCs improved their understanding of the concepts (Figure 21.2). In 2007, when in-class refinement exercises were added, the average response to statement 3 (*I am more comfortable working computer exercises outside of class because I used tablet PCs in class*) increased to 4.5 (on a five-point scale) over an average of 4.1 in 2006.

Figure 21.1. Average Score on the Refinement Homework Assignment in Solid-State and Materials Chemistry.

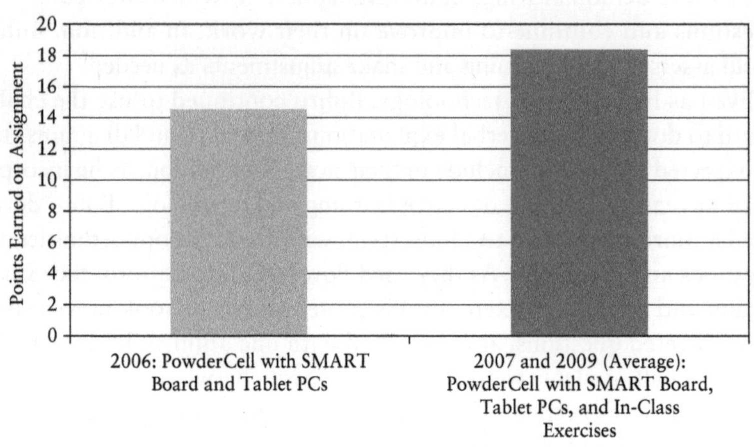

Figure 21.2. Student Perceptions of Tablet PCs in Solid-State and Materials Chemistry (Average Values, Spring 2006 and Spring 2007).

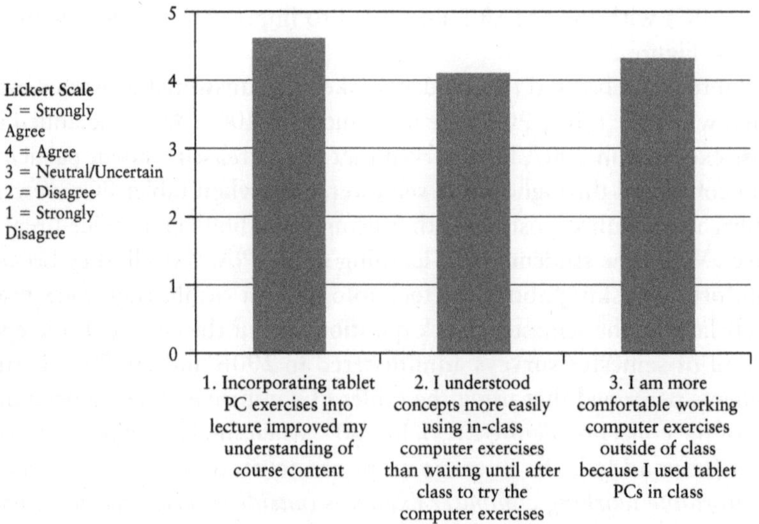

The integration of active learning and flexible technology into Solid-State and Materials Chemistry has led to a gradual but profound course transformation. Students gain hands-on computer-modeling experience combined with visualization and problem-solving skills that are essential to their understanding of solid-state structures and to their future course work and research. Increased student participation and collaboration, along with improved homework scores, have convinced Buhro of the effectiveness of active learning with the SMART Board and the tablet PCs.

Molecular Mechanisms in Development

This upper-level, writing-intensive biology course has been taught since the mid-1990s by K. G. Miller, and it was cotaught between 2008 and 2011 with D. J. Frank. One of Miller's goals for the course is to teach students not only "what we know" about developmental biology, but also "how we know what we know"—or how new knowledge is produced through laboratory research. This vision of science as a process of discovery informs the teaching goals of many science faculty. Another course goal relevant across many disciplines, including the humanities and social sciences, is to teach students how to integrate facts into broader ideas and arguments.

Early on, Miller realized that her students tended to demonstrate their knowledge by listing facts rather than by synthesizing facts into broader arguments. Therefore, she began to redesign the course in a writing-intensive format—a process that began with her participation in the Teaching Center's workshops on teaching with writing and continued in a series of consultations with Frey. The result of these consultations was a redesigned course in which students no longer took exams but instead wrote a series of essays in which they presented and supported arguments about current research articles in developmental biology.

The course redesign process continued as Miller moved away from a traditional lecture format toward a format combining lecture and discussion. After using the SMART Board to diagram experiments and document ideas generated during class, she found that her active engagement with the material led her students to be more actively engaged. She developed a series of questions that she could project on the SMART Board when starting the discussion of each article. The SMART Board provided a means of displaying these questions and documenting students' answers, with annotations that could be saved and distributed to the students using the wireless network, e-mail, or the learning management system (Figure 21.3). Repeated use of these questions allowed Miller to teach her students a structured habit of questioning that they

Figure 21.3. **Annotated Slide from Molecular Mechanisms in Development.**

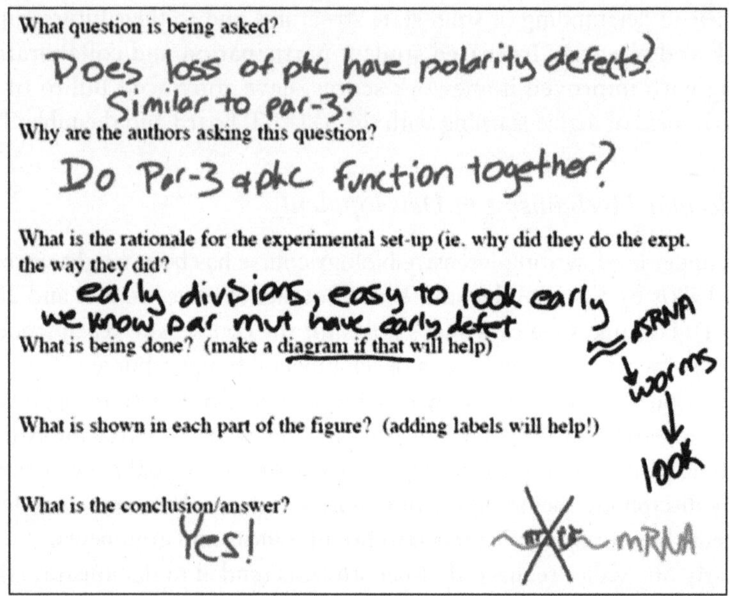

Note: *To see this figure in color, go to http://teachingcenter.wustl.edu/flexible-technology/bio3191/questioning*

could use whenever they read and wrote about scientific literature—both during and outside class.

Miller also used the SMART Board to annotate figures from research articles, thereby modeling another form of annotation that students could emulate. Miller observed that her capacity to annotate figures on the SMART Board during class encouraged her students to annotate and think about the figures. After a preliminary phase in which Miller's students annotated the slides on black-and-white handouts, Miller worked with Frey to integrate student use of tablet PCs for this purpose. With this innovation, students could use the tablet PCs and take notes on slides that Miller made available to students using the learning management system. Initially students were trained by Teaching Center staff on how to use tablet PCs during the first week of class. More recently, instructors have provided training during active-learning activities designed for the opening week. Throughout the process, Teaching Center staff prepared technology "help sheets" for the instructors and the students.

We have found that annotating with the SMART Board and tablet PCs offers four major advantages over other tools such as handouts, chalkboard, and iPads. These advantages are relevant to teaching in a range of disciplines, including science and mathematics, humanities, art and architectural design, and any other course in which students learn to analyze complex visual images or lengthy text passages. First, the figures analyzed in Miller's course are often difficult to reproduce on a chalkboard. Second, the SMART Board and tablet PCs can be used to project the figure as a full-color digital image, crucial in Molecular Mechanisms in Development because laboratory techniques often use color to indicate important information (for example, immunofluorescence to show localization of proteins). Third, both the SMART Board and tablet PCs allow users to annotate using multiple colors and save the annotated slides in electronic files that students and instructors can access outside class and that instructors can refer to when preparing to teach the course in future semesters. Fourth, when the instructor is working at the SMART Board, the students can observe her making annotations directly on the projected slides or figures. Just as in Solid-State and Materials Chemistry, this capacity makes it easier for students to follow, emulate, and refine the instructor's annotations than it would be if the instructor were annotating on a document camera or a tablet device, such as an iPad, at the instructor's desk while students were watching the annotations appear on a projection screen.

In the next phase of course redesign, Miller increased opportunities for active learning by incorporating in-class, small group discussions during which students built knowledge collaboratively through peer discourse. After developing group work with Frey in 2008, Miller has added more group work every year. In 2009, Frey suggested using a wireless network, allowing students to present their annotations to the class using a data projector.

During a typical discussion, Miller divided the students into groups of four or five and assigned to each group a figure from the day's article and displayed on the SMART Board two or three questions, such as, "What is shown in this figure?" and, "How does this figure support the authors' thesis?" She gave the groups ten to twelve minutes to annotate the figure and answer the questions and then asked a spokesperson from each group to explain the annotations, which were projected using the wireless network (Figure 21.4). During group discussions, students engaged in

Figure 21.4. Figure Illustrating a Direct Physical Interaction Between Two Proteins of Interest, Annotated by a Student During a Small Group Discussion.

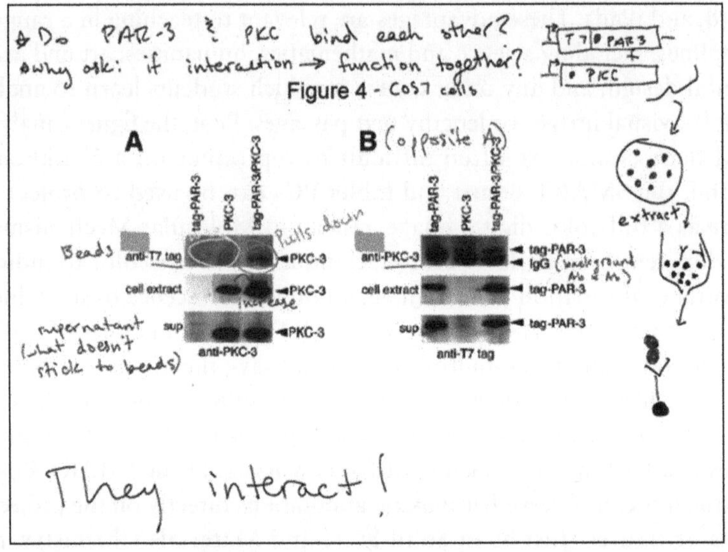

Note: *To see the figure in color, go to http://teachingcenter.wustl.edu/flexible-technology/bio3191/group-work*
Source: *Tabuse et al. (1998). Reproduced and adapted by permission of The Company of Biologists Ltd. http://dev.biologists.org/content/125/18/3607.full.pdf+html*

thinking out loud as they explained the factual research findings and how those findings supported the authors' arguments.

Using the SMART Board in combination with tablet PCs during class has been instrumental in helping students in Molecular Mechanisms in Development build critical thinking, argumentation, and communication skills that they further develop when writing essays on current laboratory research. Miller and Frank have observed that in-class use of the SMART Board and tablet PCs has increased student participation and engagement. Postsemester perception surveys administered in fall 2008 and 2009 demonstrate that students perceived active learning with flexible technology to improve their learning and engagement (Figure 21.5). In addition, students believed that tablet PCs enabled them to take an

Figure 21.5. Students' Perception of the Use of Tablet PCs in Molecular Mechanisms in Development (Average Values, Fall 2008 and Fall 2009).

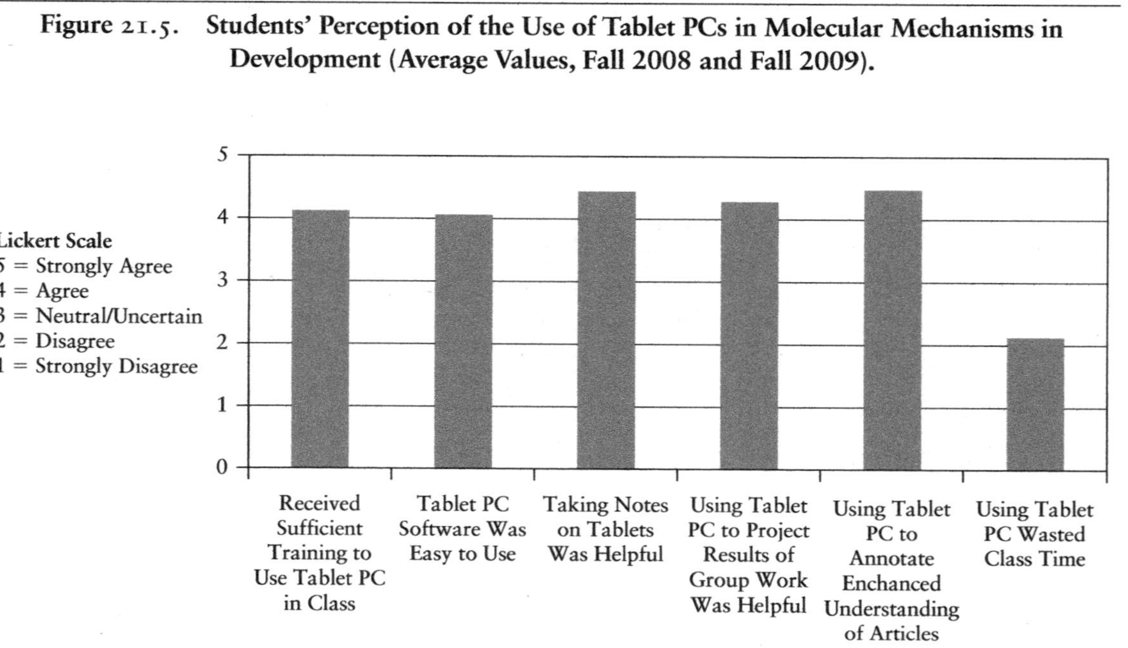

active role in class and to create personalized annotations that reflected their evolving knowledge of developmental biology. These preliminary results, along with instructor observations of improved learning, have led Miller and Frank to design a more formal evaluation of their instructional methods in a study that is currently under way.

Reflections on Active Learning with Flexible Technology

Variation among the methods implemented in these two courses suggests that the Teaching Center's collaboration with faculty to develop an incremental approach to integrating active learning is versatile enough to fit a variety of pedagogical purposes and teaching styles. Furthermore, both instructors introduced active learning incrementally, over an extended period of time, allowing them to blend active learning into their respective teaching styles. Both still use lectures for a number of purposes, such as introducing new content, making connections between new and prior knowledge, and helping students refine knowledge and skills developed during active-learning activities. Gradual integration of active learning has made the process of course redesign more manageable and allowed each instructor to observe and evaluate results of each innovation and make adjustments based on these evaluations.

The SMART Board and tablet PCs are flexible tools that can facilitate hands-on active learning in the classroom. The former allows the instructor to move around the room and interact with students rather than remain behind a computer. In addition, when the instructor uses the SMART Board, students can readily follow and emulate his or her use of the technology—whether using computer-modeling software to visualize and analyze chemical structures or annotating figures to analyze research articles. Student use of tablet PCs, in coordination with the instructor's use of the SMART Board, allows students to immediately put into practice and then refine the skills that the instructor is modeling. The tablet PCs do not block the students' views of the instructor (or vice versa), or of one another. Therefore, tablet PCs do not hinder interaction among the students or between the instructor and students, as is often the case in a classroom with desktop computers, where students are often working with their backs to the instructor or working behind large monitors, thereby making it difficult for the instructor and students to see each other. Whereas using technological devices in the classroom can increase communication barriers, using tablet PCs in active-learning activities appears to break down such barriers, whether perceived or physical. Students find tablet PCs easy to use and preferable to using paper notebooks in some cases. At the same time, the small size of the tablets means that the students can easily move between using them and taking notes on paper and between taking notes and participating in group discussions.

This process has demonstrated that flexible technological tools can benefit a diverse range of students and courses, and it has produced methods that may be implemented with a variety of high-tech and low-tech tools. We have found that the flexibility of these tools and the design of multimedia in our classrooms increases the cost-effectiveness of instructional technology. Moreover, as university-specific data from the 2011 Educause Center for Applied Research (ECAR) study demonstrate, our undergraduates rate the technology skills of their instructors more highly than do undergraduates nationally (S. Grajek, personal communication, July 26, 2011).

The active-learning methods used in these two courses have led students to develop meaningful and transferable technology skills as they learn disciplinary knowledge. These methods include authentic tasks, such as manipulating widely used computer-modeling software and analyzing and explaining complex figures and arguments. We believe that these authentic uses of technology have immediate relevance and intrinsic interest for students. The postsemester survey results suggest that students in each course perceived the active-learning strategies and use of technology as integral to the course and to their learning within and beyond the course. Survey results also confirm national ECAR data demonstrating that undergraduates find instructional technology effective when it allows them to exercise control over their own learning (Dahlstrom et al., 2011, p. 24).

Broader Impact: Dissemination and Adaptation

In addition to descriptions of the instructional methods that appear on the Teaching Center's Web site (http://teachingcenter.wustl.edu/flexible-technology), the center has produced six videos, also available on our Web site, in which Buhro and Miller describe their courses, including how they use active learning with flexible technology (http://teachingcenter.wustl.edu/teaching-strategies/commentaries). Teaching Center staff have incorporated these videos into workshops for graduate students and postdoctoral appointees and into consultations with junior faculty.

Analysis of our Web site use demonstrates that these videos have generated interest within and beyond the university. Moreover, Miller, Frank, and Frey have presented insights from the redesign of these courses to interdisciplinary audiences at our university's biennial faculty symposium on teaching. As a result of her role in helping Miller and Frank to document instructional methods employed in Molecular Mechanisms in Development, the Teaching Center's associate director of academic services, B. Fisher, has adapted some of their active-learning methods for her writing-intensive American literature course. For example, her students use tablet PCs, in coordination with the SMART Board and wireless network, to annotate literary texts and historical images and to complete in-class writing exercises.

Recommendations

The following recommendations are based on our experience collaborating with faculty to design active learning with flexible technology:

1. Start the redesign by assisting the instructor in defining learning objectives or course goals, and then collaborate to identify what students could do during class to build the knowledge and skills identified in those objectives.
2. As you work together to develop specific active-learning activities, recommend integration of these activities with other methods. For example, discuss how the instructor might combine lectures with discussions, problem solving, or group work.
3. Help the instructor develop a plan for gradually integrating active learning. An incremental approach allows the instructor to add a new method, evaluate its effects, and make any necessary adjustments before adding the next innovation.
4. As the use of active-learning strategies increases, assist the instructor in reducing the amount of material taught. Incorporating active-learning methods often means covering less material. Faculty developers can assist with this transition by meeting with an instructor to review lecture notes and identify specific parts of the lecture that convey knowledge students could derive or discover through in-class work, whether individually or in groups.
5. Discuss specific ways in which incorporating active learning can require stepping outside one's comfort zone to develop a more interactive style:
   - Address common pitfalls and how to avoid them. For example, help instructors avoid relying solely on lecturing by developing

strategies to increase student participation, such as sequencing questions from easier to more difficult and allowing students sufficient time to complete active-learning activities and compose thoughtful answers.

- Help the instructor develop active-learning activities that are well designed, clearly structured, and actively facilitated by the instructor. Instructors should give students clear instructions and time limits and should develop specific strategies for integrating results of active learning—from asking students to summarize what they have learned, to asking follow-up questions of each group and the larger class.
- Suggest specific ways to achieve student buy-in from the start of the semester. Familiarize the instructor, for example, with research showing that participation in active learning can lead to deeper learning. In addition, suggest that the instructor explain to students the purpose behind the active-learning strategies and that the instructor incorporate active-learning exercises on the first day of class and frequently thereafter during the first few weeks of the semester.

6. Determine whether technology can provide useful and flexible tools to facilitate active learning. Again, it is best to use multiple tools. We recommend, for instance, that instructors combine use of a SMART Board and tablet devices, or laptops, with low-tech tools such as the chalkboard or handouts. The document camera is another flexible tool that instructors can use to project anything from a printed image to three-dimensional models and demonstrations.
7. Collaborate with classroom technology staff to ensure that the technology is designed to be intuitive and easy to use. In addition, anticipate and plan for technical and logistical issues. These issues include determining what hardware and software are needed, which classrooms are appropriate, whether in-class technical support will be needed (and when), and whether the instructor and students will need training on specific tools or software. Classroom-services staff should also create brief "help sheets" containing essential technical how-tos for the instructor and students.
   - Encourage the instructor to allow time before the semester to be trained on any new technology tools and to practice teaching with these tools.

- With the instructor, develop a plan for providing students with any needed training by the instructor or classroom services staff. Provide training gradually, teaching students what they need to know when they need to know it.

8. Encourage the instructor to evaluate innovations. Evaluation can take a range of forms, all of which faculty developers can assist with—from observing a few classes, to administering a student-perception survey, to developing a formal study evaluating the effects of a teaching innovation.

Conclusion

We believe that our approach to collaborating with faculty to design active learning using flexible technology has been successful for several reasons. Although these reasons are specific to our approach, they suggest a philosophy that can be readily adapted by faculty developers at other institutions. First, the process is driven by the instructor's specific goals for student learning and interest in finding innovative, effective, and meaningful methods for helping students achieve those goals. Second, consultations with each instructor are truly collaborative—bringing together the rich, discipline-specific experience of each instructor in teaching a particular course with the diverse expertise of Teaching Center staff. Third, the process focuses on the development of active-learning methods that can be integrated with other pedagogical methods and implemented with tools that are flexible and unobtrusive in the classroom. Fourth, the process follows a principle that guides our consultations with faculty who are designing or redesigning a course: new methods and tools should be introduced incrementally to allow gradual adjustments in course content and the instructor's teaching style. By lowering perceived barriers to trying new methods, an incremental approach can lead to profound change over time.

Beyond the improvements in student learning and engagement that we have observed, the success of our approach can be seen in the emergence of what Lee Shulman called "teaching as community property" (1993). The innovations developed by these professors in collaboration with the Teaching Center have transformed teaching into scholarship that can be documented, opened to peer review, evaluated, and improved on. Our collaborative approach to course redesign has not only made visible the innovative and effective teaching of outstanding instructors; it has also extended outward to inspire other faculty and graduate students to explore new and innovative ways to improve teaching and learning.

REFERENCES

Bonwell, C. C., & Eison, J. A. (1991, September). Active learning: Creating excitement in the classroom. *National Teaching and Learning Forum.* Retrieved from http://www.ntlf.com/html/lib/bib/91–9dig.htm

Bransford, J., Brown, A. L., & Cocking, R. R. (Eds.). (2000). *How people learn: Brain, mind, experience, and school.* Washington, DC: National Academy Press. Retrieved from http://www.nap.edu/openbook.php?record_id=9853

Cooper, M. M., Cox, C. T., Nammouz, M., Case, E., & Stevens, R. (2008). An assessment of the effect of collaborative groups on students' problem-solving strategies and abilities. *Journal of Chemical Education, 85*(6), 866–872.

Dahlstrom, E., de Boor, T., Grunwald, P., & Vockley, M. (2011). *The ECAR National Study of Undergraduate Students and Information Technology, 2011.* Boulder, CO: Educause Center for Applied Research. Retrieved from http://net.educause.edu/ir/library/pdf/ERS1103/ERS1103W.pdf

Eberlein, T., Kampmeier, J., Minderhout, V., Moog, R. S., Platt, T., Varma-Nelson, P., & White, H. B. (2008). Pedagogies of engagement in science. *Biochemistry and Molecular Biology Education, 36*(4), 262–273. doi:10.1002/bmb.20204.

Gafney, L., & Varma-Nelson, P. (2008). *Peer-led team learning: Evaluation, dissemination, and institutionalization of a college-level initiative.* New York, NY: Springer.

Hockings, S. C., DeAngelis, K. J., & Frey, R. F. (2008). Peer-led team learning in general chemistry: Implementation and evaluation. *Journal of Chemical Education, 85*(7), 990–996.

Michael, J. (2006). Where's the evidence that active learning works? *Advances in Physiology Education, 30*(4), 159–167. doi:10.1152/advan.00053.2006.

Michael, J. (2007). Faculty perceptions about barriers to active learning. *College Teaching, 55*(2), 42–47. doi:10.3200/CTCH.55.2.42–47.

Moog, R. S., & Spencer, J. N. (Eds.). (2008). *Process oriented guided inquiry learning (POGIL).* Washington, DC: American Chemical Society.

Prince, M. (2004). Does active learning work? A review of the research. *Journal of Engineering Education, 93*(3), 1–9.

Shulman, L. S. (1993). Teaching as community property: Putting an end to pedagogical solitude. *Change, 25*(6), 6–7.

Smith, S., & Caruso, J. (2010). *The ECAR Study of Undergraduates and Information Technology, 2010.* Boulder, CO: Educause Center for Applied Research. Retrieved from http://net.educause.edu/ir/library/pdf/ers1006/rs/ers1006w.pdf

Tabuse, Y., Izumi, Y., Piano, F., Kemphues, K. J., Miwa, J., & Ohno, H. (1998). Atypical protein kinase C cooperates with PAR-3 to establish embryonic polarity in *Caenorhabditis elegans. Development, 125*, 3607–3614. Retrieved from http://dev.biologists.org/content/125/18/3607.full .pdf+html

Weimer, M. (2002). *Learner-centered teaching: Five key changes to practice.* San Francisco, CA: Jossey-Bass.

Yoder, J., & Hochevar, C. (2005). Encouraging active learning can improve students' performance on examinations. *Teaching of Psychology, 32*, 91–95. doi:10.1207/s15328023top3202_2.

Zhu, E. (2008). Breaking down barriers to the use of technology for teaching in higher education. In D. R. Robertson & L. B. Nilson (Eds.), *To improve the academy: Resources for faculty, instructional and organizational development, Vol. 26* (pp. 305–318). San Francisco, CA: Jossey-Bass/Anker.